W9-CLQ-869

BATTLE YET UNSUNG

BATTLE YET UNSUNG

*The Fighting Men of the
14th Armored Division
in World War II*

By
Timothy J. O'Keeffe

CASEMATE
Philadelphia & Newbury

Published in the United States of America and Great Britain in 2011 by
CASEMATE
908 Darby Road, Havertown, PA 19083
and
17 Cheap Street, Newbury, Berkshire, RG14 5DD

ISBN 978-1-935149-44-6

Cataloging-in-publication data is available from the Library of Congress
and the British Library.

10 9 8 7 6 5 4 3 2 1

Printed and bound in the United States of America.

For a complete list of Casemate titles please contact:

CASEMATE PUBLISHERS (US)
Telephone (610) 853-9131, Fax (610) 853-9146
E-mail: casemate@casematepublishing.com

CASEMATE PUBLISHERS (UK)
Telephone (01635) 231091, Fax (01635) 41619
E-mail: casemate-uk@casematepublishing.co.uk

Mixed Sources
Product group from well-managed
forests and other controlled sources
www.fsc.org Cert no. SW-COC-002283
FSC © 1996 Forest Stewardship Council

CONTENTS

This book is dedicated to the men of the 14th Armored Division who fought valiantly in France and Germany during World War II. This work is especially dedicated to those men who gave their lives or were seriously wounded in the fighting. This last group experienced a lifetime of sacrificing their health and wholeness.

It is also dedicated to the families of all of these men who went overseas, families which had to worry and pray that a telegram from the War Department was never delivered to their door.

Finally, this work is dedicated to two men, the late Sgt. and Dr. Robert Isaac Davies, my brother-in-law, and to his Battalion Commander, Lt. Col. Bob E. Edwards, who was an inspiration to all his men in the 68th Armored Infantry Battalion of the 14th Armored. This book is about the men of all the combat battalions in the Division, yet these dedications could go on to include the brave soldiers who risked their lives for God and Country in all the battalions that served in World War II in both the European and Pacific Theaters of Operations.

A PERSONAL INTRODUCTION

It was in 1999 that I first met Robert Isaac Davies. Bob had grown up in a Welsh community in Poultney, Vermont, a small town where slate mining in the local quarries was the primary source of income for most families. Many grandparents in the town, including Bob's, had been raised speaking Welsh around the kitchen table. He had spoken only Welsh until his first grade teacher sent a note home indicating that students had to learn English. Bob Davies' account of his linguistic transformation recalled his grandfather's announcing to his household, "There'll be no more Welsh spoken in this family." Bob's wife also remembered, like other kids, speaking Welsh.

In the small elementary and high school classes in Poultney, the average number of pupils was only twenty-five. Everybody knew everyone else, and the sports teams had rosters, especially football, that named almost every boy in a given class. Bob grew up an avid reader, thanks to some of his teachers, many of whom he remembered with respect and affection. He also loved to play sports, especially football, basketball, and baseball, the latter being the one he hoped to pursue professionally as an adult. Instead, after he finished high school, he entered the army in 1943 and shipped out from the train station in the nearby city of Rutland. His life would change dramatically in the next several years.

It was decades later, in 1999, that I first met Bob, being about fifteen years younger than him. At the time I was unattached, with four adult children miles away from me. I, to use an old-fashioned word, was courting Marilyn Frances Balducci, a younger sister of Olive (Jo)

Davies, whose family was still connected to Poultney. Bob and Jo had been married after World War II, when Bob returned home from the European Theater of Operations (ETO). He had stepped on a Schü mine in Alsace, France when he was a Sergeant of the 68th Armored Infantry Battalion of the 14th Armored Division, then with Seventh Army.

We all met at Bob and Jo's condominium in Satellite Beach, Florida, where Marilyn introduced me to the couple. As a retired English professor, I regarded it as a signal privilege and great honor to get to know a wounded combat veteran, and more so later to become his brother-in-law. I am one of the generation of the famous military historian Stephen Ambrose, who, like me, grew up as a child during World War II. I can still remember the drama in my living room listening to our cathedral-shaped radio which announced the Japanese attack on Pearl Harbor on December 7th, 1941, "a date which will live in infamy," as President Roosevelt phrased it.

Ambrose would go on in his professional life to produce several excellent books on the fighting in Europe, and what he said of the combat veterans of the war, both British and American, typifies my feelings and those of most of my contemporaries: "It has been a memorable experience for me. I was ten years old when World War II ended. Like many other men my age, I have always admired—nay, stood in awe of—the G.I.'s. I thought that what they had done was beyond praise. I still do."

When I was a kid, a few years younger, I was entranced by action scenes in films, of which there were many about World War II in the decades after the fighting. Living vicariously through someone else's heroism filled my thoughts and dreams as it did thousands of other young boys. This glorious and harmless view influenced our vision of war years and even decades later.

However, as happened to countless other families, the tragedy of war struck home as well. Sometime in May of 1944, my mother, father, brother Dave and I were returning home from seeing a movie. When we entered the hall of our home, there was a telegram on the small table with the lace doily in the hall. It informed my mother, considered next of kin, that my Uncle John, her kid brother, was dead. He had been an artilleryman with a National Guard Division and had spent two years in the hellhole of New Guinea fighting the Japanese. John, we were informed, had died of a combination of malaria, typhoid fever, and pneumonia. I was later to discover that at least half of the deaths of soldiers in places like New Guinea were caused not by some noble flesh wound in the tradition of Homer's Iliad but by invisible bacteria. Some time later a Purple Heart Badge was mailed to my mother, but it could not undo the broken heart that she suffered. Such experiences were commonplace for mothers and wives across the country, a theme dramatized in the recent documentary The War by Ken Burns.

In my uncle's case, the grim irony was that he hadn't had to serve in the Armed Forces. He, like all his sisters and brothers (six in all) was an immigrant from Ireland and was, like his father and one other brother, a carpenter, living in Brooklyn and patiently awaiting his US citizenship. His death, in another sense, was not ironic at all. The pattern had been set years, decades, and even a millennium earlier. Both my father's side of the family, the O'Keeffes, and my mother's side, the O'Sullivans, had participated in combat as early as the Danish invasion of Ireland in the tenth century.

The fondness of the Irish for keeping historical (sometimes mythologized) track of its people produced ample documentation of their sometimes violent record. Only a few years ago during a trip to that country did I discover from a cousin that the Cork City Museum had a display of explosives employed by my father to blow a bridge in 1921 to interdict a unit of British Auxiliaries, the notorious "Black and Tans." Although in daylight hours a country blacksmith, at night he fought with the Irish Republican Army to end English domination of his country. After the end of fighting, he left his country for the United States, refusing ever to return to a land that had seen so much pain and suffering.

Ironically, only a few years earlier, my mother's oldest brother, James O'Sullivan, had had his jaw shattered by a shell at the famous and painful World War I battle at Gallipoli, a campaign that failed terribly. Sadly, the pattern continued not only with my Uncle John in New Guinea but also with my cousin Mickey O'Sullivan, who disappeared when a mortar shell landed in his foxhole in Korea.

On my father's side, his brother Jack, who had emigrated to the United States years before my father, had, with his wife Alice, as many as nine children. Four of them, including a daughter, served in World War II; she a WAC and the rest in the Army. One served with Patton's Third Army, to which Bob Davies' 14th Armored Division was attached in the spring of 1945. Miraculously, they all survived without a serious wound or being killed in action. The prayers of their parents had clearly been answered.

My life as a child and as a teenager seemed to be saturated with images of combat and wounding, both victory and defeat. I found it everywhere, or perhaps it found me. At age twelve or thirteen, as a conscientious altar boy, I met the real thing, a combat wounded veteran, but in a strange kind of appearance or apparition. This last word is not hyperbolic, for there came to our church a Father Matthew Taggart. My parish was used by the Archdiocese as a kind of rest home for recuperating priests, some physically, some psychologically unwell. Father Taggart, a very tall, thin, and sickly man, was assigned to St. Frances. In contrast to the pastor and the other priests, he was very interested in children, boys especially, in a healthy way. For the first time, he organized a boy's basketball program, and the altar boys and others responded enthusiastically. He made sure that we had decent basketballs and coached us. We thought the millennium had arrived. We didn't need trumpeting angels, just some court time.

Alas, it was not to continue, for Father Taggart had been seriously wounded in France in the last year of the war. He never mentioned that fact, but the story got around. In my own febrile mind, I didn't know how to react. I served on the altar with him, struck by his genuine piety and serious dignity. It was a privilege for me. And then he was no more. Taken to the hospital, he died shortly afterward. I was shocked with surprise and grief. How could this happen? Why would God allow this?

But the denouement to the drama would come. Only a day later, the rectory announced that the radio (no TV involved then) was going to broadcast a dramatization of the action in which he was terribly wounded. All the radios must have been on in our community to hear the brief drama. The voices and the sounds of battle revealed the desperate situation in which Chaplain Taggart found himself on the fields of France in 1944 or 1945.

The American advance was suddenly stopped by the Germans, and infantry units had to retreat. Left in what was now a no-man's land was a barn full of wounded GI's. Evidently the medics must have been driven out. A decision had been made that fighting through to them was impossible, and so they would become prisoners of war. At that point, Chaplain Taggart volunteered to work his way back to the barn and bring out at least the walking wounded. He did so but in the process became seriously wounded himself.

The funeral took place a day or so after the radio broadcast. I had been chosen to serve as first altar boy, responsible for, among other things, carrying the heavy poled crucifix both in the church and at the cemetery where he was to be buried. This was the same cemetery where my Uncle John was buried and later my parents. There was heavy emotional weight on my shoulders. By the time the firing squad had fired a volley and the American flag had been folded into its customary triangle, I was awash in tears. I would never forget that day.

And so it was no wonder that I was thrilled to meet Bob Davies in Satellite Beach. I brought with me a new edition of the famous World War II cartoons of Bill Mauldin, which were a favorite of GIs like Bob. We both laughed over the picture of the seedy GI with the unmilitary growth of beard, shielding his eyes as he prepares to fire his Colt .45 pistol into the chassis of his old, reliable warhorse–his jeep. For Bob, memories lingered of a favorite GI war correspondent, Ernie Pyle, who chronicled the war in Italy. He made the mistake of moving over to the war in the Pacific to cover the fighting there, and was killed by a Japanese sniper or machine gunner. Bob and I immediately warmed to each other: we both had Celtic family backgrounds, both had retired as professional people after educating ourselves out of the working class, and both shared an abiding interest in the war in Europe. But we were looking at it from different ends of the telescope, he as a wounded participant and I as a cousin and nephew of several participants of Bob's age.

Over the years, as we got to know each other better, we shared other interests such as carpentry and house building. I was mostly a listener, for Bob Davies had the most inexhaustible fund of stories of anyone I had ever met. And he was very funny both narrating yarns and doing imitations of characters he had known. True to form, though, I was very attentive to those stories growing out of Bob's wartime experiences. Some stories pertained to the life that Bob and Jo had after he returned home suffering from the loss of his leg. Evidently, as might be imagined, he had to adjust himself psychologically to his wound and to the realization that his dream of playing professional sports was over. The transition had not been easy, but instead he employed the benefits of the GI Bill to put himself through medical school. He became a successful radiologist, and his charm and warmth made him outstanding with nervous and wary patients.

During the summers my wife Marilyn and I spent our days at the log home I had built in the southwestern corner of Massachusetts, in the foothills of the Berkshires. This location was about a three-hour drive to Lake St. Catherine, Vermont where Bob and Jo spent the summer. Visiting them, I heard more stories about the 14th Armored Division. Having been an avid reader of military histories of the Second World War, I was frustrated because I could never seem to find any books or materials that mentioned Bob's division, even in many of the official histories of the war published by the Center of Military History in Washington. Thus, getting together with the Davies and their gifted children and grandchildren during the warm weather, although producing references to battles at Ober Otterbach, Rittershoffen, and other places, didn't advance my understanding. Researching further, I realized that Bob's division had followed up the invasion of southern France of August 15, 1944, the operations known sometimes as Anvil/Dragoon. The landings of General Alexander Patch's American Seventh Army besides the French First Army under General Jean de Lattre had been the most successful in World War II in any theater of operations. I knew that the French had not forgotten it, for a small news item dated August 16, 2004, recorded the following memorial:

> France yesterday honored soldiers, including tens of thousands of Africans who staged an assault on the French Riviera 60 years ago to break the Nazi grip–one of the least remembered military operations of World War Two. . . . the belated tribute to the Aug. 15, 1944, landings in Provence—code-named "Operation Dragoon"–which helped change the course of the war. . . .

It was no surprise that the only country to pay tribute to the invasion, the subsequent fighting up the Rhone Valley into central France through Alsace, and the violent struggle to cross the Rhine and enter Germany, was France. In the United States there is barely a mention of this fighting except in a few military histories. At the time I remembered the powerful story of fighting in Audie Murphy's book To Hell and Back and the subsequent movie, which saw his 3rd Infantry Division through to the fighting in the Vosges Mountains. Bob had mentioned those mountains, and so here was another clue, but no mention of the 14th Armored.

I finally asked him if there was a regimental or divisional history available to read. He responded, "Sure, if I can find it in my study." On the next morning over breakfast, he handed to me a photocopy with cardboard spiraled cover of "Unit History: 68th Armored Infantry Battalion: From Port of Embarkation to V-E Day." The text was composed of dark 6-by-9-inch pages (43 in number) with the maps so dark as to be unreadable. At the end was a list of those who had received various medals, Bronze and Silver Stars mostly but no mention of Purple Hearts. Considering Bob's sacrifice and those of others who had been wounded out of combat, I was puzzled. (Much later I discovered that it was the Medical Corps that awarded Purple Hearts based on the severity of wounds. The battalion history recorded only medals awarded by the division.) The foreword of the little History, which had been written by a Lt. Madden and Pfc. Kovanda, was dedicated "to the 619 officers and men, our buddies, who gave part or all of their life's blood for the victory we now enjoy." The book was published with the approval of the Commanding Officer, "Lt. Col. Infantry, Bob E. Edwards" in Germany but without a date. It was probably put together in the summer or fall of 1945. The brief history raised as many questions as it answered, not only about the battles but also about the context of the battles in the grand strategy of defeating Germany and the operational situation in Western Europe.

In many histories of the war in Western Europe in 1944–45, there was a virtual silence about the struggle in southern France up to and including Alsace. A study of the war written and published in 1970 by the distinguished British historian, B. Liddel Hart, pays no attention to the Dragoon Operation or the subsequent fighting north and eastward. In the text, an apparently comprehensive map, "Caen to the Rhine," pictures the advance from Normandy and the later extensions by 21st Army Group to the north and 12th Army Group in the center. This latter formation included Patton's Third Army which fought its way, with great casualties, into Lorraine, just north of Alsace, where the 14th Armored Division fought under Seventh Army, until in the spring it was attached to Third Army under General Patton. His advance, as of August 16, 1944, appears on the map, but the invasion of Southern

France on August 15 does not. Perhaps there is a little British bias here, for they had little to do with the invasion with the exception of naval support.

Admittedly, Operation Dragoon was regarded as a stepchild by Prime Minister Winston Churchill and by some on the staff of SHAEF (Supreme Headquarters, Allied Expeditionary Force), which was responsible for the prosecution of the war in Europe. There was desperate fighting from the landing in the Riviera in August to the end of the war for the various divisions, both French and American, until the German surrender in May 1945. There were thousands of casualties in Seventh Army until the men of the 14th Armored and of other divisions stacked their arms and looked forward to getting home. Forgotten was the fact that as early as November, a combat patrol of the 14th had crossed the Lauter River into what was then considered by Hitler as Greater Germany. The casualties in the 68th AIB (Armored Infantry Battalion) had been severe.

Knowledge of this kind propelled me, a retired Professor of English, to begin editing and correcting the battalion's history, but the more I worked at it, the more I realized what I didn't know. I knew a fair amount about such divisions as had been renowned on Omaha Beach or during the Battle of the Bulge and other famous operations. There were over eighty American divisions active in the fighting in World War II, however, and my question was what about the others? Celebrated divisions such as the Big Red One, (1st Infantry), the Screaming Eagles and the All-Americans (101st and 82nd Airborne, respectively) which fought, bled, and died deserve credit for what they did, but the lack of credit, testimony, or memory of what other divisions had done bothered me. I felt a need to do some serious research and write what I could to rectify this imbalance. Much of the material in the following chapters resulted from four sources: those from the National Archives II in College Park, Maryland; from the Institute for Military History in Carlisle, Pennsylvania; and those, whether in book or pamphlet form or in conversations offered by the veterans of the 14th Armored Division who have supported me in this endeavor: and finally, those from the Division Newsletter, The Liberator.

And so this modest effort is an attempt to do justice and pay tribute to the men of the 14th Armored Division who fought for their country, those who survived whole, those who suffered grievous wounds like my brother-in-law, and those who didn't make it safely to the end of the fighting. It is also correct to say that some of the wounded in any of the divisions in World War II (or other wars) eventually paid a price in the gradual deterioration of their health over their lifetimes. I believe Bob Davies did.

Several of the veterans, among whom are friends, have read various chapters and have expressed support. I am only sorry that thousands of others who have passed on will not be able to read this effort.

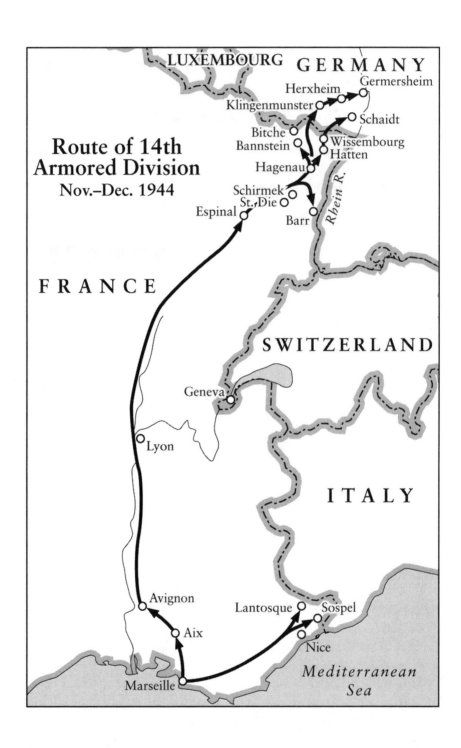

Route of 14th Armored Division
Nov.–Dec. 1944

LUXEMBOURG   G E R M A N Y

Herxheim   Germersheim
Klingenmunster
Schaidt
Bitche
Bannstein   Wissembourg
Hatten
Hagenau
Schirmek   Rhein R.
St. Die
Espinal   Barr

F R A N C E

S W I T Z E R L A N D

Geneva

Lyon

I T A L Y

Avignon   Lantosque   Sospel
Aix   Nice
Marseille   *Mediterranean Sea*

Chapter 1

FIRST DAYS OF BATTLE IN THE MARITIME ALPS

The 14th Armored Division was activated on November 15, 1942 at Camp Chaffee in western Arkansas, near the old frontier town of Fort Smith by the Oklahoma border. The following September the U.S. Army standardized its armored divisions so that each contained three tank battalions (TB), three armored infantry battalions (AIB) and three armored field artillery battalions (AFA), along with engineer, medical and ordnance battalions, a cavalry and reconnaissance squadron, an armored signal company and headquarters units. The only armored divisions that remained in the larger prior organization, with three full regiments of armored infantry, were the 2nd and 3rd Armored, which were slated for immediate support of the invasion of Normandy.

The 14th Armored sailed from New York on October 14, 1944, and began disembarking at Marseilles in the south of France on October 29. By then the Allies' June 6 invasion of Normandy had proven a success after ferocious fighting during the summer of 1944, and the follow-up invasion of southern France on August 15 had met far less resistance. Indeed, during the early fall of 1944 the Germans had seemed in head-long retreat all across France. In the south, Sixth Army Group, built primarily around American Seventh Army and French First Army, had pursued Germany's Nineteenth Army through the Rhone Valley to Alsace and the Vosges Moutain region near the borders of the Third Reich.

During fall 1944, however, as the Germans fell back closer to their supply, and the Allies advanced farther from theirs, which depended completely on a few ports or beaches, enemy resistance stiffened. A war that was thought could be over as quickly as Christmas suddenly trans-

1

formed into a bitter slogging match, even as the Germans began to pre-pare counteroffensives.

Attached to General Alexander Patch's Seventh Army after its arrival in France, the 14th Armored was quickly dispatched to the front. Per U.S. Army doctrine it was divided into three flexible Combat Commands: A, B, and R (Reserve), which initially forged inland in sep-arate columns. Most typically the 14th AD's tank battalions (the 25th, 47th, and 48th) would each be paired with an armored infantry battal-ion (the 19th, 62nd, and 68th), while the field artillery battalions (499th, 500th, and 501st) and other divisional units would be allocated to wherever the fighting was heaviest.

The History of the 68th Armored Infantry Battalion records that the battalion landed on 29 October and began its "trek to the staging area."

> Our first impression of this foreign country was one of amaze-ment, as hundreds of French urchins clustered about us, scream-ing for "cigarettes for papa," and bon-bons for themselves. Innocent and helpful, we gave until our pockets were empty. The entire battalion (of almost 700 men), a long brown line of staggering humanity, wound in dizzying circles through the town, and about the hill on which we nestled.[1]

These men, like their mates in the other battalions, would have to walk up a steep hill for about eight miles in order to set up a bivouac area. The march was with full packs, a condition which normally would not have been a problem for recently trained soldiers. However, the fif-teen days spent upon the water had gotten most of the men into soft shape, and their muscles and tendons, stretched to the extreme on the uphill climb, suffered for the exertion. The battalion, in the vicinity of Aix-en Provence, in peacetime a tourist destination, had to contend with pouring rain and the difficulty of erecting tents and protecting gear in a most unfavorable set of circumstances. There was much cussing and complaining.

All of the men in all the units had to prepare the equipment of modem war for battle, which included cleaning off the cosmolene, which protected from rust and deterioration, from guns, vehicles, and other equipment. The armored infantry had to clean their half-tracks and jeeps (called "peeps" by some armored men) as well as their guns and mortars. For the men in C Company of the 48th Tank Battalion, there was the task of cleaning and preparing their tanks and guns; for the Tank Destroyer units their vehicles and guns; for the artillery men their guns and equipment, and so on. Once everything was ready, all the guns had to be test-fired and calibrated for accuracy.

All of this work had to be conducted in weather that was becoming increasingly cold. This winter was to be the coldest on record in Europe for a hundred years, and the US Army was straining to procure and deliver the clothing and gear that the fighting men needed to keep from freezing. Spending their days boiling and heating off the stubborn waxy cosmolene during the day and trying to sleep warm at night, the GIs had all they could do to work efficiently and to get the rest needed to begin their fight with the enemy. Jim Craigmile remembers how cold it could get, even in early November:

> We slept in pup tents with army blankets spread on the cold wet ground. Soon the race was on to find something to put on the ground under the blankets. Newspapers were the best insulation, but they were hard to find. The nights spent there were among the worst I experienced, much worse than sleeping sitting in a cold tank.[2]

The other unexpected experience was the welcome from Axis Sally, who informed the green soldiers that "we would all die there." It was somewhat unnerving after all the emphasis on security, including not sewing on division patches until after they had settled into the bivouac area. The men were puzzled and frustrated that their whereabouts were no secret at all. Roger James wondered about spies and leaks, and remembered the wartime slogan (now taken facetiously) that "Loose lips sink ships." The Germans had been in France for four years and still had a network of spies, including those Frenchmen sympathetic to the collaborationist government of Pierre Laval. They had the same in Italy, right next door to the south. When the war was over, GIs would find that they seemed to have more in common with the Germans than with the French.

The 68th Armored Infantry Battalion (68 AlB) examined and prepared its equipment and supplies in the town of Lantosque, a lovely village "surrounded by snowcapped peaks." The town was situated almost directly north of Nice by land, and toward the eastern side of the Bale des Anges.

Further east were the Italian Alps and the German Army firmly entrenched in that high country. The march to Peira-Cava, diagonally southeast but toward the Maritime Alps, the French side, was characterized by hostile artillery fire and subject to ambush by German troops who had been stationed on the Italian side. The ordnance company was forced to use a much longer and more dangerous route because of the mountain roads, which were winding and narrow. There were so many hairpin turns that the drivers in the trucks and half-tracks often had to negotiate them by backing and advancing carefully four or five times. The combat infantrymen enjoyed the dubious pleasure of looking down the steep sides of the mountain as the vehicles reversed. The vehicles ascended and descended in low gear with speeds no more than five miles an hour, proving tempting targets for an enemy forward observer looking to call down artillery. The marching troops were not exempt to the shelling either. To add to the difficulties, although it was only November, after sunset in these high altitudes, ice formed on the road surface to add to the hazards and the difficulties of the drivers. Veterans of the 68th often expressed thanks to Warrant Officer Junior Grade Norman Wemple and his service staff for the reliable performance of the vehicles.[3]

As the 68th History tells, it, the men were shaken out of their "frivolous attitude" by the announcement from Colonel Bob E. Edwards, their CO, that the battalion would be moving out to take its place on the battle line. A serious mood ensued. The only significant pleasure for the men was to look out over the glorious scenery in the mountains—a spectacular view for tourists in peacetime. But this was not a civilian's activity for the GIs. The battalion's assignment was to hold the western flank of the Main Line of Resistance (MLR) to prevent the "harassment or encirclement of our northward moving forces." These were VI Corps, General Lucien Truscott's advancing divisions, which were effectively chasing the German Nineteenth Army north and east toward the Rhine River and the defense of the Fatherland. The role of the 14th Armored and the other divisions that landed in October and November was to continue Operation Anvil/Dragoon. Colonel Edwards reminded the troops of the dangers of Schü mines, which were a constant threat to maim American soldiers. The paratroopers the 68th were replacing had already been victimized by these tiny but deadly instruments of war.

Various emotions roiled in the breasts of these newcomers to battle. As the 68th history set the stage, "That was our first battle, a mental battle, waged individually. And so it was that early on the morning of the 13th (of November) we left this field that we called 'home,' loaded into our half-tracks and trucks, and set out in convoy for the Maritime Alps."

The journey, with sunny weather as a complement, provided the men an opportunity to view the "renowned hotels and resorts [which] looked majestically over the palm-lined avenues and the blue Mediterranean, apparently to receive their liberator, the American GI."[4] At least that is the idealized view of the authors of the battalion history. However, the billeting would be less than elegant, for the men assembled in an old cement factory in St. Martin du Var. The troops had to practice cliff climbing here in preparation for their deployment in the Alps. For several days a careful reconnaissance of the area was made by company commanders and platoon leaders. One of these excursions became stranded overnight in the cold hills but returned safely to bivouac. The 68th was designated to replace members of the original parachute drop on "The Blue Line" of Anvil/Dragoon on the evening of 14 August. These were the 550 Glider Infantry Battalion and the 509 Parachute Infantry Battalion. On the 16th the armored infantry battalion replaced them after it wound its way up the treacherous road and around the steep mountain. The airborne troops were only too happy to be relieved for they were quite exhausted after fighting for two months.

The authors of the battalion history waxed rhapsodic over the scenery:

> The Alps produced a different atmosphere from that we had experienced at Marseille. The rugged mountains were all around; at dusk one could sit and watch the mountains close in on him. The air was fresh and invigorating, the days were clear and cool, and the nights cold. On most nights the whole galaxy of stars could be seen; they shown brilliantly against the deep infinitude of darkness. Such was the physical environment of our first battle area.[5]

The 19th AIB also moved into their positions near Sospel but in high points above that little town. The ascent was so narrow and so steep that mules had to be employed to move equipment. As the 19th Armored Infantry Battalion history relates the trek:

> The M-8s [assault guns] were driven up the treacherous mountain trails at night during a hard rain, later described by one of the drivers as a trail he wouldn't even drive a peep [jeep] on in daylight. The next morning, 15 November, after relieving the 75 Pack Howitzers of the 51st (actually the first) ABTF [Airborne Task Force], the Assault Gun Platoon registered their guns and fired what is claimed to be the first round fired by the 14th AD against the enemy. These three guns took over positions occupied and defended previously by 16 guns.[6]

The headquarters of the two armored infantry companies were located in diminutive towns that clung to the mountain slopes: B Company (68) was situated in Turini (its name suggesting its closeness to the Italian border), and A Company settled in Rocque Bellaire (its name hinting at its beauty), with the fourth platoon in the same town. A Company's first platoon found itself in the resort town of Belvedere, and much to its delight, was billeted in a luxurious hotel in Bethmoth Les Baines. C Company was held in reserve to the rear in Peira Cava, with one of its platoons commanded by 2nd Lt. Gosselin committed to outpost duty in the town of Moulinet.[7] Yet their mood, which had been so positive before, was darkened with the accidental death of one of their own, Pvt. William M. Greene of C Company. Pvt. Russ Taylor and Greene were out in front of the line at Peira-Cava restoring the telephone lines at night. Russ was on the right and Bill was on the left as they returned to their position in a hotel surrounded by sandbags and a machine-gun position. A rifleman, probably edgy, fired at the two men and hit Greene in the chest while Taylor dove over a rise as an MG fired high over him. The third member of the patrol shouted out the countersign when they were challenged, but it was too late for Greene. Taylor asked the outpost whether they had finished shooting. He felt that they were trigger-happy. Russ Taylor is upset to this day that the incident was not recorded in either the 14th's or the 68th's histories. Pvt. William M. Greene is listed as KIA in the 14th Armored History, but the story is not told in the narrative.[8]

That History depicts the anxiety of the men:

The tenseness began. . . . The tenseness was never to leave, not completely until the war was over, the tenseness of being in combat, the uncertainty, the 'might' (the 'next one might' . . . 'they might'. . .). War seems to be nothing but uncertainty, there is no rhyme or reason to its killing, if you had been there instead of here, you would have gotten it, if you hadn't happened to turn, if your peep hadn't happened to have a flat you would have arrived earlier—life and death hang on a whole series of minor mischances; and your luck runs out—that is the tense-ness.[9]

Captain Joseph Carter's rendering of the tension of battle reflects the knowledge of war that he had gained as an officer in Headquarters Company, 14th Armored Division, from the Maritime Alps to the end of the war.

The 68th's battalion front extended incredibly long, 21 miles across the hills and valleys of the Alps. In support were the first platoon of A Company, 40th Engineers, the 601st Mountain Artillery Battalion, with their pack mules to carry the 75mm guns broken down in packs on the mules, B Battery of the 68th AAA, with their 90mm anti-aircraft guns, and B Company of the 645th Tank Destroyer Battalion, equipped with the 3-inch M-10 assault guns. The entire group was flanked on the right by the 19th AIB and on the left by the 100th Japanese-American, or Nisei, battalion of the famous 442nd Regimental Combat Team. This was the most decorated unit of World War II, with extraordinary courage and terrible losses incurred in the demonstration of that courage.[10]

Although this is to get a little ahead of things, when the 68th was later relieved by a unit from the 442nd RCT, Bob Davies, with a new sergeant's rank, was given the task of showing his replacement sergeant the area they were going to occupy. The diminutive sergeant, after about fifteen minutes of climbing up and down the irregular terrain, began to lose his breath. Bob Davies, who loved to needle people if he thought it appropriate, chided the Nisei NCO about not being in good shape. The latter then stopped, looked at Bob, and opened his fatigue jacket, expos-ing a large bandage on his chest. He then peeled back the bandage to reveal his open lung, which had been severely wounded by either a bullet or shrapnel. He then replied to Bob's challenge, "You know, I really shouldn't be in the line at all. I should have been shipped back to a field hospital. At the battalion aid station they patched me up a bit and gave me a few days to recover. Then they processed me back on the line and here I am." Bob was appalled by the story and regretted criticizing someone who should have been his comrade. Clearly the fact that the American Army and Marines were fighting a fanatical foe and that Pearl Harbor was a recent memory determined that anyone Japanese was not going to be treated, at least by some, as a comrade.[11]

It was obvious that there was little need for the tank battalions in such rugged and steep country, with little chance for maneuver on either the roads or off-road on the heavily bouldered and cratered terrain. Since Colonel Edwards had warned his soldiers of the danger of mines, there was a need for engineers to detect and disarm or explode them. It was also obvious that trying to manhandle 105mm or 155mm howitzers would be extraordinarily difficult, and so they were not brought up but fired from the rear. In their stead was the less powerful but still lethal 75mm gun complemented by the 4.2-inch mortar.

The .50-caliber machine guns were quad mounted for defense against aircraft, but they could be turned against land targets such as fixed positions and lightly armored vehicles. They were extraordinarily lethal and fearsome when employed against infantry. However, the gunners would not want to stand against any German tank or assault gun because they had so little protection. The 90mm guns were designed for an anti-aircraft role, but as with the German 88s, could be leveled and used in an anti-tank role. There were also some M-10 Tank Destroyers with 3-inch guns which could be effective as mobile artillery, but it would have been suicide for the M-10's to confront a Mark VI Tiger with its thick frontal armor. American shells had a habit of glancing off those tanks. The Mark V Panther, while not as heavy as the Tiger, would also be deadly against the M-10. Foot soldiers liked to have an M-10 behind them, usually camouflaged, to act as urgent support.

During November the Headquarters' Staff was going to have it really easy as they were stationed in Nice in the sunshine and along the sandy beaches of the Mediterranean. This was CCR Headquarters (Combat Command Reserve), which commanded both the 19th and the 68th AIB and their supporting units. The other two Commands were A and B, and although it sounds as if CCR would always be the Reserve Command, that was not always the case, especially in complex and extended battles like the nightmare at Hatten-Rittershofen in January. Any of the combat commands could be called upon, like regiments in infantry divisions, to reinforce one another or suddenly to take advantage of a gap in the enemy's lines or to plug one in their own. Cavalry units such as the 94th and the later-attached A117th, although designed primarily for reconnaissance and probes of enemy positions (with their light tanks and armored cars), could also be employed as a reserve force. Horses were no longer used in American cavalry units, but at the beginning of the war in Poland in September 1939, Polish cavalry units were directed to attack German infantry and armor—with predictably disastrous results. General George Patton still loved to wear the distinctive jodphurs or cavalry pants, and he saw tanks through the prism of horse cavalry.

Also located in Nice was the headquarters of the First Airborne Task Force, commanded by General R. T. Frederick. The Task Force, on the evening before the Anvil/Dragoon landings, had been airlifted from Rome and dropped near Le Muy. After successfully defeating German forces in the area, it had been stationed in the Maritime Alps. The 44th AA Brigade, commanded by General Tobin, relieved the Task Force along with the battalions of the Fourteenth. Most of the attention on airborne troops during the war has been focused on the 82nd and 101st Airborne, but the airborne and glider troops of the Airborne Task Force had done a commendable job in fighting the enemy.[12]

To return to the 68th in action, the Mortar and Machine Gun Platoon moved into position on the left flank of B Company atop Hill 1926. Here, on the morning of 18 November, the first round fired by the Fourteenth hit German positions. Charlie White's Mortar Platoon began shelling Fort LaForca while the I and R (Intelligence and Reconnaissance) Platoon was stationed in an observation post on the extreme right flank, overlooking two German-held forts of the Maginot Line, La Forca and Mille Forche. Both artillery fire and patrol action were ordered to feel out the German strengths and weaknesses. The Germans responded with counter-battery fire, and hostile patrol opposed friendly patrol. On the morning of 20 November, at about 2000 hours in the darkness, one of the German patrols engaged the second squad of B Company's Third Platoon in a firefight on top of Hill

1926. Although the squad was outnumbered and German soldiers had crept to within ten yards of the defensive position. Staff Sergeant Jim Miner, despite being wounded, directed the fire of his squad and repulsed the enemy patrol, inflicting heavy casualties in the process. Captain Joseph Carter describes the action in his usual dramatic and immediate fashion:

> There was the flat crack of a rifle, re-echoing past the black rock crags of the night, then the orange streaks of the automatic weapons slashing the night in streaks of light, the explosions sharp snaps of white, the smell of cordite and the clattering of sound. A German patrol was attacking quickly, savagely, and in superior numbers; at one time they were in, their dark uniforms barely visible, the endless sudden darting into light of their guns only giving away their positions.[13]

During the fight, Sergeant Cecil F. Slusher, also wounded, continued to engage the enemy from an exposed position. The 68th AIB had demonstrated courage and resourcefulness in the face of the enemy in its first experience of combat. Both Staff Sergeants, Miner and Susher, were awarded Silver Stars for their bravery and devotion to duty.

The men of the 19th AIB had also had their hands full. On 16 November a patrol of B Company, led by S/Sgts. Paul D. Brown and Ronald C. Hanwood, encountered the enemy. Both the assault guns and the 81mm mortars supported the action. On another patrol S/Sgt. Howard Nick Jonson, first rifle squad, 3rd Platoon, directed the squad against a German pillbox when

> the first quick burst of a German machine gun blasted at him (and forever after it was easy for the men to tell the difference between American machine guns—a stuttering 'Da-da-da-da-da-da-da-' and German guns—'Brrrrp,' 'Brrrrp', sounding quick and hard and flat.) As the machine gun quieted, Johnson [sic] continued to work his men ahead; with the pillbox in sight he had them cover him and made a dash for it. The Germans had pulled out. (As Johnson dived in the pillbox window, he barely missed set ting off a booby trap.)

On another patrol with the 19th, Sgt Maurice E. Short led his men near la Gonella but was wounded in the process. He organized his squad to devise a way to get back without activating a German machine gun. He told them to go back to their positions, by going on a different route than they had come. He deliberately drew the fire of the gunner away from his men, for which he would later earn a Silver Star.[14]

During this period in November, with snow beginning to fall in these regions, the German Schü mines took a toll on the GIs, for the Germans would conceal them everywhere, near trenches or bunkers, or inside them, and along trails. With the snow covering them, they became lethal weapons which took a soldier out of the fight without his ever being able to respond to the enemy who had planted them. The engineers found them almost impossible to detect because they were basically made of wood. The high explosive placed inside was equipped with a tiny igniter and a trip wire to set off the mine. They did not intend to kill but to maim, taking off the lower part of the leg and rendering the victim *hors de combat* but also removing from the immediate fight one or two other soldiers who would go to the assistance of the injured man. Even taking a medic temporarily out of the fight was an advantage in these cases. On the battlefield in the Alsace campaign, it was nothing extraordinary for German snipers to deliberately aim at a medic, even the cross on his helmet which should have made the wearer off limits to hostile fire. More than one medic would be killed later. Two members of the 68th who were victims of Schü mines were Pfc. Dake Novotny and Pfc. James Walters of Bob Davies' B Company. He found the mines especially appalling because they were assembled by school children.[15]

The authors of the 68th history recognized the contributions of Headquarters Company laying wire under dangerous circumstances, especially two Captains, Bob Hunziker and Joe Hensly, and T/Sgt. Benjamin Bloomfield and Pfc. Phillip Snoberger, Bob Davies' buddy. All of these men received Bronze Stars for outstanding duty under fire. The Communications Section laid over two hundred miles of wire, and the Supply Branch maintained a thirty-five mile communication line all the way back to Nice.

Ken Hazleton, an aid man or medic with the 68th, wrote a report which detailed the contributions of some of the aid men:

The work of [the] Baker Company aid men who had the majority of the casualties was notably backbreaking. By the aid of a ski-litter, they hauled men up and down precipitous mountains, in 3–4 feet of November snow. One memorable trip, Sgt. [Harold] Schneider, Tec 5 Goldstein [Bernard Gorstein?], and Pfc. [Allan] Simon with the able assistance of 16 linemen labored 8 hours removing two wounded men from an outpost. This was in the dark of night, the best time made for such a trip was 4 hours [presumably in the daylight]. It was indeed a rugged but beautiful country. An ambulance trip between the two [aid] stations was 30–40 miles by road, although as the crow flew, the distance was about 6 miles. The winding mountain roads with their continuous turns were a remarkable deterrent to speeding or vehicle driving.[16]

The Tenth Mountain Division, during their training in the United States, had invented the ski litter, which on all mountainous battlefields, was a godsend. The Fifth Army, fighting in the hills around Monte Cassino, would have found it so, as would the combatants in the First World War, both Austrian and Italian. The shorter the time between any kind of trauma, whether combat injuries or civilian strokes and heart attacks, the better the chance of survival for the patient.

The experience of the men of the Fourteenth Armored, especially the 19th and 68th AIB, had been a valuable preparation for entering more serious and sustained combat. The men became accustomed to mortar and artillery shells landing around them. While the fighting was nowhere near as severe as it would get later, nevertheless it served them well. The combat also welded the men together as a unit and kept them looking out for each other. Although it is a cliché to say so, even today, the men learned a genuine love for those fighting closest to them, their squad or their platoon.

And so the fighting and skirmishing continued until the first of December, when the 68th Armored Infantry Battalion was notified it would be relieved. The famous 100th Battalion of the 442nd Regimental Combat Team, tested terribly and with great loss of life, replaced the 68th on the MLR along with the 899th AA Automatic Weapons Battalion. The next assignment for the 68th was to rejoin the 14th AD in the Alsatian plains, further north and up through the Rhone

Valley. When the relief had been completed, the battalion descended for a hasty reorganization back at the cement factory. The full-track and half-track vehicles were loaded on the infamous French boxcars, the notorious "40 and 8" railway stock. In World War I the 40 referred to the human passengers, formerly the *poilu* and now the GIs; and the 8 referred to the horses of that war. The French flat cars hauled the tanks, armored cars, the half-tracks, and other miscellaneous vehicles. Bob Davies told an amusing story of how Captain M. A. Reed, the CO, couldn't wait to defecate while stuffed inside one of the stinking boxcars. In the middle of this procedure, with his hind quarters hanging out over the track and a train station full of civilians up the tracks, he asked his men for some toilet paper so he could swing modestly back inside the car. They refused and allowed him to suffer the cheers and the jeers of the French people in the station, including many women. He was not pleased, but his company thought it was hilarious.[17]

On a more sober note, when the wheeled vehicles traveled by road during the day and bivouacked by night as they passed through the country, "twisting along the beautiful valley of the Rhone, Avignon (Sur le Pont), Valence, Dijon, and Lyon," the scenery was breathtaking and "the signs of war were few." There . . .

> was a long stretch of highway, miles and miles, where General Patch's Seventh Army troops had nailed a retreating German column on the road, blocked its way by blowing bridges, then bombed and strafed and shelled the long doubled column of German vehicles (behind the 'champagne campaign' was the smell of death) knocked them out and burned them up, and then the American bulldozers had come along and scraped the hulks into ditches. There they were, rusting in the air, dead scrap of the war machine."[18]

Unmentioned in the graphic description was the large number of horses that had also to be killed along with their military masters. Despite the popular impression that the army of Blitzkrieg was a mechanized army, throughout and to the end of the war, horses continued to be employed to carry equipment and pull guns. Nobody has counted the number of horses that were tormented and killed in the maelstrom of war. The same thing had happened in the pursuit by Third Army of the

German divisions that had tried to escape the double envelopment in the Falaise Gap. Not only machines but also innocent, dutiful animals were burned or ripped to shreds.

In the French towns as well, specifically in Charmes, as the 14th's History points out, the beautiful facades of 18th century houses had been smashed, "and here was the full desolation of war":

> Here was not simply bombing; here had been infantry and artillery firing at defended positions, and Charmes did not simply have blocks of houses ruined by a bomb hit; here houses had been flattened, leveled, reduced to senseless piles of rubble by the deadly pounding of artillery, and here were holes where strings of machine gun bullets had sprayed. Here were only a few civilians, watching the up-moving troops with weary eyes, here was waste and full destruction.[19]

The 68th's History passes by the ruination cited above and concludes the journey through Luneville, Sarrebourg, Saverne, and ending in Schwindratzheim, calling it "uneventful." The last leg of the trip, after Einvaux, had been conducted in the halftracks, which smelled more pleasant than the railroad cars. Casualties for the Maritime Alps had been comparatively slight, although not slight to those who were wounded or to the families of those who were killed. The total of those wounded or injured was eleven, and killed in action were three. Quite a few of the wounds were caused by the hateful Schü mines. The 68th History concludes: "It was quite an experience to leave a French-speaking country and find ourselves confronted with a new tongue, namely Alsatian."[20]

Chapter 2

TRAGEDY AT BARR

While the 68th AIB was engaged in infantry action in the Maritime Alps without the usual accompaniment of a tank battalion, the three organic tank battalions of the 14th Armored Division—the 25th, the 47th, and the 48th—were active elsewhere. The 48th was paired with the 62nd AIB, which joined them in action during November in Alsace. This would lead to the tragedy at Barr on 27 November. Each battalion had fifty-three Sherman M-4 medium tanks and 17 Stuart M-5 light tanks. Each tank battalion also had six medium tanks armed with 105 howitzers. Also attached to the Division was the 847th Tank Destroyer Battalion, which was designed to fight tank-versus-tank against panzers. In April 1945, the 636th TD Battalion would also be added to the 14th.

In the ideal armored situation, according to tank doctrine, armored forces were to slice through the enemy's Main Line of Resistance and cut through to rear areas to sow confusion and disarray. This was the theory promoted energetically by General George S. Patton. In Alsace, as well as in the rest of Europe, small roads led through towns of various sizes, and every town or city could be a chokepoint for tanks and armored vehicles, and an occasion for an ambush when the enemy chose to attack. In Normandy, in the summer of 1944, both tanks and infantry had been stifled, frustrated, and defeated because of the hedgerows and sunken roads built over centuries by Norman farmers to mark and negotiate their land. Casualties were high for the American divisions trying to break through because it was sometimes impossible to make headway against hostile positions that were carefully dug in with pre-registered fields of fire for machine guns, mortars, tanks, and artillery.

But the breakout from Normandy in August changed all that.

In Alsace, where nothing much had changed, by 22 November, the whole of XV Corps had passed through the area of the Savrne Gap onto the Alsatian plain; the Saales Pass was taken the next day by the Third Infantry Division (of Audie Murphy fame); and by the end of the week, all the passes had been stormed and taken. The key city of Strasbourg fell between 23 and 25 November.[1] However, none of this had been easy, for when XV Corps attacked between 11 and 14th November, the gains were less than impressive. In an unusual maneuver, the commander of the 71st Division, Major General Robert L. Spragins, ordered the 114th Infantry to cross in front of his other two regiments and penetrate the defenses of the 553rd Volksgrenadier Division "from the flank and the rear." As the Official History of the campaign in southern France appraised it:

> This somewhat unorthodox—if not dangerous—maneuver proved successful; by the evening of the 15th, the 114th Infantry had gained a mile and a half to the east, northeast, and north of Leintrey, thus dislocating the German defenses in the rising, partially wooded ground. On 16 November the 114th Infantry and the 106th Cavalry Group mopped up on the division's left, and the next day the 324th and 71st Infantry continued their advance east, passing through the wake of the 114th, which reverted to its reserve status.[2]

Everything seemed to be going the way of the combined French and American divisions in Alsace. The armored columns, with tanks, half-tracks, self-propelled guns, and trucks were motoring along expeditiously except for some manned roadblocks which held out for a while but then retreated under pressure to the next town and the next roadblock.

One of the tank battalions speeding ahead, along with its partner in the 62nd Infantry Battalion, was the 48th. The 48th had left New York with the rest of the division on 14 October and arrived in Marseilles on 29 October. In action already in November, the 48th exchanged one tank company for an infantry company to assist in the advance, which would take it through several contested towns. Company A-62 would work with the 48th Tank Battalion. Of critical importance to the relatively inexperienced tankers and infantry was the need for the infantry and reconnaissance elements to identify enemy anti-tank positions and panzers, which could literally be lurking around the corner in an Alsatian town with narrow streets and hidden alleys. Without men on foot, armor was near blind in built up areas or in woods.

The 48th liberated such towns as Rambervillers, Blamont, and Schirmeck and then were ordered to assault "to take and hold the town of Selestat," north of Colmar. Around 26 November, General Friedrich Wiese's German Nineteenth Army held the city, "a critical rail and road junction city . . . ten miles south of Barr." Two infantry divisions, the 103rd and the 36th, assisted by the Fourteenth Armored Division, were ordered to take the key city. Major General Edward H. Brooks, commander of VI Corps, ordered the division "to secure the section of N-83 (highway) south of Erstein behind the main German defensive line," which would lead to the fight at Barr. The operational purpose was to help the French Second Armored Division seize Selestat, north of Colmar.[3] Resistance in the town of Valff caused the 48th on 27 November to disengage and try another route through Obernai and Bernandsviller "only to meet disasterous [sic] results from the enemy at Barr," according to the unit history of the 48th published after the war. The unit history of the 14AD also characterized the event in ominous tones: "The 48th Tank Battalion column had meanwhile run into trouble, serious and deadly trouble; and its name was Barr."[4]

As it happened, the 48th and A Company of the 62nd AIB constituted the main element of one column, with Lt. Col. Edwin H. Ferris in command, and the rest of the 62nd AIB rode with Company B of the 25th TB, under the command of Lt. Col. James H. Meyers. After the order to seize Schirmeck in order to block the German retreat came down and was carried out, the result was that many casualties were incurred at another roadblock. This roadblock was only conquered by the heroic action of S/Sgt. Samuel E. Boyden, who, in the second tank, fired on the roadblock and blew it away. However, he had to dismount the tank to clear the barrel of the gun and was then killed by a sniper. For this action he was posthumously awarded the Bronze Star.

In addition to this courageous action, the division history further described how the 48th TB, with the third platoon of Company B of the 94th Cavalry Recon, entered the town of Valff, with Sgt. Charles Small of Company A, the 48th, in the lead. His tank was hit by a panzerfaust, with Tec/5 Raymond Polanowski dying as a result of the high-explosive (HE) projectile. Sgt William E. McCauley then put his own tank on point. Company A of the 62nd AIB, with Captain Daniel R. lannella in command, rode on top of the tanks and prepared for further action. McCauley's tank's machine gun then "cut down an enemy bazooka team." The juxtaposition of town buildings and alleys with the lethal nature of the panzerfaust made it a very unforgiving situation for the men in and on the tanks.

The driver of McCauley's tank, no doubt apprehensive about anti-tank guns as well as panzerfausts, skidded his tank into a ditch to get defilade protection. Sgt. McCauley then instructed his gunner, Corp. Esthe P. Hamman, to fire on German troops near a stone cross, but the gunner, a pious soldier no doubt, protested against firing on a holy site. "It's a piece of stone with Krauts around it. . . . Fire!" McCauley himself fired four times with the 30 cal. machine gun mounted on top and killed four soldiers in Feldgrau uniforms as they mistakenly popped their heads up over a wall. Lightly defended roadblocks after this incident slowed the column only slightly, but on 26 November the tanks and infantry arrived at the town of Barr, France.[5]

The 48th was divided into its four tank companies, and an infantry platoon of Company A of the 62nd AIB was matched with each. The people in Barr knew that the town was defended by "infantry and grenadiers of the German 10th Volksdivision supported by tanks and anti-tank guns and bazookas [panzerfausts], men, snipers and machine gunners, road blocks, artillery and mortars. The German had power there, power he was instantly to unleash; and his strength was underestimated."[6] It is also an "underestimation" to equate the American bazooka with the German panzerfaust; the latter were much more deadly then the American weapon because of their large hollow-shaped charge which could penetrate up to 200mm (7.8 inches) of armor and could be fired easily by one man.

The concept of underestimation is an understatement for another reason. On 26 November at 10:00 p.m. a message arrived in Barr, presumably at the train station, that a train carrying anti-tank weapons was due to arrive soon. Clearly the Germans were going to oppose the armored column with everything at their disposal. The FFI (French Forces of the Interior, or "the Resistance") had also detected at Goxwiller, not that far away, several tanks and a detachment of troops from the SS Feldernhalle Division. An account of this event from the French perspective was accompanied by the statement, "The Americans had to be forewarned . . . that they should expect a dynamite [?] attack [which had to be especially dangerous in a town or city.]" The FFI, to their credit, made a decision to destroy the railroad track between Eichhoffen and the pass at Mittelbergheim in order to frustrate the German defenses.[7] Fortunately, the train never arrived, but it is a puzzle why the FFI did not send a message to the advancing American column warning them of the trap ahead.

The Monthly Report of the Division coolly recounts what happened to the armored column, first on 27 November and then on 28 November:

MONDAY NOV 27, 1944.
LOCATION: Vic: Valeff [sic] and Meistratzheim
TROOPS: Add 69th AFA

ACTION: At 0800 head of column crossed IP and advanced toward Obernai thence to vicinity of Valeff where Bn again met heavy resistance of heavily protected road blocks and artillery fire. After several conflicts, Bn withdrew to vicinity of Meistratzheim where Cp was set up in village and outposted for night.

TUESDAY NOV 28, 1944.
LOCATION: Vic: BARR
TROOPS: No change

ACTION: Bn moved toward Obernai and continued advance toward Barr.* Light resistance was encountered along the route consisting of defended road blocks and bazooka fire. Upon reaching Barr well concealed AT guns opened fire on our tanks inflicting great loss in men and equipment. AT's were protected by small arms fire and bazooka fire. On contacting the EXO, [Executive Officer] with his authority the Bn regrouped outside the village of Barr [more a town or city] and on completion of same, withdrew to Bernardsviller where CP was set up in a school house and the village was outposted and was immediately replaced by Div on this date.[10]

Then S/Sgt. Pete Lakey, only a few years ago, wrote of his memory of Barr from the perspective of a member of A Company of the 62nd: "On the 27th of November, we entered Barr riding on the tanks of the 48th. At the outskirts of town we were told to drop off the tanks and follow them. The tanks ran into stiff opposition in town and many were lost."[11]

As B Company of the 48th entered the town of Barr under Captain Menefee E. Blackwell, with Lt. Lawrence F. Doyle in the lead, an anti-tank round smashed into Doyle's tank. The driver, Tec.14 Mike Bellish, careened the tank into a ditch to save the lives of the crew. The second tank, under Sgt Hubert V. Summers, lashed back with a "streak of flame" to destroy the enemy gun and crew, "which erupted into the air." Corp. Raymond O'Donnell's tank got a lucky hit and exploded an ammunition dump, with smoke and flames billowing into the sky. There erupted then a cacophony of small arms fire in a "hysterical continuous chatter," along with the boom of artillery rounds. The infantry of the 62nd suffered terribly from the artillery fire as they tried to escape into the ditches beside the road. Members of the 94th Cavalry uncovered and destroyed the gun but not before it had knocked out a friendly medium tank.

As the 14th AD's history continued, "The fierceness, the intensity of the fighting that developed in Barr is impossible to describe; like a beaten, bleeding and bloody fighter, the tank column fought its way into that boiling inferno on sheer nerve, inch by hellish inch."[8] What the officers in the column did not know was that there was a battalion of the S.S. Feldernhalle Division in the town who were dedicated to the destruction of the American force. German anti-tank guns, panzer-fausts, and at least one panzer, probably a Tiger, were ingeniously concealed within or behind the buildings of the town, including and especially the hospital, as the story will unfold.

The battalion commander's tank was smashed at a roadblock, with Lt. Col. Ferris wounded in both legs. Although the men in the tank had known the location of the anti-tank gun that had hit them, the tank gunner missed his target, but the AT gunner did not. Lt. George H. Herbert tried to swing his tanks down another street, but they were also fired upon and struck, and he was killed in the fight as "the inferno closed in on him." S/Sgt William Winslow fired into a house, but an AT gun destroyed his tank with three rounds, "and it burst into flames the sudden incredible way a tank burns," as Captain Carter put it. The habit of referring to the Shermans as "Ronsons" or "Zippos" was validated in this clash when the gasoline tank must have exploded. Captain Blackwell had nine tanks in flames and a total of ten eliminated from the fight. Carter quoted from the official report of the action: "The Company was in bad shape. There were only five tanks in operating condition and the morale of the men was at its lowest ebb."[9] It was no wonder that the spirits of the men would be down after the devastating losses they took from a largely concealed enemy.

Company A's experience was both heroic and tragic. After having two vehicles wrecked by enemy fire, Sgt. Forest Gable moved into the town and fired into a suspicious looking house. Later it would be discovered that a hidden AT gun had been obliterated. Moments later his tank moved into the open town square where another AT gun fired from the window of a hospital. According to the Director of the Hospital (as we shall see later) there was a tank hidden behind a wall at the hospital, and perhaps this was the source of the cannon fire. The facade of the hospital was hammered by cannon fire from the Shermans in response to the panzer's fire. The enemy gun was apparently knocked out in any case, and Captain Carter portrays an enemy soldier with a panzerfaust emerging from cover. "Pvt. Dennis L. Hennessey, loader and radio tender, cut him down with a machine gun; and at the same moment the tank was hit in quick succession by two enemy bazooka rounds." Carter repeats the words of the citation for Sgt. Gable:

Distinguished Service Cross awarded posthumously to Sergeant Forest Gable for extraordinary heroism on 28 November 1944. While advancing into the town of Barr, France, through intense enemy artillery and mortar fire, Sergeant Gable's tank was hit twice by enemy bazooka [Panzerschreck, similar to the U.S. bazooka) fire which disabled the tank and injured three members of the crew. Sergeant Gable immediately directed artillery fire against the hostile position, thereby enabling the wounded men to escape. When his 75mm ammunition was exhausted, he crawled to the rear of the tank and despite intense automatic weapons fire, he continued to fire his .50 caliber machine gun. Disdaining retreat, he held his position until killed by enemy fire. By his extraordinary heroism and unselfish sacrifice,

Sergeant Gable enabled three wounded comrades to escape and effected the successful withdrawal of his platoon.[12]

Others, impelled by the hellish experiences they had undergone, or their family members, vividly replayed the scene. Michael Taxman, the son-in-law of Pfc. Elton C. Ross, Company D of the 48th TB, summarized what he understands happened to one of their loved ones:

> On November 21, 1944, his company first engaged the enemy outside of Schirmeck, France. Six days later, his company entered the town of Barr, France. His [Ross's] tank was struck by bazooka fire and burst into flames. My father in-law, a bow gunner, proceeded to rescue the tank commander and driver, but was unable to pull the gunner from the burning tank. Severely injured, he spent the next 45 days in a hospital in France, after which he insisted on rejoining the battalion, then in the midst of battle. For his actions, he was honored with the Bronze Star and the Purple Heart.[13]

Corp. Knott Rankin, who was Sgt. Gable's gunner, "stayed at his sweating, death-ridden seat" until all his ammunition was expended but was killed as he tried to escape the deadly trap of the burning tank. For his action he posthumously received the Silver Star.

In the confused melee, Lt. Edgar Woodward's platoon was ordered to escape the area but wound up in the middle of Barr. Fortunately for both the tankers and the infantry, the tank platoon encountered some men from the 103rd Infantry Division. The officers on both sides decided to form a tank-infantry team. A squad of infantry under Sgt. Joseph J. Costa of B-48 started forward on a reconnaissance mission when they saw someone in civilian clothes running across the street. They ordered him to halt, but he refused. Upon opening fire, the squad received what was described as "lashing fire" from two German machine guns at the end of the street. The infantry suffered several casualties before a Sherman pulverized the machine gun emplacements with cannon fire.[14]

During the night the German soldiers began to retreat from the town, and the men from the 103rd searched the town house by house. The 48th also returned to find nineteen comrades, many wounded, who had had to hold on in enemy territory all night. As the 48th returned to the attack, two light tanks were knocked out by mines, with several casualties. These would have been M3 Stuarts which had a small 37mm gun along with three .30 caliber machine guns and 1.5 inches of armor. Bob McClarren remembers Capt. Andrew Winiarczyk (25th TB) calling the light tanks with the 17mm guns as "kiddy cars with pop guns." It was considered "Obsolete as a combat tank by 1944" by another source. Obsolete or not, the 14th's tank battalions were equipped with them with all their vulnerability. They were often used as command or scout cars.[15] After the light tanks were wrecked by the mines, S/Sgt. Othello Comprino earned himself a Bronze Star for taking a leadership position.

To turn attention to the infantry of the 62nd AIB, Captain Joseph Carter wryly observed, "The 62nd column did not have a much better time." It was led by Lt. Willard G. Bowsky's Cavalry platoon from Company B of the 94th, with C-48, C and Headquarters Co. of the 62nd, and Capt. Andrew Winiarczyk's C Company from the 25th Tank Battalion in the rear. Between the darkness and the fog, the visibility was quite uncertain, with a dark woods to the front. The column had passed two destroyed French reconnaissance cars and the bodies of their occupants, for the French had been through here earlier on their way to Strasbourg. Carter's prose is graphic in painting the picture of what happened next:

> The patrol flushed its first Germans. The atmosphere tensed in the burning stink of the recent fighting, you could smell something ahead. A string of rifle shots like firecrackers came back from the head of the column; the column halted, stopped by a minefield covered by fire.

Carter again: Lt. Bowsky volunteered to examine the minefield to clear a route through it. Someone ordered the convoy to turn on its blackout lights and all hell broke loose. Only a hundred yards away a German machine gun opened up on the column, and outside of town the GIs could see a horse drawn artillery piece ahead of it on the road. The armored cars of the 94th's Company B fired as the lights went out, and "the flat hard bark" of a 37mm broke the momentary stillness, "and the sound did not carry but hung in the air, the flames suddenly sparked up and die, the ragged yellow fingers of the machine guns jabbed instantly through the night," in Carter's words. The fighting continued in a madness of destruction. Men were wounded and killed on both sides, as well as the many horses that pulled the German artillery pieces. The Germans were apparently withdrawing and in a vulnerable position.

Nevertheless, the Germans had one of their deadlier weapons, the four-barrelled flak wagons, two barrels up firing tracer and two down firing ball ammunition (20mm). Originally designed for antiaircraft purposes, it was sometimes employed with deadly effect against infantry. An American bazooka team, led by Pfc. Roy W. Barbee, fired two rounds into a house when fire could be observed. Every conceivable weapon, the 20mm guns, anti-tank guns, bazookas, mortars, machine guns, machine pistols, and rifles were flinging steel and lead throughout the nightmarish light. Lt. Bowsky and several of his men were killed in the action, with Bowsky later receiving a posthumous Silver Star. Many more were wounded and killed until Lt. Marion H. May led C Company of the 125th Armored Combat Engineers into the fight, and the second platoon of C-62 passed through the tanks and dug in. Any thought of a respite from the fighting was dashed when a 62nd mortar platoon started firing and the Germans responded with counter-fire, causing still more casualties. Two scouts then established that the enemy had erected a roadblock about two hundred yards down the road. Carter's description is again apt: "The volume of fire continued to increase in the mad, ghastly, nightmarish baffle of the fog."[16]

The Shermans continued to fire at gun flashes from the German positions, but the enemy gunners employed one of their favorite nighttime tactics, firing MG tracer to see fiery ricochets of the Shermans' armor and then firing cannon at the identified target. In an impossible situation, Lt. Russell Watson ordered his platoon of the 48th TB to fall back, despite difficulties with turning the vehicles under accurate enemy fire. Several more men, including Lt. Watson, were killed or wounded. The battle would continue for a while, but it would take another day to eliminate the enemy from the vicinity of Barr.[17]

Another element in the story of the battle at Barr was the participation of units of underground Resistance fighters such as the "Regiment de Marche de La Legion Etrangere, the first battalion, Organization des FFI." These units operated against German forces in Occupied France, which in 1944 was all of France. These guerilla units provided important assistance to the Allies by rescuing downed flyers, communicating useful intelligence, sabotaging railways, bridges, and tunnels, and, when the time came, fighting alongside the Allied armies as they liberated France from Nazi domination. The particular unit in Alsace had members in eighteen towns, including Barr, who eagerly awaited the arrival of the French and American forces. German troops had retreated from Barr on 23 November with a variety of vehicles including bicycles and baby carriages, according to a pamphlet published in the 1980's in Alsace.[18] Captain Karrer, the commander of the FFI battalion, would play a decisive role in getting the townspeople organized after the battle for Barr was completed.

The actions of the Resistance and the townspeople add a substantive dimension to the Barr tragedy and to the fate of one or more of the wounded tankers. As has been said, it is unclear whether or not the Resistance had made any contact with the lead column motoring toward Barr. The Germans had indeed retreated from the town during the third week in November in some disarray, but they had returned in force to defend the town by 26 November with anti-tank guns, at least one tank, and a detachment of troops from the Feldhernhalle Division. US Army Intelligence was apparently unaware of this change to the tactical situation. The German battalion had as its motto, "bis zum Sieg" ("until victory"), an appropriate slogan for an SS unit. The German troops entered the buildings and the houses along the main street, setting up machine guns and small arms positions and several anti-tank guns in well-concealed positions, with a tank around the corner next to the hospital waiting to pounce on the unsuspecting GIs.[19]

Although the account of the fight is treated briefly in the history of the 48th Tank Battalion, it does relate the basic problem:

> Here well concealed anti-tank and bazooka teams [panzerfausts] located at strategic dug-in positions completely foiled our advances. In addition to the Battalion Commander's tank [that of Lt. Col. Ferris] being knocked out, and he seriously injured along with his crew, the companies suffered severe losses in men and equipment.[20]

One of the few survivors of the initial onslaught was Howard Knapp, a private in the 48th's Headquarters Company. He remembers dramatically what happened: seventeen tanks of B Company entered the town in the late afternoon of the 28th without sufficient awareness of the German presence. The anti-tank guns and the panzer opened up on the unsuspecting Americans of B Company and Headquarters Company, and destroyed all seventeen tanks and wounded or killed 85 men, of both the tank and the Infantry (?) Battalion, with only two survivors including Knapp.[21] He also wrote a brief summary of what happened to him on that calamitous day:

> I was the radio operator in the lead tank of the 48th Tank Battalion, 14th Armored Division. Lieutenant Colonel George Ferris was the battalion commander and I was in his tank going to battle at Barr. Leaving Obernai, we headed toward Barr. Colonel Ferris ordered reconnaissance of the city and scouts reported back that there was no enemy in the area. Company B then was ordered to enter [the city]. I was unable, in my tank, to secure radio contact with the tanks of Company B. I could hear, over the radio, echoes of battle but communications were not possible. I reported this to Colonel Ferris and he decided to go see what had happened to Company B. We entered the city and saw numerous tanks burning in the streets. We continued to advance while continuously returning fire. We had almost reached the far side of the city and should have turned left but there was a barricade there and an emplaced anti-tank cannon. Our cannon returned fire, a near miss, but the anti-tank cannon's aim was better.

And then Private Knapp, who had been wounded in the arm by shrapnel in an earlier engagement, described this terrible wounding and near death:

> Our tank took several direct hits and caught on fire. A medium tank carries a crew of five men. Lieutenant [Robert J.] Kaufman, the battalion radio officer, was an extra passenger. He had requested to accompany us into battle and Lieutenant Colonel Ferris had acquiesced. Lt. Kaufman was staying close to me; we were pressed side-by-side, two men occupying the space intended for one. As the tank caught fire, Lt. Kaufman had just

sat down. I jumped on him, grabbing his vest and pushed him upwards out of the manhole. As his legs passed my vision, I could see that he had suffered the loss of one of his legs and I pushed him as hard as I could out the man hole [the turret hatch], and I tried to exit, myself. As I was half emerged, there was an explosion which fully ejected me. I found myself on the ground outside the tank and lost consciousness, I was now blind and hurting badly. Lt. Kaufman was lying next to me and said he had lost a leg. I could not help him as I could not see and my hands were burned, He kept talking for hours then he stopped. After a while I heard the sounds of boots on pavement and thought German soldiers were approaching. I asked them for a drink; they gave me not a drink but were interested in my papers. One of the soldiers said in English, 'poor guy.' I asked him how my companion was but he did not answer as his steps faded away. Even blinded I could sense that night had fallen and it was getting very cold. I called for help.[22]

This eloquent and heart-rending story of the struggle is amazing in that Knapp was able to survive at all. But his story reveals two important tactical pieces of information: one, that Lt. Col. Ferris had sent scouts into the town, and, two, that radio communication had broken down. These two failures were tragic elements in this drama, and, added to these is the absence of a warning from the FFI that the Germans had reoccupied Barr on 26 November after having left it on the 23rd.

Another survivor of the carnage, Pvt. Jack E. Reinhart, remembers his tank being hit by a panzerfaust and the molten steel entering the compartment, with the result being one dead, one seriously wounded, and one less seriously wounded. There were no visible wounds on Pvt. Vern Hanheider, but he could have died of shock, concussion, or a heart attack. T-5 driver Andy Bedient was seriously wounded in the head.[23]

An extraordinary document was published after the war, a treatment of the battle in Barr written by Dr. Marcel Krieg, the Director of the hospital in the town during the fighting. It is valuable for two reasons: one, it adds to the battle scene in which the American tankers and infantry were engaged and, two, it provides a dramatic picture of the suffering of the people in the town, the destruction of their buildings and property, and most important, it renders in heartbreaking terms the injuries and deaths of American GIs, especially the tankers in the blast-ed streets of the town. It begins by lamenting the fact that the Red Cross sign painted on the roof and the Red Cross flag flying at the entrance of the hospital did not protect either the building or its occupants: the medical personnel and the sick and the wounded.

The inhabitants of Barr had looked forward to liberation by the Allies after the liberation of Paris and the approach of both the American Seventh and the French First Army. The rapid advances of August and September by both the American Third Army from Normandy and the Sixth Army Group from Provence had given way to apparent stalemate because the Germans had regrouped and the Allies suffered problems of supply. The German propaganda machine cranked out continually the message that the province of Alsace would stay in the hands of German Army Group G, with its combined First and Nineteenth Armies. For weeks on end before the end of November, the townspeople could watch from a distance "fireworks" illuminating the Vosges Mountains and hear the sounds of heavy artillery to the west. Those Frenchmen who were able to work were dragooned by the Germans to construct fortifications (the younger men had already been conscripted to serve in the Wehrmacht). The skies were full of Allied fighter planes strafing any vehicles that appeared to be employed to transport military equipment, supplies, or personnel. At this stage of the war, the Germans were still using horses and wagons for transportation, but so were many of the French farmers in the area.* Alsace was a dan-gerous place for both combatants and noncombatants.

For Dr. Marcel Krieg and his assistants and nurses, it was risking their lives to venture out except in darkness, and they sometimes used motorcycles to get around to treat their patients. Near Bourgheim and Barr, at night, the villagers could see Allied aircraft returning from mis-sions to the east, some of them flying low and desperately trying to reach their bases safely. Two of the bombers, Dr. Krieg remembered, had crashed into the peak of Champ-du-Feu, not far from La Chaume des Veaux. German trucks bringing materiel to the front travelled by night, as did most German vehicles because the American IX Tactical Air Force had, for the most part, driven the Luftwaffe from the skies.

The Volksturm, although mostly elderly, sick, or very young troops, made their presence felt, and Nazi Party officials menaced the popula-tion with threats. In the "scrub bush of Barr" [translator's phrase], there were hiding some three hundred Wehrmacht deserters, who could sometimes be careless about their own security. The FFI, under the command of Captain Karrer, had great difficulty keeping them hidden. This sounds like an unusual arrangement, but the war seemed to create them all the time. The closer the Allies came to the vicinity, the more desperate was the situation for the deserters and even the FFI, trying to protect them.

During the week of 19 to 26 November, the inhabitants learned on the BBC Radio that French troops had advanced into Sundgau, not far away from Barr. On Sunday the 19th, fighter aircraft (what Dr. Krieg called "mosquitoes"):

> . . . crisscrossed the skies without letup. The most dangerous moment so far occurred when, around two o'clock in the afternoon, "two shadows" [aircraft?] flitted past the window. A huge explosion erupted in the garden of the Kayser brothers, scattering wood, metal, and earth into the air. Three more explosions followed as the aircraft dropped two more bombs in the vineyard behind the Kormann house on Dr. Sultzer Street. The family was badly shaken, and a short time later they realized that a bomb fragment "had traversed the corridor to the garden where our little girl was lying in a carriage."

She was apparently unharmed.

As Dr. Krieg's story continues, on 21 November, the city of Mulhouse was lost to the enemy, and the area simultaneously was hard pressed by the Allies. Workers who had been at the front returned to Barr and informed everyone that "the collapse of German resistance was imminent." Word was received that General Andre LeClerc's forces had wrested Strasbourg from Nazi control, and a cyclist "confirmed" the news of the welcome by the French of General LeClerc's armored division into the city's environs. As well—on a more ominous note—the exits from Barr toward Heilienstein and Gertwiller were blocked, with barriers constructed on Dr. Sultzer Street, at the end of the platform of L'Abattoir (the meat market), in Vandenberg Street (Poststrasse), and on the Station (Gare) Street. Evidently the Burgermeister and the German civil authorities had forsaken the town and sought respite in Selestat.

Then there was a change in the German plan:

On Saturday, in the streets, we witnessed a spectacle reminiscent of the dark days of June 1940 [when France fell]. Hundreds of German soldiers, some carrying backpacks, most with ripped uniforms, exhausted, others pushing baby carriages or pulling carts, retreated for hours thru the streets of the city. We learned from them that the German front had collapsed, that the battle had been hard. These soldiers evidenced the terrible hours they had endured; making their way towards the Bade [unidentified] region to regroup.[24]

Dr. Krieg's story goes on. A German ambulance, employed to transport patients to their homes in neighboring villages, was parked at No. 4 Vandenberg Street. The French medical personnel and the German medics became quite friendly as they sometimes worked on the same patients. The Germans informed Dr. Krieg that their troops were retreating from Barr and wished Dr. Krieg good luck with the arrival of the Americans. At this juncture, there were only a few troops still occupying the telephone exchange and some of the barricades.

The hospital was filled both with surgical and sick patients, who had no idea what was going to happen when the American column arrived in the town. However, Dr. Krieg and his assistants strengthened the hospital cellars with beams and girders to protect the occupants. Ever since the earlier bombardment by U.S. artillery, all occupants were moved into the cellar next to an emergency medical center in one corner of the building. The medical staff had reason to worry about both artillery and air bombardment. On 3 October, during an overflight by a large formation of bombers, probably American, two heavy bombs fell close to the hospital and shook it to its foundations. Dr. Jean-Paul Wagner, who had chosen Barr as a safe area, assisted Dr. Krieg in treating his patients during surgery. Both physicians were very concerned that if any light escaped from the operating room, they could be bombed again.

During the nights of 25 and 26 November, Saturday and Sunday, the intensity of the bombing increased and artillery shells fell on several houses to cause both injuries and death to the people of the town. The bell tower of the Catholic church suffered serious damage. As Dr. Krieg explains:

Sunday morning, the city looked dead. Four Austrian soldiers, who wished to escape the Wehrmacht, had hid themselves in the basement of the hospital near the heating plant. On the afternoon of the same day, Captain Karrer assembled the members of the FFI to brief them on their response to the advancing American column. The latest news from Strasbourg was that the Germans would make a stand in Barr and Dambach and that they would prepare defensive positions in the two towns to stop the American advance through the Ville Valley, the Hohwald, and the Bruche Valley. The enemy also wanted to have complete surveillance of the plain when the American forces arrived.[25]

It would be intriguing to know whether there was any discussion of warning the advancing Americans.

During these days American artillery fired from the heights of Sommerain at the same time as a German battery on Gutleutrain engaged it with counter-battery fire.

The townspeople could only pray that the artillery bombardment would not focus on the town, but the night passed and the city was quiet, with the few remaining German soldiers under cover. As artillery shells whirled over the roofs of the houses, it seemed as if dawn would greet the departure of the last German soldiers. Unfortunately, at about 10:00 a.m., an unusual commotion was heard: "Numerous marching boots, rifle fire, the noise of caterpillar tracks [armored vehicles], heavy boots kicking in doors and loud guttural orders shouting, 'everyone in the cellar, open the door, close the blinds'."[26]

Even more troubling to the townspeople, the young troopers forcing their way into the houses were dressed in SS camouflage fatigues. Occupying the first floors as defensive positions, they appeared quite menacing and shouted Nazi slogans of, as Dr. Krieg put it, "extreme fantasy." These were members of a battalion of the SS Feldherrnhalle Division, Sturmgruppe Biedermann apparently, dedicated to evicting the Americans from Alsace. Their motto, "Bis zum Sieg," indicated that they would do so with all the energy at their disposal. The level of anxiety of the poor Alsatians heightened measurably.

On Monday morning, the 27th, the artillery bombardment suddenly stopped. Dr. Krieg was in, what he called, the Peterhouse at the end of Quai de L'Abbatoir, and he could see that his planned route to the hospital was now quite complicated. At the hospital, the occupants thought that they were safe in the hope that the Americans would liberate them from further fighting and death. But it was not to be. Dr. Krieg could see a German tank prowling on Promenade Street, appearing, for just a moment, to be above the wall of the hospital, "with his cannon pointing menacingly toward the city."[27]

Suddenly in the afternoon, the people heard cannon fire alternating with machine-gun fire from the direction of the town of Gertwiller (to the east). Machine guns volleyed along the Quai de L'Abbatoir, "punctuated by cannon fire." Suddenly a violent explosion reverberated along the buildings. The people later discovered that the German gunfire had come from the Kimeck bridge. Climbing to the housetops, the civilians were able to see many fires illuminating the city, along with plumes of smoke and the scent of incendiary devices. "Fighting raged throughout the afternoon," Dr. Krieg observes sadly. American artillery intensified over Gertwiller and Barr, with many shells exploding over both towns. As night arrived, the fighting subsided momentarily, but the Allies, whom the citizens hopefully expected, did not appear. The Germans were still entrenched, and the American assault on Gertwiller had apparently failed.

Around ten o'clock in the evening, German soldiers hammered on Dr. Krieg's door and demanded to see him, admitting that they had "numerous wounded" but no medical resources. They ordered the physician to follow them, and so, carrying his medical bag, he proceeded towards Allmendweg Street. "Just as we passed under the railway bridge," he noted, "machine-gun volleys whistled over our heads, striking the steel bridge beams and the railway ballast" with what must have been a shower of ricocheted sparks.[28] The group then had to crawl on the ground in the vicinity of the water-filled ditches on either side of the road. The Germans informed the Doctor that Gertwiller was partially occupied by the Americans and that the whizzing bullets were no doubt from a machine gun on a tank, presumably American. It would have been a great tragedy for all if Dr. Krieg had been accidentally killed by what should have been for him "friendly fire."

Dr. Krieg requested that the wounded be taken to the Heinrich house on Lycee Street. There he discovered that the soldiers' wounds were quite serious, and thus they were immediately evacuated to the hospital. It happened that several days earlier the Doctor had hidden a young deserter who was a "colleague," presumably a medical person. The deserter was hidden in the nuns' compound on the second floor of the Hospital. Dr. Krieg nevertheless summoned him to assist in caring for the patients. Both of them began treatment of the wounded presently in the building, but once word leaked out that there were medical personnel available, more wounded arrived. Operations continued throughout the night. Perhaps miraculously, the electricity remained operative, but the crowding in the medical center became very difficult for all concerned.

Once in a while SS soldiers came to see a comrade who was wounded or to stay awhile in order to warm up and drink some hot coffee. It was bitterly cold outside. Even the SS were nervous about the conditions, despite their earlier bluster. Dr. Krieg recalled one or two, formerly visitors, who were brought in seriously wounded. Nevertheless, "their fanaticism hardly abated." One in particular, entered with a wounded comrade, and after gulping down a cup of hot coffee, he left, announcing "Heil Hitler" as his exit anthem. Yet he too would return later with a foot wound. He was repaired temporarily with a bandage, but then he took the boot of another wounded man lying on a cart and returned to battle.

The doctors and nurses distributed the wounded among the sick and surgical patients lying on mattresses, and the commotion prevented anyone from getting rest due to the constant shuffling back and forth. The four Austrian deserters, who had been stowed behind the heating unit, remained concealed, and the medical personnel had all they could do just to persuade the young SS soldiers to leave their weapons at the entrance and not wander about the medical center. Dr. Krieg felt great sympathy for what he called "our poor Austrians," who were terrified of exposure, which would most certainly have meant death by firing squad. They remained safely hidden for three days, but the medical staff was quite worried about their welfare and their own since they were guilty of harboring deserters from the German Army. As morning approached, "a quiet calm" descended and no more wounded appeared.

On Tuesday morning, the 27th, Dr. Krieg took advantage of the lull and proceeded to his home in order to gather his wife and children and bring them to the hospital for safety. En route, he could see that the barriers were well manned, but no other soldiers could be observed. The

German tank maintained its ominous position by the wall of the hospital, a sure menace to advancing American troops whether on foot or in armored vehicles. The street pattern of the town was somewhat irregular, especially the main street, with curves and intersections ideal for ambush, On his return, Dr. Krieg also noticed that the enemy occupied the agricultural building and had placed machine guns on the first floor pointed toward the town. He regarded this development as especially worrying for troops advancing against the building. Yet that morning remained eerily quiet with only a few sounds of gunfire in the direction of Geriwiller. Fortunately, as the doctor saw it, the weather was cloudy, a situation which prevented aircraft from flying. But, since most of the tactical planes were American, usually P-47 Thunderbolts, the overcast presented a distinct disadvantage for the approaching column. That disadvantage would prove costly.

The nursing nuns and their helpers prepared meals and assisted in the medical treatment that day. By this time the entire basement was covered with mattresses and stretchers, making it difficult for them to circulate among the patients. Although the electric power was still on, there were flashlights, oil lamps, and candles available in case of a power loss. Anxiety pervaded the hospital, and time dragged on interminably. Artillery fire suddenly hammered the calm, and from the first floor of the hospital, the medical staff could see fires flaring again in Gertwiller.

Dramatically, at two o'clock in the afternoon, "intense fighting resumed." Cannon fire and machine-gun fire from the direction of Heiligenstein (to the north) became more and more threatening. From the first floor windows fires could be seen flaring up on the Sultzer Street heights, on the north side of town, in the Stoffel and Kleinmann houses, with shells exploding dangerously. Loud noises from tank tracks erupted along Sultzer Street, and more chaos sounded from an artillery barrage at the barrier on that street.

The intensity of the fighting seemed nonstop, accompanied by more sounds of approaching armored vehicles. Dr. Krieg descended into the basement as the noise appeared to be nearing the hospital. "Suddenly, violent impacts on the front of the hospital, both cannon and machine-gun fire, shook the structure."[29] This report appears to describe the conflict between B Company of the 48th Tank Battalion with defenders from the Waffen SS. The American armored column had come down

Route du Vin, Highway 35, into town.

At this point, German machine guns in the agricultural building where animals were apparently housed, commenced firing, and the panzer behind the hospital fired, inciting exchanges of cannon fire from tanks and guns on both sides. Dr. Krieg was grateful that the rear basement entrance was out of the line of fire. However, the hospital's facade continued to receive hits without interruption, evidently American tanks trying to silence the concealed panzer. Windows shattered, and cannon blows were heard even on interior walls. Suddenly the entire glass facade which enclosed the first two floors collapsed into the basement, and an instant later three explosions of enormous volume shook the building. The next day's light would show that it was the blasts from the destruction of three tanks, American Shermans, one in front of the Post Office, another by the hospital, and a third by Eugene Bossert's house on Railway Avenue, "all within a radius of fifty meters." The explosions continued as the north wall of the hospital was struck and the electric lights were immediately were extinguished.

Panic seized the civil and military surgery patients and the other sick while the nuns fell on their knees and prayed out loud. They were then joined by all the other occupants of the hospital. Dr. Krieg remembered it as "a moment of intense emotion with everyone lying around haphazardly in the basement."[30] At once, the door opened and an orderly entered, announcing that the Agricultural Building, which was full of hay, was burning. He had managed to release the cows and a bull and the hogs, but, as one might imagine, the poor animals were frantically running wild in the chaos. The orderly asked for help in trying to capture them and put them safely out of the way. Through the doorway immense flames could be seen racing to the sky and threatening the hospital with destruction. Between the threatening fire and the nightmare of battle outside, the panic now reached new heights while Dr. Krieg and the other medical personnel tried to calm things down.

The Doctor remembers that "We have lost all sense of time as the battle drags on," and darkness gradually enveloped the town. On the streets which housed the Railway Station and the Post Office, the blast from exploding munitions, machine-gun fire, and cannon fire continued for hours. The citizens of the town and the people in the hospital found out later that the munitions were blowing up inside the tanks. Only later would the people of Barr discover that many of the fatalities on the

American side would be from these explosions as well as those of panzerfausts and anti-tank rounds. Only with the activation of emergency
lighting, apparently from a generator, would the treatment of the
patients continue. When the cacophony of battle subsided, a sense of
calm returned, and some of the patients fell asleep, thoroughly exhausted. The staff was able to serve hot drinks and food, but the patients,
their emotions run rampant, were so distraught that they were incapable
of digesting any food.

Dr. Krieg, ever in control, climbed the stairs to the first floor and
saw that the Agricultural Building was now "fully engulfed" and continuing to burn. Thick smoke covered the whole town, punctuated only
by the light of innumerable fires. "An even more intense light emanates
from the city hall plaza as the city hall burns, and the appearance," at
least to the Doctor, "is eminently 'lugubrious'."[31] A few sporadic bursts
of small arms fire interrupted the momentary quiet. In front of the hospital itself, tanks were engulfed in flames, and the city was yet being
shelled by artillery.

One of the townspeople, Emile Haberer, informed Dr. Krieg that he
had heard foreign speech behind the hospital wall, a language which
seemed to him to be English. He also reported that the German tank had
left the hospital area and that the German troops seemed to have withdrawn. Mr. Haberer also had heard cries for help coming from the railway street (on the west perimeter of the town), and he had left to inves-
tigate them. Moments later, he returned, carrying on his back an
American soldier, "badly burned about the face," whom he had found
next to a burned out tank near Eugene Bossert's house. This badly
wounded GI would turn out to be Pvt. Howard Knapp, a 19-year-old
loader and radio operator in Lt. Colonel Ferris's tank. This was the tank
that had come late to the action after radio transmissions indicated a
fierce battle for Company B. Mr. Haberer went back to find other badly
wounded, mostly burned, tankers lying on their tanks or in the street.
Others were beyond hope.[32]

The doctors and nurses laid the first GI on the operating table and
removed several layers of uniform (because of the early cold) and determined that he had severe burns about the face and hands, knee frac-
tures, and a fracture of the right leg and wounds about the hips. These
injuries were no doubt caused when Howard Knapp was blown out of
the tank. In an interview at a 14th Armored Division Reunion in

January of 2005, Howard told this writer that his head and ears had been protected from the blast and the burn because, underneath his tanker's helmet, he wore a German wool cap and his own wool cap to keep his head and ears warm. He also had a black German uniform under his uniform, and a sweater.

First aid was immediately given, but he could not open his eyes. Because he had no injuries to his stomach, he was able to receive a hot drink, but he was unresponsive after having lain several hours in the street temporarily blinded and crippled. A shot of morphine dulled his pain somewhat, and he was placed on a mattress and covered with a blanket.

Forty years later, Howard recalled those painful moments:

> In spite of not being able to see, the memory of that night is still clear in my mind. It seemed to me that they had put me in a large basket and hidden me under the table. I could hear footsteps and I understood German. I heard German soldiers discussing wounded American soldiers. Dr. Krieg did not engage them and I fell asleep. On awakening the next day I learned that the city of Barr had been liberated. I will always owe a debt of gratitude to the residents of Barr and to Dr. Krieg for saving my life. I named my only son Barton [a contraction of Barrtownj in honor of the city.[33]

Emile Haberer—though not a soldier, still a hero—returned with a second wounded American, an officer with his right leg "ripped off" (probably the communications lieutenant, who was already dead). The heroic Emile went out into the night again, and he returned accompanied by M.M.J Bossert and his brother, Freddy, carrying two more wounded Americans. One was the Battalion Commander, Lt. Col. Ferris, who was in charge of the attack in Barr. His tank, the same as Howard Knapp's, had been hit by a round from an anti-tank gun in front of Mr. Bossert's house, which blew up the tank and ejected both Knapp and Ferris. The residents of the house had dragged him inside their cellar through an opening caused by the explosion of a cannon round.

Taken to the hospital, he was treated along with several other wounded who were saved by the townspeople. Dr. Krieg recalled how, through the tarp shielding in the operating room, the silence would be interrupted by requests for "scalpel," "pincers," "sutures," and "bandages." More room was made in the basement for the wounded, both German and American. The medical staff was concerned that if more arrived, there would be no more place to put them. Some time in the night, a townsman came to warn the Doctor that a German officer was seeking to meet with him. The first thought in his mind was, "Are they still here?" The German, it seems, was a medical officer who presented himself and a medical corpsman to Dr. Krieg. The officer was informed that the hospital was treating German soldiers who had been wounded in the battle, and he asked to see them. By the illumination of the emergency lighting, the medical officer and Krieg were able to interview both the German and the American wounded, asking their names, serial numbers, and unit assignments, which the German officer noted on a pad. Although the German wounded gave all the requested information, the Americans contributed only their names.

Unable to transport the German wounded, the officer left them in the care of the Alsatian physician. He asked that the Doctor sign an official receipt for them and that he turn them over to the Americans, who would arrive in a few hours. The officer established the fact that the German forces had removed themselves from the city. The two men emerged into the street, eerily lit by the burning tanks and other fires. Dr. Krieg walked with his opposite to the railway station, where the German's vehicle was parked. As he departed, he took Dr. Krieg's hand and thanked him for the care given to the German wounded, but the physician said emphatically, "Go now and be certain never to return." The officer smiled, and his receding steps echoed in the now quiet night.[34]

The orderly who had accompanied him returned as a prisoner two days later, and he was assigned to care for the German wounded. Treatment continued for the remainder of the night. Next morning, about eight o'clock, an American Second Lieutenant arrived, and he asked for two rooms in the hospital to set up an emergency first aid station. He took over two rooms on either side of the facade of the building. The area was quickly cleared by more Americans, and the US medical officer arranged his equipment in the space provided. Dr. Krieg was astounded by the sophistication of the first aid equipment, especially the intravenous and transfusion apparatus. The Alsatian Doctor had been separated from his source of medical supplies since the German invasion of 1940.

"A veritable convoy" of ambulances began bringing wounded soldiers for medical care and returning to the front those whose injuries had already been taken care of. The American medical personnel then departed, with Lt. Colonel Ferris thanking the hospital staff for all that they had done for them and for him. However, the work was not over as wounded German soldiers continued to be delivered to the hospital while others were evacuated. All of those staying were placed on mattresses which had just been emptied of the previously injured. All of this activity continued while German artillery still pounded the town.

An inspection of the exterior of the hospital revealed that not a single window or shutter remained on the façade, and that the interior walls of many rooms had been pierced by both artillery shells and heavy machine-gun fire. The main operating rooms on the first floor had endured multiple hits and were in very poor condition. Surrounding the hospital were the "burned out hulks of tanks, some with turrets drooping, burned bodies of American soldiers, with other bodies draped around the tank engines. Some of the bodies were totally burned, just pieces of flesh remaining. Other bodies were missing arms or legs and were horrible to see," as the Doctor observed them.

Dr. Krieg then responded to a call to treat those civilians who had suffered during the conflict in their city. He witnessed the mess on the Main Street, Taufflieg Street, and City Hall Place: houses on fire, the City Hall with windows and doors exploded. In all of these streets there were yet more burned out American tanks. The guns and the panzerfausts had been well concealed on the first floors of the buildings in the town and evidently escaped the observation of the infantry scouts sent into the town before the battle.

The Doctor carefully advanced up the Main Street despite two more artillery volleys and provided care for the civilian casualties by bringing them back to the hospital. Local residents began to emerge from their cellars, and the firefighting equipment, which had been summoned during the fighting, continued to extinguish the fires. American infantry and tanks crossing through the city advanced south toward the towns of Mittelbergheim and Epfig. Captain Karrer of the Resistance Battalion took charge of municipal services in Barr.

Dr. Krieg approached an American officer responsible for "Civil

Service," and he provided stocks of serum, sulfanilamide, and emergency bandages. The medical staff of the hospital turned over the Austrian deserters to the American authorities; the deserters had tears in their eyes as they left. The FFI took prisoner various wounded German soldiers who had been scattered in vineyards around the city. Despite the continued shelling, the source of which is unclear, and the numerous American bodies still lying in the streets, the residents kept emerging from their cellars and expressing their thanks to the American soldiers despite the damage done to their lovely city. They had come to the conclusion that the Germans were driven out by the Americans, who had paid a very heavy price for the liberation of Barr. The count of destroyed tanks in the streets was seventeen, with five dead crewmen found in addition to losses in the armored infantry and the reconnaissance units.

For the next few nights, despite the medical staff's armbands, both FFI and Red Cross, it was still dangerous to walk about the town. Dr. Krieg saw that the American troops, no doubt jittery, fired into every enclosure and doorway where they could see light. According to him, "These men were from faraway Texas and hearing German spoken all around them, [they] believed they were in Germany already." Fear was high.

At the hospital the staff covered the broken windows and doors with cardboard and boards in makeshift fashion. On the following day patients who had undergone sham surgeries to prevent them from being drafted by the Wehrmacht departed. Also, patients who had been diagnosed as having infectious diseases left. Captain Karrer was assigned the task of overseeing the civilian uses of the hospital pending the day when a "normal administration" could be put in place. He also insured that the townspeople had sufficient supplies for heating in the unseasonable cold weather.

An especially vexing problem involved some aged Germans who had been evacuated from hospices in northern Germany on account of the heavy bombing by both American and British long-range bombers. They had been transported to and found refuge in hospitals in both Andlau and Barr, but they were despondent. An old German colonial doctor, 85 years of age, attached himself to Dr. Krieg while he was making his rounds. The elderly German doctor described his experiences as a physician in a former German colony in South Africa. The two medical professionals became "great friends," especially because the

German was very lonely as his connections with his family had been broken. The staff attempted to console these people, who still had to endure many long weeks and months before they could return to their former homes.

Nevertheless, not everything was pleasant and positive. As Dr. Krieg characterized it, the atmosphere was "poisoned by the population purge" that emerged once the Germans seemed to be gone for good. Orders were delivered, from whom is not clear, that the inhabitants of the cities and villages themselves would effect retaliation against those seen as cooperating excessively with the German occupation—those deemed "collaborators." This activity was not to be influenced by any outsiders, and so a vigilante mood "opened the door to all manner of excesses, personal vengeance, and the threat of summary executions." Such actions were not confined to Barr and surrounding towns but took place all over France and other occupied countries that had been dominated and degraded for four years and more.

The war damage to the hospital was slowly repaired as both time and building materials became available. Of signal importance, the heating plant kept functioning during the cold winter days that deepened into December. The hospital gradually recovered its services, and a sense of normalcy returned to both staff and patients. This transformation was most fortunate, for at the end of the year and into January, Barr served as a refuge for hundreds of people evacuated from Benfeld and Selestat. These refugees in January were no doubt produced by the German offensive known as "Operation Northwind," about which more will be said here in a later chapter. There would be more pain and death for the combatants and for the innocent civilians from the region.[35]

Yet military reports and histories maintain a safe distance from the suffering. One cryptic message, sent from Division to Sixth Army Headquarters, briefly said, "Town Barr taken this afternoon 1600.00 pm by 1-2-7 lnf. Btls, and 7th C.C. of 103rd. I. D. –out—."[36] The Monthly Report of the 14th Armored Division summarized 29 November, the day after the battle:

LOCATION: VIC: BARR
TROOPS: No change.
ACTION: Again the Bn [the 48th TB] advanced toward Barr;

passing through Heiligenstein and after being held up for road blocks and very light resistance Barr was entered and outposted. The AT guns and their protection had withdrawn and only slight sniper fire was found.[37]

The very late Official History of the war in southern France and Alsace, published in 1994, sketched the battle at Barr and appended a grim conclusion:

Throughout 28 November heavy fighting took place at both Barr and Erstein. At Barr the 411th Infantry [Battalion] battled into the town from the west, attempting to clear each house and building one by one; meanwhile, the supporting CCA [including the 48th] entered the city from the north and east; this proved a costly mistake. With little accompanying infantry, the armor found itself out of place in the narrow streets and lanes; it lost eighteen tanks in the course of the day, eight of which were abandoned when Company B of the 48th Tank Battalion was forced to withdraw from the town, leaving behind most of its equipment and many of its dead, wounded, and missing. The following day, 29 November, the 103d Division's foot soldiers finally cleared Barr, and the armored unit was fortunate enough to recover all eight of the abandoned medium tanks, still in serviceable condition as well as nineteen of Company B's tankers. The men of the 14th Armored Division were acquiring their experience the hard way.[38]

The most personal comments immediately after the fact were by comrades of the tankers of the 48th TB and of the 62nd AIB's infantrymen. Peter Lakey, of the 62nd, "recall[ed] seeing many knocked-out tanks as we moved into town with tank crew members burned or shot as they tried to get out of them. We encountered little resistance other than taking a few of the enemy as prisoners near the post office in the center of town." And Fred Peiper, a Sergeant with the 48th's Headquarters Company, in charge of a mortar squad, recalled, "My mortar squad had the dubious honor of recovering the dead from destroyed tanks and other places. Pulling a mess trailer behind our half-track we hauled approximately 120 dead back to graves registration."[39]

Because both the French Dr. Krieg and the American soldier, Pvt. Howard Knapp, wanted to share with others their difficult and painful experiences at the end of November 1944 in the town of Barr, we know how hard the suffering and the dying were.

Chapter 3

OBER-OTTENBACH: THE ONSLAUGHT[1]

After the debacle at Barr for the 48th Tank and 62nd Armored Infantry Battalions, the Seventh Army's advance in Alsace continued, with more hard fighting but significant progress toward Germany, and even into it across the Lauter River. As the Official History comments, by "12 December Major General Edward H. Brooks, VI Corps Commander, "decided to insert the 14th Armored Division between the 103d and 79th Divisions . . . to provide the armored division with a sector of its own . . ." On 13 December it moved to Hagenau to "attack northward at daylight" to "secure crossings" for the two infantry divisions.[2]

"Both Combat Commands of the 14th Armored Division [CCA and CCB] were operating in Germany on the morning of December 16." On 13 December CCA was ordered to attack Wissembourg from the direction of Surbourg to the southwest. The 62nd encountered resistance at Soultz including "heavy artillery fire." The 500th Armored Field Artillery Battalion had tremendous difficulty supporting the action because of "seas of mud," and two companies of the 62nd had great difficulty crossing an icy stream and a "soggy marsh between Soulz and Schoenberg."[3]

As the surge forward continued, C Company of the 62nd reached the town of Riedseltz, but the Germans were ready for them. When the GIs entered the town, the two bridges going out of the town were blown, and immediately artillery rounds began to fall on them. C Company, after "the bitter business of fighting from house to house" slowed them down, managed to take the town by nightfall. The War Diary of the l4AD succinctly comments on the actions of 14 December:

CC 'A' seized and occupied lngolsheim, Hermerswiller, Hoffen and Reidselz. Some elements of the Combat Command reached Oberseebach. CC 'B' seized and occupied BuhI, Trimbach, Siegenand, Oberlauterbach, while elements of the 19th AIB reached their objective—Salmbach. CC 'R' moved to vicinity of Niederbetschdorf."[4]

The History of the 14AD continues to trace the seemingly inexorable movement of the tank and infantry battalions and their support, although the enemy was exerting maximum pressure to stall the tanks, half-tracks, and soldiers. The area was laced with ponds, lakes, streams, and rivers, and so bridges were destroyed before the advancing forces, sometimes to trap units for extermination by heavy artillery fire. At Hoffen the bridge was blown, but C Company of the 125th Combat Engineers installed a bridge extending for thirty feet. At dawn, on the 15th the column, with the 25th Tank Battalion in the lead, was rolling through Oberseebach when, "Rounding a turn, there was the sharp, loud, flat crack of an 88 and Lieut. Klinefelter's tank was burning; and Sgt. Manuel Mello's tank, behind him, had received two hits." Both men survived their wounds. A melee ensued with tanks, assault guns, and mortars "opening up a savage counterfire." The Germans further responded with artillery and mortar fire. Two rescuers, S/Sgt. Preston Rensch, a medic, and Lt. Fred Gisse in a "peep" combined to get the wounded out of the sector and back for treatment. Fortunately for the wounded remaining, darkness fell. As the column lagered for the night, it was suddenly attacked by six hostile tanks, two of which were destroyed, with the rest retreating. By morning the Germans had vacated the town, and the column was able to continue its motor-march to Wissembourg. At Reidseltz the same kind of charged battle transpired, again with artillery and mortars falling on the men of the 14th.[5]

The German construction company referred to as the Todt Organization, named after the master engineer Fritz Todt, had built the fortifications and gun emplacements in the area in which the 14th was struggling. Although General George S. Patton had thought that the guns in the Siegfried Line had been removed to the Eastern Front and that therefore the Line "was an empty shell," it was not. The guns still fired. The desperate fighting continued through town after town, and it is possible only to mention seriatim some of the actions. At Reidseltz, after the engineers set a bridge in place, the enemy fire was extremely intense, and the infantry could only hold where they were. Tanks of the 25th fought their way across the bridge but could not spot targets because of the fog rolling in. At Ingolsheim, the combat infantry was able to proceed several hundred yards into town. S/Sgt. R.J. Adcox called in mortar fire on some enemy soldiers several hundred yards ahead. T/Sgt, Newton L. Houchen and S/Sgt. Thomas Walsh "called down mortar fire that they saw blow a German burp gunner out of his foxhole [but] the Germans did not withdraw."

In the approach to Wissembourg, a key town for both sides, C Company of the 62nd and the Anti-Tank platoon were instructed to outflank the enemy. The plan was for the latter platoon to lay down a base of fire with .50 caliber guns as the 3rd Platoon assaulted the enemy. "No sooner did the scouts move out than they drew heavy sniper and machine gun fire; the platoons worked their way forward in the merciless cross-fire." Pfc. Adelbert Brott, who had had to take over a squad, was killed, and practically every man in the squad was wounded. Brott was posthumously awarded the Silver Star.[6] The 14AD "Diary" once again provides a skeletal version of the heroism and suffering of the advance for 15 December:

> CC'B' completed occupation of Salmbach. CC'A', halted by enemy fire from vicinity of Oberdorf, dug in. The 62nd AIB was under heavy SA, artillery and mortar fire but advanced toward Wissemberg [sic]. CC'R' moved up to Oberseebach and established patrols west of Schleithal.[7]

The 68th moved under CCR's control into Schwindratzheim, where the first platoon of B Company cleared roadblocks on the road into Hagenau Forest. Some prisoners were taken, and the battalion feinted in the direction of Strasbourg with its vehicles "to give the appearance that we would attack in that direction." As implied above, the 68th as part of CCR, traversed the road from Betschdorf to Oberseebach. At the same time, the 68th history notes, the 62nd "was busy clearing the town of Wissembourg. To the east the 19th was struggling with the enemy in Salmbach."[8]

In Wissembourg, the enemy tired of the fight and retreated while the inhabitants of the town, overjoyed at what they hoped would be the end, at least, of their war, flew flags. "In the distance a single church bell tolled. A ripple of rifle shots sounded above the grinding of the steel track treads on the stone streets." It was also an auspicious moment for the GIs when "Headquarters Company fired its first rounds into [greater] Germany." The tanks of C Company of the 25th Tank Battalion "crossed the German border at 1030 . . . no resistance was encountered." However, the game was not over by any means. When B Company of the 62nd progressed halfway up a hill beyond Rechtenbach, the Germans let loose volleys from snipers and machine guns, and mortars began falling along the road close to the half-tracks. "The men boiled out and the half-tracks turned to go back to Rechtenbach (three vehicles were helplessly mired)."

The 14th Armored History summarizes the events of 16 December:

> Troops of the 19th AIB pushed first 14th Armored Division troops into [greater] Germany. CCB crossed patrols to the north bank of the Lauter river near Salmbach and Schleithal . . .The 62nd AIB proceeded to Scimergen, Rechtenbach and Haftelhof. The 25th Tk Bn reached the outskirts of Schweighofen.[9]

This was a tough and difficult advance against increasing hostile pressure, but it appeared that the enemy was retreating steadily. Unfortunately, he had the Westwall (Siegfried Line) at his back. "The Germans had been driven back to the forts of the Siegfried, a few kilometers inside the border and roughly running parallel to it." And so it was no surprise that a steady and severe rain of shells from various types of gun tubes was pouring down on the advancing soldiers. "As night fell the enemy laid in rockets on the buildings, and mortars and heavy caliber howitzers, and an 88 was firing from an opposite slope two thousand yards away."[10]

The Wehrmacht was embedded in prepared fortifications with pre-registered fields of fire for all of the guns just mentioned and including, of course, criss-crossing MG-42 machine guns. The Nebelwerfer rockets whooshed off sets of launchers with a frightening shriek (and so were called "screaming meemies"). These were not notably accurate weapons, but combined with the firing of the other guns, they could be quite unsettling to soldiers who had never been exposed to them before. Apropos of the density of fire the armored infantrymen were facing is the statement by the French philosopher Andre Maurois that described modern war as an attempt to force as much steel as possible to penetrate human flesh.[11]

The Siegfried Line was known to the Germans as "Der West Wall," designed by Adolf Hitler's engineers to protect Germany's western flank in the event that it had to wage war in the east against the Soviet Union. German's aggressive tendencies in the 1930's would propel that nation against Poland in 1939, and thus, in advance, protection was necessary against Germany's likely adversaries in the west, the French and the British Armies. Historically the Rhine River has been the border between France and Germany, but the border had been adjusted several times in previous wars. When Hitler occupied the Rhineland, that extended the borders of Germany, and in Alsace the border ran along the Lauter River, several miles west of the Rhine in some places. Thus, after elements of the Fourteenth crossed the Lauter, they were in Greater Germany. After that came the Siegfried or Westwall, which had to be breached in order to get to Germany proper.

After World War I, the Treaty of Versailles declared that the Rhineland was a part of France despite the fact that there were many loyal German residents living there. Thus there was a bulge for many miles west of the Rhine. When the Westwall was constructed, beginning in May 1938, it was designed to cover as much of that territory as possible. The Todt industrial organization "had 100,000 military engineers, 350,000 men . . . and he had many thousands of the Arbeitdienst working for him [Todt]. From May 1938 to August 1939." As Charles Whiting wrote of the wall, "these busy workers used eight million tons of cement, over a million tons of steel and iron and nearly a million tons of wood to construct 14,000 bunkers and piliboxes, over thirty-five per mile, along a line of four hundred miles in length. The cost was estimated to be 3.5 billion marks. It was the greatest construction program ever undertaken in Germany's history." The Westwall was built in depth, an average of two and one half miles "of hundreds of mutually supporting pillboxes, observation and command posts, linked by concrete roads, with troop shelters and bunkers. . . .The typical Todt bunker was about twenty-one feet wide, eighteen feet high and forty-two feet deep, with 11 walls and roofs of reinforced concrete up to nine feet thick."[12]

In front of the bunkers and pillboxes were rows and rows of "dragon's teeth," concrete abutments about five feet high and two feet wide at the tapered top. At Ober-Ottenbach there were seven rows. These were designed as tank and tracked-vehicle traps which ran for hundreds of miles from the border with Holland, snaking south and southeasterly until they terminated at the Swiss border. This line reflected the old trenchlines of World War I. The name "dragon's teeth" was a reminder from Greek mythology about the dramatic founding of the Greek city of Thebes. According to the story, the Oracle at Delphi had advised Cadmus, who was seeking to find his sister, that he was to found a new city. In the adventure, Cadmus had slain a dragon who had blocked his search. After the beast was dead, Cadmus took its teeth and sowed them in the ground. From these ungainly seeds a race of armed warriors was born. They, in turn, fought with one another until only five were left. These became the royal line of the kings of Thebes, including the great warrior and king Theseus, who would slay the dreadful Minotaur on the island of Crete, the domain of King Minos. The name of the tank traps was terribly appropriate, for many men, most of them American, who would die, figuratively impaled by machine-gun fire while mortar and artillery tore them to pieces.

In late 1944 and the spring of 1945, the line was attacked in many places from north to south by American and British arms, with the 5th Armored Division sending a patrol through in September. One of the officers, Charles MacDonald, who later wrote about the fighting, described the wall in the vicinity of Aachen, a locus of deadly combat many miles north of where the 14th Armored would find itself fighting in Alsace:

> We crossed a slight knoll and the antitank wall of the Siegfried Line came suddenly into view. It was like a prehistoric monster coiled around the hill sides; the concrete dragon's teeth were like scales upon the monster's back—or maybe headstones in a kind of crazy cemetery.[13]

As might be expected from the German side, all kinds of mines were planted in front of the dragon's teeth to torment the attackers, demoralize them, and tear them to pieces. An infantry lieutenant remembered the horror when one of what the GIs called "bouncing bellies" would explode. This type of mine was designed to "bounce" upon activation several feet in the air to rend the body in horrendous fashion. When the explosion signaled to the German infantry that somebody was in the minefield, machine gun, small arms fire, and mortars would open up, freezing the men in place. "It was no use attempting to drop. The soldier doing so ran the fearful risk of exploding another Bounding Betty. Scared out of their wits, men would remain perfectly erect under shellfire [at night] rather than drop on the mines."[14] This hell was similar to that experienced by Bob Davies' squad, in February in the minefield outside Pfaffenhoffen.

But to return to the narrative and the combined battalions of the 62nd AIB and the 25th TB: in support, the 500th Armored Field Artillery fired its first rounds in response to the heavy fire coming from the Westwall against the "doughs" of the 62nd. These were taking a beating from the German artillery:

> The infantrymen, laid on the floors of the thick-walled farm houses, close by the walls; waiting between the screams and explosions of the artillery to look out; and the artillery ripped gaping holes in the walls, showering the men with plaster and smashed at the fragile tile roofs and debris fell into the streets.[15]

In order to force an avenue through the dragon's teeth, Company C of the 125th Combat Engineers fashioned over two tons of explosives into charges to blow a way through. Meanwhile the 25th had advanced through Wissembourg in the direction of Schweighofen. Under fire from that town, the tank battalion sent a platoon under Lt. Gisse to open counter-battery fire. They were assisted by Lt. John R. Martin's Assault Gun platoon of the 25th Tank Battalion which "dropped timed fire and white phosphorus in the town. Darkness fell and the column set up security for the night." On 16 December, A battery of the 500th "fired direct on the dragon's teeth and pillboxes." As the 14th's History continues in ominous tones: "A combat force was formed to test the Siegfried."[16] It is always facile in hindsight to question an order over half a century later and without the thorough understanding of officers who were there in front of the Westwall. Yet it should be said that the decision to "test" it with the forces at hand represented too positive an evaluation of the battle situation.

Major William E. Shedd, Ill, formed a force containing the following elements:

Troop C of the 94th Cav and Recon,
1st Platoon of medium tanks, the 25th Tank Battalion,
1st and 3rd Platoon of lights [tanks] from C-125,
two rifle squads from A-62,
two combat engineer squads from C-125,
a tank dozer and two assault guns. . . .

When this aggregate force was forwarded through Schweigen and Rechtenbach and on to Ober-Otterbach, "and hit in the Siegfried Line," it was met by a terrific storm of artillery fire. As the 14th's History drily observed, "the Siegfried had more tricks than that, they were to find." The narrative continues:

The scene was almost deceptive, the flat, open patch of country and the farm houses, the Dragon Teeth seeming only a few inches high, and a camouflaged gray-green pill box half hidden in the furrow of a hill; but every inch of that flat open country was covered by machine guns in casual curves of the earth, and artillery hidden far back, and some of the neat little farm houses turned out to have walls of reinforced concrete seven feet thick; and if you assaulted one pillbox from the flank you were under cross-fire from two others.[17]

Almost before they got started, hostile rounds of artillery came in, and the troops were withdrawn to Schweighofen itself. There was no question that the ground forces needed help. An air liaison officer arrived after a hazardous journey to the CP, and after some analysis it was announced that a bombing run was to be made on the Westwall:

The ground troops pulled back and watched the formations of two-motored silver bombers drone slowly across the clear skies; the bombs fell and the watching men could hear hollow, empty explosions, feel the earth shake and see the black smoke billow skyward.[18]

The concise summary of this action in the 14th's "Diary" for 17 December reads:

> Division CP moved to Leiterswiller. CC'A' reconnoitered north of the Lauter river, then withdrew 500 yards for a bombing mission. Artillery missions were fired at pillboxes of the Siegfried Line. Task Force Shedd was dispatched from Rechtenbach to Ober Ofterbach and Berg-Zabern. The 25th Tk. Sn attacked east from Schweighofen. The entire Combat Command back to the line Schweigen-Schweighofen for bombing mission.[19]

The only way, unfortunately, to determine whether the bombing mission had been successful was to advance into the dragon's teeth. "At 1330 the Combat Command attacked again." Company C of the 62nd in their half-tracks, with some men riding on the point tanks, advanced through Wissembourg while anxious civilians, with carts, baby carriages, bicycles, and wagons, retreated south in fear that the Germans were counter-attacking. "The offensive ground to a halt outside Rechtenbach." When evening came, the 62nd was relieved by the 68th. B Company of the 25th joined with the infantrymen in preparation for an attack on 18 December, as the 68th History says. B and C Companies of the 68th exchanged with the respective companies of the 62nd. Lt. Graham P. Madden, who would later write the history of the 68th, and Lt. John F. Kraker of the 94th Cav. and Recon. led these patrols to determine "enemy dispositions." They returned at 0600 hours "on the morning of the 18th." Again, the word "test" is used with reference to the tactical intentions of CCA toward the Westwall. At 0745 hours, it was planned, "to penetrate the Siegfried Defenses and capture the town of Bergzabern."[20] Unfortunately the bridge over the River Oaur had been blown, which made tank support limited.

The two companies of the 68th moved out cautiously and met very little resistance for the first hour as they proceeded in two columns on either side of the road leading into Ober-Otterbach. The tanks of Company B, the 25th, were in support. Once through the town, as both the 14th's and the 68th's histories agree, all "hell broke loose." The enemy was ready for them:

> Artillery and mortar fire blasted the ground, machine gun and

rifle fire cut through the men; the bridge over the Oaur was blown and so the tanks and infantry were separated. The tanks fired fast, the brass casings piling up in the firing compartments and the stink of cordite cutting the nostrils, but the German fire did not diminish in intensity, the wounded and the dead of the 68th lay among the Dragon's Teeth and on the winter ground (the 68th took 102 casualties in the action) and the fire was so savage that the closest of comrades could not get to wounded friends. The German was in his forts and trenches, his observation was perfect and he laid murderous fire across the face of the earth. The order was given to consolidate; but the fire was so intense that not even that could be done successfully; some of the men got back to Ober-Otterbach and others were left in the field.[21]

Tec 3 Carlyle P. Brown, a member of the medical detachment assigned to the 68th, the 84th Medical Battalion, had moved up with the armored infantry. He noted that A Company did not join the assault with B and C Companies. His account of what happened on the early morning of the attack follows:

> We got near the Siegfried Line, into the Dragon's Teeth, when the Germans hit us with everything they had. Companies B and C fell back and dug in outside the small town of Ober-Otterbach. We had left several wounded in the town . . . , and that night [2nd Lt.] Glenn Scott went in to see if he could find them but they were missing. Companies B and C lost almost 20% of their men, killed or wounded in the engagement. We stayed there about five days and received lots of mortar and artillery shelling. Lieutenant Kirby and Sergeant [Robert D. of Hdqrs. Co.] Colburn of the 25th Tank Battalion were the first men treated by me in Kapsweyer, Germany.[22]

Ken Hazleton, a medic with the same medical detachment, also wrote about the coming action. This being his first serious battle, Hazleton regarded the coming action in romantic fashion: "Finally the day arrived—commitment to battle and like countless other soldiers we whispered to ourselves 'This is it'." The medics for the 68th took over the facilities of the 62nd's medics and prepared to receive the wounded:

Dec. 18th was a cold, wet, windy day as the troops jumped off for battle. Rechtenbach was secured and at the Weinter [?], where an ambulance post was established, the medics of the aid station sweated out casualties and the few 88's that came their way. The wait was not long. Over the radio came the call 'Medics needed'. Off went the ambulances and crews . . . to gather the first of the stream of wounded. So many came in that the aid station was swamped. We worked hard and fast, ably assisted by Chaplain [Maj. Matthew J.] Casey. Many of our friends came to us that day [as patients]. Neither did the detachment escape without casualties. Pfc. Wayne Lehman, aid man with 'B' Company, was killer [sic] by a sniper while going to the aid of the wounded.[23]

Later, in the battle for Ohlungen Forest, the Germans would observe the rules of the Geneva Convention and respect the medics, but not this day. A stray shot can be considered accidental but not the bullet of a trained and equipped sniper. The infantry were pinned down among the dragon's teeth, which provided limited cover, and the snipers fired into those exposed among them, and this situation, in turn exposed the medics to the deadly fire.

At this point, the German infantry counterattacked, cutting off two platoons. Then the 68th retreated to a position 800 yards on the other side of the town. The situation had become desperate because the tanks could not cross the river to give close support to the men trapped in the dragon's teeth. Sgt. David F. Kennedy earned a Silver Star by staying with and reorganizing his men despite the fact that he had suffered wounds to the arm, cheek, and leg. Although he was in a weakened condition, he "spent the night in a freezing, water-filled foxhole, and refused to leave until he got a flat order." The tanks tried to support the infantrymen, but "The supporting tanks fired round after round on known emplacements, but were only answered with continuous enemy mortar and artillery barrages." The critical fault at this stage of the battle was that the tanks could not cross the river. It might not have been possible under enemy observation to have bridged the river before the assault had been launched, but perhaps it should have been tried.

As it was, only a portion of the 68th was able to withdraw out of the dragon's teeth, and the rest, including Bob Davies' squad, were stuck in the open and attempting to dig in. As the 14th's *History* sketches the outline of this effort,

> Trying to dig in on the high ground behind Ober-Otterbach was a difficult task. The men used entrenching tools, knives, canteen cups and helmets to get shelter in the frozen earth. For five days and nights the battalion held these foxhole positions, five miserable, hellish days and nights in the close, cold, frozen earth of a water-soaked foxhole, five days and nights of nerves, terror, wounds and death while the Germans screamed over their artillery and mortar shells and you heard the scream and forgot to shiver for the cold and felt the blast of the earth; and your clothes were frozen and wet and stiff, and always cold and hungry and not wanting to eat and afraid, always afraid and waiting.[24]

A small group of men found safety in a house in Ober-Otterbach, some of them wounded. Here Lt. Glen W. Scoff not only treated the wounded who were brought in but went out in search for more in the open ground subject to hostile observation and fire. The other "aid men" or "Medics" recounted the courageous actions of "Scottie" as his comrades called him. He was attached to C Company of the 68th:

> Casualties occurred within the village and in open fields. He brought all of them from exposed positions under fire to safety in the cellar of the last house in town, within sight of the dragon teeth. There he treated the wounded and started the walking [wounded] back on their painful way to the aid station. Those who could not be evacuated he left in a safe place and followed his platoon in the withdrawal, treating casualties as he went. The next afternoon it was decided to attempt evacuation from the village. Sgt. Scott led the patrol with his Geneva [Red Cross] flag but was fired upon as they approached the town. It was then decided to try again under cover of darkness with a small patrol. Scott again led a partol [sic], this time of four men, into the village to find the wounded. They met a few walking slow-

ly on the way back, but when they arrived at the cellar they found that the wounded had been removed. All that remained were several dead whose names were secured from their dog tags. For this action Sgt. Scott was awarded the Silver Star for gallantry in action and later commissioned 2nd Lt. MAC. It was said that Charlie Company wanted him second only to their company C.O. Capt. Broadwater.[25]

In an effort to allow those stranded in the foxholes desperately dug near the Dragon's Teeth and in other hastily chosen areas around the town, the tanks of B Company, the 25th, laid down a smokescreen for cover. They needed it. In addition to the mortar, rocket, and artillery shells, the MG-42, the deadly machine gun, fired rounds at the rate of 1200 per minute with an effective range between 600 and 3500 meters, almost two miles. The German soldiers called it "Hitler's Saw" because it could cut a human body in half. Charles Whiting described the awful situation in front of pillboxes and bunkers for attacking troops:

> It was basically an infantryman's war. Occasionally a tank would rumble up and help them out with a few quick shells from its 75mm gun before scuttling off to safety again; for the tankers knew that Germans armed with the one-shot panzer-faust . . . lurked everywhere . . .
>
> Here a few Germans could hold up whole companies, and the capture of every single pillbox became a carefully planned operation involving the use of mortars, flame-throwers, a great variety of high explosives. . .[26]

The 68th never got close enough to the pillboxes to employ a flamethrower, and the available records of the Ober-Otterbach fight don't mention mortars except for those of the Wehrmacht. The fight continued nevertheless, and the forward observers of the 500th Artillery tried again and again to maintain an OP but had buildings blown up around them. None of them, surprisingly, were killed. One survivor was Captain Donald C. Alexander, a recipient of the Silver Star, who established an OP on the left flank of C Company. "Each time the 'Krauts' either shot away his position or attacked with small arms, but by moving frequently he was able to maintain excellent artillery support."[27]

There were many individual stories of foot soldiers trying to survive for five days and nights of shelling, some of them amusing and some frightening. Of course, we usually know stories from those who survived the ordeal and not always those who didn't. As the 68th's *History* put it:

Despite all the misery, there were examples of grim humor. At one point of the assault on the town Pfc Fossitt of the second platoon, B Company, ran quickly over to see one of his buddies, Pfc Crockett, of the same platoon, who was firmly imbedded against a haystack, and hurriedly said, "Whew! that was close." Crockett very nochalantly [sic] turned to him and said, "Well, Pal, these aint exactly mothballs hitting around here."

A tale twice told, once in the 14th's and once in the 68th's History (and there are many others), was that of "Rifleman Adolph A. Cacchione," like Fossitt and Crockett, a member of B Company, Bob Davies' company. In the middle of a thunderous barrage, he left his foxhole because he thought he saw his sergeant gesture to him. He immediately "crawled out of his foxhole" to the sergeant's foxhole. It turned out that the sergeant had not asked him to come over. When Cacchione returned to his foxhole, "he found it had been greatly enlarged to a shell hole."[28]

Another hazardous experience related by Clifford Hansford of C Company years later matches almost exactly the story of Pvt. Adolph A. Cacchione:

I had that same experience at Ober-0tterback [sic]. We were dug in on a hill at the end of the first day of baffle there. I did not understand why, but felt that I just had to get out of that foxhole! Calling to my buddy, Thomas 'Mac' McKee, I asked him if there was room for two in his foxhole. He answered back, 'Cliff, come on and we'll make room for two.' I had no sooner got into his foxhole when a large round came in, throwing dirt all over us. Mac stuck his head out and said, 'look at your foxhole!' It had been greatly enlarged.[29]

And Hansford's adventures were not over yet, for on the same day, "shrapnel from a tree burst made a big crease in my steel pot and a mortar round had blown off part of my boot heel."[30]

Others were not so fortunate. Lt. Paul Dixon was killed, and Lt. M.A. Reed took over command of Bob Davies' Company B. Bob would comment later what an extremely "tough customer" Reed was. Many men, including Bob, would develop cases of trench foot in this baffle after being crouched in a foxhole partially filled with icy water. The 68th set up a refuge in Schweigen to relieve those who could be relieved and restore them with a few hours' sleep, hot food, a bath, and a change of clothes. Medics were quite busy taking care of "the rapidly mounting cases of trenchfoot."[31] For Bob Davies, his particular case would come back to haunt him later in the campaign and in his life, but this is to get ahead of his story. As a result of the exposure to the prolonged bombardment, his hair turned white, the result of a change in his body chemistry. Later it would return to its normal color. The final story in the Ober-Otterbach fight is Ken Hazleton's narrative of what he called "The mystery of the disappearing patient." A round from an 88mm gun had wounded a guard at the Battalion CP:

> The station moved en mass [sic] and dressed him where he fell. Tenderly lifting him to a litter and assuming the shelling was finished, they carried him out to the ambulance. Just as the back doors gaped wide the now familiar unmistakable whine was heard again. All hit the ground and after the shelling was through, Tec 5 [Edward P] Sellen couldn't find his patient. He was found safely inside, having 'git thar' so swiftly that no one had seen him.[32]

On 23 December, the battalion, after taking a bad beating, was relieved by the 3rd Battalion, 315th Infantry, 79th Infantry Division. The relief was carried out in blackout conditions, for the enemy artillery was still a dangerous weapon in the hands of experienced gunners. The redeployment was carried out safely, and the 68th settled in the vicinity of Merkwiller. As the writers of the 68th History put it, "Thus we had ended our formal christening or baptism of fire and had given and taken more than a man should be able to endure." The 14AD's History remarked that "The 68th Infantry, at Ober-Otterbach was having so many casualties that a detachment of men . . . were ordered up to help the aid station. Casualties were treated there in 12 hours."[33]

Casualties for the battle were as follows:

Wounded in Action	63
Injured in Action	3
Killed in Action	7
Died of Wounds	1
Missing in Action	28
TOTAL CASUALTIES	102[34]

Unknown to the men of the 68th, although perhaps known to their General Officers, Hitler's surprise attack north of Alsace, in the Ardennes, had begun early on the morning of 16 December, with two American divisions neutralized in the first twenty-four hours. Although surprised at first, General Eisenhower ordered the movement of an armored corps from General Patton's Third Army to break off an attack and swing north to attempt the rescue of the airborne units around the Belgian town of Bastogne. As a result of this movement, as shall be shown in later chapters, Sixth Army Group, under General Devers, was ordered to extend his MLR in Alsace to cover the right flank of Patton's Third Army. This extension forced both VI and XV Corps to become overextended and vulnerable to attack by Germany's Army Group G. Before the end of December, Hitler and his General Staff would plan and execute an attack against Seventh Army and its two above-mentioned Corps which would put such pressure on them so as almost to break them.

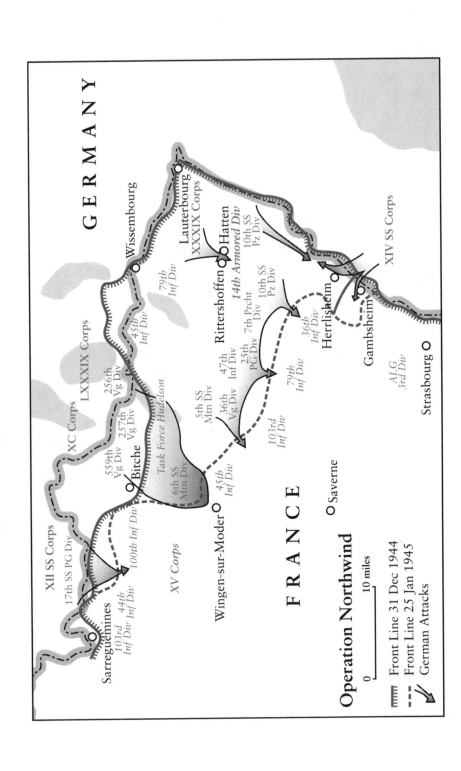

Operation Northwind

Chapter 4

TASK FORCE HUDELSON AND OPERATION NORTHWIND

After an anxious blackout drive through Wissembourg and Soultz-sous Forets, the 68th Armored Infantry Battalion column closed in on the towns of Merkwiller and Diffenbach-les-Woerth, France in the early hours the day before Christmas. Few of the men knew that their shift west to this area was intended to plug the opening formed by the Vosges Mountains on either side of the Wissembourg gap, the target of a new German offensive. For the average GI or "dough," as he was sometimes called during the war, it was a relief from the torments of Ober-Otterbach and the impenetrable Siegfried Line. They had fought hard and bravely there, but caught in the open under relentless enemy fire, they had had to endure five days of pain and shock. This was where Bob Davies' hair had turned white from the shock to his system. They had not broken, but they needed rest, reorganization, and replacements.

Most of their officers and some of the enlisted men knew that military strategy in the Vosges Mountains was always a matter of gaps in either direction. Historically, French and German armies had attacked each other through them. Further south was the famous Belfort Gap, a popular artery for assault and defense. In November of 1944, both the victorious Americans and French had sliced through the opening called the Saverne Gap. In December, however, fresh and important intelligence was being analyzed and communicated to the American Sixth Army Group and Seventh Army. Critical command decisions were being made, and troop movements quietly effected to repel what was supposed to be for German Army Group G a surprise slash through Seventh Army in what was ultimately designated "Operation Northwind."

In order to comprehend what happened during January 1945 in the Vosges Mountains and on the gently rolling plains of Alsace to the east, it is useful to review General Eisenhower's and SHAEF's plans for General Devers' Sixth Army Group as a result of the surprise attack early on the morning of 16 December 1944—what journalists at the time described as "The Battle of the Bulge." Previous to this massive armored assault with three Panzer armies, Ike's strategy, first, was to leave the Colmar Pocket in the vicinity of Strasbourg and south to the divisions of the French First Army. It was, second, to stretch Seventh Army thin in order to free up divisions to assist Gen. George Patton's Third Army after it had had a terrible time in front of the rat's nest of fortifications around the ancient city of Metz. Seventh Army's Sixth and Fifteenth Corps to the south of Third Army had to make do with fewer troops than was necessary to continue offensive operations against the enemy.[1]

A German intelligence estimate of the American troop situation in the Vosges area estimated, pretty accurately, that with the combined losses to Seventh and Third Armies from 12 December to the inception of Operation Northwind at the end of the month, American strength had been reduced by six infantry and two armored divisions, leaving a "total of not more than eight infantry and three armored divisions."[2] And now Sixth Army Group was ordered to go on the defensive, a turn of events which Devers deplored. He was an offensively oriented general and felt that his troops could push the Germans back across the Rhine and hasten the end of the war in Europe.

A brochure from the U.S. Army Center of Military History points out the painful gap between what had been hoped for by General Devers and General Alexander M. Patch, commander of Seventh Army. At the beginning of 1945, "Lt. Gen. Jacob L. Devers' 6th Army Group in the Alsace region would also [in addition to 12th and 21st Army Groups] launch attacks and additional Rhine crossings from their sectors." Cirillo emphasizes the fact that:

Patch had been ordered not to cross the Rhine, even though his divisions were among the first Allied units to reach its banks. In November the Seventh Army had been the Western Front's leading ground gainer. Yet when Patton's Third Army found its offensive foundering, Patch, again following orders, had sent a

Corps northward to attack the Siegfried Line's southern flank, an operational lever designed to assist Patton's attack.[3]

This decision led to the abortive attempt by the 14th Armored's 68th Armored Infantry Battalion to break through at Ober-Otterbach, and more frustration for Major General A. C. Smith, the 14AD's commanding general.

Devers bitterly resented being stripped of more divisions in order to assist Twelfth Army Group, and being ordered to withdraw from the Rhineland into the Vosges Mountains in a defensive position:

> The Sixth Army Group, having created its successes, and about to exploit them, has been disappointed for the second time, as on November 24 when our mission was changed before. Then the Seventh Army was poised to strike across the Rhine in the vicinity of Rastatt, turn north and outflank the Siegfried Line. Events at this moment prove that that maneuver, thoroughly planned and taken boldly, would have been successful. I am also confident that the 3rd Division [battle-proven in North Africa and Italy], debouching from the Vosges Mountains, with direct orders to cross the Rhine, would have forced the bridges at Strasbourg before they could have been blown there, providing a blocking force so that any troops coming from the south would have had to go back through the Black Forest. This would have automatically relieved the Colmar pocket and given the French an opportunity to close up on the river. All facts indicate that this estimate of the situation was correct and would have been successful.[4]

To be sure, Devers' conclusions are hypothetical, and he wouldn't be the first or the last general to justify his actions or himself for posterity. Yet more than one historian, including Douglas Porch (to be cited below) thought Devers was correct. As a Patton biographer has written—to add insult to Devers' injury—"Patch's Seventh Army was threatening the Westwall south of XII Corps, an area where the line was not strongly fortified, . . . [Lt. General Hermann, German commander of Army Group G] shifted Feuchtinger's 21st Panzer Division remnants and the 404th Volks Artillery Corps to reinforce the threatened area" around 15 December, just one day before the Germans launched their Ardennes Offensive farther north.[5]

Eisenhower's order of 19 December was based on the desperate need to race north and rescue the airborne and armored troops holding out under extreme circumstances around Bastogne in Belgium. As a result of the order, General Alexander Patch's Seventh Army had to displace further north into the icy mountains on frozen roads, in blizzard conditions, and foot-freezing temperatures in order to maintain a very thin line of defense against a sneak attack. Estimates of the distance between foxholes of the cold and tired soldiers ranged from fifteen to twenty yards. One squad leader claimed that his squad had to cover a thousand yards of front. Another armored infantryman related that when the men were dug in to repel the violent assault of the panzer grenadiers, they could not see the foxholes of their fellows on either side of them. Not only were the distances and the frozen conditions a problem, but the fog obscured everything in the dense fir forest.

A further complication of the troops' new alignment was that Eisenhower wanted the French to evacuate the critical historical city of Strasbourg, which he initially saw as of limited military value. However, when news of the planned withdrawal reached the French Provisional Government in London under the leadership of the imperious General Charles de Gaulle, he and the French leadership were incensed at the plan. The loss of Strasbourg would have enormous political consequences for them. French divisions had only recently liberated the city, and if the German forces returned, there no doubt would have been nasty reprisals for all of those Frenchmen who had leapt from anonymity to assist the combat troops of the First French Army.

The French and the Germans had shed quantities of blood over this city and region for centuries, and the local people could have given the Americans a history lesson about their beloved Alsace, where most people spoke French or German or both languages in their own dialect. Most of the place names in the area sounded German, but that meant nothing to the French, who were up in arms. The French government in exile took the position that French troops would refuse to leave Strasbourg and instead defend it to the death, creating a "Stalingrad." SHAEF responded obtusely by threatening to cut off their supplies and ammunition. DeGaulle, in London, called on British Prime Minister Winston Churchill to support him in the contretemps with Eisenhower and SHAEF.[6] Finally, the general from Kansas, ever politically sensitive, changed his mind:

> After closely studying the French views in this matter, and recognizing the political importance of Strasbourg, I felt compelled to alter the original plan for withdrawal. Originally, I had considered that the matter of Strasbourg was merely a conflict between military and political considerations and that I was completely justified in handling the question on a purely military basis. However, as I studied the French views, it became evident that the original plans for withdrawal might have such grave consequences in France that all our lines of communication and our vast rear areas might become seriously affected through interference with the tasks of the service troops and through civil unrest generally. Clearly the prevention of such a contingency became a matter of military as well as political necessity.[7]

Churchill agreed with Eisenhower's decision and told him that he had done the right thing, but only after SHAEF had threatened to cut off support for the French First Army. Yet such support from the Prime Minister was reassuring to the Americans, considering that on another occasion he had quipped that the Americans had always done "the right thing," but only after they had exhausted all other alternatives.

And so the VI Corps, which included the 14th Armored Division, returned from the exposed area known as "the Lauterbourg Salient," on the Eastern Alsatian Plain. Its left flank was now fixed in the Vosges in the forested country around the town of Bitche, where there was still a fortress from the days of Vauban, the great fort designer. It was a matter of some concern to the men of the Corps and the Division that they now had to relinquish to the Wehrmacht territory they had fought, been wounded, and died for. The 14th AD's earlier progress toward the German border and the Rhine had not met with consistently strong opposition because the German Nineteenth Army had needed time to consolidate its new positions. It had been chased, since August, up the Rhone Valley by VI Corps, then led by the very competent General Lucius Truscott. On the American side of the hill, the 14th's 68th Armored Infantry Battalion had been bloodied at Ober-Otterbach in

December, and although the first run through the town of Barr for the 48th Tank Battalion had been relatively easy, the second advance at the end of November had produced a calamity.

Earlier that same month reconnaissance elements of the 14th had reached the Lauter River, then the border with Germany, and sent patrols over it. Yet SHAEF had never seriously considered a major attack up from the south of France, with Seventh Army traversing the Rhine after penetrating the Siegfried Line. General Sir Bernard Law Montgomery's 21st Army Group in the north had been given precedence in the assault against Germany proper. It is doubtful that many American officers with SHAEF in England or fighting on the ground in France thought that Monty could do it—no matter how much support he received by way of infantry, armor, artillery, paratroops, navy boats, and supplies for the great Rhine leap. Certainly General Patton didn't think so. For Americans in the ETO, the Twelfth Army Group was considered the favorite. It would cross in March over the now famous railroad bridge at Remagen, but not now in winter, with the Ardennes campaign causing general officers to bite their fingernails down to the nub about the powerful thrust of Hitler's panzer armies in the "Bulge."

There was yet another element to ponder about General Devers' Sixth Army Group and the original invasion of southern France the previous August. One of the strongest arguments for that invasion had been that French troops, especially the Colonial troops from North Africa, had performed with distinction in Italy fighting with General Mark Clark's Fifth Army, including the bloody morass at Monte Cassino. They had fought with notable bravery, even recklessness, in their effort to defeat Les Boches. Additional motivation for native French troops was their earnest desire to return to their fatherland and to rid it of their detested historical enemy, Germany. By the middle of 1944, it was apparent that French units would be pinched out of the fighting in northern Italy when the Allies reached the Appenine Mountains. For them to fight successfully up the Rhone Valley and, along with American divisions, push the enemy out of Strasbourg was calculated to reinforce their sense of mission. To be told then by Les Americaines that they would have to relinquish the city was entirely too much for them to accept.

Eisenhower's intent was consistent throughout late 1944 and early 1945 in that he wished to exercise maximum pressure against German units all along the line (much as General Grant had in Virginia during the last year of the Civil War). General Montgomery, on the other hand, believed in a sudden, bold thrust through stubborn enemy fortifications. Eisenhower felt that he could not count on any one force with enough energy to establish a bridgehead on the other side of the Rhine. He also saw that by lining the western side of the Rhine and the Siegfried Line respectively he could establish contiguous defensive positions just in case the always dangerous German Army suddenly struck back. However, like almost all his intelligence sources, he was surprised by the eruption in the Ardennes on 16 December.

Two other factors affected the situation. The positive was the opportunistic crossing of the Rhine at Remagen in March; the negative was the extremely high infantry casualties suffered by both the British and American Armies in their dramatic sweep from Normandy through central France and Belgium to the border with Germany. The lethality of the fighting in the hedgerows of Normandy and the stubborn defense of the Landsers (German infantrymen) even in retreat enforced a caution in Eisenhower and his advisors.

And so, to return to the campaign in the Vosges and Alsace, the rapid advance of Seventh Army was not seen as an opportunity to strike but rather as a source of both fighting divisions and individual replacements for transfer. This was what incensed General Devers. As he put in his diary entry for 19 December:

> The low infantry strength of the Third Army makes my problem particularly difficult since I will have to furnish replacements ordinarily coming to us to help them out. On the other hand, the Seventh Army has been admirably led [by General Patch] and tactically and strategically sound, and as a result their divisions are in excellent condition. Infantry replacements must be secured.[8]

Although the 14th Armored had forged ahead to the edge of the Reich and more, Ike's plan was for Seventh Army to bend northward to support Patton's Third Army in the Saar region. That support resulted in Seventh Army's being stretched taut along a winding front in the Vosges Mountains eastward and down into the Alsatian Plain. Too few troops in VI Corps meant that the 14th Armored would be asked to hurl back a violent attack at any incised point along the MLR.

At a meeting at Verdun on 19 December, Devers heard the bad news. After Eisenhower cautioned Patton about his radical shift from west to north toward the site of battle in the Ardennes,

> Patton blithely waved aside the difficulties. "I'll be in Bastogne before Christmas," he said. Eisenhower warned him of the great strength of the German assault and then turned to Devers, who commanded the army group south of Bradley [commander of Twelfth Army Group]. "Jake," he said, "you'll have to thin out your lines so you can take over the big gap left by George. And if you're attacked, give ground even if you have to move completely back to the Vosges Mountains."[9]

According to Eisenhower's son John, writing as a historian decades later, Hitler had resurrected an old plan of attack into the Vosges Mountains. Sixth Army Group was now vulnerable: both the Seventh Army in the north, adjacent to the Saar region, and the French First Army, stationed north and west of Strasbourg on the Rhine, outside the Colmar Pocket to the south and southwest. The two German armies opposing Devers' forces were the Nineteenth under General Friedrich Wiese in the Pocket, supported by two panzer corps on the east side of the Rhine. Immediately to the north was the First Army under General Hermann Balck, which was composed of three corps, the 13th SS, the 82nd, and the 90th, totaling nine divisions, six infantry and three panzer. While it was true that these divisions were nowhere near full strength, they still represented a formidable force against the weakened US Sixth Army Group.

General Eisenhower's decision in October and November not to exploit the enemy weakness in the Vosges and Alsace by thrusting Seventh Army aggressively toward the Rhine to outflank the German forces west of the river has been criticized by more than one historian. One of these, Douglas Porch, argued that "Eisenhower's decision not to unleash the Seventh Army across the Rhine enabled Hitler to prepare a counterblow, one that brought Franco-American relations to a crisis point." Porch also contended that Ike made a mistake because "within less than a week, the Ardennes offensive had begun to lose momentum."[10] Yet that is a debatable conclusion about the fraught situation around Christmas, when major issues in the Bulge were still unresolved. It is doubtful that any readers would find that historians of the campaign like the younger Eisenhower, Charles MacDonald and Danny Parker agreed with Porch.[11] The northern and southern shoulders of the Ardennes salient were still not stabilized, the situation at Bastogne was still a nail-biter, panzer armies were still in Belgium, and there yet remained the possibility that the German war machine, in one last gasp, could advance to and cross the Meuse River, giving Hitler a huge strategic opportunity.

Charles Whiting remarks on the fact that the German command was well aware that the American Sixth Army Group's territory had been stripped of more than a few Divisions:

> SS Colonel Linger, commander of the SS Grenadier Division, who was later captured in Alsace, told his interrogators: "When the breakthrough in the Ardennes had been stopped by the Allies, it was realized that several American divisions had been sent north to aid the Americans in their defense. It was therefore decided to launch an attack against what we felt was sure to be a weak position."[12]

Nevertheless, preparations for Operation Nordwind (Northwind), an opportunistic scheme, were hampered from the start by General Balck's ignorance of what was going to happen on 16 December in the Ardennes. He opened sealed orders on that date which announced

> ... the beginning of the Ardennes offensive and advised that a relaxation of enemy pressure along the Army Group G front could be expected with the progress of the offensive. The Führer's order was given only in general terms, but it did not leave the army group much freedom of action. Deciding the objective of the offensive and its date was left to Hitler himself.[13]

About 20 December Balck removed two divisions from the tine, the 251th Panzer Grenadier and the 21st Panzer Divisions, two elite, although weakened, units, and positioned them east of the Vosges, west of Pirmasens, and north of Bitche. Later Bitche would become a key hinge in Operation Northwind, also known as "10 May 1940," the date of Hitler's invasion of France in 1940. A decision was made not to attack along the Saar River but to drive westward toward the Vosges Mountains, which the Germans called the Hardt Mountains, and on to Saverne to cut off the US forces strung out in the Lauterbourg Salient to the east. General Gerd von Rundstedt, Commander in the West, gave Balck permission for such an attack since German intelligence had concluded that an American corps in Third Army had begun moving northward toward the Ardennes and that the American Sixth Army Group appeared to be going on the defensive.[14]

As an SS battalion adjutant in the 6th SS Mountain Division, Wolf T. Zoepf, who had fought in Northwind, commented decades later after a careful examination of the evidence:

> On December 22, Hitler ordered a feasibility study of an attack by two armored divisions and three infantry divisions from the vicinity of Bitche toward the south. The objective of this attack was to thrust into the rear of the American forces deployed on the Alsatian Plain near Wissembourg. He further ordered a high level of activity along the entire Group G front to deceive and contain the enemy.[15]

But there was no end of surprises for the hasty implementation of Northwind. Suddenly Hitler replaced Balck with Generaloberst Johannes Blaskowitz as commander of Army Group G. On 23 December, with slightly more than a week to prepare the operation, Blaskowiz, deciding to follow Balck's strategy to attack toward Saverne, ordered the First Army to advance to the south in order to link up with Nineteenth Army. The objective was to "annihilate the U.S. VI corps in Alsace." There were two options in the operation to seize Saverne and the key pass there. One armored force was coming down toward Saverne from the northwest, between Wingen-sur-Moder and Sarrebourg (the 21st Panzer and the 25th Panzer Grenadier Divisions), and the other was streaming down from the northeast, due south of Zinswiller (actually the same divisions depending on what happened with the initial attack).

As part of the final preparations, the 6th SS Mountain Division (the third battalion in which, Adjutant Zoepf served) was to arrive from

Finland on New Year's Day. It didn't arrive on time. It was also esti-mated that five infantry and three mobile divisions were available, the aforementioned 21st Panzer and the 25th Panzer Grenadier as well as the 17th SS Panzer Grenadier Divisions. Artillery support was available, but there were some reservations about the possibility of reinforcements in both personnel and materiel, and a serious concern about the lack of self-propelled guns.[16]

Nevertheless, Hitler ordered the operation to commence regardless of these uncertainties. Even more uncertain was the weather, which could prevent the movement of American armored vehicles and the sup-port of "Jabos," the German slang term for American fighter bombers like the P-51 Mustang or the P-47 Thunderbolt. The latter were more common in this theater than the former. The historically bad weather throughout the winter of 1944–45 favored the German forces in gener-al, but in this attack the weather and the icy road conditions caused problems for German armor as well.

To shift focus to the American side and to the 68th Armored Infantry Battalion, its history showed the men to be completely unaware of the great decisions taken beyond their ken. Operational details and complexities swirling around army, corps, and division staffs, not to mention their own battalion staffs—of these they were blessedly unaware. The GI's in the 68th and their comrades in the other division units—tank, cav and recon, artillery and so on—enjoyed momentary amenities in the small Alsatian villages where they were billeted. Certainty there were plenty of fir trees in the area, and for Christmas, Sergeant Bob Davies of B Company, the 68th, was decorating one with whatever shiny scrap metal the men could find. To the far north, in the Ardennes, once the great enemy assault had begun, it was most difficult for units isolated there to decorate any trees. Tree bursts from German artillery provided a grim counterpart to the shiny Christmas trees in Alsace. (In a grim irony of war and literature, the name "Ardennes" is the same as the word "Arden" in some of Shakespeare's comedies such as "A Midsummer Night's Dream," with its gamboling fairies and quaint night creatures.)

However, the company officers of the 68th had other plans for the men. They had trained in sabotage school, designed to teach them to protect themselves and their half-tracks and jeeps from the eyes of enemy reconnaissance teams. And so they practiced concealing vehicles, supplies, ammunition, and fuel from hostile patrols and possible Luftwaffe reconnaissance. The men also knew that there were local residents who might harbor sympathies for the Third Reich (as was the case in the Ardennes) or who might just want to appropriate useful goods for themselves in an especially cold winter. The headquarters staff and company officer worked out detailed training schedules. The I and R Platoon (Intelligence and Reconnaissance) kept the frontline troops aware of local German positions by actively patrolling and by ascertaining the best routes for advance or withdrawal if it came time to do such.

SHAEF and Sixth Army Group and Seventh Army knew from ULTRA that the German First and Nineteenth Armies were planning an attack in Alsace to retake Strasbourg, drive in the flanks of Seventh Army, and roll it up to eliminate Sixth Army Group from the American Order of Battle. Major General William W. Quinn, Intelligence Officer for Seventh Army, after noting that the enemy in December–January was putting most of his energy into the Ardennes campaign, stated that in the Vosges Mountains, "the day after Christmas aerial photographs revealed new enemy forward emplacements for artilllery. Then we also captured two German parachutists and other agents who were trying to find out the location of our reserves to determine how they could isolate these forces after a breakthrough." (Quoted from the U.S. Army's "The Big Picture—The Seventh Army Story" television series, 1950–1975). For the Allies in Alsace, the German command did not observe the absolute radio silence which enabled the initial stunning success of the German armies in the Ardennes. American intelligence passed on this critical information to Devers in December. He was instructed to stop his advance and take up defensive positions. Eisenhower told Devers at the Verdun meeting on 19 December, alluded to previously, that "he must on no account permit sizeable formations to be cut off and surrounded."[17]

In contrast and most unfortunately, American intelligence in Twelfth Army Group in December had been largely overconfident and casual when it came to the possibility of a major German offensive. The thinking was that the Wehrmacht had been demoralized after its retreat across France. That "the boys would be home before Christmas" had been the mantra of both the leaders and the led. Indeed, Eisenhower had a bet with Montgomery based on this optimistic assessment. However, when the German attack smashed into the unready American lines, Ike comprehended the nature of the threat almost immediately while General Omar Bradley, commander of Twelfth Army Group, did not. By that time one infantry division, the 28th, and a significant portion of another, the 106th, had been cauterized from the ensuing struggle.

General Blaskowitz's Army Group G, composed of the First and Nineteenth Armies, did not take to heart the lesson of the surprise to the north—it did not observe radio silence. Unknown to the men in the American divisions on the ground was the fact that their key commanders, Patch and Devers, had been given specific information about enemy troop movements in the Vosges that led the two generals to take preventive measures against the planned German attack. It would occur at midnight and in the early morning hours of New Year's Day, 1945.

What would only be revealed decades later was the existence of the amazing code breaking system called ULTRA, situated in Bletchely Park on the outskirts of London. The story of this remarkable secret, maintained throughout the war, began with the German invasion of Poland in 1939 and the capture by Polish Intelligence Officers of a German coding machine called Enigma. Once Bletchely Park had cracked the secret of Enigma it allowed for the interception of radio messages broadcast by all of Germany's armed forces including the Kriegsmarine and Luftwaffe. Some of these messages were decoded by the English and American codebreakers even before the messages were received by their intended German recipients. The story has been told elsewhere and more than once about the outstanding analytical achievements of the mathematical geniuses at the Park. The detailed planning and preparation in late December by units such as Task Force Hudelson and other units in the snowy mountains of the Vosges were made possible by ULTRA and other intelligence sources.

As early as 20 December, General Devers knew that he had a monumental task ahead of him, but he recorded positively that "We have a difficult job ahead of us, but with the spirit and drive displayed by my commanders and staff, I feel sure that we will get marvelous results." A day later, because of the chronic infantry shortage, he insisted:

My staff is now beginning to worry about my well-being. I am determined that I will not pull troops off the front to guard my headquarters. We will guard it with our own personnel. We need every fighting man to help bring this war to a close, and I am sure that will be done in the not too distant future.

This comment perhaps refers to rumors that the English-speaking German commandos led by the exotic SS Colonel Otto Skorzeny had been infiltrated into American rear areas to, among other things, assassinate Eisenhower and other key Allied personnel.

On Christmas Day he expressed more confidence in the coming challenge:

Careful inspection of the northern front gives me confidence that we will hold the position. However, we are very thin. The Seventh Army has done a magnificent job in shifting troops, getting organized in depth, taking every precaution. We have made the most with little.[18]

In order to determine whether Devers' confidence was justified, it is useful to examine two reports produced after Northwind by Seventh Army, one entitled "Now It Can Be Told" after the fact, and the other, "Hudelson Task Force, 21 December–2 January," written by Lt. Col., Infantry William B. Goddard, an Army Historian. The last one, earlier in time, has a cover letter addressed to "Commanding General, 14th Armored Division [A.C. Smith]." Both of these reports provide sometimes firsthand and always first-rate accounts of what transpired in the Vosges Mountains in the Bitche Salient from the last week in December 1944 to 2 January 1945.

The "Now It Can Be Told" report, providing the strategic context of Northwind, recapitulates the details of both the intelligence and the deployment of troops to meet the imminent threat revealed by the intelligence. The second report, what can be called the "Goddard" report by Seventh Army Historian Col. William B. Goddard, delineates the assault against Task Force Hudelson and its response. The "Now" report reveals in detail how Seventh Army and the French First Army had forced their way into Germany around Bobenthal on 15 December, cleared Strasbourg, and faced northwest. The dangerous German pocket around Colmar, known by that name, reaching to the south and southwest and including Strasbourg, was left to the French First Army to excise. The American Seventh Army at the time was composed of six infantry and two armored divisions in VI and XV Corps. The flank of VI Corps was positioned adjacent to the Rhine and included the 3rd, 45th, 79th, and 103rd Infantry Divisions and both the 12th and 14th Armored Divisions. The Army front was 47 miles wide, and the VI Corps had "a 32-mile frontage," and XV Corps "a 16-mile frontage." The right flank of Seventh Army "extended along the Rhine for 36 miles" and was held by some infantry regiments which were new and untested in combat."[20] Also untested was the 12th Armored Division, and the 14th had only recently engaged in battle.[19]

The Goddard report stated that Task Force Hudelson (TFH), which had been culled from the 14ths CCR or Reserve Combat Command, was set in place between 21 December and 2 January, with most of the time devoted to preparing for the expected attack:

> On the VI Corps left flank, holding a frontage of about 10 miles in the lower Vosges-Hardt area was the Task Force Hudelson. It consisted of Combat Command Reserve, 14th Arm'd Division less one tank battalion; Co. B, 645th Tank Destroyer Battalion; Co B, 83d Chemical Mortar Battalion, Co A, 125th Arm'd Eng Bn, 1-540 Combat Engr, 94th Cav Sqd (-) [,] 62nd AIB and the 117th Cav Rcn. Sqd all under the command of Colonel D. H. Hudelson.[20]

Colonel Daniel H. Hudelson was the able commander of CCR of the 14th Armored Division.

Looking at the defensive arrangement from a larger perspective, the Lower Vosges bisected the Seventh Army sector with the axis of advance (or retreat) parallel to them and dividing the two Corps, the XV and the XVI. To the east were the plains of Alsace and to the west the "gently rolling Saar River Valley." In the area east of Bitche, the Maginot Line, running roughly northwest and southeast, mostly remained in the hands of the Allies, but the Germans controlled it in a few places. Thus the MLR during January would be quite confusing at times during the upcoming battles at Hatten-Rittershoffen and at Germersheim bordering the Rhine River. The "Now" report's analysis specifies two reasons for the blunting of Northwind by the VI Corps: the accurate intelligence before fighting erupted and the heroic stand made by the mixed group in TFH, by other units of the 14th Armored, and by other divisions, mostly infantry like the 79th and the 42nd, but also by the 12th Armored Division, which would be hurt by the enemy campaign. This green unit would suffer terribly around Germersheim but would stand their ground as long as possible. In the bitter cold of the end of December and throughout most of January, the tank and armored infantry battalions of the 14th would battle against, among others, the vaunted tanks and grenadiers of the 21st Panzer Division and other units of Army Group G.

The "Now" report recapitulates how Seventh Army had split the Nineteenth and First German Armies, and when the Seventh turned northeast, it "virtually destroyed" the 361st and 553rd Infantry Divisions, whose responsibility was to protect the Siegfried Line near Karlsruhe. The German retreat had been very rapid up the Rhone Valley in the fall, when VI Corps, then under General Truscott, had pursued them in relentless fashion. It wasn't so much that the German Army had been routed as much as its orders were primarily to protect the Fatherland at Karlsruhe. Nevertheless, the German forces were badly mauled. These divisions were temporarily replaced as a screening force by 11th Panzer, 25th Panzer Grenadiers, and the 130th PG Divisions until the 256th and 245th Volksgrenadier (VG) Divisions arrived from Holland. The enemy withdrew from contact when it reached the Vosges Mountains, where the terrain, supply problems, and weather for the American VI Corps conspired to stall the 3rd, 36th and 45th Infantry Divisions in their pursuit.

Yet the German divisions vigorously attacked the French First Army in the Colmar Pocket to the south, seeking a way to keep the Allies away from the Rhine River so that thorough defensive preparations could be made. German POWs informed US Intelligence Officers that they had been ordered to withdraw to the Westwall by 16 December, the date of the German irruption into the Ardennes. There, they were told, "you shall fight and die." But some German divisions had not yet been pinpointed by American intelligence, and the question remained whether they would rotate north to the Ardennes or pivot into the attack in the Vosges Mountains and Alsace, which would be Operation Northwind.[21]

As a result of the information gathered, during December Sixth Army Group and Seventh Army set in motion a number of critical rearrangements of both fighting and support units before the threatened

German assault. On 18 December, Seventh Army was ordered to extend itself left to St. Avoid and to switch to a defensive posture. On 21 December XII Corps relinquished control of its area in the Vosges to Seventh Army and gravitated toward Luxembourg to break through to the surrounded American divisions at Bastogne. By then XV Corps of Seventh Army had identified the 17th SS Panzer Division and the 347th Infantry Division "in its widened sector."

General Devers reported on 27 December about a meeting in Paris with Eisenhower, who had demanded the defensive posture of Sixth Army at Verdun. It is not clear as to the exact date of this meeting, but it was probably on 19 December.

> Took off for Paris where I had a long conference with Eisenhower and Bull. Eisenhower was very definite [underlined by hand in the text] that I must move my troops back to the Vosges line and hang on, that I would not get many replacements—in fact they were taking replacements from me—I would get no more ammunition and no more help; that I would undoubtedly be threatened down the Saar River Valley and that I would have to stop the drive. . . . I am not interested in territory and so informed Ike. I am interested in the integrity of my troops and the protection of the people I have liberated. We are preparing positions in depth and will try to pull back slowly; it cannot be done rapidly unless I am forced to do so, because of the terrific rearrangement we have gone through in the past few days to get out reserves for Patton. Our dispositions are sound for, if they had not been, I would not be able to set up a corps of two divisions for the use of SHAEF immediately.[22]

By 26 December, Seventh Army's front was 84 miles from the Rhine to a point near Saarbrucken to the northwest. VI Corps, now under Major General Edwin H. Brooks, "held a line from the Rhine River to Bitche, with the 79th and 45th infantry Divisions in the line with 14th Armored in reserve," as the "Now" report phrased it. The composite force, Task Force Hudelson, was assigned to the MLR in the vicinity of Bitche. The right flank on the Rhine was held by Task Force Hams and Task Force Linden from the 63rd and the 42nd Infantry Divisions respectively, a role that would prove both costly and bloody. The 42nd was still waiting for support units and its artillery which had debarked at Marseilles later than the infantry battalions. In the conflict ahead, their assistance would be sorely missed.

The critical nature of the situation, already stressed by Devers, was reinforced in a letter quoted in the "Now" report from Sixth Army Group dated 21 December, which grimly declared that it should "be prepared to yield ground rather than endanger the security of its forces," an echo of Eisenhower's order to Devers. The Goddard report quotes this letter with only minor verbal changes. As a result, tons of supplies were loaded and transported rearward to keep them out of the hands of advancing enemy forces while engineers and ordnance personnel raced forward with mines, barbed wire, fence pickets, concertina wire, and explosives to make the charging foe pay dearly for any risk he might undertake. As the Goddard report continues, preparations intensified as the hours passed:

"Road junctions were prepared with craters and demolitions to make the roads impassible for enemy armor. Timber was felled, with the branches sharpened and pointed in the direction of the attack. T.N.T charges

> were tied to trees which would be blasted to fall across all avenues of approach. Roadblocks of tanks and [a] trench system were organized. Anti-tank and personnel mines were strategically placed to supplement concertina wire and trip flares as precautionary defensive measures. Listening posts were established. Patrols were ordered to take prisoners for identity of opposing forces and information regarding enemy positions and intentions.[23]

On 28 December, within hours of the expected attack, General Devers held a 'War Room Conference" with five other generals (not identified) to parse carefully the strategic and operational range of options available to them:

> Drew up order for the defense. We went into great detail. This is necessary because it is our first defense order and because it was necessary for me to make clear that Eisenhower wanted to give up the whole Alsacian [sic] plain and to fall back upon the

line of the Vosges. The position I give up is much stronger than the one to which I go. Both have hinges, but the hinge in the Vosges is weak. I gain some in the front to be covered. However, we shall go back to the line of the Vosges just as fast as sound tactics will permit.[24]

The timing implied by the above must have proved painful for officers and men alike, for they all had just 72 hours at the most to make the move and prepare for the attack, and try to get some rest in between.

The intelligence situation was still fluid and ambiguous as staff officers tried to locate and track enemy divisions. Some enemy divisions, such as the 6th SS Mountain Division were still en route to the area, while two others were en route from Holland. Charles Whiting cites orders on 29 December from Devers to Patch, the Seventh Army commander (after the 28 December conference), enforcing the necessity of keeping a major reserve force:

A hostile attack against your flank west of Bitche may force you to give up ground from your main position. To meet such a possibility it is necessary that your west flank be protected by a reserve battle position. With this in mind, reconnaissance and organization of a reserve battle position will be instituted without delay. . . .[25]

With all of this frantic activity occupying the troops and their company and field commanders, none of the intelligence officers from Army Group down to Division to Combat Commands or Regiments knew the degree of importance which Hitler himself was attaching to Operation Northwind. Colonel Joseph E. Lambert, the S-3 (Operations Officer) of the 14th Armored Division, researched the subject soon after the war in Europe was over while files were still active. He cites the following statement:

Hitler, in a speech made to Army, Corps, and Division Commanders on 28 December 1944, stated among other things:
"Gentlemen: I have asked you to come here before an action on the successful conclusion of which further blows in the west will depend.

". . . Thus the task allotted to the new offensive does not exceed the capabilities of the forces that are available. We are committing eight divisions on our side. With the exception of a single one . . . from Finland [6th SS Mt. Div.]. The other seven are, of course, battle worn, too. One division is an exception; it is located directly at the Rhine. One will have to wait and see how it is going to stand up. There is also the 12th American Armored Division which is not committed. At any rate it is still a new unit which has not been in combat yet. But outside of that, the other units at the side of the enemy are battle worn, too. We are sure to get into a ratio here which we could not wish to be any better. . . .

"This second attack [after the Ardennes strike], then, has a very clear objective, the destruction of the enemy forces. There is not a matter of prestige here. The point is to gain space. It is a matter of destroying and exterminating enemy forces wherever we find them. The question of liberating all of Alsace at this time is not involved either. That would be very nice; the impression on the German people would be immeasurable, the impression of the world decisive; terrific psychologically; the impression on the French people would be pressing. But that is not important. It is more important, as I have said before, to destroy his manpower. . . .

"I fully approve of the measures that have been taken. I hope that we will succeed especially to push the right wing ahead fast, to open the roads to Saverne. Then push at once into the Rhine plains to liquidate the American Divisions. . . . I don't have to explain to you the second time just what depends on it. The success of the first operation, too, is very dependent on this. Because as soon as we finish these two operations, A and B, and if they succeed, the threat to our left flank will vanish automatically. . . ."[26]

Whatever the Führer's alleged descent into madness and delusion in the spring of 1945, in December 1944 his command of the strategic and operational situation seemed secure. He knew what Northwind would attempt to do, but he seemed to have no illusions about its capacity, if rightly fought, to wrest all of Alsace from the Allies and possibly to destroy the American Seventh and the French First Army. Notable also is his regarding Sixth Army Group as representing "a threat to our left flank," something that Eisenhower and SHAEF apparently did not.

Hitler's speech notwithstanding, Seventh Army intelligence discovered that the 21st Panzer Division "had not gone north." By 29 December, a little more than 48 hours before the anticipated German campaign, it also uncovered a definite enemy buildup in the East Rhine Valley and in both the Colmar bridgehead and the Saarbrucken region. ULTRA Intelligence Officer, Major Donald S. Bussey, drew his conclusion about the serious danger of a possible hostile slice into the Saar River Valley—it was both serious and likely. General Patch, the Seventh Army commander, was most concerned about an assault dividing his Army, "a penetration that could split his forces and leave the VI Corps stranded on the Alsatian plains."[27]

All told, there were elements of nine enemy divisions of the First German Army arrayed against the American Seventh Army. The capabilities of these forces were outlined in the "Now" report at the end of the war:

> (1) to attack South from Bitche-Sarreguemines with 5 to 8 divisions to seize Saverne pass and lngwiller pass," the objective of which was "to cut off and destroy Seventh Army and to recapture Strasbourg.
> (2) to make limited attempts to keep Seventh Army in place to help the German Armies fighting in the Ardennes.

This last option was considered more likely than the first, but there was still some unease at the buildup of hostile troops in Alsace and at the fact that the German Army still held a strong bridgehead in the Colmar region. The shortening of communication and supply lines for the Wehrmacht only made this possibility more threatening. Also considered was the implication that any kind of enemy victory in the Seventh Army's sector would provide a boost to German morale. In order to prepare for either eventuality, "A Sixth Army Group Letter of Instructions dated 28 December . . . laid down successive withdrawal positions and specified that the main defensive line would follow the Eastern slopes [of the Vosges]. A Combat Command of the 14th was moved to Phalsbourg. A firm MLR was to be established on the

Maginot Line, but it was not to be held to the death" unlike the command to the German troops in this operation.[28]

A reader can only imagine what might have happened to American troops at the point of attack if there had been no warning by SHAEF Intelligence to Sixth Army Group. In fact, Devers' Diary entry for 1915 hours on 30 December states that [General] Patch called me and said the attack was coming during the night; in any case, the following night. I agree." A similar call came the following day, Sunday, New Year's Eve, 1944.[29]

Down at the division level, things were also moving expeditiously. A "Diary" of the 14th Armored Division, extending for only a few typed pages from 14 December to 27 January, adds a few details of what transpired in the days before and during the German effort against VI and XV Corps in the Vosges. On 28 December, CCA, composed of the 48th Tank Battalion and the 68th Armored Infantry Battalion, C Company of the 125th Combat Engineers, B Company of the 136th Ordnance and Maintenance Battalion, and "detachments of the 154th Signal and MPs, moved to vicinity of Phalsbourg and was attached to XV Corps." In addition, the "Diary" specifies that

> 14th Armored Division not operating as a unit. CCR, under name Task Force Hudelson, holding part of VI Corps front around Baerenthal. CCR composed of 62 AIB, 94th Cavalry (Mczd), 500th AFA Bn, 1 Co. of 125th Armd. Engineers, and normal attachments of Signal personnel and MPs plus other units outside of Division.[30]

This list does not include the attached 117th, Cav and Recon, the 83rd Mortar Battalion, the 1-540 Combat Engineers, or Co. B of the 645th Tank Destroyer Battalion, units noted in the Goddard report, but it does mention the 500th AFA Battalion, which the Goddard report did not.

On 30 December, a radio message was sent to all divisions ordering them to establish a reserve division force from the already designated "Reserves," half of them east of the axis Kandroff-Benestroff-Saar Union-lngwilter. And so Seventh Army placed the experienced 36th lnfantry Division and the inexperienced 42nd Infantry Division on that tine. The 12th Armored Division was taking a defensive posture along with the infantry divisions, but the VI Corps directive to the 14AD was quite different in that it was to act "as a counter-attacking force in the event of an enemy breakthrough in the XV Corps zone." (Of course, the division had been reduced by its contributions to Task Force Hudelson.) On New Year's Eve, the Army commander, General Patch, personally traveled to XV Corps Headquarters in Fenetrange. There he informed both XV and VI Corps commanders, Generals Wade H. Haislip and Edward H. Brooks, "that an enemy attack was to be expected during the early hours of New Year's Day." Such a move by the Seventh Army commander indicated how grave was the threat to his troops. The "Now" report then concludes portentously, "insofar as was possible, Seventh Army had made itself ready."[31]

In the Task Force Hudelson area, "The 62 AIB was placed on the right of the sector, the 117th Cavalry Squadron the left and the 94th Cavalry Squadron in the center, but the lines were described as "paper thin" according to the Goddard Report. The combat engineers were responsible for maintaining the bridges and acting as a reserve.[32]

Vernon H. Brown, Jr., a gunner in the 94th, who was stationed in the area with Troop D, felt the collision of the German assault with his unit:

> On December 31, 1944, New Year's Eve, Platoon spotted an enemy patrol around mid-afternoon equipped with full field packs instead of the usual equipment. Guard was doubled for the night. I was sleeping fitfully just before midnight when [Corporal William D.] Cage, who was standing watch on the machine gun in the dugout, kicked me awake. Heavy "incoming mail" of all sorts was now landing all around us, and as I struggled up to a sitting position I could see the stuff bursting in the woods in great balls of orange fire. [Pfc.] Bill Tauber was hit by flying shrapnel. We could hear a heavy fire fight going on out on the left flank. GI machine gun fire, grenades and rifles, answered unmistakably by Kraut burp guns.[33]

The history of the 68th AIB records simply that on New Year's Day the reinforced battalion left Schoenbourg and motored to Rahling, a crossroads town just west of the Vosges and Bitche to provide XV Corps assistance in repelling an attack in that Corps area. The men in the battalion did not know what had happened the evening before, but those at the point of the offensive were agreed on the fanatical even suicidal, nature of the charging grenadiers: "the extremely idiotic and senseless manner in which they [stood] right up . . . and simultaneously called the defenders vile names and fired into their positions. . . . In many cases even the wounded who were unable to get to their feet continued firing into Company K (397th Bn.) [42nd Infantry] positions."[34]

As the US Army History of the war in southern France and Alsace describes the action, "The German attack barely made a dent in the beefed-up Allied line. In some cases the SS troopers advanced in suicidal open waves, cursing and screaming at the American infantrymen who refused to be intimidated."[35] Other troopers in the 42nd experienced the brunt of this special madness: "First we heard 'em shrieking like Indians. Then they came rushing in waves waving their guns right in the sights of our machine guns. . . . Those guys acted like they had just had a shot of something."[36] Captain Horace D. Orr, a medical officer with the 500th AFA Battalion and not directly involved in the fierce combat, was stationed near Baerenthal and heard the commotion:

> About midnight I began to hear the sounds of 'burp' guns in the distance but thought no more about it until about 6:00 a.m. I was awakened by GIs coming to our aid station who had been wounded by enemy fire. (It must be remembered our defense lines were very thin.) In about two to three hours, artillery fire began to fall around us and [the] order was given to pack up and retreat. This we did and soon our unit was on the road.[37]

Because of the lengthy irregular front, punctuated by hills, valleys, streams, and dense stands of evergreens, organizing a line of "sufficient depth" had been extremely difficult. As the Goddard report remarks, "Indications of an enemy attack were not lacking. Aerial observers had noted the movement of German troops in the few days of flying weather which prevailed during the traditional foggy and rainy month of December. Enemy patrols were active during the period and hostile artillery registration fire on villages and cross roads was reported."[38]

The enemy surge had begun with six divisions; the 256th Volks Grenadiers, the 361st VG, the 559th VG, the 17th SS Panzer Grenadiers, and the 19th and 36th VG Divisions. Like the other separated units of the 14th Armored Division, Task Force Hudelson, which was deployed from Bitche to Neunhoffen, "was little more than a trip-wire running through mountain forests," and the men of the Task Force, freezing in their foxholes, agreed with the men of the 42 that "It was an attack by madmen through their positions." The intent of these wild infantry assaults was to open the "seam" between XV and VI Corps. "The 62 AIB of the 14th, along with 117th Cavalry Recon., linked Task Force Hudelson to the 100th Division's 399th Infantry. The Cavalry fell back to a place north of Mouterhouse. Col. D. H. Hudelson had established a series of strongpoints on the mountain roads that entered the sector from east and west. . . ."[39] This displacement of the 117th peeled back the flank on that side and caused some consternation that the line could become undone.

As the Goddard report reminds us, the 17th Panzer Grenadier Division, which was "up to strength and newly fitted," was assigned the mission of piercing the MLR on the eastern side of the Hardt/Vosges mountains in order to provide an avenue for 21st Panzer to debouch into the Saar Valley. Prisoners of War later admitted that the attack was designed to provide "a diversion for the Belgian offensive, thus relieving the pressure Von Rundstedt's armies were receiving in the north and to give a cheap political victory to bolster German morale on the home front."[40] However, the evidence behind the argument in Col. Joseph E. Lambert's essay supports the opposite conclusion—that the primary aim was the destruction of the American Seventh and the French First Army, i.e Sixth Army Group. Hitler's speech indicated clearly that he was not interested in a propaganda victory either.

The flexibility of the instructions given by General Devers' Sixth Army Group not only protected Task Force Hudelson and the other units at the heavy point of the spear but also frustrated German intentions to bypass strongpoints to surround and annihilate them. This maneuver blunted the enemy's goals, but there was enough hostile infiltration and confusion so that many American units, especially Col. Hudelson's troopers, had to fall back very rapidly in order to regroup. In the zone of the 42nd Infantry Division near the Maginot Line, the first attacks had occurred in darkness in the fog-shrouded mountains, with both sides barely able to see each other. By all accounts, the German grenadiers charged into the open without much cover and suffered terrible losses for their efforts, with dead and wounded soldiers draped over barbed wire, some dead but some moaning in pain. One machine gunner in the 397th Infantry, "Pfc. Leon Outlaw . . . alone dropped over one hundred Germans in front of his position."[41]

At the Hudelson positions, C Company of the 62nd AIB was under attack before midnight:

> About 2400 on 31 December the 62d Battalion C.P., located in Phillipsbourg, received a telephone message that 'C' Company was undergoing a servere [sic] enemy attack. Lt. Col. J. [James] H. Myers (Comdg. 62 AIB) immediately issued instructions for two platoons of Troop A 117th Cav Rcn Sqwdn to occupy previously selected positions in 'C' Company's area.[42]

The task of these platoons, which were attached to CCR, was to seal off the highways leading in and out of the area.

The History of the 14th Armored Division by Captain Joseph Carter also reports on the hostile strike into the 62nd's positions. The action began with a trip flare illuminating the night in front of A Company's defenses. The flare revealed a German patrol fifty yards away and crawling in their direction. The GIs had been warming their weapons inside their clothes to prevent the mechanisms from freezing, but now they had to be wrenched out suddenly and put into action. Carter's writing sketches the drama that ensued:

> The chatter of a single machine gun, first, then all the guns slashed through the night; the flares of the muzzle flashes laced through the woods and darted through the night.
> The Germans attacked, yelling and screaming, firing automatic weapons. It was an attack by madmen.[43]

C Company of the 62nd AIB's response to the "initial enemy attack" was to employ four half-tracks with their .50 caliber machine guns cross-firing against the enemy troops when their outpost position was assaulted "in and around the hotel at Lake Et de Hanau." The combination of this fire with small arms fire raked the advancing German infantry. "The Germans crumbled into the snow under the Americans volley of fire."[44]

Captain Carter repeats the account of the retreat of the 62nd and their coverage by the cross-firing .50 calibers on the half-tracks, but he also records the difficulty of withdrawing under the intense pressure of hostile gunfire. "The minute the outposts moved, the Germans, following in hot pursuit, began to infiltrate the lines along the front." C Company's First Platoon "was surrounded and cut off, and C Company was hurt."

Carter also notes how, along with the friendly .50 caliber fire, shooting intensified with the addition of .30 caliber machine guns, which fired relentlessly at the advancing grenadiers along with submachine gun and rifle fire. "Germans crumpled to the ground and the snow stained brown." As friendly artillery fire began to fall in front of the 62nd's positions, the company began to exfiltrate as the fire from the enemy became extraordinarily intense—from burp gun to artillery. "The 62nd was undergoing such pressure from enemy infantry that "C Company (62) had called artillery fire down on its own positions and the German artillery came in on top of it."[45]

As the story continues, when the 62nd was driven back to Bannstein, the fighting continued under a savage hail of German artillery fire. At this point, the reserve of Task Force Hudelson, the 125th Combat Engineers, also of the 14th AD, was committed to battle. The charging enemy infantry repeated the habit of the earlier assault troops by shouting out profanities and threats against the American defenders: "Yankee bastards! Die, Sons of bitches!" Their profanity notwithstanding, they were cut to pieces as they poured into the fringes of Bannstein and forced the GIs to abandon equipment and supplies. As was the case with other units in the MLR around Bitche, because of good intelligence on German intentions in Northwind, the GIs fought as long as they could in their prepared positions and took a grievous toll of the enemy. Then, as a contingency plan had laid it out, they exfiltrated back through the hills and woods to fight another day. It wasn't pretty or smooth, but the plan worked.[46]

Although the grenadiers had initiated the assault without artillery support in order to surprise what they thought would be unwary and unprepared American troops, Colonel Hudelson had no such reservations when he called in artillery fire to support the withdrawing GIs. The 17th SS Panzer Grenadiers were in the vanguard of the advance, and they were accompanied by Jagdtiger Assault Wagons. Fortunately for the defenders, nature would be evenhanded: just as GIs had to abandon some of their vehicles in their swift withdrawal because of icy roads, so too would these behemoths have trouble maneuvering on the same treacherous pavements now covered with snow.

During the advance against C-62, after the grenadiers had been shredded by machine-gun fire, one of the company's officers at the OP demanded that the Germans surrender. Col. Goddard recreates the scene:

> Six green-clad soldiers advanced with hands held high. The Americans held their fire and watched the Germans advance in the moonlight.
>
> Other enemy forces opened fire on the surrendering soldiers. None of the Germans were hit however. The[y] hit the ground and crawled over the snow to the American forces.

The surrendering infantry claimed that they were part of a battalion attacking the 62nd. Before they were surrounded, the outpost group withdrew to the MLR on the Bannstein highway. Friendly artillery (105 and 155mm) supported the withdrawal.[47]

But the action was far from over as enemy soldiers infiltrated the lines "through the eastern section of 'C' Company's lines." Men of that Company later told Lt. Col. Goddard that a German infantry squad had tried to fool them by shouting out "Hold your fire" in English. The GIs did hold their fire momentarily but resumed when they realized that they had been tricked into a momentary ceasefire.

The Goddard report commented further that "The scene was one of confusion as the white clad, German figures 'romped all over the place' [to use the language of the men of the 62nd] firing automatic weapons and hollering 'Die—Yankee bastards' and ganster [sic] -bitches'."

With the threat of being surrounded imminent, half-tracked vehicles were ordered to evacuate the men to Bannstein, but a German "bazooka" round disabled the first half-track. Immediately the friendly response was machine-gun fire, which caused the Germans to pull back. The armored infantry followed in the same direction in their retreat to Bannstein. When the troops reached their own lines at a roadblock, they endured a burst of "friendly fire" from the nervous defenders. Nevertheless, the beleaguered 62nd men crawled forward and gave the password "Baloney," which produced the countersign "Dot." They continued "along the icy highway" towards Phillippsbourg. Attached 117th Cavalry and organic 94th Cavalry units were sliding in their vehicles in the same direction, creating a hazard for those on foot.[48]

The Goddard report also describes how other elements of the 62nd in the area of Bellerstein, northeast of Bannstein, were also being undermined by enemy infiltration from the north. The pressure on Company C, commanded by Capt. Howard A. Trammel, was relentless. Trammel wrote a detailed account of what happened to his Company during the fight. When orders were given to pull back, Pfc. Donald E. Allen, on outpost duty, reached a gully but was wounded in the leg. While being taken to the rear in a half-track, the vehicle was hit by a panzerfaust. Allen was "blown out of the halftrack and after regaining consciousness, heard his name being called." It was the voice of Tec. 5 Vincent R. Dorior, who was driving a second half-track, who would save Allen from capture or worse.

Staff Sergeant Edward W. Faytak was a squad leader in the Second Platoon. He had been feeling edgy most of New Year's Eve and repeatedly checked on the men on outpost duty. Around midnight, a grenade exploded in a place where his men had set flares to detect the enemy in motion. As he painted the picture,

> After the grenade went off, all hell broke loose. The Krauts were tripping the wires. They were coming from all over—through the woods, down the hills and across the lake. We never did get orders to get out of there, but we were over-run with Krauts in white, screaming and yelling—they acted crazy.[49]

Faytak and his squad made it back to the CP, but he was wounded severely in the shoulder and lungs, and although losing consciousness periodically, he managed to find safety in a house. He was attended to by a woman and a girl but was captured by the Germans after the women left because of the shelling.

Capt. Trammel was having an extremely difficult time maintaining radio or telephone contact with Third Platoon. (Radio conditions in forested mountains in winter were problematic at best.) Trammel directed its Platoon Leader to withdraw across the road and over the railroad tracks to Bannstein. Trammel also ordered him to take all personnel in town to establish a position on high ground covered by woods south of the town. Yet the Captain had his own problems because he was cut off from that position by hostile forces. As he characterized the problem, he had to stay at the CP for two reasons:

(i) The withdrawing Second Platoon would be moving toward the CP from the direction of the lake, and, and he needed to be at the CP to redeploy the Platoon.
(2) All his communications to "higher headquarters" were through the CP, and to leave it would be to cut his Company off from re-supply and reinforcement and, most immediately, from "the very effective artillery fire support."[50]

Elements of the Third Platoon found their way into Bannstein and were joined by those from the First Platoon. This group moved to the high ground stipulated by Trammel and then continued southwest, "being closely pursued and fired upon." After Requesting "artillery concentrations" north of the town to harass the advancing Germans who were moving south, he left the CP to rendezvous with the Third Platoon leader. However, he was diverted by burp-gun fire in between him and the rendezvous point, but nevertheless managed to reach the road junction which led to Baerenthal. Here friendly troops told him that their orders were to locate any Company C troops and take them to Phillipsbourg. Trammel got there along with the stragglers, which he then organized.

Meanwhile the Platoon Sergeant of First Platoon (not identified) led some of his men, who had also been cut off, to temporary safety in Bannstein. As Trammel noted, the Sergeant was awarded a Silver Star and later a battlefield commission.

Fortunately for a squad led by Tec. Sgt. Dale F. Phipps, he was able to guide his patrol to safety by effective use of his command of German. Encountering a hostile patrol, he told its members that he and his squad were dressed in American uniforms to create havoc and confusion among the "Amis." They were evidently convinced by his flawless German and by their knowledge that farther north, in the Ardennes, this tactic had been attempted by a special unit under command of the notorious Col. Otto Skorzeny. After two more days and nights evading enemy outposts, Phipps' squad, although having no food and only snow to drink, managed to return to the friendly side of the line.[51]

Other small groups off American soldiers did their best to get to safety, and some of them managed to inflict serious casualties on the grenadiers who were pressing them. Still others were menaced by German tanks and found out to their dismay that their 2.36-inch rocket launcher or bazooka was useless in the face of heavy panzer armor. A friendly rear guard was set upon from the flank as they circled around a hill. Hostile fire made it impossible to escape, and about a dozen men were captured.

Captain Trammel summarized C Company's condition in a morning report for 6 January, five days or more after the enemy assault against his Company:

> The morning report of 6 January 1945 for Company C shows 2 officers and 139 enlisted men present for duty. At the start of Bannstein the Company was under strength by 35 enlisted. Of those missing, the officers were the 1st and Anti Tank Platoon leaders. Missing in enlisted were 7 squad leaders and 9 halftrack drivers. Thus, reconstructing the Company after Bannstein, it was necessary to replace these key personnel.[52]

After half a century and more, Lt. Colonel (ret.) Trammel still feels that the efforts of his company were not appreciated and even insulted. This issue will be taken up later in this chapter under the rubric of the intelligence available to his battalion and company before the commencement of Northwind.

To return to the fight and the Goddard report, a defensive posture at Bannstein had been established to exercise control of the road arteries leading in and out of town. The defensive force, somewhat bare, composed of only 24 men and nine half-tracks, fired on the charging grenadiers, who insisted on forcing their way despite the intense hostile machine-gun and small arms fire. The story must sound familiar to the reader of this chapter:

The Germans were "persistent" and continued to charge across the snow covered fields toward Bannstein. Firing automatic weapons and yelling in frenzied tones, "Yankee bastards—Die sons-a-bitches," the enemy forces continually tried to cross the bald surface. The Americans successfully held the enemy off until the morning hours of New Years Day.[53]

It is perhaps the moment to discuss a sore point for veterans of the battle in the Vosges Mountains from New Year's Eve 1944 until at least the day after New Year's Day. Those involved with Task Force Hudelson, including and perhaps especially those from the 62 AIB of the 14th Armored Division, have been quite unhappy and in sharp disagreement with the British historian Charles Whiting's account of the early morning assault against the positions of the 62nd, the 94th Cav and Recon, and the 117th Cav and Recon attached to the division. A fair estimate of the battle situation would conclude that in the face of overwhelming strength, including enemy armor and superior firepower, these units had no chance to survive except by withdrawing. They had been emplaced from the beginning as a screen, almost as a large number of pickets, and their explicit orders from the top were to give up ground rather than risk the loss of substantial units. Whiting's judgement is needlessly harsh and unfair; "When Task Force Hudelson left the line, it would be a beaten and decimated formation."[54] Even if one concedes that the New Year's Day action represented a tactical defeat, it can still be regarded as an operational and strategic victory.

In sum, the intent of Operation Northwind had been to penetrate the mountain passes in the Vosges and to destroy Seventh Army, but neither of these goals was achieved. The grenadiers and the panzers may have won the immediate ground but lost the ultimate goal of the campaign. In the process, they suffered absolutely terrible casualties for temporary gains. When ultimately Himmler refused to allow the panzer divisions to advance on the icy roads toward the strategic passes, especially the Saverne and Ingwiller passes, a great number of German soldiers had died in vain. But to return to the fight at Bannstein, German infantry, reinforced by "four armored vehicles," started to systematically blast the buildings in the town, and the only response available to the GIs was to fire at them with bazookas. The rounds failed to explode "because of the freezing temperatures."

The troops began to withdraw under "flat trajectory fire" (which sounds like 88mm fire), that prevented the removal of friendly vehicles. Small groups of men siphoned their way out of the town and had to leave behind fifteen halftracks, two trucks, and several jeeps.

In case of capture, the retreating soldiers threw away their German souvenirs. All, however, was not lost in retreat as American tanks and tank destroyers reinforcing the 62nd, the 94th, and the 117th units, withstood the challenge of the German troops to control the highway. This stand enabled the withdrawing GIs to find a wooded path over the hill toward Baerenthal. Lt. Col. Goddard interviewed both men and staff from the 62nd and staff from the 94th and 117th and received firsthand information about the fight. Evidently, Goddard never interviewed Capt. Trammel, the commander of C-62, or at least neither man mentions that as happening.

Goddard's report outlines what events occurred to A and B Companies of the 62nd. About midnight on 31 December 1944, some 300 enemy foot soldiers attacked both companies. The 83rd Chemical Mortar Company "harassed the invading horde in the vicinity of the open ground around Neunhoffen." Tree bursts from the mortars were hitting dangerously close to the "friendly troops so the fire was withheld." 'A' Company managed to repulse the enemy assault "with machine guns, hand grenades and small arms fire."

According to Lt. Col. Goddard, in the thinly manned line, German troops infiltrated behind the two companies' positions and fired wooden bullets against them, presumably to avoid hitting their own soldiers attacking from the front. B Company withdrew and "flanked the rear of 'A' Company clearing out infiltrators." A common line was then refused, and help was received from the 75mm guns of American armor and from 4.2-inch mortar fire. The enemy still persisted in harassing GIs, who were dug in and returning masses of fire.[55]

More danger was to threaten as five panzers had reportedly "broken through north of Phillipsbourg and were traveling south in the direction of that town." If they had reached it, they could have cut off both A and B Companies of the 62nd. In reaction to this threat, two tanks, a 57mm antitank platoon, and two bazooka squads formed a roadblock northwest of Phillipsbourg. Although the menace never materialized, a large number of enemy infantry approached the valley. Both armor and friendly infantry fired against them and killed an undetermined number and captured 150 of them, hardly the reaction of "a beaten and decimated formation," to employ Whiting's phrase.

At the conclusion of this struggle, troops from the 275th Infantry

Regiment replaced the armored infantry of the 62nd and adopted a defensive posture on an east-west line north of Phillipsbourg.[56]

Although attacks in the area north of the 62nd were repelled and the enemy was retreating to Neunhoffen, the momentum of the German thrust, as has been noted, had still carried to Bannstein and was threatening both Baerenthal and Phillipsbourg. Communications between many units were lost. After Lt. Col. Hudelson requested assistance to rectify the situation, the 19th AIB and A Company of the 25th TB of the 14th were on their way to stabilize matters.[57] At 0800 on 1 January, the 19th arrived in Baerenthal. Two companies were ordered to counterattack on the left flank of the Task Force in the 117th Cav and Recon's zone of responsibility. The 19th was directed to restore the main line of resistance which had been overrun in many places. . . . The other company of the 19th AIB was to attack in the vicinity of Bannstein in order to relieve pressure on [Capt. Trammel'sj 'C' Co of the 62nd."[58]

The result off these tactical counter-moves was limited as the enemy force "had by this time grown to sizeable proportions. . . . Meanwhile the friendly troops still in Bannstein were isolated because the enemy had cut the main highway leading from Bannstein to Phillipsbourg." The situation appeared parlous since the enemy had slashed through the crust of the Bannstein defenses and was throwing in rounds of artillery and bombs from mortars. Once Bannstein was ordered evacuated, the men literally took to the hills. Enemy patrols were ever present, and "GIs helped each other along across the snow covered and hilly terrain," a scene reminiscent of what happened in the Ardennes on 16 and 17 December. German outposts controlled the key highway between Bannstein and Phillipsbourg and the region immediately to the south and east.[59]

Pinned in the middle of this turmoil, between the 117th Cav and Recon and the 62nd AIB was the 94th Cav and Recon Squadron. The evening before the battle began, 30 December, its patrols had reached Stockbronn and the elevation above Camp de Bitche. They discovered a well dug-in enemy in the woods near Equelshaardt. Manned roadblocks composed of felled trees and machine guns stopped the progress of these patrols, During daylight hours on 31 December, the sounds of German tanks and even railroad trains could be heard, a sure indication that more trouble was coming. Friendly artillery fire was called in, and the sounds subsided.[60]

However, as it had done to the other units on the MLR, soon after midnight on the last day of 1944, enemy infantry charged the zone of the 94th, setting off trip flares which illuminated the entire area. Then there was silence until 0300, 1 January, when enemy activity was reported in the 117th positions, "with considerable small arms fire to the west." Lt. Col. Goddard summarizes what happened at the point of the attack based on interviews with some of the men of the 94th:

> B and D troops received orders to withdraw to a secondary position to stem the enemy advance. While B troop covered with machine gun fire from their armored vehicles, D troops infiltrated to a secondary line of defense. Several armored vehicles had to be abandoned because they could not get through the snow covered woods. Tank crewmen removed the machine guns from the vehicles and carried the weapons back with them.[61]

Although their comrades from the 19th AIB were rushing to the rescue, their own efforts to hold out proved insufficient. Even though the 94th Cav and Recon had assault cannons firing against the swarming grenadiers, "the enemy's drive was pushing forward relentlessly, driving everything in its path," as Goddard characterizes the desperate situation. By the afternoon of 1 January, the 94th reached its secondary MLR, the road extending from Mouterhouse to Baerenthal. This would all have been to the good except that the enemy had interdicted it. The GIs divided into "small groups, employing the available defilade and cover" in the woods to hasten cross-country towards their destination, Sarreinsberg. On the original typed copy of the report, Goddard stated that the infantry "drifted southward behind the 94th Cav troops." The handwritten revision changed the wording to "covered the withdrawal of the 94 Cav troops."[62] Perhaps the change was made to suggest hopefulness to the events depicted, but there was little good news on New Years Day for the men of the 94th.

As it turned out, just as the 62nd AIB was hammered, so was the 94th in the middle of the line at Bitche. In D Troop was Corporal James Minn, Jr., who kept a diary of his experiences in the battle. On the evening of the 31st, he was on outpost duty, doubled in this threatening atmosphere, when at 2320 hours, "heavy mortar and artillery fire came

from the Germans. . . . Very heavy accurate enemy fire." Minn's partner on guard, "received a very serious arm wound from the German
88's," a wound which was finally bandaged by his comrade, Tec 5 Ario
P. Venturelli. After some confusion the injury was stabilized. At 0145
hours the Third Platoon and the First Platoon came through their position. The machine gun squads were instructed "to set up 3 machine
guns to fight rear guard actions, so that the others could have an orderly withdrawal." Tec 5 Vernon H. Brown, Tec 4 Edmund E. KarwoskI,
and Minn were selected for the MG on the left of the road. "We sat
waiting for the enemy and froze. They did not try to sneak up on us. At
4:30 a.m. they came through the woods shouting and saying that they
were coming to get us. . . . We thought they were drunk and doped up."
The action continued in frantic moments:

> [Staff Sergeant Earl D.] McTee's machine gun opened fire and
> the Germans returned fire. Then the Germans shot up flares,
> and we tried to remain motionless, so that we wouldn't be spot-
> ted. From the changing direction of fire, McTee thought that the
> Germans were trying to outflank him, so he crept up the road,
> to ask [unidentified] Grandin for permission to withdraw to a
> safer position. Now [Pfc. Thomas S.] Jones thought he was a
> German soldier and shot him with a machine gun across the
> thighs. McTee was lying on the road screaming that he was
> bleeding to death. Grandin went out onto the road, picked
> McTee up, gave him first aid, and sent him back to the medics
> in a Jeep. Jones went to pieces when he found out that he had
> shot McTee and he had to be sent back, too. We kept with-
> drawing and setting up new positions and the Germans kept
> pressing forward. [Sgt. William L., Jr.] Pemberton killed a good
> many with his machine gun, but he had to withdraw under
> increased enemy machine gun, grenade, rifle, and time fire.[63]

Eventually most of the men in D Troop and the other Cavalry
Troops would exfiltrate back to prearranged positions and continue to
take a toll on the enemy, especially with indirect artillery fire from the
500th Armored Field Artillery Battalion, a part of the Task Force. The
Forward Observers did an excellent job of spotting German attackers
and bringing down fire on them. The enemy, with good reason, had a

very healthy respect for the accurate and explosive power of American artillery.

As has been seen, the fight at the CP in Bannstein was a close call, with the defenders fighting off enemy swarms with machine guns and small arms fire. It was only the rescue by tanks of the 14th Armored Division's 25th Tank Battalion that saved the men in the headquarters. Goddard again: "Advancing over the icy terrain the armored unit destroyed the German forces surrounding Baerenthal." After those two tasks were completed, one platoon of medium tanks rushed off to "relieve pressure" on the 62nd's remnants in the area of Phillipsbourg. Yet danger still hung in the air since communications were out between the Task Force Commander and the Cavalry troops near Mouterhouse. Consequently, help was not sent immediately to relieve them. The History of CCR of the l4th argued that help for the right flank was instantly necessary so as to gain control over "at least a part of that sector."[64]

By dusk on 1 January, hostile shellfire probed the friendly units, but it did not inflict any serious harm according to the Task Force staff's responses to questions by Lt. Col. Goddard. VI Corps Headquarters ordered the relief of the remaining elements of the Task Force by the 275th Infantry Regiment. That unit was ordered south to the vicinity of Reipertswiller to rebut enemy attacks and to hold the line there. It was to confront the highly experienced and well-armed battalions of the SS Sixth Mountain Division recently entrained from Denmark. Radioed orders to Hudelson's Force had them withdraw "upon relief' to deploy in the area of Zinswiller. The various routes of withdrawal of different units were in a southerly direction into the Lower Vosges.

Because communications had not been restored with the cavalry units, the 94th and the 117th Squadrons did not receive these orders. With the Task Force headquarters' arrival at Reipertswiller, the CO directed the remainder of Company A of the 19th AIB and A Company of the 125th Armored Engineers (part of the original reserve) to take up defensive positions a mile north of Reipertswiller. This composite force was later assaulted by an estimated battalion of enemy grenadiers, but they "held their ground and prevented the hostile force from reaching Reipertswiller."[65]

In his conclusion, Lt. Col. Goddard reported that during the night of 1 January, the 275th Infantry extended the process of replacing the troops of the Task Force. At the same time, both Cavalry units fell back "to a line running generally Strasbourg [sic]-Wingen-Ulimmenau [sic] before the relief was effected." The line appears to be quite irregular, something like a 100 degree angle south from Sarreinsberg to Wingen and then east to Wimmenau, somewhat north of the line which the 68th AIB of the 14th was holding. This deployment, although not stated in the two reports cited in this chapter, would have given the Task Force the strength of the 68th as an additional line of support. As Lt. Col. Goddard continues, "The 62nd could not be relieved until the following day because of the icy terrain and the fact that the 62nd was in close contact with the enemy in their area."

His report puts a note of finality to the efforts of Colonel Hudelson's improvised group:

> With the alleviation of their positions by the 275th Infantry, Task Force Hudelson was dissolved as per instructions from VI Corps Headquarters which put the official time of 0001 on 2 January 1945.
>
> The Germans had paid heavily in their New Year's assault on the American lines. They gained several thousand yards of terrain in the attack but the cost had been great in number of casualties inflicted on his forces. Some estimates placed the figure as high as 1,500 along the Task Force front, which limited the penetration south through the Vosges mountains to merely local gains instead of its anticipated large scale campaign.[66]

It is time to address a problem which was raised several years ago by Lt. Col. (ret.) USA Howard A. Trammel, who was the commander of Company C of the 62nd Armored Infantry Battalion. Above was cited Lt. Col. Trammel's disagreement with the unkind assessment of Task Force Hudelson's condition at the end of the fight in the snowy woods and icy roads of the Vosges by Charles Whiting. Trammel differs with the conclusion repeated here and elsewhere that Allied military intelligence knew that German Army Group G was going to make a major attack in January, whether the intelligence was from SHAEF, based on ULTRA, or on other sources of intelligence available to the American Sixth Army Group or Seventh Army. Indeed he repeats the argument popular in early December 1944 that the German Army was incapable of a major offensive and the fact that many officers believed it. He argues that no intelligence was available to him and presumably to other company and battalion commanders under CCR, the parent of the Task Force.[67] Yet Colonel Hudelson was a member of CCR's staff, and it is difficult to understand how information about a serious enemy threat could or would have been kept away from field and company officers. All of the preparations cited in the Seventh Army report by Lt. Col. Goddard have been itemized here, including the setting of mines and the preparation of TNT to fell trees along key roads. Also cited earlier in this report was evidence that the enemy was pre-registering fire on key roads and crossroads, not to mention the movement of supply dumps further away from the MLR.

Also quoted here in several places were entries from General Jacob L. Devers' Diary for the month of December 1945 including conferences with other senior officers and one or more telephone calls between Devers and Lt. General Alexander M. Patch, commander of Seventh Army, indicating a keen awareness that a German offensive was imminent in the last hours of before New Year's Day. Clearly down the line, from Devers to Patch to Hudelson, accurate intelligence was communicated. It is true, and the authors of the official history of the campaign in southern France agree, that, as Lt. Col. Trammel argued, intelligence focuses more on the capability of the enemy than his definite intentions. Devers and Patch were not absolutely sure of precisely where the New Year's attacks would come, but the official history does concede that "Devers' decision to rush the nine brand-new regiments into the line before the attacks had even begun was perhaps his most important contribution. . . ."[67] Devers, in an entry in his diary on 26 December, was certain that "The Germans will undoubtedly attack me now down the gap west of the Vosges and I must stop them at the start."[68]

The official history, while emphasizing the uneven quality of the intelligence during the month of January, concedes generally:

> ULTRA, nevertheless, performed a valuable function, enabling its users to verify the welter of often conflicting information that poured in during the battle from POW reports and other conventional sources. In these matters, experience and common sense were more valuable to intelligence officers than exotic sources of information.[69]

Probably more critical than the intelligence question is the strength of the American forces in the Vosges on New Year's Eve. On 20 December Devers exclaimed in frustration, "Losing troops when you are already thin and loyally carrying out orders which are foreign to your nature is no small task, but we will be in there pitching, and as far as we are concerned [there] will be no letdown."[70]

The basis for the weakness in the defensive posture in the Vosges for the American forces, especially Task Force Hudelson, was the stripping of divisions from Seventh Army in favor of Third Army and secondly the redeployment of an armored corps from the latter army to the Ardennes. One weakness led to another weakness. This is the source of Devers' frustration. Trammel is perfectly correct in saying that the "Sector of Responsibility . . . was too large." If Seventh Army had not been reduced in strength of divisions, it might have been possible for VI Corps to have fixed in defensive positions all three Combat Commands of the 14th Armored Division and not just a picked over CCR for the Task Force in the zone of Bitche-Bannstein-Baerenthal. To have had the 62nd, the 94th, and the 117th buttressed closely by even one of the other two Armored Infantry Battalions (the 19th or the 68th) with appropriate support units, then they would have been able to hold their ground much better than their perhaps chancy dispersal on the line allowed. Consider hypothetically the ability of 14th Armored to add one more Combat Command, whether A or B, with organic tank and artillery support, and the Task Force could even have thrown back the "romping" grenadiers. The 14th Armored Division was to have been the reserve for VI Corps, but it was divided up piecemeal and scattered in the snowy mountains. Of course, all of this, as said, is hypothetical.

Not so hypothetical was the role of the 68th Armored Infantry Battalion. Sgt. Bob Davies' recollection of the role of his battalion was somewhat hazy in that he thought that his unit was a part of the Task Force. It was not. On 1 January it was stationed on an axis from Ingwiller to Wietersville, running north and south but west of Col. Hudelson's force. Its evident mission was to block the German advance in Northwind with the purpose of preventing hostile armor from breaking through the pass at Ingwiller in the Vosges Mountains. After all, it was the vital passes at Ingwiller and Saverne that motivated Hitler's plans and Himmler's desire to sever communications behind Seventh Army and Sixth Army Group in order to annihilate the American and

French divisions holding much of Alsace.

The S-2 & S-3 Journals (Intelligence and Operations) for 1 January delineate the defensive nature of the assignment. (The original wording with abbreviations is maintained for the purposes of immediacy. Abbreviations are explained in the Glossary):

> C-68 moved into new positions. 68 to establish holding position on commanding ground in present sector using AT Guns, AG, Mortars, Cal 50, Cal 30 MG's and SA wpns for close-in defence. Mission of 68 to establish center of resistance from which tks can maneuver, attacking from S, Sw, or E thru our position. Our dispotion [sic] to hold a fixed defense so tks can attack. Reconnoiter road system to E, SE of present position to E, SE of present position to E boundary of XV Corps because if ey atks thru woods, AT Guns and Bazookas of this unit may be ordered to E against flank of such an attack. This unit to be prepared to drop back to alternate positions vic Schmidtville, similar to position in Rahling area, to repel Counter-attack. See atchd overlay of roving patrols of C-94 connecting to OP's. Ey positions at. . . [map coordinates]. Six ey tks at (650563) about 1125. Two knocked out by direct 155 hits. Eleven tanks were committed against our center division early this morning PW taken by that division says real ey attack will be tomorrow, 2 Jan-signed 1512-msgr [messenger].[71]

It was critical for the 68th both to maintain the line to the east with XV Corps and to do the same with C Troop of the 94th Cav and Recon of the 14th's CCR. Just like Task Force Hudelson, their task was defensive, but the advantage for the 68th was that they had solid tank support as well as the same fine artillery support as the Task Force.

On 2 January the 68th with C Company of the 94th, which had been attached to it, motor-marched to Niedersoultzbach to establish a command post. Hostile forces were busy infiltrating Reipertswiller, "with fire fights going on in town." Captured enemy prisoners testified that the entire 6th SS Mountain Division was deployed in Equelshardt and Sturzelbroun.[72] B Company of the 68th (Bob Davies' company) was outposting the area "to prevent e[nem]y infiltration from woods from NW or thru our flanks. A battalion of 12 SS. Regiment was believed to be on a key hill . . . and heavy pressure was being exerted by the German troops at Phillipsbourg. Baerenthal was already taken by the enemy" (S-2 & S-3 Journals, 2 January).

Enemy armor was prowling in the vicinity, and as previously noted, two had been hit directly by rounds from 155 mm. guns, a comfort to the friendly infantry. On 4 January 4 Mark VI Tigers were rumbling south toward the 68th's positions but were then hammered by the even larger eight-inch guns of VI Corps. The ability of the 499th and 500th AFA Battalions, as well as Corps artillery, to spot enemy targets and deliver accurate fire on them was simultaneously consistent and remarkable. German commanders were most concerned about this effectiveness. On 4 January they "called off the effort." General Blaskowilz of Nineteenth Army decided "not to throw the German armored reserves into the battle."[73] What might have happened had Himmler and his generals gambled for high stakes and committed them can only be a subject for conjecture.

Even so, the battlefield situation remained in crisis for American units in the Baerenthal area in that enemy troops had cut the lines of communication between Phillipsbourg and Baerenthal and between Mouterhouse and Baerenthal. Strong hostile forces occupied those key roads. It is seldom that an American reader is presented with the prospect of American troops being "methodically mopped up by the hostile forces," but that grim assessment appears in Lt. Col. Goddard's report. The Task Force Hudelson CP was both surrounded and besieged by enemy artillery and small arms fire. Even worse, all radio communications were out with the exception of the 62nd AIB. As later Lt. Col. Trammel of the 62nd remarked, "communications were tenuous, being mostly by wire," and telephone lines were easily cut, sometimes scissored by hostile artillery rounds. Goddard remarks, "strong enemy attacks [were] overrunning 'C' but 'A' and 'B' Co's still holding out."[74]

The 19th Armored Infantry Battalion was notified very late in the game, on 30 December, that it was needed to support the Task Force at Baerenthal. It moved on that same day to Redheim, where plans were made to march the next morning to Baerenthal with the following distribution of troops: "Company 'A', 3rd Platoon, 'B' Company, and 'A' Company-25th Tank Bn, less one platoon were attached to Task Force Hudelson at Baerenthal; the rest of the battalion (Companies 'B' less 3rd platoon, 'C' less 1st Platoon, Headquarters, Service, one platoon of 'A'-

25, and 19th Med. Det.) were attached to 117th Cavalry Recon Squadron commanded by Lt. Col. Hodge at Mouterhouse, France."[75]

In the extreme cold on the icy roads, all of the vehicles had difficulty climbing, and the tanks, moving extremely slowly, had to pull off and allow the half-tracks, and the other vehicles to pass. The tanks would never get into the oncoming fight. The assault guns and the heavy weapons platoons made the advance successfully and lagered north of Mouterhouse. The 19th's history mentions the degree to which units and various guns, tanks, tank destroyers, and other vehicles were scattered all over the mountainous forest surrounding Mouterhouse in a complex network of roads. To make matters more strained, "intermittent" artillery and mortar fire was falling on the troops in dangerous tree bursts. When Major Forest T. Green, the commander of the 19th, drove to Mouterhouse to get clarification about the battlefield situation, a sharp attack on the right flank of the combined 19th and other troops on the line suddenly exploded. While the vehicles of the 117th Cav and Recon pulled back to get out of the way of the armored infantrymen, the fight raged on "when Major Green returned and ordered a withdrawal."[76]

As the unit history put it, "There was complete confusion until the other units had moved their vehicles and personnel out of the way." Then B and C Companies, in an orderly manner, established alternating positions until they were able to fix an anchor on high ground northeast of a road junction west of Mouterhouse. Mouterhouse was almost directly south of Bitche and slightly northwest of Baerenthal. The 19th was thus quite in the middle of the disorganized activity generated by Northwind on New Year's Day. In fact, the Recon Platoon under Lt. George K. Beine, who earlier had been near Zinswiller to the southeast, in trying to return to the battalion at Mouterhose, ran into the conflict at Baerenthal and assisted A Company of the 19th, which was in turn assisting the 62nd AIB.

After the initial attack on that town was repulsed, the Recon Platoon left in their "peeps" in the icy, winding roads but were taken under fire by unidentified American half-tracks with .50 calibers doing the firing. A number of the men, including Sgt. Gregory Guzey and Cpl. William H. Monks, were hit, and Monks was thrown into a ditch. He would survive that unsettling experience, but Guzey would not. Plc. Robert Thogmartin suffered similarly and was "evidently knocked unconscious." Later he would be reported missing in action. Sgt. William Dougherty, who was sitting in Thogmartin's peep, leaped out and returned fire. Several of the other men in the platoon grabbed the light machine guns off the vehicles and cut down some of the advancing infantry. Evidently the grenadiers had made good use of captured American half-tracks to support their assault. Eventually the men in the Recon Platoon managed to cross a field and escape, with Pfc. Edgar Meyers getting first aid after suffering a head wound. Pfc. Robert Housh was able to reach CCR Headquarters to report what had happened. The other men stayed to fight, and the wounded men were able to reach Reipertswiller and receive treatment there.[77]

B and C Companies of the 19th, meanwhile, scrambled down a frozen hillside to a creek and continued down the valley to Sarreinsberg just south and west of Mouterhouse. A rear guard and the assault guns allowed the companies to establish a defensive perimeter around 2300 on 1 January in darkness.

Company A-19, whose responsibility was to support C-62 at Bannstein, had the mission of seizing high ground west of the Fomeau Neuf-Bannstein road. The First Platoon had to hold that ground while the rest of the company marched to Bannstein. At 1000 hours, the Second Platoon was then assigned a new task—"to repel Krauts one kilometer east of Baerenthal." The Company reached Fomeau neuf. The First Platoon moved out to take and hold the ridge in the area, and the Third and Anti-Tank Platoons followed but were then subjected to hostile artillery fire. After some mired vehicles of the AT Platoon were extricated, it was decided to send the Third Platoon to Baerenthal to aid in the defense there.

With Lt. Jack R. DeWitt busy getting orders, one of the noncoms took over the responsibility of defending the headquarters there:

> In the absence of Lt. DeWitt, T/Sgt. Junior Wright hurriedly and expertly set up the platoon to defend the town. He placed all the drivers on the .50 cal. machine-guns on the half-tracks and had each squad put their .30 cal. light machine-guns into action. After he assigned the mortar squad its positions, S/Sgt. Welson Schickel asked what targets he was to fire on. Wright replied, "Oh, just drop them anywhere in those woods; there are so many Jerries up there you couldn't miss if you tried." When Lt.

DeWitt returned, he found the platoon already hard at work.[78]

DeWitt, highly regarded by his men, would become the most decorated member of the division, earning a Distinguished Service Cross, the
British Military Cross, and other awards.

However, things were not going very well in Bannstein, where Capt.
Ernest M. Spokes found the S-3 (Operations Officer) of the 62nd, who
told him that his battalion had been driven out of the town. It was in
the process of reorganizing on the high ground on the south side of the
Baerenthal-Mouterhouse road. Spokes was unable to find the men of his
battalion (the 19th) but saw a hostile column moving south. "Fomeau
neuf was alive with Krauts," as the 19th's history phrased it. Spokes
gravitated to the west, where he eventually found the AT Platoon. A
squad of six men was sent out to locate any platoons in the area under
the command of Lt. Harris Loken or Lt. William C. Hodge. Lt. Joseph
Osbom of Company C led a mounted squad to a house at a road junction just south of Fomau neuf, but the men of this squad were unable to
maintain their position because of severe enemy pressure.

At 1630 on 1 January, the Second Platoon of A Company of the
19th was ordered out of town and proceeded toward Reipertswiller but
were impeded by tanks stranded on an icy hill. The platoon managed to
skirt around them and reached Reipertswiller. The Second Platoon
remained concealed in their positions and allowed a considerably superior force (perhaps the 2nd Battalion of 6th SS Mountain Division) to
bypass them "as it was too big a force to tackle." After the platoon dug
in overnight, in the morning they were confronted with an unfriendly
column, which was then fired upon and stopped." When the column
sent up an armored car to neutralize the platoon's forward outpost,
"Sgt. Elmer Bruns and Pfc. Richard Hoff stopped it with effective
machine-gun fire, and Pfc. Edward J. Chittendon damaged it with a
bazooka." When German infantry assaulted the left flank, Pvt. Felix
Gomes, "waiting until they were dangerously close to his position, hit a
large number of them with his BAR and forced them back. Upon orders
to withdraw, the platoon did so after T/Sgt. William Driscoll "called for
and adjusted a very effective barrage of artillery fire to cover his
retreat."[77]

A company of the 19th also had more than its hands full. Like most
of the small units in this region of mountainous forests, it was outnum-

bered; discretion indeed had to be "the better part of valor." On a hill near Baerenthal, Lt. Hodge sent out a patrol to find out what had happened to two men sent to coordinate action with Capt. Spokes. It was discovered that the platoon "was completely surrounded by the enemy. As yet the platoon had been unnoticed." Lt. Hodge made the decision to shift the platoon to Reipertswiller during a night with the moon shining brightly. Luckily, the men quietly managed to find their way across an open field which was mined. Pfc Ed Shannon somehow maneuvered a path which brought them to the other side of the field. The adventure, however, was not over. At one point a German staff car passed by without discovering them. As they passed an enemy outpost, a guard asked them where they were going. The last man, a member of the 62nd AIB, "miraculously could speak German; he told the guard they were going to the front, so the platoon passed by unmolested."[79]

Effectively, this action represented the end of the 19th AIB's contribution to supporting their beleaguered comrades in the 62nd in Task Force Hudelson. Despite the crazy quilt pattern of fighting and dodging necessary to maintain the integrity of the Task Force, if the 19th had not assisted in the struggle at Baerenthal, a deep gash might have been cut in the defensive line of the Task Force. As a result of all the confusing movement of forces, the general picture for General Blaskowitz was confusing. He was not sure of what the initial penetration of the MLR had achieved. Heinrich Himmler, nervous about this operational uncertainty, refused to unleash the German armor in the vicinity of Bitche, Bannstein, Baerenthal, and Mouterhouse. Had he done so, the whole front could have been compromised for American forces.

Keith E. Bonn has provided an astute analysis of why Operation Northwind was doomed to failure. He calls attention to what might be called a double equation. This equation parallels the original Allied campaign, Operation Dogface, that had successfully penetrated the Vosges Mountains in early November with the Wehrmacht Northwind campaign, which attempted to reverse the first part of the equation, the victory of the American VI Corps. To follow Bonn's analysis, Army Group G is credited with its original "skill at delaying numerically superior Seventh Army in terrain eminently suitable for such operations." Yet Seventh Army's "pursuit proved their relentless tenacity and skill at preserving sufficient combat power and morale to penetrate the same fortified positions their opponents had failed to dent four and a half years earlier [the Maginot Line forts]. When Army Group G attempted in the winter of 1944–45 to penetrate the American defenses in the Vosges with superior numbers, they were unable to do so. Thus Bonn's conclusion: "Flawed in concept from the start, Operation NORTH-WIND was a resounding failure." The reasons for this failure were serious:

> Poorly trained and organized units conducted attacks in amateurish and wildly wasteful manners, sustaining heavy casualties that they exhausted themselves in two or three days of combat. Oversupervised by the army group headquarters, the subordinate commands' chances of success with incompletely trained formations almost disappeared with the sacrifice of mid- and low-level planning and doctrinally required reconnaissance in deference to vain hopes for tactical surprise.[80]

Because Seventh Army was deprived of air support due to the terrible weather, Bonn's *When the Odds Were Even* demonstrated the combat excellence of Patch's soldiers without it. However, the fighting wasn't over by any means in the rugged fastness of the Vosges after three or four days. By 5 January, the 68th AIB and the other battalions in the mountains were primarily sending out patrols to determine the enemy's intentions. The 180th Regiment, attached to Task Force Hudelson now, was preparing to step off to clean out remaining unfriendly troops in Wingen. More important for the immediate future of the 68th was the following message in its journals:

> E[nem]y has been infiltrating strong patrols up to 50 men strong across the Rhine between Kilstett and Rosenheim. . . . FFI [the French Forces of the Interior] reports our troops in Gambsheim . . . Surrounded. 7th Army believes ey may attack crossing of Rhine in Vosges. . . . One Bn ey crossed and is pushing west (S-2 and S-3 Journals 5 January).

This message dramatically indicates that there has been a major shift in the focus of the German attack in the first week of January. This was an ominous development since both Allied forces were already stretched paper thin and enemy supply lines and artillery range from east of the Rhine favored those soldiers wearing feldgrau or SS black and not those wearing khaki. Operation Northwind had changed.

The significant movement of hostile troops in those areas adjacent to the Rhine and north of Strasbourg indicated, as Seventh Army reported, that the German command in the west had shifted the axis of the Northwind strategy from the axis north to south in the mountains to that running east to west on the plains of Alsace. The inability of the German mass to break through to the passes in the Vosges persuaded General Blaskowitz and Himmler to reorient the attack. The latter would later be criticized for putting his troops piecemeal into Northwind and not concentrating at the proverbial "Schwerpunt" or heavy point of the spear. Still, the powerful forces at his disposal were capable of inflicting serious damage to VI Corps and its weary and cold armored and infantry divisions.[81]

General Blaskowitz and his staff at Army Group G Headquarters had already concluded that the assault in the lower Vosges had failed and that Northwind would have to change both its focus and the location of a new attack to break the American Seventh Army. Both the 21st Panzer Division and the 25th Panzer Grenadier Division, which had originally been dedicated to breaking through to the Saverne Gap, were moved on 6 January to the west and onto the Alsatian Plain. This formidable force was to attack from an assembly area north of Wissembourg in a southerly direction on 7 January.

Directly below Wissembourg on the map are two small farming towns a kilometer or so part, and here Sixth Corps, including elements of the 42nd and 79th Infantry Divisions and the Corps Reserve, the 14th Armored, would fight a bitter fight for the better part of ten days which would engulf Hatten and Rittershoffen, two communities which had previously escaped the violence of war, in bombardment and fire that would destroy them.

On 6 January, the 68th, still in the mountains, continued patrolling and noted the fall of enemy rounds, but the messages coming into the CP indicated more ominous activity near the Rhine: "Fighting continues around Gambsheim. None of our troops in town yet. Ey attempting to re-inforce this action with troops crossing the river in barges. One barge was observed with gun mounted on it. No info on ey activity N or S of this point." Because of this enemy activity, the 68th displaced from Neidersoultzbach to Soultz-sous-Forets, spotting nine hostile tanks at dawn. As German units filtered through the region, "Throughout day unit and attachments remained alert for forthcoming missions." Further messages from the S-2 and S-3 Journals of the 68th for 6 January indicated that strong enemy units could jeopardize Task Force WahI, to which the 68th was attached—especially the "unlocated 22d Panzer Regt'."

On 9 January came the clarion call to the 68th: "Alert your unit to be ready to move at 0815 to SE," and another message later recorded that the pastoral town of Hatten, the town closest to the Rhine of the two (Rittershoffen the other) was being assaulted from the west and northwest. At 0910 panzers were located in the vicinity of that town," emerging from the woods. "Our heavy arty put on them and TD's [Tank Destroyers] alerted." Then there were even more reports of enemy armored movement, as many as fifteen German tanks. Finally, the critical message arrived: "One company of the 827th Tank Destroyers and Company C of the 48tt Tank Battalion of the 14th departed from Soulz-sous-Forets to vic of Hatten to support tk battle north of Hatten and relieved from this unit." The 94th Cav and Recon also reported that seven enemy tanks were burning from an engagement with its light tanks around 1500 hours. The battle of Hatten-Rittershoffen, with dire consequences for both American and German soldiers and especially for the trapped citizens of these small farming communities, was about to unleash a scene of bloody carnage and fiery horror not exceeded in intensity in the European Theater of Operations.

VI Corps, Seventh Army, the 14th Armored, the battered nucleus of Task Force Hudelson, and units like the 68th AIB and other attachments had successfully blunted Operation Northwind in the Vosges and interdicted enemy entry to the mountain passes. In some sense Himmler and Blaskowitz had blinked and not sent in their powerful armored forces to conclude the mission. Strategically and operationally, Northwind had failed and caused significant German casualties as well. Contrary to the contention of Charles Whiting, the men of the Task Force and other units in the snowy hills had taken a hit but had still recovered to fight off significantly superior forces. The task of the American units now would be to frustrate again the German Army on the rolling plains of Alsace in the second week of January 1945.

Special Epilogue

On the retreat of Task Force Hudelson to Phillipsburg on 3 January, 1945, Pfc. George B. Turner, of the 499th Armored Field Artillery Battalion, performed such feats of valor, at age 46 years of age, that he was given by the President the Congressional Medal of Honor, which citation follows:

Pfc. George B. Turner
C Battery, 499th Armored Field Artillery
Recipient of the Medal Of Honor

Pfc. George B. Turner, the 14th Armored Division's only recipient of the Medal of Honor, earned the respect and admiration of his comrades in arms long before he committed the acts that earned him the nation's highest award for heroism.

Turner joined the Marine Corps in the First World War, but the war ended before he got overseas to join in the fighting. When the U.S. entered the Second World War, Turner volunteered once again to defend his country. This time he joined the U.S. Army. During training, many of the young soldiers and officers with whom he served came to admire his quiet strength and dedication to duty. Turner soon gained the reputation of being a good soldier who truly wanted to come to grips with the enemy. He lived up to that reputation, and more. At 46 years of age, he may have been the oldest recipient of the Medal of Honor during the Second World War. Regardless of age, Turner's deeds were, and remain, timeless.

[Signed]
President Harry S. Truman

(See last page of the photo section in the center of this book.)

Chapter 5

THE HATTEN-RITTERSHOFFEN INFERNO

Slipping Into the Fire

Lt. General Jacob L. Devers, commander of Sixth Army Group, expressed his views and his reservations about the situation in his command, especially that of Seventh Army, in his Diaries. He had had to relinquish control of several divisions, especially to Third Army because they were short of divisions in November 1944 due to the costly fighting in Lorraine. Later he would lose several more as a result of General Patton's sending a corps toward Bastogne in mid-December to prevent a German victory there.

A recent analysis demonstrates the way in which the German General Staff took advantage of Devers' weakness:

By 21 December Hitler had decided on a new offensive, this time in the Alsace region, in effect, selecting one of the options he had disapproved due to Dietrich's failure to break the northern shoulder [in the Ardennes Bulge], and with no hope of attaining their original objectives, both Hitler and Rundstedt agreed that an attack on the southern Allied front might take advantage of Patton's shift north to the Ardennes . . . [1]

This attack was designed to hit VI Corps in its southern flank.

After the fight in the Vosges repelling Northwind diminished in intensity and threat, Devers, in a diary entry on 8 January 1945 expressed his concern about a new assault on the Alsatian plain near Rimling, on the border between XV and XX Corps. This was to be an

111

extension of Northwind although Devers couldn't foresee this. General Alexander M. Patch, commander of Seventh Army, according to Devers' Diary, was confident that the 79th Infantry Division could stop the assault at that point in the line. After a conference with Patch, in whom Devers placed great trust, he confided to his Diary for 16 January:

> In my conference with Patch we again pointed that our present position is the strongest position we can occupy; that two American infantry divisions, the 79th and the 45th, had withstood 9 German divisions since the 1st of the year successfully; that the fighting had been tough; that they had been assisted by two armored divisions, the 12th and the 14th; that the Germans had brought in a new corps consisting of the 6th SS Mountain Division, the 7th Paratroop Division, and possibly the 10th Panzer Division; that all of these were big divisions, not small divisions; and that now we needed [the] help of at least one infantry division on this front; that as long as [Gen. Omar] Bradley was in trouble to the north we gave and gave and gave until we were stretched too thin; but that now that he is out of trouble we felt that we should be given a chance to push the Germans back on the defensive and we believed we could do this with very little; that it would pay great dividends in the future; that we could release this division by the 1 of February; that giving up terrain was a terrific slap in the face to the soldiers who had fought so hard and so well to retain it; this caused, more than any other thing, a great lowering of morale, and it is morale that wins battles. . . .[2]

It is puzzling that Devers could be so confident of things on the 16th, when the very enemy divisions he was citing were causing such trouble in the Hatten-Rfttershoffen sector, where the 14th Armored and units of the 79th and 42nd Infantry Divisions were fighting a desperate battle for their very existence. Never mind the idea that they were capable of defeating a foe that outweighed them in every department. To bring this question up now may seem strange, but it suggests the degree to which Seventh Army and Sixth Army Group seemed to be insulated from what was happening to those soldiers who fought hard and suffered and died at Hatten and Rittershoffen. Even the Official History,

Riviera to the Rhine, devotes only a few pages to the fighting that occurred there in the second and third weeks of January 1944. This chapter will respectfully attempt to redress that imbalance.

The summons to action for the 68th AIB and other units of the 14th came on the morning of 11 January, when the battalion was ordered to help stem the offensive not too many miles west of the Rhine in the vicinity of two sleepy farming towns, Hatten and Rittershoffen, about a kilometer apart, respectively, west to east. The two towns were situated close to the axis of the Maginot Line, which here ran generally but not entirely north and south. The initial phase of Operation Northwind had developed from the north and northeast in the vicinity of Bitche in the Vosges Mountains, known as the Bitche Salient. The new German assault, starting in Gambsheim, adjacent to the Rhine River, had begun on 5 January. The advantages of this battle plan were twofold: the lines of communication and supply were quite short, and German artillery from across the river was capable of shelling Gambsheim and all the other small towns in the area. The other key town, north of Gambsheim, was Herrlisheim, which would later cause so much grief to the green 12th Armored Division.

As has been previously mentioned, in the crazy-quilt pattern of authority and power in the Third Reich, with all its fiefdoms doled out by the Führer, there was a desperate competition among the traditional Wehrmacht, the Waffen SS Divisions, the Luftwaffe (with its ground troops), and even the late and lowly Volksturm (the recent amalgam of the very young, the very old, and the very sick) for the implements of war. Heinrich Himmler, in addition to his other responsibilities, was in charge of these last two forces, most importantly the SS Divisions, which were the best equipped of all units. Hitler had given Himmler command of Army Group Upper Rhine, which was active in Operation Northwind, despite his lack of proper military training and experience.

As Richard Engler reminds us, he determined to discontinue operations in the Bitche Salient because of the stubborn resistance of the GIs and the difficulty of moving armored and other vehicles on icy roads with frequent snowfall. What had made it difficult for American vehicles also made it difficult for the panzers, a problem that similarly bedeviled the panzer armies up in the Ardennes. The Northwind offensive accordingly was switched from the mountains to the plains on an axis from Wissembourg south to Gambsheim—"the most fateful deci-

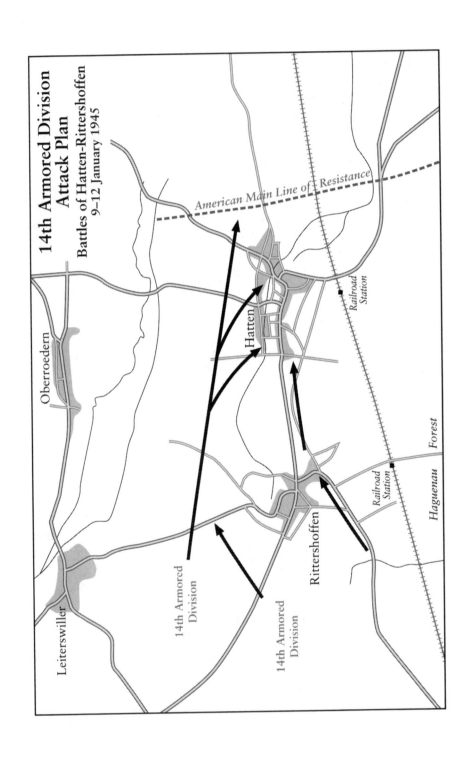

14th Armored Division
Attack Plan
Battles of Hatten-Rittershoffen
9–12 January 1945

American Main Line of Resistance

Oberroedern

Leiterswiller

Hatten

Railroad
Station

14th Armored
Division

14th Armored
Division

Rittershoffen

Railroad
Station

Haguenau Forest

sion of the entire campaign!" American infantry, including elements of the 42nd, of which Engler was a member, and the 79th Infantry Divisions, had been holding the Maginot forts for the most part since November. Himmler wanted to break through not only at Gambsheim but also through the Line—an effort which would consign these units and the 14th Armored Division to a fiery inferno.

Flares signaled the attack on the twin towns on 9 January.[3] Engler, who has argued that the 42nd was besieged beyond measure, remarked that the 242nd Regiment's Journal reported that 28 German tanks were bypassing Hatten and aiming toward Rittershoffen to the west, with ME-262 jet aircraft flying overhead in support of the thrust toward the town. In a very short time, two out of three American anti-tank platoons were eliminated from the contest, manning under-powered anti-tank guns. The Cannon Company of the 242nd Regiment fired "point-blank" at the advancing panzers but with little effect. A terrified private later remembered what he called "the poise of cooler heads":

> The tanks were right on us and firing point-blank, and a lot of men were going down. Our captain just went berserk. He rushed out and started throwing snowballs at the tanks. He was cut down quick. A sergeant brought us out with most of our vehicles. I was sure he was taking us in exactly the wrong direction. But he got us out of there. Later we went back and retrieved the guns we'd left.[4]

The ultimate intent of the German Command in the West was the capture of Strasbourg, just short miles to the south of Gambsheim—not only primarily to destroy the First French Army defending Strasbourg but to outflank and defeat the American Seventh Army. On 2–3 January, Major General Edward H. Brooks' VI Corps had begun its transfer from the Vosges Mountains toward the Maginot Line. Seventh Army, after it had delegated responsibility for Strasbourg to the French, planned a new MLR, a fallback position along the Moder River. Ironically, after the battle of Hatten-Rittershoffen, that is exactly where they would be anchored, for the 14th Armored, the 315th Battalion of the 79th Infantry, and remnants of the 42nd Infantry Division would be forced to take up defensive positions along the Moder River, well north of Strasbourg in the vicinity of Hagenau Forest.

However, in the meantime, between the 9th and 20th of January, those units cut off in Hatten especially but also in Rittershoffen, including soldiers from the 42nd, struggled to hold out. They received supplies by airdrop but not much else support until the 14th Armored battled vigorously to get to them. The unit historians of the 68th Armored Infantry Battalion, Lt. Madden and Private Kovanda, liked to employ the image of a roving back (presumably in American football) to charge quickly to any critical spot in the MLR which needed sudden defense or an immediate offensive thrust against the enemy. As it developed, the entire 14th would be needed dramatically to rebut the hostile assault and rescue those men in the two infantry divisions trapped there in the twin Alsatian towns. The division was not committed as a whole at one time in a powerful charge but fed piecemeal into the fight, mostly with a tank battalion customarily paired with an armored infantry battalion. Other units, like the 94th Cav Recon, not only did scouting but also took on enemy tanks whenever possible. The 125th Armored Combat Engineers performed their usual tasks besides fighting in place as infantry or in reserve. After the war there would be criticism of this gradual deployment of forces, but at the time it seemed the only way to prevent those cut off from being overwhelmed and swallowed by the maw of war.[5]

Another grim irony of this grave situation was that the 48th Tank Battalion had figuratively waltzed through the towns only weeks earlier, before the enemy had had a chance to regroup after being chased up the Rhone Valley by Truscott's VI Corps. There would be no waltzing of any kind when the Americans returned in frigid January, a month that broke century-old records for freezing temperatures. Of the American divisions fighting in this sector, only the 79th Infantry could be said to be battle-wise. The 14th had learned as much as they could since disembarking in October; the 12th Armored had no experience to speak of. They were pitted against a strong and dangerous force which dominated the rolling farmland north of the two towns on the high ground near the towns of Buhi and Stundwiller. This position gave the enemy an enormous advantage in spotting for artillery and mortars, and it had ample ammunition for both. In place were the 21st Panzer Division, considered a crack outfit, and the 25th Panzer Grenadier Division.

Before the commitment of the tanks from the 48th Tank Battalion on 9 January and other units of the 14th AD on succeeding days, there were only the remnants of the 242nd and two battalions of the 315th Regiment, respectively of the 42nd and the 79th Infantry Divisions. But they were, unsupported and no match for the panzers and the artillery arrayed against them. The Hagenau forest just to the south of the towns and a number of Maginot forts almost touching the towns were supposed to be defended by the 42nd Division, but the fight for the forts, although causing serious German casualties, led to their abandonment. Those infantrymen who could sought shelter in the two towns, but as Richard Engler described the situation, these men were in a parlous state with German armor flowing through the area.

Orders were issued to the 14th AD to redress the situation, but at first it was only C Troop of the 94th Cav Recon acting as reconnaissance and patrolling the north edge of the forest. Following on was the 48th Tank Battalion. The German attack against the dug-in GIs in Hatten possessed overwhelming tank and artillery superiority, which kept the desperate Americans pinned down in the houses of the town hoping for the best awaiting rescue. The unit history of the 48th Tanks characterizes the fearful situation of the "doughfeet":

They were pretty green to begin with, not their fault, and they'd been kicked around in a couple of other engagements; in short, they were pretty easy meat for even the ordinary run of Heinie guts and tricks. Then one night Jerry pushed into the east edge of Hatten (the other little town) where the battalion in that sector had its Command Post in a cellar by the church near the center of town. At first the next morning it looked rough for them, and then it didn't, then it did. And during that night and the next day the battalion was cut off, the remainder of the regiment was beaten back and Heinie was in Rittershoffen too. But's that's too fast for the story because we got tangled in it soon after Heinie threw himself into Hatten.[6]

Tec 5 Vernon H. Brown, Jr., with D Troop of the 94th Cav Recon, observed the beginning of the action when the men of the 242nd Infantry stepped off on 7 January:

Before long the firing started and shortly after that a procession of peeps pulling little trailers reappeared down the road bringing casualties to the rear. The infantry had jumped across frozen fields whereupon the Krauts caught them with machine gun and tank fire. When they moved into the woods the mortars sought them out with tree bursts. The ones that had thrown away their entrenching tools had no choice but to run for it, and the situation went from bad to worse. Eventually the infantry was able to disengage and pull back through our screen [of light tanks and armored cars], and as the enemy made no attempt to follow up, much to our relief we also returned to Weyersheim.[7]

There was then and still now, among some veterans of the 14th AD, reluctance to give much credit to the men of the 242nd Regiment of the 42nd Infantry Division. Richard Engler wrote *The Final Crisis* to rebut this negative picture of his regiment's and his division's fighting ability, and to correct, from his perspective, the record as a combat veteran fighting in cold Alsace in the winter of 1945.[8]

To return to the combat, the 48th TB of the 14th made a serious effort to help those American soldiers trapped in the two towns, which previously had enjoyed relative peace with the war flaring around it. The unit history provides a graphic picture of the initial efforts on 9 January to stem the tide of the panzer juggernaut. "A" Company was assigned the task of leading a counterattack to assist and rescue the men of both the infantry divisions in the towns. The tankers had been resting and refitting in Kuhlendorf, where Bob Davies' 68th AIB had been doing the same thing. That town is northwest of Rittershoffen about three kilometers away. From that "good pivot" at 0930 hours on 9 January, A Company had been rushed to assembly positions east of Rittershoffen," all set for a big Jerry drive through and past the doughfeet [infantry] MLR." As the 48th history breathlessly continues, "It was 1300 sharp when Captain Ace [Joel P. Ory] quietly told 1st Platoon leader [Lt. Edgar P.] Woodard to bring the boys back up with a hell of a bang while he whipped over to Hatten in the peep [jeep] to talk to the doughfeet Colonel."[9]

When Captain Ory made contact with the infantry in Hatten, he could feel the nervousness, almost panic, in the air. The fear was understandable when soldiers are almost completely surrounded by German tanks and half-tracks crammed with infantry and under intense German shelling. There was in place a friendly Tank Destroyer Battalion on the west edge of Hatten, although its commander was reluctant to engage the enemy. Fortunately, one Sherman tank commander put his gun in the right direction and "sent the lead [hostile] half-track up in a shower of sparks, range 75 yards. . . ."[10]

A humble corporal of the 48th's A Company, Franklin J. McGrane, kept a diary (although orders forbade such recordkeeping) of the fighting on that as well as other days:

> This was friendly country, we knew that. We had passed through it a few weeks before and gone beyond the Maginot Line, those forts that followed this entire area along the northern edge. We had been untouched, we pushed north—toward the Rhine. To the south stretched the forest [of Hagenau], a coniferous snow covered group. A valley lay tranquilly between the forest and a snow-padded highway which seamed the North and South sectors together. Between the Maginot and the forest at either end of the road sat two towns, foreign as yet to war's destruction, Rittershoffen at the west, Hatten at the east. The country between the chain of forts to the north and the wooded sector on the south rippled gently.[11]

That tranquil scene would not last as Company A went to work. A recon officer jumped out of a jeep. He shouted that there were German tanks to the right, in the valley: "Tanks on your right—German tanks—in the valley—Get 'em Get 'em! . . ." Corporal McGrane and his fellow tankers couldn't believe it. "They couldn't be there. . . ." Nevertheless the tank platoon swung to the attack in a position overlooking the valley. "These were ours, of course—they weren't ours! Fire! Gunner, Fire! Five tanks spat flame, one still on the move. It was a two-minute job—."[12]

Three factors allowed the instant success of Corporal McGrane's platoon:

(1) The M-4 Sherman tanks in January of 1945 were late models of that standard tank, and they possessed a new 76mm gun, which had increased muzzle velocity to penetrate the

armor of the German Mark IV panzer.

(2) The reconnaissance of the Americans in this instance was superior.

(3) The Shermans were equipped with an electric traverse, which allowed the gunners to get off the first shots. The panzers were equipped with only a mechanical traverse, more laborious and slower.

The heavier Mark V and Mark VI, the feared and infamous Panther and Tiger tanks, might have provided a more deadly challenge to the Shermans, even the up-to-date "Easy Eight" Shermans, since the German panzers possessed up to six inches of armor on their front slopes, several more than any of the American or British tanks. The thick armor on the Panther's glacis was set at an angle to encourage enemy rounds to glance off the surface. The only real chance for a Sherman was to get a lucky shot off the sides or rear, which were much less protected. There was more than one complaint by American tankers that their rounds just bounced off enemy armor.

But to return to this stage of the battle in Alsace. The German offensive had to be stopped, and the "lost battalions" in the two towns had to be rescued. "It was time to seize the initiative and restore the MLR by committing the power of an entire armored division." The orders from Major General Edward H. Brooks of VI Corps to the 14th AD were to "pass through the 79th Division positions and attack to capture the line Stundwiller-Buhl-Forest of Hatten."[13]

The Germans, however, were busy as well according to Colonel Hans von Luck, the leader of the "Kampfgruppe" named after him, a miscellaneous group of soldiers who had been driven back from Normandy over the summer and fall. Just as the Americans had to rescue some of their men, the enemy had to rescue combatants from the 25th Panzer Grenadiers, who held the southern portion of Hatten. By the evening of 9 January, "only a small breach" had been made. The 25th PGD with von Luck's troops tried to force their way into Rittershoffen and capture the Maginot bunker line running north of the town. Von Luck's parent division was prepared to take the town on 10 January, but the 192nd Regiment, which had been assigned the task, had failed in its mission. On the following morning, Major Spreu of the 192nd took the bunker and captured its occupants by employing anti-tank guns and machine guns against the apertures in the concrete structure. Major Spreu's account is as follows:

> At first light I moved up with the platoon of engineers while my heavy weapons company fired nonstop at the gun-ports of the bunker. We charged through the snow and within a few minutes were at the bunker. The engineers threw hand grenades into the ports, while others ran around to cut the barbed wire and cleared mines. When we ran around to the rear entrance, the door opened and a white flag appeared with five officers and a garrison of 117 men.[14]

The besieged Gis, before surrendering, managed to call in artillery fire on their own positions and caused some serious casualties among the attacking grenadiers. After many of the bunkers were overrun, the infantry of the 242nd had retreated to the town of Rittershoffen and took to the houses to employ as fortifications, but the Germans were "lodged firmly in the railroad station." The wounded were removed to the few bunkers still in American hands. The battle for Hatten had already become disjointed and disconnected, and although the rallying cry at American higher headquarters was to "restore the MLR," in truth there was no discernible line to restore.[15] Once the fighting invested the two towns, they were doomed to a terrible fate.

Colonel von Luck continues his account of his Kampfgruppe's struggle in Rittershoffen. On 10 January, his regiment made their attack, and by evening it had forced its way into the farming village, "but there too, just as at Hatten, the enemy held out in the houses and at once mounted a counterattack with tanks and infantry [the 48th TB and the 2nd Battalion of the 315th regiment]. This hit my II Battalion in particular, which had established itself in the center near the church." From von Luck's perspective, as a seasoned veteran commander on several fronts, "There now developed one of the hardest and most costly battles that had ever raged on the western front."[16] Von Luck construed the American effort as designed to recapture the Maginot Line bunkers and pillboxes, but as the fighting continued, it was more a matter of taking houses and sections of the two towns. Soon it would simply be a matter of clusters of soldiers on both sides trying to survive, with foes only yards apart and sometimes on different floors of the same building.

Both sides employed incendiary shells and the Germans flame-throwing tanks, even phosphorus grenades thrown into doorways and windows. It would be no wonder that the towns would cease to exist except as burned and shattered rubble. Tactical urgency overcame any other military considerations.

The most distressing element of the battle was the suffering and dying of the civilian population and their domestic animals and livestock:

> Even now the civilian population remained in the two villages. Women, children, and old people, packed in like sardines, sat in the cellars of the houses. Electricity had been cut off, the supply of food was short, and there was no water for the pipes were frozen. We [the German troops] tried to help as much as we could. By day any movement was fatal; our supplies could be brought up only by night in armored vehicles. In this we were helped by a hollow [supply road] which concealed us from the enemy, whose flares threw the area into brilliant light.[17]

The fiery stalemate forced Major General Edward H. Brooks, commander of VI Corps, to commit the 14th Armored Division to fight, beyond the initial action of the 94 Cav Recon and Company A of the 48th Tank Battalion. The fight was eating up infantry at an alarming rate. General Albert Smith's order to his division stated, "Div attacks R-H: CC abreast, daylight 12 Jan 1945 to restore VI Corps MLR."[18] However, as Richard Engler and others recounting the battle were to conclude, there was no MLR to "restore." The combat was disorienting for the troops, and commanders at any and all levels on both sides could not change the disorientation.

Before the morning of the 13th, the 14th AD had not committed all of its armored infantry battalions, but everyone was on alert, and it was just a matter of time before these were thrown into the cauldron. The S-2 and S-3 Journals of the 68th AIB had reported the action between A-48 and the panzers on 9 January at 1315 hours: OP's report 16 Mark IV Tks, 9 personnel carriers, 8 half-tracks moving toward Hatten. . . ." Elements of the 827th Tank Destroyer Battalion were advancing toward the combat. Formal armored doctrine ordained that in cases where a tank versus tank clash was anticipated, tank destroyers were to be favored. The TD's possessed a 76.2mm gun and later in the war a 90mm gun, and before the Sherman was upgunned to the 76mm gun, the TD possessed more hitting power. However, the armor was at the most only one and a half inches, so they were not safe places to be when fighting against panzers was imminent. Eventually, by the end of the war, the Tank Destroyers would be phased out, but that didn't help the crews at Rittershoffen and Hatten. The 68th's S-2 and S-3 Journals intercepted a message indicating that more TD's of the 827th's TD Company B had shifted toward the fight and that Company C of the 48th TB was doing the same.

At 1500 hours, the 94th Cav Recon reported to CCA Headquarters that "7 ey tks now burning at (165430)—time 1500." This report was the result of the good work of Corporal McGrane's A Company, for which its First Platoon would receive the following citation:

Recipient: 1st Platoon, Company A, 48th Tank Battalion, Lt. Edgar D. Wood ard, Pl. Ldr., for outstanding performance of duty in action on 9 Jan 1945, near Hatten, France. Assigned to the mission of repulsing an enemy attack, the 1st platoon, consisting of four operating medium tanks, moved rapidly and decisively to the support of friendly infantry already partially over run by enemy armor. Displaying great skill and superior marksmanship, the platoon engaged sixteen Mark IV tanks in a deadly firefight, and without loss of men or equipment, destroyed four enemy tanks which the Germans were attempting to evacuate.

The critical reconnaissance work done by Troop C of the 94th Cav and Recon also received a citation in that they "supplied higher commanders with rapid, accurate information of the attack on Hatten by an estimated three armored infantry battalions of a Panzer Grenadier Division."[19]

Corporal McGrane of A Company of the 48th continues his vivid account of the scene after the counterattack begun at 1710 on the same day:

We left our commanding ground and eased down its sloping sides toward the valley floor past the smouldering Jerry tanks which burned like huge torches to guide our way in the gathering darkness. Doughfeet walked behind us, five to a tank. Now and then Heinie ammo within the flaming tanks would explode and throw hot metal into the sky to make of the sky a blanket of twisted colors. The night was cold; the wind was sharp. We stamped our feet against the floor as our tanks munched through the snow, exhausts coughing at their heavy vents. We pressed forward along the valley floor, going due east now. Our right flank, the forest wall [of Hagenau Forest], was close but invisible, it blended into the night.[20]

Charlie Company of the 48th was to assume the role of attacker on the following morning, 10 January. It didn't jump off until 1600 hours and advanced "due east, north of the Hatten-Rittershoffen Road into the teeth of German tanks and anti-tank defenses," as the 48th's History characterizes the situation. This time the panzers were not taken unawares, and they had three Mark V Panthers, possibly the best tank in the Wehrmacht arsenal. Corporal McGrane summarizes the furious action: "Within two minutes the Panzers were flaming coffins. Then Heinie struck back. Concealed antitank guns (you don't see the flashes) took three of our tanks before we could recover." Ever since the tank war in the African desert, German panzers had used the tactic of drawing enemy tanks onto the "stakes" of anti-tank guns after creating the appearance of a tank-to-tank battle. McGrane's Sherman was hit twice by another camouflaged gun (or so he thought at the time), but it proved later that there were two captured American tank destroyers, with larger and more deadly guns than McGrane's gun.[21] Why the American crews of the TD's, if they were physically able, did not neutralize the gun on their vehicle before they abandoned it is a puzzle.

The orders to the German divisions designated to make the attack on the tenth: the 7th Parachute, the 47th Volksgrenadiers, and the 2nd Mountain Division came from Hitler himself. He directed them to surge out of the Hagenau sector west to push the Seventh Army back to the Vosges Mountains and in the process cut if off between the Rhine and the mountains. If that gambit succeeded, the First French Army defending the Colmar Pocket would have been outflanked and either forced to withdraw or to stand fast and be destroyed. General DeGaulle had suggested that the French were willing to turn Strasbourg into a

"Stalingrad," but the costs would have been staggering and fruitless. To reinforce his attack, Himmler now received the 10th SS Panzer Divsion, the 21st Panzer Division, and the 553rd Volksgrenadier Division.[22]

Between the Hammer and the Anvil

In the battle soon to be engaged, the Americans were seriously outnumbered, and the fighting in and around Hatten-Rittershoffen would take a terrible toll on both sides as well as on the civilians. Some veterans of the combat considered it one of the great tank battles of the war, especially those who fought amid the streets and houses, whether as infantry or tankers, whether engineers of reconnaissance troops, headquarters or ordnance troops.

One of those who was there was Sgt. Darrell E. Todd, a loader in a Sherman tank in C Company of the 48th Tank Battalion. He was one of those involved in the fiery contretemps on 10 January. His tank scored a hit on a panzer, which set it aflame. His friend, "Mac" McAfee told him that the tally of three destroyed tanks was his birthday present, his twenty-second. Despite this small victory, Todd's Company rotated back to Rittershoffen after their failed attempt to take Hatten. The Germans continuously fired what the GIs called "screaming meemies" (from the Nebelwerfer multiple rocket launcher), missiles that were less lethal than more accurate mortars or artillery rounds but which kept the men on edge with their eerie scream. Todd remembers the attack:

> The next morning, 11 Jan was foggy with 8 inches of snow on the ground. The Germans had sent in screaming meemies all night and at 0630 hours started their attack against our positions. Their tanks were painted white, ours were covered with OD [olive drab] sandbags; and their infantry wore white parkas. The first German tank I spotted was 75 yards in front of my tank. Through my telescopic sight I could see my tracer disappear into the Kraut tank turret. I traversed left and fired [the] 2 rd into the next tank turret.[23]

Todd had been promoted to gunner in December and had learned well his deadly trade. But again, the enemy was about to surprise the American tankers, who learned the hard way of the ingenuity and deception of their stealthy foe. Todd's tank was hit by a round from a captured American tank destroyer—another instance of a captured TD inflicting harm on a Sherman:

> I spotted what I thought was a German tank with their gun tube pointed in our direction. Before I could fire Lt. Stair shouted that it was one of our attached tank destroyers. At this time I traversed left to search for more targets and our tank was hit by the TD, which we later learned was abandoned by the American crew and manned by a German crew.[24]

The TD hit on Todd's Sherman would result in of several serious problems for its crew as the tank started to burn and then explode stored rounds inside the tank. When Pvt. Nathan McAfee climbed out of the top hatch he was hit by machine-gun fire. Todd and the other crewmembers descended out of the bottom hatch, the safer exit. He managed to crawl into a potato furrow about eight inches deep and, although freezing, reached the safety of the other tanks in the platoon. During the ordeal depicted by Todd, according to the 14th AD's History written by Capt. Joseph Carter, "Multi-colored German tracers criss-crossed in the dawn. A tank burst into flames. A corporal gunner remarked, 'I sat in that seat and picked a spot on the steel side of the tank where I figured the first 88 would come through. I cursed the mist on the sight'."[25]

The S-2 and S-3 Journals of the 68th Armored Infantry Battalion recorded what was happening from a message from CCA to the 68th. Enemy artillery, approximately 250 rounds, fell on the 48th TB's positions from the direction of the Rhine to the east. "At 0810 about 200 ey began an atk on Hatten from the East. They have fire support from S of town which may develop into an attack."

It most certainly would, according to the 68th's history: "The summons came the morning 11th January and we were ordered to stem a German offensive in the vicinity of Rittershoffen. We moved up and dug in positions east of Kuhlendorf. The stage was set but little did we know that this time what a tremendous job had been cut out for us. . . . to relieve the pressure on the 3rd Battalion, 315th Infantry, 79th Division."[26] The specific instructions from CCA to the 68th articulated the need for the 48th TB and the armored infantry to coordinate their movements: "48 will hold positions strongly vic Rittershoffen, preventing both enemy armor and inf. from moving to W or NW. 68 complete its defense positions and hold this position, preventing any movemen [*sic*] to W or NW past it. Both Bns be prepared for hvy ey armored atk that is likely to come at any time today [the 11th]. Both Bns make plans for C/Atk to E and SE. Boundary between bns to be E-W 34 grid line. This C/Atk will be launched only on orders from this Hq. . . ." (S-2 and S-3 Journals, 11 Jan. 1945).

According to the 14th's *History*, 0630 on the morning of 11 January, Company C of the 48th was assaulted by "a company of German tanks [approximately 16 or 17] and 300 infantrymen supported by a heavy artillery concentration. The attack was repelled at 0730" (n.p.). This is the attack which destroyed Darrell Todd's tank and took the life of his friend "Mac" McAfee. The First Platoon now had only two tanks, the Second one, and the Third three, and so the company was ordered back to "the high ground north of Rittershoffen." S/Sgt. Robert M. Winslow sketched the fight from his perspective:

> We were to move south across the railroad track, then due east across the "pool table"—flat, treeless land around Rittershoffen and Hatten. Our objective was the Hatten-Seltz road that A Company had cut the first night, It wasn't very far as distance goes, perhaps two kilometers away.
>
> As we moved out into the open the Germans began laying artillery, but we received no direct fire from Rittershoffen. When we reached the point where we were to cross the tracks, my section went across the line, covered by the other section. The other section 1st platoon was moving east, south of the tracks. As my section crossed the track, we were fired on from somewhere on the south or the west of Hatten. My section apparently got out of the traverse of these guns but as we moved up 100 yards further two more German flat trajectory guns opened up on us. Behind me, Captain [Robert G.] Elder's tank was hit twice in quick succession. Four more tanks were hit and we still couldn't pick up the flashes. It's a strange feeling to see a shower of sparks cover the turret of the tank in front of you. Your whole whole body goes tense, you are scared to your fingertips. "Driver, back! Hard right! Move out straight! See that

knocked-out Kraut tank? Get behind it, kick hell out of it. Communications went out. You're helpless then. Darkness came down like a blanket. (Carter, n.p.)

The 68th AIB's unit history explains that its infantry attack was scheduled for 1545 hours, "with two platoons of A Company on the left, C Company on the right, and one platoon of engineers in reserve. We jumped off."[27] B Company advanced along with the 48th TB in order to make a similar move from the south side of Rittershoffen "All went well until the orchard on the west edge of Rittershoffen was reached, and the 'Kraut' from his high vantage point opened up with terrific mortar and artillery barrages and grazing small arms fire." C Company had only managed to capture two houses in the southwest part of town. "This strong defense, plus the oncoming darkness forced us to consolidate our positions. Digging in the snow-covered frozen ground was a task in itself."[28] S/Sgt. William D. Rutz of C Company and a small group managed to find cover in a barn on the outside of town. Rutz and two other sergeants spotted a panzer and grabbed a bazooka and a small amount of ammunition to kill the tank, but they were unsure of what was following the tank and went back to get some more rounds for the bazooka. As Sgt. Rutz delineated the event:

Sergeant [Martin C.] Diers was the lead guy going back, and as he jumped up and had taken three or four steps to cross the alley, the tank had moved and had visibility at that point and fired a direct hit on him. It must have been only 30 or 40 yards away. He was so close to the muzzle of the gun that he was covered with black gun powder. He didn't make a move.[29]

Sgts. Rutz and Elmer C. Bullard made it out of that harrowing situation, but Rutz was wounded by a shell that exploded in a building where he and his squad were housed. Worse, on the next day Sgt. Bullard was killed. Sgt. Rutz was taken to hospital and returned to the fight six weeks later.

The open flat ground around Rittershoffen and Hatten to the north, except for the protection of Hagenau Forest to the south, gave little protection to the infantry. The German artillery observers had a clear field, and the frozen ground made it difficult if not impossible to

Pvt. Bob Davies stateside before going off to war along with millions of his comrades in the Armed Services between 1942 and 1945. *Photo courtesy of Dr. Olive (Jo) Davies, his widow.*

Below: Lt. Colonel Bob Edwards, pictured here as a Major before going overseas. He was the much respected and beloved commander of the 68th Armored Infantry Battalion, 14th Armored Division, who in turn much respected and loved his men.

Lt. Col. Edwards earned a Silver Star, with oak leaf cluster; a Bronze Star; a Combat Infantry-man's Badge; and a Croix de Guerre. A career officer, he would go on to serve his country in Korea. *Photo courtesy of his son John and his wife Cindy, who miss him.*

The hill town of Sospel, France in the Maritime Alps near the area where both the 19th and the 68th Armored Infantry Battalions were stationed to acclimatize them to infantry action. *Photo courtesy of Philip Snoberger, formerly of C-68 and a close friend of Bob Davies.*

Some of Bob Davies' squad in colder weather, probably in December 1944. The tree in background appears iced, which would be typical for a winter that was classified as the coldest in Europe in 100 years. *Photo courtesy of Richard Green, son of Chet Green of B-68.*

Unidentified soldier from B-68 manning a .50 caliber heavy machine gun mounted in a half-track, the vehicle used to transport armored infantry (envied by regular infantry soldiers). Mechanization such as this allowed infantry, artillery, and engineers to move rapidly along with the tanks in an armored division. The machine gun, though slow-firing, shot large hard-hitting rounds, and German soldiers hated and feared it for the damage it could inflict on a human body. *Photo courtesy of Richard Green.*

Bob Davies with his infantry squad from Company B-68 with a snowy mountain in the background. The typical 12-man squad carried grenades in bandoliers as well as M1 rifles. One man probably has a BAR. Identified are (back row) Privates John Chester ("Chet") Green, left, Bob Davies, second from right; (front row) Johnny Garrett, left on one knee, Peter Cuomo, kneeling center. Squad leader SSgt. Willard R. Kirchner is in the picture but not identified. Ass't. Squad Leader Sgt. David F. Kennedy appears on one knee lower right. *Photo courtesy of Robbie Davies and Richard Green, sons of above men.*

A bridge across the Lauter River near Salmbach, blown by the retreating Germans and repaired by B Company of the 125th Armored Engineers in December 1944. This repair allowed 14th AD patrols to enter Germany. Around this time General Jacob L. Devers wanted permission to continue forward, cross the Rhine in force, and flank the German Army. SHAEF refused to give it. *Photo courtesy of 14th Armored Division History.*

Another AIB in the 14th AD was the 62nd, always competitive with the 68th and the 19th. In this picture is a gun crew, part of an Assault Gun Platoon of Headquarters Company. The gun is a 105mm howitzer mounted on an open M4 tank chassis. In the back, from left, are Fred H. Harshberger, Don Glosh, and Gordan Bryant. Adjacent to the gun barrel are Lee Oster and John Helper. The name of the gun is "Headache," whether to the crew or its target is not specified. *Photo courtesy of Fred H. Harshberger.*

On December 29, two days before German Army Group G would initiate Operation Northwind in the Vosges Mountains, Fred Harshberger's SP crew decided to hunt deer in the snowy woods but got a wild boar instead. They shot the boar with an M1 rifle but then found that skinning it was difficult. Some locals, including a young boy, volunteered to show them how to do it. Because of the enemy assault, the crew never got to eat the meat. *Photo courtesy of Fred H. Harshberger.*

On December 16, 1944, infantry of the 62nd AIB advanced through Wissembourge, France, accompanied by a tank from the 25th Tank Battalion, its gear stowed neatly on the rear, called the "bustle." The men at the front left may be 125th Armored Engineers carrying timber to support another crossing. *Photo courtesy of Stillpix, National Archives II.*

A restored M3 light tank, known as a Stuart, with a 37mm gun and three machine guns. Thousands of these were used in combat, and each tank battalion had a company of them. Because the gun and light armor were insufficient against German tanks, it was replaced by the M5, which had more armor and a stronger engine, the model issued to the 14th. The Stuart performed a variety of duties, such as reconnaissance, guarding flanks, or as a command vehicle. *Original photo courtesy of the General George Patton Museum.*

On February 11, 1945, an M4A Sherman tank with a long-barreled 76mm gun sets up to fire on a target outside Hurtendorf, France. Note the sandbags piled up for additional protection. The tank belonged to the 25th TB, 14th Armored Division. *Photo courtesy of Stillpix, National Archives II.*

A mortar squad of Co. C, 68th Armored Infantry Battalion, 14th Armored Division, fires on Bitschhoffen, France on 23 Feb 1945. There are four men in the squad who appear to be firing a 60mm mortar while protected by a sandbag emplacement. *Photo courtesy of Stillpix, National Archives II.*

In late February and early March, movement in Alsace for the 14th Armored was difficult. There was much mutual shelling in the Pfaffenhoffen area. As the men of the 68th AIB reach that town, "the leather center of France," engineers of the 125th Bn. on March 10 "detonate 300 M Wurfkoerrerspreng" (evidently a large mortar bomb or round) which lodged in a roof of a house." *Photo and comment courtesy of Stillpix, National Archives II.*

A wrecked 88mm gun at Herxheim on the west bank of the Rhine. The Wehrmacht fought hard to maintain a river crossing at that point, and the town itself was incorporated into the Siegfried Line. Tanks from the 47th Tank Bn. and men from the 19th AIB worked to clear the heavily defended town around March 21, 1945. *Photo courtesy of Captain Joseph Carter's History of the 14th Armored Division.*

At the end of March 1945 after the battle at Steinfeld, when the 14th AD cracked the Siegfried Line, Fred Harshberger took this picture of his Company commander, Capt. Willard C. Robinson, and Lt. (later Capt.) John Ryan, a Platoon Leader of the 62nd AIB. His comment on the back of the picture: "This was the first line of dragon's teeth on the Siegfried. Just one more shot from our tank fixed the building."
Photo courtesy of Fred Harshberger

A watercolor of armored infantry in March 1945 around Bitschoffen. The original 14th History presented colorful pictures without identifying the artist. Later it was printed only in black and white, a real loss to the book's quality. The artist, according to Bob McClarren, was Robert Taylor, an art student from Northwestern University, a bow gunner and assistant driver in McClarren's tank while at Camp Chaffee. Taylor's work was not credited in the 14th's History. *Photo courtesy of Captain Joseph Carter's History.*

14th AD infantry advancing on April 6, 1945 toward Hammelburg, Germany to rescue Allied POW's. They are passing a knocked-out light tank of General Patton's forces, which made a rash previous attempt to free the prisoners, who included Patton's son-in-law.
Photo courtesy of Stillpix, National Archives II.

Armored infantry waiting outside Gemunden in early April until artillery of the 499th Armored Field Artillery Battalion can soften up German positions. The 14th AD had just liberated the camp at Hammelburg, men of many nations who were jubilant at their release. The 14th's proud nom de guerre is "The Liberators." *Photo courtesy of Carter's History.*

Men of the 62nd AIB fight their way through Gemunden on April 8, 1945. The German commander said one reason for the collapse of his defensive position was the volume of artillery fire. This picture confirms his opinion. *Photo courtesy of Stillpix, National Archives II.*

Another watercolor by Robert Taylor of a 14th tank column forging its way in April 1945 on the Autobahn in their workhorse Sherman tanks. By this time newer models had wider tracks, improved suspension, heavier armor, and a better gun and ammunition. In the foreground are men of the 154th Armored Signal Company working their radio with its large antenna.
Photo courtesy of Carter's History.

A tank destroyer, probably the very capable M-18, on April 8, fires in support of friendly infantry advancing on the left, probably the 19th AIB (the number crossed out in the Signal Corps description). It notes that the TD belongs to the "17th Tank Bn.," but more likely as a TD, it belonged to the 636th. *Photo courtesy of Stillpix, National Archives II.*

On April 26, having crossed into Germany on Easter Sunday, "units of 14th Armored Division, 3rd U.S. Army [no longer Seventh Army], advance along a road after crossing the Altmuhl River." The prison camp at Moosburg, Stalag VIIA, with 100,000 prisoners, was liberated three days later. *Photo courtesy of Stillpix, National Archives II.*

At a Luftwaffe field near Amphing in May, with the war just over, Pvt. Philip Snoberger and Tech. Sgt. Benjamin Bloomfield of C-68 relax in a jeep next to a three-engined Ju-52 transport aircraft. *Photo courtesy of Philip Snoberger.*

A sure sign that hosilities have ended. Fred Harshberger's friend, Dina Ludmilla Krackminof, stands atop what appears to be a Jagdpanzer IV, a lethal tank destroyer for the Wehrmacht, with a height of only 6'1". The large, lethal 75mm gun provides a sober contrast to the pretty girl on top, whose White Russian family had fled the Red dictatorship of Joseph Stalin. *Photo courtesy of Fred H. Harshberger.*

Pfc. George B. Turner of Battery C of the 499th Armored Field Artillery earned a Congressional Medal of Honor during the fighting in Operation Northwind. On the retreat to Phillipsbourg on 3 January 1945, he performed such feats of valor, at 46 years of age, that he was given the medal by President Truman. (The Presidental Citation appears at the end of Chapter 4.) *Photo courtesy of The Congressional Medal of Honor Society.*

dig in. Sometimes only a slight furrow of ground, dug by an Alsatian farmer, offered protection for the stranded GIs. B Company seemed especially exposed to German fire.

Further complicating the situation for Battalion, Combat Command, and Division commanders was the fact that C Troop of the 94th Cav Recon had been trapped in the town of Hatten by their opponent's combined tank and infantry attack that had already cost the 48th TB losses in men and vehicles. The troopers had managed to slip west into the town of Rittershoffen, but that was a dubious sanctuary after they lost Sgt. Leslie E. Koontz, suffered several wounded, and forfeited both an armored car and a peep.

The attack would continue regardless, and orders issued on 11 January at 1415 by CCA to the 68th AIB provide specific instructions for the taking of Hatten: "68 to move rifle co's SE along creek line to position SW of Rittershoffen. 68—Above co and Co A south and push on to East and capture Northern half of Hatten" (S-2 and S-3 Journals). This would prove to be a tall order, and by the end of the fighting neither the Americans nor the Germans could control either of the towns entirely.

Nevertheless, a Citation in February 1945 read the action somewhat differently:

> By 1630 the enemy was so mauled by tank fire that he was forced to fall back into the village. The tanks were in the assault wave and, by their determination, indefatigable spirit and initiative, were able to establish a foothold in this sector of Rittershoffen for the first time. The infantry could now move in, take up positions and carry on the attack under more suitable close-in fighting conditions. . . .[30]

Whether the troops stuck in the hell of the two towns until 20 January would agree that such "close-in fighting conditions" were "more suitable" is highly doubtful. Even the 14th AD's Commander, "General Albert C. Smith later described the impending operation as '. . . about as prolonged and vicious an engagement between armored units as we can cite in the military history of our Army'."[31] In another context, during a conversation between a tanker and an infantry soldier, when the tanker protested about the thinness of the armor on his tank, the "dogface" pointed to his shirt and asked, "How thin is this?"

Robert H. Kamm, a "buck sergeant" as he remembered himself, from A Company of the 68th, survived the onslaught in the orchard and the entrance into the town: "I can remember being pinned down in the orchard and trying to dig in the frozen ground. I remember the German tanks and the flame-throwers, and also in taking part in trying to clear the town house-by-house, only always to pull back. I thought then that we'd never get out of there. I lost a dear friend in that battle, Pfc. Henry Houselog from Chicago."[32]

S/Sgt. Donald L. Haynie, also of A Company, and also the target of a multiplicity of projectiles from small arms to rockets, protected himself but saw others terribly wounded and killed:

> I made myself as flat as I could and, I believe, dug into the ground with my belly to afford as small a target as possible. My companions all around me were being hit. I saw one of them being picked up by the medics. As he was being loaded into a jeep, I saw him reach down and bring his newly severed leg into the vehicle.[33]

Once he and his squad got into town, they tried driving hostile artillery observers from the belfry of the Lutheran Church, without much success.

Overnight, between the 11th and the 12th, C-68 Company patrols were able to reach some soldiers from the 315th Regiment, who had been trapped in the town, and to reassure them that at 0800 the following morning the rest of their battalion would arrive and relieve them. There were also troops from the 94th Cav Recon who were holding out in town after they had been cut off.

The desperate cold, darkness, and the mist made life miserable for both infantry and tankers, causing dangerous frostbite to the feet whether inside a tank or in a ditch. For the gunners in the tanks, the sights misted over and the lubricants in the guns congealed. Yet in the morning, the next attack began, with A Company of the 68th providing "protective fire." B Company, combined with the armor of A Company, the 48th, made the assault under a tremendous array of enemy gunfire.[34]

The 14th's commander, General Smith, issued orders for the morning of 12 January: "CCA attacks at daylight, seize R; protect right flank of Div; screen passage CCB in attacking H. . . . attack in column of battalions, leading battalion to seize H and screen passage of following battalions; second battalion cut roads E of H and restore MLR. . . ." On the left of CCA, Company B with the tanks of Company A of the 48th, were to attack along the main road from the west. "The main effort" by Company C of the 68th was to be closely articulated with the tanks, with C divided into four teams of two infantry squads, two tanks each, four light machine-guns and one rocket launcher (bazooka) per team. With Company A of the 68th providing a base of fire, the houses in the town of Rittershoffen would be cleared. A would then follow C into the town with the mortars, machine guns, and assault guns of Headquarters Company in support. An anti-tank platoon was designated to protect the flanks of the assault, and a platoon of the 125th Battalion of Combat Engineers would follow 300 yards behind as a reserve. The 62nd AIB with the 25th TB of CCB would bypass Rittershoffen to attack Hatten.[35]

As Richard Engler, one of the isolated 42nd Division infantrymen struggling to survive, saw the situation, the tanks of the 25th were about 1000 yards behind the infantrymen of the 62nd in a field of white frozen ground. The Germans were able to fire on these exposed troops from fortifications and anti-tank positions. After they commenced firing on the 62nd AIB, its A Company lost some seventy men. The 25th lost five tanks. CCR, however, did not get involved in the fight on 12 January. Medical supplies were fired in by artillery shells during the night of 12 to 13 January, to treat the wounded, but little of this material got to them. Finally, CCR moved up in preparation for an attack on the thirteenth.[36]

With all the casualties so far, there were many tragic stories of the heroism and sacrifice of soldiers, and one of these was that of Harry and Larry Kemp of Company C of the 68th, twin brothers from Lakeland, Florida. Both served in the 68th AIB along with Bob Davies. In December, after being trapped in a foxhole partially filled with icy water for five days in Ober-Otterbach, Harry developed symptoms of pneumonia. As he told the story to the Augusta (Ga.) Chronicle, he regretted being off the line:

"I didn't want to leave my brother, but I was on the verge of getting pneumonia, . . . It was more or less an order from my platoon leader."

While Mr. [Pvt., later Lt.] Kemp was recovering in an Army aid station in a French village, a captain informed him of his brother's death.

Mr. Kemp had to go back to the fighting the next day. His brother's body was sent to an American cemetery [at Epinal, France].[37]

Harry informed this writer verbally that his brother had been killed outside Rittershoffen while acting as an exposed artillery observer protected by a tank, but a sniper managed to shoot Larry in the head and kill him instantly. Especially painful for Harry was to try to see his brother's body before internment. The officer in command refused to allow Larry's face to be seen since the sniper's bullet, presumably, had terribly damaged it. The loss of his brother made Harry especially anxious to inflict as much damage on the enemy as was possible. While the fight was still raging in Rittershoffen, he had his chance:

One day in Rittershoffen a German halftrack pulled up and parked about a block away from my position. The halftrack was loaded with German soldiers. An American Sherman tank was parked behind the house where I was located. The tank commander had his hatch open so I told him about the German halftrack and he pulled up to where he could see it and blew it to kingdom come with one shell from his tank.[38]

Thus was the departed twin avenged by the surviving twin.

It was in the nature of the fighting in the twin Alsatian towns that both sides had infantry, either on foot or in halftracks, and tanks and other vehicles hiding around the corner from one another and waiting for an opportunity to kill their opposite numbers. Some combat events occurred on purpose, but others just seemed to be the result of chance, which the alert fighter had to take advantage of chance opportunity, or else be victimized by the same.

For example, there was the wounding and survival of Bob Davies' co-platoon sergeant of Company B-68. Neither one wanted to be NCO

Platoon Leader but agreed to serve together with each other. On Company B's advance into town on 12 January, Chet Green was hit in the forehead by a sniper's bullet that, by good fortune for Green, had already passed through a seriously wounded comrade, who would die from the bullet. That comrade was S/Sgt. Willard R. Kirchner, Bob Davies' assistant squad leader, who was recorded as killed in action on 13 January, a day later. While wounded and lying on the ground and "playing possum," Green was then hit by mortar fragments and by more bullets fired evidently by the same sniper. Furious at this punishment but acting dead, Green waited for the sniper to show himself. Green then shot the sniper, who tumbled out of a barn window, dead.[39]

During the advance into town, some of the 68th's armored infantry had fallen behind the protective cover of the tanks of the 48th TB, but C Company continued toward the town, where they were sorely beset yet again in the town by enemy fire from multiple weapons. A Company of the 68th reported that "most of one plat are casualties and several casualties in balance of platoons," but C-68 was "coming along fine; 5h/t's [half-tracks] in town. C-68 CP located in bldg in Rittershoffen (S-2 and S-3 Journals, 12 January). C Company was able to progress because of the covering fire of Company A and the screening efforts of B Company, all of which produced so many casualties. One of the patrols encountered a squad of hostile infantry and three Mark IV tanks in town and were instructed to eliminate them. By this time, around 1100 hours, there were both tanks and infantry from both sides in Rittershoffen or in the process of moving into town from Hatten to the east. Artillery was falling on the town from both armies, some of the hostile rounds fired from a streambed to the east. CCA ordered "C/Btry on ey arty" and the tanks of A-48 to "fire to knock steeple off church in Rittershoffen." The battle was becoming a confused meleé, with both sides risking hitting their own troops in the town.

Following the American armored doctrine of combined arms, "Tank-infantry teams," with eight men to each tank, moved down the dangerous streets, each protecting the other. The infantry spotted hostile tanks and gun positions or concealed infantry with panzerfausts, and the armor blasted away with its main gun or machine guns to provide some safety for the foot soldiers. Each house was becoming its own fort and had to be challenged and even totally destroyed to insure safe passage. As the *History of the 14th Armored* fashioned the scene:

The tanks inched ponderously a few yards down the street, heavy cannon searching out machine gun nests, enemy strong points; the infantrymen moved along with them, running, dodging from building to building, throwing grenades in the cellar windows, going through each farm house room by room, rifles at the ready, hand grenades ready; the artillery and mortar fire screamed into the street and exploded the roofs; and the German machine gun fire swept the street in quick nasty blasts.[40]

A new horror in Rittershoffen was the enemy's setting on fire any house that they abandoned. In addition, friendly tanks were being knocked out by concealed anti-tank guns and panzerfausts. These last were most hazardous to tanks because a single German soldier could pop out of a concealed position behind a door or in an alley and fire the weapon. The charges in the weapon were often fatal. The 48th Tank Battalion attempted several different vectors to enter the town and support the infantry, but as darkness fell, the tanks retired to relative safety over the brow of a hill.[41]

The light tanks of the 94th Cav Recon had slightly better luck than those of the 48th. With armor on both sides suddenly appearing out of nowhere, it seemed, luck came to those who could get off the first shot. As mentioned earlier, the electric traverse of the Shermans allowed their gunners a moment of advantage denied to the panzer gunners, who were forced to use a manual crank. As Pfc. William Z. Breer recounted it, the 94th, lightly equipped as it was with thinly armored tanks, armored cars, half-tracks, and open peeps, managed to get lucky in the orchard where previously friendly tanks and infantry had been savaged by enemy fire:

> The orchard was on top of a hill and our tanks were able to fire a round from the crest of the hill directly at the enemy tanks and, then, reverse below the line of sight before the Germans could "zero" them in and then, repeat the procedure over and over from different positions, until we had knocked out several of their vehicles (both tanks and half-tracks).[42]

The authors of the 68th's history pause at this stage of the action to relate the newfound importance of this suddenly key town:

> Rittershoffen was a small Alsatian town occupying no strategi-
> cally important position, no communications center, no railway
> hub; it did not even afford the superior positions from which to
> attack or defend. Yet it had to be held at all cost until a strate-
> gic position could be dug in, for should the "Kraut" break
> through at this point, his offensive would probably have carried
> him to our rear installations [presumably Kuhlendorf]. . . .[43]

With members of the 68th occupying houses in Rittershoffen on
the western edge of town, there were still significant numbers of civilians hiding in the cellars and anywhere else they could find shelter from
the relentless artillery bombardment and house-to-house fighting. A
friend of Sgt. Bob Davies, Sgt. James F. Kneeland, was out on patrol at
night when he heard what sounded like a distress cry. He asked permission from his Company Commander, James M. Reed, B Company, to
crawl into the cellar from which he had heard the cry. Although this
could have been a clever trap, Reed assented, and, after the patrol, Jim
crawled into the darkened cellar and found a woman and child in
pitiable condition. They were eating melted snow to stay alive.
Kneeland took them out and put them in a reasonably safe place and fed
them.

The 68th was directed to make a second attack, along with tank
support, to begin at 0800 hours on 12 January. With A Company laying down a base of protective fire, C Company plunged into the town
again to "exploit the gains of the previous night." The Company
achieved the advantage of a few more houses in the southern part of the
town down the main street—east and west. Then A Company joined the
assault and redirected it from the east to the north. The exact time
sequence is a little ambiguous.

The 68th's history tells a story of what happened on the night of
the 12th to C Company:

> During the first night a "Kraut" patrol made their way to our
> OPLR [Outpost Line of Resistance] and into a cellar, after
> killing Pvt. [Joseph P.] Gorman who was guarding the door.
> This cellar was occupied by Lt. [Charles E.] Bailey of C

Company, and part of his platoon. This patrol, reportedly clad in GI uniforms, heralded their approach with, "Are there any Yanks there." The reply of "Yes" was met with a hail of "Potato Mashers" [grenades] and spraying of Burp Guns, seriously wounding Lt. Bailey and Pfc. [Phillip H.] Anderson of the Medical Detachment. The enemy patrol was wiped out.[44]

Both the German and American infantrymen, in the close confines of the town and its narrow streets and small houses, favored short-barreled weapons: for the Americans the carbine, the Thompson submachine gun, and the notoriously ugly and unreliable M-3, the "grease gun"; the Germans preferred the Sturmgewehr 44 and the Schmeisser machine pistols or "burp guns," effective weapons with a high rate of fire.

The general mayhem continued unabated. On the second night for the GIs in the town, 12–13 January, a German combined infantry and tank attack, including flamethrower tanks, roused the friendly units in town to a frenzied response. As the 68th AIB's history relates it, artillery was called in, and preregistered 105mm rounds hammered the tanks and decimated the German panzer grenadiers. C-68 bazooka teams neutralized some of the flamethrower tanks with their hollow-shell projectiles. When tanks were introduced by the British in World War I, at first infantry fled at the sight of the approaching monsters; but in January 1945 both sides had rocket weapons that a single infantryman or a two-man team could use to destroy tanks. Still, it was not a picnic in Rittershoffen since the anti-tank teams had to get pretty close to get a shot at the tank to hit one of its vulnerable spots. The presence of flamethrowing tanks introduced a powerful element to terrorize infantry.

Despite the agonizing tension of that night, the men of the 68th and their other comrades in the infantry and tank battalions and the 325th Engineers in reserve would get no rest the following morning. The division had been given the difficult assignment of driving the Germans out of both the towns of Hatten and Rittershoffen. Over the coming days, all the armored infantry battalions, the 19th, the 62nd, and the 68th, and the tank battalions, the 25th, the 47th, and the 48th, would be committed to the inferno, and only the 325th Combat Engineers would remain in reserve. Thus, the division which was the reserve of VI Corps would itself have to call upon its reserve to extricate it from a battle which could at best result in a draw. The continual refrain from the commanders would be to "restore the MLR." The enemy was placed in a similar conundrum: it was supposed to drive VI Corps and Seventh Army off the Alsatian plain and back to the Vosges Mountains to the west. The German forces also faced the prospect of a disappointing stalemate after the expenditure of ordnance, armor, and infantry in a demanding effort, perhaps beyond what they were capable of achieving.

Soon after the war, an analysis of the battle by Committee I of the War College reflected the Operations Intructions No. 10, published 122000 January:

1. CCA would continue its attack "at daylight to clear RIT-TERSHOFFEN. . . ."
2. Combat Command B was to attack both towns 'by fire only along the RITTERSHOFFEN-LEITERSWILLER road"
3. "The Reserve Command was to make the main effort on the 13th. Colonel Hudelson would assemble his forces in the vicinity of NIEDERBETSCHDORF prior to daylight and then attack around the south flank of the Division at daylight to seize HAT-TEN; rescue the remnants of the 2nd Battalion, 315th Infantry, still isolated in town [apparently in addition to those already rescued by the 68th on the twelfth]." CCR would, among other things, secure the right flank.
4. Two troops of the 94th Cavalry would also protect the left flank.
5. The fire plan for the attack included the support of VI Corps artillery. Some 8-inch howitzers would be used in the close support of the troops in HATTEN. [These guns were necessary to fire on the solidly built old churches and other massive targets that demanded large caliber rounds to destroy them.[45]

Committee 1 saw this plan for January 13th as similar to that on the 12th, the major difference being the vector of the assault from the south and the employment of more and heavier artillery. At this stage of the fighting, it would seem that it was like "making the rubble bounce."

Lt. Col. Joseph C. Lambert, G-3 of the 14th, also sketched the plan for the morning of 13 January, which developed from the south, between Hagen-au Forest and Rittershoffen. Armored cavalry patrolled the right flank at the edge of the forest while Combat Command B made a demonstration on the left flank and provided a base of fire. CCB also had to be on the alert for a German threat from Wissembourg to the north. Snow had fallen that night, and the infantry had had a long march the day before.[46] Nevertheless, the attack would be launched. The 62nd AIB was paired with the 25th Tank Battalion, with A and C Companies of armored infantry in tandem with C Company of the 25th, the 62nd's B Company and the remainder of the 25th's tanks in support. As the 14th's *History* narrates, "The 62nd's attack managed to get 1000 yards past the line of departure: the men clad in OD's stood out like targets on a rifle range against the white snow, and the German fire cut them down; artillery fire, mortar fire, small arms fire sweeping the open flat land."[47]

Colonel Francis J. Gillespie, Commander of CCB, responding to a question about the operation, grimly replied that

> It was snowing heavily at the time of our attack. We moved directly from the road, from march formation, to the line of departure, and attacked on time. The attack was not successful, but it undoubtedly relieved the pressure from the troops in RITTERSHOFFEN and HATTEN. At times, because of the snow, we could not see more than a hundred yards in advance. The ground was frozen and there was no opportunity to take cover of any sort, which considerably worried the troops. There was no evidence at the time that the holding attack had been launched; and as far as I could find out, the holding attack, if at all organized, had not gained ground.[48]

The "holding attack" evidently refers to the support given by B-68 and the rest of the 25th tanks, which did not have any appreciable effect on the primary effort.

A Company of the 62nd AIB had suffered the worst casualties, losing about seventy men and a beloved leader, Captain Daniel R. Iannella, and the tanks of C Company, the 25th, also took some serious losses. Captain Iannella had been seriously wounded but couldn't be evacuated because of the intense hostile fire. Several tanks were hit and began to burn, including that of Lt. Gisse, the 2nd Platoon Leader, already noted in previous action. Later, when B Company of the 62nd, along with more tanks of the 25th TB, advanced again, the result was basically the same: as soon as the tanks and artillery made their way into the open, they were scathed by fierce enemy fire, not only machine-gun, mortar, and artillery fire, but also fire from captured American anti-tank guns. Like the men, the tanks were especially vulnerable in the near white-out conditions because of their standard O.D. (olive drab) color. They were in the open, but their opponents' guns were camouflaged both by the snow and their own usually effective masking techniques.

Part of the assault, largely to take some fire off the 62nd, was the march of the 68th AIB, which jumped off at 0800 hours and immediately gained lodgement in a few houses in the town. By noon the men had advanced 400 yards, and a CP was established. The battalion made contact with elements of the "lost battalion," the 315th of the 79th Division. By 1900 the western side of Rittershoffen was cleared, at least partially due to the able support of the 500th Armored Artillery Battalion. The 68th, which initially in this fight had been attached to Task Force Wahl of the 79th, was now under the direct control of General Smith, commander of the 14th Armored Division. By evening the 62nd AIB was dug in on the Rittershoffen Leiterswiver Road, while the 25th Tank Battalion retired to Hohwiller for resupply. By the end of 13 January, the second battalion of the 315th was relieved. All in all, there was a slight positive movement in Rittershoffen for the American troops, but the cost had been high, as well as for their foes, battered by heavy tank and artillery fire.

Richard Engler, with elements of the 42nd Infantry Division still trapped in Hatten, comments that one of the purposes of the attack on 13 January was to retake the Maginot Line forts lost earlier. CCB was limited in its aggressive potential because of damage suffered the day previous, but it would attack by fire along the road between Rittershoffen and Leiterswiller. The vehicles of CCR managed to crawl over icy roads during the night to their assembly point in Niederbetschdorf. Captain Joseph Carter, Headquarters Company, who would later write the outstanding unit history of his division, was in one of the tanks:

If you were a driver, you saw nothing except the vagueness of the fields alongside, the dark strip of road a few feet ahead, the deeper black of the woods. All the light in the world was the twin red blackout-tail-lights of the vehicle in front and the indirect glow of the dials on the instrument panel. If you were a vehicle commander, you stood up every now and then to check your column—it was too cold to stay standing. You could see the long line of tanks and half-tracks behind you, creeping ominously along through the blackness, blackout lights just barely visible. Every now and then you heard the angry howl of a 500 horse tank engine as the driver shifted for a bad stretch of road.[49]

The men of the 19th Armored Infantry Battalion knew little about what was ahead of them in the attack on the 13th. Colonel Hudelson of CCR sent a ten-man patrol ahead to answer many questions about the roads, road junctions, the woods, and the streams in the Hatten area, in addition to discovering the disposition of enemy forces, but there was not a great deal of information which the patrol could collect. The 19th was teamed up with the 47th Tank Battalion along the railroad tracks to the south of Hatten. Company A was on the left, B on the right, C in reserve. The Assault Gun Platoon, the machine-gun platoon, and the mortar platoon supported the attack. The third platoon of the tankers of C-47 supported 19-A and B with a total of five tanks. While the men of the 68th AIB remembered well the battle of Rittershoffen, for the men of the 19th Armored Infantry, their special trip into hell was aimed at Hatten. As the unit history of that battalion sets the scene for the attack and the grim results:

At the same time that our battalion jumped off on the south side of the railroad, the 47th Tank Battalion had jumped off on the north side to proceed to a high ridge just west of town from the south. They did partially reach this ridge, but were stopped cold by a hail of anti-tank gun and direct tank fire. A look, out across the fields on both sides of the railroad tracks, would make anyone shudder, for artillery and mortar fire was falling everywhere, and tanks were being knocked off one right after another in the exposed fields. The enemy just had too many anti-tank weapons and tanks well placed, dug in, and on the commanding ground. To add to the fury, a raging battle was also going on with CCA in Rittershoffen, the next town to our west, but we were too busy to pay much attention."[50]

The unit history of the 47th Tank Battalion describes what happened to 2nd Lieutenant Seth D. Sprague, Platoon Leader of Third Platoon, C Company when it began its advance on the morning of 13 January:

His radio is crackling softly and then the green light on his receiver flashes on and he hears his call word crackling. "Move out! Move out!" "Wilco," he says, and switches to interphone. "Move out," he says to the driver, "Move out."

The tank engine roars suddenly in his ears and he does not hear the driver shift into gear. The tank lurches a little and pulls ahead. He feels its familiar grating progress as the steel tracks claw at the ice-hard roads. The engine roars again and the driver shifts to third. Sprague's head is even with the windows of the houses and he can see the road better before him. . . .

At 0913.

"Heavy enemy artillery fire," he says. "Can't see, visibility poor, all I know is that it's coming in!"

The enemy is on the high ground to his left; they are behind him now, in Rittershoffen. He is in his tank, the engine roaring hot behind him, creaking and jolting over the frozen ground. His turret hatch is closed now. He cannot see the infantry, but he can see the craters suddenly appear in the frozen ground ahead of him. He can feel the lift of the tank sometimes as one hits close, and he can hear the shrapnel smash angrily at the armor sides.

At 0930.

Captain Persky is on the air. "Can't contact Sprague," he says. "I've lost two tanks out of his platoon." Later it turns out to be three and fourteen men.[51]

Pfc. B. J. Trauner, Company C of the 19th, remembered waiting in the woods for the attack to commence:

The worst place to be during an artillery barrage is in a forest. With tree bursts some shrapnel sprays down so there is no protection like you might ordinarily have in an open field where you can drop flat when you hear a shell coming in. Tree bursts explosions are especially loud and visible and you can hear the chunks of shrapnel as they rocket all around you. You find yourself continually saying your little prayers, not knowing just when the end will come and how much it's going to hurt.[52]

For an infantryman it was an impossible situation: tree bursts in the forest, no protection on the frozen ground, clothes the wrong color for winter, and an enemy that seemed to have both the high ground and a vast supply of ammunition.

Companies A and B of the 19th were able to advance about 300 yards but were then caught in a withering hail of machine-gun fire both from the front and the left, and even C Company in reserve was pelted with tree bursts. It was next to impossible to find safe ground, and so the numbers of killed and wounded began to mount. Many men were occupied tending to the wounded along with the aid men, who were overwhelmed, and there were few places of refuge. B Company's communications were severed, and T/Sgt. John J. Conroy "volunteered to run the gauntlet" to re-establish communications in order to get supporting fire to allow the company to withdraw. Recorded in the unit history are acts of bravery by Pfc. Roy Thompson, S/Sgt. Raymond L. Hart, Pfc. Samuel L. Lhober, and Pfc. Jan Braley, as well as others crushed between the hammer and the anvil. Lt. Robert L. Policek and Pfc. Frank S. Bonnano ran over a field exposed to enemy fire to get some direct tank fire and artillery fire. They succeeded in bringing smoke to cover a withdrawal and shellfire to make the enemy pay for the damage they had just done to the 19th AIB. Lt. Policek, the Forward Artillery Observer, was killed later that day trying to enter Hatten in a halftrack.[53] During the carnage, one soldier watched the helmet of Pfc. Zolen Newman of B Company, "victim of a direct hit by an 88," as Carter puts it, spinning in the air.

Later in the day, at 1500 hours, General Smith, commander of the 14th AD, ordered another attack—to chase the Germans out of Hatten and "secure the forts of the MAGINOT LINE north of HATTEN." Colonel Daniel H. Hudelson, who had led the fight in the Vosges on New Year's Day with his hard-pressed task force, was given the job of leading the attack. In his own words, he details what happened:

Due to the extremely heavy small arms, mortar, tank, anti-tank, and artillery fire falling in the area of CCR, I decided to delay the attack until dusk. The Light Tank Company of the 94th Reconnaissance Squadron (12 tanks) and two companies of the 47th Tank Battalion (23 tanks) were assembled in the woods 800 yards south of HATTEN. The remaining combat troops of the 19th Armored Infantry Battalion were loaded on these 35 tanks under the command of the 19th AIB Major Forest Green at 1700 hours 13 January 1945. These tanks, loaded with the infantry, dashed into HATTEN at top speed. The infantry dismounted and was engaged in a bitter house-to-house fight within a matter of minutes. . . . By 2400 hours our attack lost its momentum. About three-fourths of the town was then in our hands. 73 casualties were incurred by the armored infantry during the house-to-house fighting prior to 2400 hours. Three of the five tanks that had been left in HATTEN were knocked out and were replaced immediately. 126 Germans were captured. 91 dead Germans were found in that portion of Hatten held by CCR at 2400 hours on 13 January 1945.[54]

But this hellish day was not over by any means. At 2115 hours, German troops attacked again, "with flamethrowers, tank and artillery fire," driving more GIs out of Hatten even as friendly artillery fire tried to protect them. The enemy thrust forward also in Rittershoffen, pushing back the 68th AIB and the 48th TB, but CCA and the third battalion of the 315th held on.

With German heavy artillery weighing in, hostile forces, as Col. Joseph Lambert reported, "converged on the Reserve Command (CCR) from Buhl and from the direction of Seltz (to the north). One-half the gain [of the 14th's attack] was lost."[55] The 68th in Rittershoffen was now proceeding house by house—progress was made slowly against a cacophony of various fires. Two enemy tanks were eliminated, and then a smokescreen was laid which allowed the battalion to reach the church in Rittershoffen. However, the third battalion was still encountering ferocious resistance. The 48th Tank Battalion, with seven medium tanks, forced its way to the road between Hatten and Rittershoffen. The German counterattack, which had driven back the 19th AIB and the 47th Tank Battalion, hurled itself against the 68th and the 47th. Both division and corps artillery responded vigorously to stifle the counterattack. In Rittershoffen, C Company of the 68th employed bazookas to stop the hostile tanks in town while A Company, still trapped in the orchard, fought alongside the 48th's tanks and terminated the enemy assault.[56] The 68th's S-2 and S-3 Journals record that 16 P-47's dropped supplies to "isolated troops of the 315 lnf." The Forward CP reported to the Rear CP, "We are held up by hvy fire from bldgs which we are attempting to destroy." As a Seventh Army History characterizes the combat:

> The battle thus boiled down to a desperate infantry fight within the towns, with dismounted panzer grenadiers and armored infantrymen fighting side by side with the more lowly infantry. Almost every structure was hotly contested, and at the end of every day each side totaled up the number of houses and buildings it controlled in an attempt to measure the progress of the battle.[57]

Committee I of the War College rendered this verdict on the action of January 13th: US artillery had fired 6,142 rounds in support of the effort and though the gains of the attack were "negligible," "a major enemy counterattack had been stopped" and American positions had increased in strength (at a high cost indeed). All of those writing about the action agreed that there would still be another week of desperate and bloody fighting. The Commander of CCB, Brig. Gen. Charles H. Karlstadt, urged the following approach to the situation: "Our battalions will seize anything in R that can be taken without undue loss of personnel. Attack by fire. There will be full watchfulness for enemy attacks, and buildings and grounds now held will be maintained. The impression of the usual attack will be given without excessive fire. Organizations will be kept in hand, in full strength to meet probable enemy attacks."[58]

The above represented Committee l's reading of the situation by 14 January. Perhaps General Karlstadt's policy at the time would not have earned the satisfaction of General George Patton in its measured caution. However, by this time the already dangerous foe, who had put up such a fight, were being reinforced by the 104th Volksgrenadier Regiment and the 47th Volksgrenadier Division.

In response to enemy tactics, CCA instructed the 68th AIB to fight toward the center of Rittershoffen, the location of the key enemy strongpoint, the ancient Lutheran church with stout stone walls. A 155mm SP (self-propelled gun) was ordered in to destroy the church, but it was "A Mighty Fortress" as Luther termed "our God." Bob Davies remembers advancing down the street carefully with one eye on the steeple of the church and the others on windows and doorways where a nervous Volksgrenadier might be waiting.

Robert H. Kamm, a "buck sergeant" in A Company of the 68th, as he portrayed himself, had survived the onslaught in the orchard and the dangerous entrance into the town: "I can remember being pinned down in the orchard and trying to 'dig in' in the frozen ground. I remember the German tanks and the flamethrowers, and also in taking part in trying to clear the town house-by-house, only always to pull back. I thought then that we'd never get out of there."[59] Corporal Earl Hardin of A-68 vividly relived the fight in town:

> I was in the fourth platoon, as part of the anti-tank crew. We didn't have it as rough as the riflemen and the machine-gunners. . . . We went into Ritershoffen on a Saturday night in January of 1945. I will never forget that night. It was after dark when we set up our 57mm gun in between the third and fourth houses on the edge of town. We had a little field of fire over in the old orchard. There was a German tank about one hundred yards away and it was on fire.[60]

One of the most amazing stories is told by Pfc. David Groves of B Company of the 19th, which was trapped in Rittershoffen, now mostly destroyed. Almost no activity, he wrote, could be conducted during daylight hours, whether the movement of tanks or armored infantry or bringing up supplies or evacuating wounded. The German guns were firing at everything that moved more than an inch, and there were no white or Red Cross flags to allow the transfer of casualties. Everything was done in darkness. The enemy had brought up some heavy tanks, Panthers or Tigers, and these prowled the streets at night after their foot patrols had located the houses in which the GIs were ensconced. Then the panzers destroyed those houses with shellfire, thus forcing the American infantry to keep rotating from one house to another.

This nocturnal routine, of course, got on everyone's nerves, waiting inside of a house or in the street for the tank to blast them. Groves again:

> One large tank, in particular, would come up the street directly in front of us at night. The tank would fire three or four rounds into our positions and then retreat. The tank had a special muffler that had been muffled. Even though we knew it was coming, and knew the approximate time, we often missed it in the shelling and firing. Again and again we suffered the loss of position and the loss of lives because of the quiet and effective movement.

One of the men, the smallest in the platoon, a man Groves calls Aaron (but not his real name) got thoroughly fed up with the situation and hatched a plan, known only to himself. He went out two nights in succession and dug a hole in a part of the street over which the tank would pass, covering it during daylight with a sheet from a closet in the house in which the men were staying. "And then he told us 'Tonite, I'm going to take out Jonah's white whale.' He picked up a couple of bazookas'." Groves especially noted that they were German bazookas, not the American bazookas so must have been either panzerfausts or panzerschrecks.

The story continues with Aaron, on the third night of the shelling, venturing out with his two weapons and climbing down into his "own private foxhole." Then he covered the hole with the white sheet and waited:

> On schedule the large, white, German Tank [sic] came up the street in the cover of darkness. After all, had it not been successful each night in destroying our positions; had it not been effective in killing or maiming us and putting us out of action; after all had it not come and gone at its own pleasure without any successful action to deter it on our part.

Aaron quietly waited in the dense darkness until the monstrous tank was just past him, with its vulnerable, less armored rear, open to Aaron's almost biblical determination to kill it:

Though we had not been able to perceive its previous comings, we did hear the explosion—that great explosion. . . . And in the light of its burning, we could see its silhouette. The tank was destroyed. The tank crew was dead. Death by that enemy vehicle would come no more.[61]

That one gratifying but small victory would not slow down the hostile juggernaut of armor and infantry. The S-2 and S-3 Journals of the 68th AIB record the messages at the end of that terrible day, the 13th of January:

2323 "Enemy tanks through L-31 5. Careful."
2344 "Additional enemy tanks and hltracks entering Rittershoffen from Hatten."

The last message for the day from the Rear CP to the Forward CP was "Order for tomorrow, 14 Jan 45, continue the attack. . . ." Neither side was willing to give a centimeter for the two towns that neither considered, of themselves, essential.

Hanging On for Dear Life

The image of hanging on for dear life applies first to both of the armies locked in a death struggle, the American and German, each of whose soldiers were suffering terribly in the conflagration in the two towns and out on the frozen ground, where there was little protection. Second, it applies to the unfortunate citizens who had not made the choice to engage in battle, mostly old men, women, and children frightened out of their wits; third, the livestock in the barns and in the fields died by the score, sometimes frightfully in the artillery barrages and other kinds of fire. For soldiers, civilians and animals alike, life was becoming a proposition without guarantee.

The American forces attacked first at dawn on January 14. CCA and CCR, which was reinforced by infantry from the 79th Division (those rescued earlier from the towns), launched coordinated attacks, CCA on Rittershoffen and CCR on Hatten. The CCA gambit was frustrated because German infantry had transformed a medieval stone church and a "stone-walled cemetery" in the western town into an impregnable stronghold. No matter how much artillery was fired at that church, it seemed invulnerable even to heavy rounds. The CCR attack in Hatten at first seemed to be going well, when by 1100 two-thirds of the town was captured "in house-to-house fighting and by mouseholing (blowing small holes in walls to gain entry) from house to house. Then came the counterattack. Preceded by intense artillery of all gauges and supported by heavy tanks and flame throwers. . . . One-half the gain was lost"[62]

On the same day, Sunday, the 19th AIB and the second battalion of the 315th Infantry, 79th Division, coordinated an attack delayed until 1100 but were driven back by aggressive counter-fire. The 19th's unit history traces what happened. Its A Company, supported by two medium tanks, cautiously traversed a road to get to their destination, the north road. The road became a street in Hatten, but when the men of A Company got there, they were met by an impenetrable curtain of fire. Bazookas blasted holes in houses where the doors or windows could not be used, with hand grenades following into the interior of the house. The two tanks sprayed the buildings with machine-gun fire, but one of the friendly tanks, although warned about an enemy tank nearby, could not fire against it and was then hit by the opposing panzer. The crew bailed out but ran the wrong way into a house and was presumably captured. A bazooka team then savaged the panzer while other men threw grenades at the exposed crew.

The always helpful S-2 and S-3 Journals of the 68th show that the action for them on the 14th began only an hour and a half after midnight, when "ey flame thrower tk in vic of church [in Rittershoffen]. One tank with Inf (Co A team) knocked out one ey tak. Four ey tks knocked out by A-68 with a bazooka within one hour after ey C/Atk. Tk with Co C Team does not know whether it knocked out ey tk or personnel carrier, either one or the other. At 0100 ey activity more or less ceased. Cannot give anything on casualties. A-68 has about thirty men left and C-68 about 60 men. Approx 100 ey killed. [A casual count of the men of A Company recorded in the 14th's History suggests that the company had lost as much as 75 or 80% of its authorized strength.] Probably knocked out two ey tks 2 ey personnel carriers and I ey self propelled gun." It was clear that no tank or half-track or other vehicle could survive in the towns or the open area, especially to the north. The CCA attack outside of town was stopped by artillery and tank fire and anti-tank guns. Likewise, the Shermans and the tank-hunter teams in the towns had taken a toll on enemy vehicles. It is difficult to know how many of the Shermans were equipped with the new, more powerful 76mm guns, but they could be deadly in a close encounter. Regardless, neither side was able to push the other out of either Alsatian town.

The petering out of the attack was recorded in the 19th's unit history. After some confusion about whether some hostile troops were friendly, two men, Lt. Robert Donovan and T/Sgt Robert Anderson, were both hit by enemy fire. Next:

> The attack continued slowly and under heavy fire. When contact was finally made with E Company at the road junction, both companies continued on down the street until after dark, when a German counterattack with infantry and tanks started from the north. E Company pulled out, leaving the right flank exposed. It was a desperate situation; A Company was ordered to withdraw immediately back down to positions on the north side of the street. The withdrawal was somewhat disorganized, but the company managed to get back across the wooded area to the road to join the rest of the battalion.[63]

As another source put it, ". . . the fighting was at very close quarters with heavy defensive fires placed on enemy troops just across the street from friend-forces." A counterattack by the 20th Parachute Regiment of the Seventh Panzer Grenadier Division was contained, and "Houses were set afire by incendiary bullets and flamethrowers," according to another.[64] How long this mutual savagery could continue was doubtful.

The rest of the day was a deadly cat and mouse game between infantry, mortar crews, machine-gun squads, and roving tanks, each looking to gain some advantage against his equally determIned enemy. In Rittershoffen the 68th AIB destroyed an enemy flamethrowing tank. Yet hostile anti-tank crews remained a similar problem for friendly Shermans. Small groups of soldiers tried to locate panzers to put fire on them from mortars or artillery, even 8-inch guns. Machine-gun fire stifled these efforts at times, but the fire from 81mm mortars and 75 or 76mm tank cannons suppressed every anti-tank fire. The enemy was busy as well. Burp gun fire was coming in from the right, and mortar rounds were also dropping on the men of the 68th—"intense" fire as the

S-2 and S-3 Journals reported. Friendly artillery fire silenced the enemy fire temporarily.

Over in Hatten the 19th AIB fight with the enemy continued. Staff Sergeant Bernard J. Trauner of Company C outlined what happened as the company advanced down the street. The infantrymen sprinted, ducked, and took cover wherever they could on the dangerous street, and then, Trauner wrote, "a German panzerfaust shell landed right in front of me that did not explode," much to his safety and relief. His squad retreated to a substantial house to find that there were three more squads from the 19th occupying the house. "We could see American artillery barrages land on the church every so often just to keep the Germans from using the steeple as an observation tower." As the combatants changed position to gain some advantage, their opponents could hear each other in the same buildings. When things momentarily quieted down, some of the men risked their lives to pull bodies out of burned American tanks until hostile fire drove them back. Trauner was impressed by the German grenadier's or parachutist's ability to dart from cover to cover moments before an American infantryman could aim and fire at him.

Later that same evening a German tank rumbled down the street and parked, and several of the tankers dashed into a house. Lt. Robert E. Lingle, the platoon leader, ordered Trauner and S/Sgt. Joseph E. Thibodeau, the bazooka team, to try to take out the tank. Trauner relates what happened then:

> We crawled to within about 40 yards of it expecting to get shot at any time but it never happened. I held the bazooka to my shoulder. Joe quickly loaded and wired it and tapped my shoulder. I took careful aim and fired. The shell glanced off the top of that tank without exploding. Since a bazooka fires a rocket shell that leaves a bright flash it would have been suicide to stay and fire again. We dashed back and literally dove into "our" house.

Artillery was called in, and one of the shells destroyed the tank but also hit the house in which the GIs of the 19th were holed up. This shell tore a hole in the leg of Frank Harris, another Staff Sergeant in Company C. He was taken out to the halftrack that served as an ambulance. (The Germans were firing on all ambulances.) Later, a mortar shell landed in the halftrack, killing almost all of the occupants—medics and patients alike.[65]

At this stage of the battle, on the 14th, there were infantrymen in every conceivable place in the towns while their comrades were dug into foxholes mostly north of Rittershoffen in the frozen ground of the orchard and the meadow. Only the lucky ones were resting back in Kuhlendorf with warm food and shelter. The fight, however, was far from over, and every GI knew that no man was safe anywhere from German artillery, mortars, tank fire, or even strafing from the new Luftwaffe jet fighters.

About nine o'clock in the evening, both the regular and the armored infantry and the tankers had to endure another hostile action by the 20th German Parachute Infantry. Both sides were struggling largely over rubble, for the towns had been pulverized and incinerated into only shadows of what had once been a lovely farming community in the gently rolling hills of Alsace. The Journals of the 68th reported enemy tank movements, and artillery was called in, a surprise which discouraged the panzers.

On the evening of 14 January in Hatten, the men of the 19th AIB were having a bad time from all the shelling, and the unit history remarks that a light tank from the 94th Cav had to make the trip with wounded thirteen times because of the enemy heavy and small arms fire. Just as had happened to the 68th on a previous night, an enemy patrol, this time of ten men, threw grenades into the OP and into a vehicle outside. There were no casualties, and the patrol was beaten off, leaving a blood trail. Another enemy patrol suffered the loss of four captured and five killed.

For the still combative 2nd Battalion of the 315th, the early morning hours produced a hostile attack with flamethrowers and German bazookas. Although F Company had to withdraw from several houses, it "beat off" the attackers. As the 19th unit history comments on this incident, "This was merely one of numberless attempts by the Germans to attack and set fire to our buildings with flamethrowers, bazookas, and by any other means possible to deny us use of the houses."[66] If the enemy could not drive the GIs out of the houses of the two towns, it would simply destroy them and push them out indirectly.

To indicate how determined the German command was, CCA

reported overnight to the 68th Rear CP that the 125th Regiment of the 21st Panzer Division was in the area, with two companies committed to the struggle in Hatten as well as a Mark V Panzer from the 22nd Regiment. The S-2 and S-3 Journals continue: A PW (prisoner of war) "believes 22d Pz Regt is in Rittershoffen with 14 Mark IV's." The attack on Hatten cited above was made known to CCA at 0545 as was its repulse by the men of the 315th.

The German command also sent reinforcements from the northeast toward Rittershoffen, and the 14th's commander, General Smith, ordered the 68th to "First bring every appropriate fire against them. Then whenever practicable follow with sml C/Atk (a small counter attack) covered fully by arty, mortar and MG fire. . . ." Both 81mm mortars and assault guns were directed to fire on the advancing enemy force. The 68th was then ordered to attack north and northeast against that force, coordinating with the fire of 155mm guns and tank fire "against church; rush in and capture church bldg and bldgs immediately surrounding." The 68th and those men of the 315th in Rittershoffen together were supported by a platoon of three to five tanks from the 48th Tank Battalion while the rest of the 48th's tanks were ordered to prepare for a counterattack. A radio intercept revealed that tank fire had shattered the steeple on the church and that mortar fire "dropped WP into church. Ey sniper fire holding up friendly troops in vic of church. Around 1630, the Forward CP informed the Rear CP that 'We are making preparations for strong defensive system for tonight'." There was some small patrol action in Rittershoffen, but things generally seemed to have settled down. Fatigue on both sides was perhaps beginning to set in as well as the sense that neither side could budge the other from its positions.

The stalemate continued in Rittershoffen on both Monday and Tuesday, 15–16 January. Some of the tank companies were now operating with minimal or no infantry coordination and support. For example, the First Platoon of C Company of the 47th Tank Battalion was brought up along with the one remaining tank of the third platoon by Captain Harold D. Persky to fire against German troops in Hatten. The 47th's unit history provides the scene:

That night Hatten was to be attacked from two directions— from the west along the main East and West road and from the south. Into the inferno came Capt. Persky with all of the available tanks of the company, attacking the southern edge of town. It was dusk, visibility was poor, and there was no supporting infantry. They penetrated about two blocks but lost three tanks in doing so. The voice of Capt. Persky had come over the radio. . . "Can't see anything. Smoke is too bad, smoke is too bad." Then, as he got through the smoke and into the fire: "Christ, there are millions of them up here. They're everywhere, they're all over the place. . . Johnny, Johnny, there's one now, get him, get him . . . ! Can't see anything, can't see anything. Smoke is too bad, smoke is too bad." And his voice went off into abrupt silence.

Three C Co. tanks were knocked out that night and Cpt. Persky and Lt. Hack were among the casualties.

The mortar platoon firing in support of the tanks got "so hot that the grease boiled out of the base caps, leaving the barrels loose."[67]

Colonel Joseph Lambert summarized the situation from the 14th to the 19th:

And so for the next five days there were attacks and counterattacks. What had been intended as a skirmish to restore the MLR had turned into a major defensive battle. The toll of friendly troops mounted and mounted. The houses in the towns, the churches, the public buildings gradually began to disintegrate under the constant artillery, phosphorus, air and flame throwing attacks. Blocks of buildings were destroyed to establish fields of fire. One hundred fifty-five[mm] self-propelled rifles were utilized to penetrate walls of strong points and phosphorus fired through the holes. The enemy continued to commit fresh troops while the strength of the friendly troops dwindled after each attack. The friendly garrison in Hatten was reinforced by a troop of cavalry [of the 94th] and Rittershofen was reinforced by armored engineers.[68]

CCB remained on the defensive northwest of Rittershoffen. With the commitment of the 125th Combat Engineers, the division, part of VI Corps reserve, had committed its own reserve, leaving essentially no reserve in place. The only other Corps reserve, the 12th Armored, was already committed and suffering badly in the Gambsheim-Herlisheim area near the Rhine.

Captain Joseph Carter's account of the fighting in the division history compliments the men of the Battalion Maintenance and Service Companies, who would venture out into the battle areas to bring supplies and retrieve tanks and other vehicles wrecked in the fighting. In the US Army in Europe, a high percentage of these vehicles were returned to combat, but Carter returns to the infantry in his re-creation of the fighting and the suffering:

> The tenseness and the fighting went on.
>
> The artillery still came in with its endless scream and whoomp! and the small arms clattered endlessly; and the enemy was in the house next door.
>
> We would be on one side of a wall and the enemy on the other and you would try to lob hand grenades over, and the infantry would set up a mortar and take off all the increments except one and try to lob shells over one house onto the next. The dead lying in the street began to get on your nerves and the tenseness of always looking down the sights, always waiting, and the artillery always coming in, and it was only a question of time before one landed in the house you were in. The fighting had reached such a vicious pitch that they [friendly artillery] tried to range in eight inch howitzers on a single house, which is sometimes like trying to hit a fly with a shotgun.[69] (Yet this howitzer was considered a very accurate weapon.)

On the evening of the 16th, at dusk, the Germans attacked again. After an initial artillery barrage there could be seen "the quick gray shapes of the enemy running, as Carter limns the picture, and next the friendly artillery rebuffing the assault. But it was not just a fierce fight between soldiers because "You could hear the shouts and the screams through the gun fire, and the screams of women trapped in the cellar of a burning house, set afire by phosphorus," a deadly element which burned almost like the neverending fires of hell—through the skin and into the bones.[70]

The intensity of the fighting became so severe that Col. Hudelson had to rescind an order to evacuate shock cases because anyone who was there qualified as a shock case.'[71]

As the battle chewed up more men, vehicles, and equipment, it became obvious that there was a desperate need for reinforcements and resupply. On the same day as the combat sketched above, as the 14th Division History has it:

> . . . an additional infantry battalion, fresh from combat in the Vosges Mountains, [the 1/315 Bn] was committed, supported by tanks, to take the northern section of Rittershoffen. One man of the assault company returned. Nine more tanks were lost. Sorties by jet planes (German) were becoming more and more frequent. Friendly air missions were flown on the enemy-held section of Hatten, on Buhl, and Stundwiller. The aid station in Hatten with medical personnel and patients was destroyed by enemy mortars. Medical aid men removed all conspicuous markings as they were fired on indiscriminately. Evacuation and resupply continued to be effected by tank and halftrack. An attempt to resupply Hatten by air drop was unsuccessful.[72]

On 17 January, the 47th Tank Battalion, minus A and Service Companies, advanced to attack toward the southeast of Hatten in order to "relieve pressure on the troops fighting in the town." The medium Shermans led the attack with the light tanks behind to provide additional firepower. When they reached the cemetery which had been a strongpoint for German infantry, all guns opened fire. But the concealed anti-tank guns were going to take a toll on the friendly tanks. As the unit history pictures it, there was ". . . a quick glimpse of figures leaving a tank; men running with blood streaming from their faces. . . . Suddenly more men of the platoon are seen on the ground. Sgt. Tom Manley crawling slowly forward, Cpl. [Wallace K] Reinert limping but moving toward a shell hole to escape the little fleks [sic] of dust which spurted and followed his movement." The debacle continued, with more tanks, both light and heavy damaged or destroyed, and men wounded and killed. "From the flank another anti-tank gun opened up, and more tanks were knocked out. 'Move back, Move back', and the remaining tanks began gyroscopic maneuvers in an attempt to dodge the shells coming in."[73]

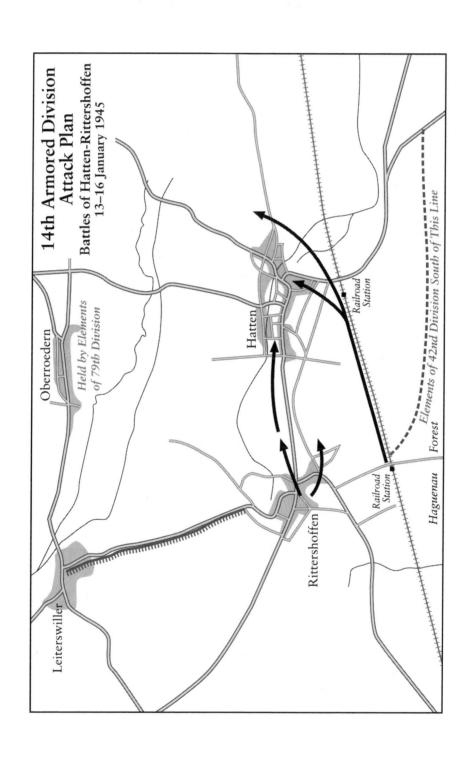

14th Armored Division
Attack Plan
Battles of Hatten-Rittershoffen
13–16 January 1945

Oberroedern

Held by Elements
of 79th Division

Leiterswiller

Hatten

Railroad
Station

Rittershoffen

Railroad
Station

Elements of 42nd Division South of This Line

Haguenau Forest

Captain Carter relates how Lt. Francis E. Marshall of C Company worked relentlessly to locate the anti-tank guns taking a severe toll on the friendly tanks. He located the guns and radioed coordinates to the artillery battalions, and they fired at the targeted guns. Nevertheless, a short time later the guns were firing again. He couldn't determine whether the artillery rounds missed or the Germans were replacing the guns and the gunners after the originals had been decimated. It took Lt. Marshall the whole afternoon to get his three remaining tanks into the town. As Carter typifies the action, "All afternoon there was fighting and all day there was dying. It is not possible to tell everything that happened. There was a Division in there and each man could tell you his own story a different way. Each man was afraid in his own way, or cowardly in his own way."[74]

The extreme horror of the struggle fostered a total candor on the part of Carter, a candor that is sometimes missing in writers on World War II. The late Stephen Ambrose's extremely positive characterization of the American soldier as superior to all others is too inflated, but, on the other side, the negative reporting of Charles Whiting, the British historian, provides a foil, the opposite picture of the American fighting man in Europe. This is too long and complex a subject to continue here, but suffice it to say, the GI's stayed in Hatten and Rittershoffen and fought as long and hard as possible. Carter has it about right.

Also on the same day, the 17th, the second battalion of the 315th executed a small attack but with little to show for it, and that sort of progress, characterized the fight until the withdrawal ordered for the 20th by Seventh Army. Grievous casualties continued to mount, due not only to wounds but to frostbite and trenchfoot, not to mention the shock cases. A number of enemy tanks and halftracks were put out of action by patrols with bazookas. Company C of the 125th Combat Engineers, which had been held in reserve, moved into Rittershoffen to destroy the bridge between Rittershoffen and Niederbetschdorf, and a large minefield was laid between Rittershoffen and Leiterswiller. The intent of army command now was to prepare to withdraw, and there was a need to interdict enemy intervention by severing the routes he might employ to prevent a successful movement back to the line of the Moder River.

An aggressive posture, however, had to be maintained. From the 17th to the 19th, as the 68th's S-2 and S-3 Journals reflect the situation, that battalion was active in maintaining it's position in Rittershoffen and patrolling actively to ascertain enemy activity. Sniper fire as well as anti-tank fire remained a problem for those maintenance personnel attempting to retrieve a damaged tank with a recovery vehcile. Companies and squads, including members of the 62nd AlB, were still embedded in the town, and requests for artillery support were often turned down because the recommended targets were too close to friendly tanks and infantry. This key instruction from the 2nd Battalion of the 315th Regiment via a messenger is revealing: "Operational Instructions for 18 Jan—Hold the ground already secured." Late in the day on 18 January, as both sides exchanged heavy artillery fire, this order came through: "Co 68 [Col. Bob Edwards] will assume responsibility for defense of ground now held, to hold at all costs. . . ." The wounded were being removed to safety as much as possible, but the 19 January S-2 and S-3 Journal entry for 1515 hours is significant: "Ambulance knocked out on last trip to Ritter shoffen." Also of import is the terse message of 1605: "(Via Officer) "One copy Secret Mine Field overlay." Clearly a withdrawal was imminent.

On 19 January, "the day of the big barrage," as Richard Engler termed it, 10,000 rounds of German artillery, mortar, and tank fire were hurled at the American troops crouched in protective positions. Friendly artillery fired only 3000 rounds. Trucks ran the road all the way to Marseilles "and returned with artillery ammunition dug out of the surf at the landing sites of the invasion of Southern France." The Gls of the 14th Armored and the 42nd and 79th Infantry Divisions were trapped for hours in an area of 400 by 200 yards in Hatten along with their dead and wounded. When aid stations were destroyed, medical personnel and patients had to relocate to other buildings, which were also under fire. When some men of the 2nd Battalion of the 232nd Infantry, freezing from the cold, built a fire to keep warm, they were spotted by the enemy, and an artillery shell landed in the fire and killed four men instantly. "The medic who rushed in to help became unhinged when he saw the carnage."[75]

The entry in the S-2 and S-3 Journals for 2100 on 19 January indicates a careful awareness of enemy troop movements outside the Hatten-Rittershoffen sector. A decidedly unfortunate event happened at Herrlisheim to the east of the two towns to the inexperienced 12th Armored Division: "Reported at Herlesheim [sic]-Gambsheim area ey

captured one Armd Inf Bn and one Tk Bn. Ey has taken Sessenheim."
This report would turn out to be correct, an event that General Devers
had suspected might happen to his inexperienced divisions. This disas-
ter possessed double import for the GIs at Hatten-Rittershoffen: first,
that two towns southeast of them on the Rhine were in enemy hands,
with strong armored and infantry units available to further threaten
Hatten-Rittershoffen; and, secondly, for the members of the 14th
Armored Division, it meant that their fellow armored division, con-
ceived, built, trained, and equipped just like them, had suffered a terrible defeat and loss of men, vehicles, and equipment. If it could happen
to the 12th, could it happen to the 14th?

The official history of the campaign in southern France tells the
grim story of what happened in the attack by the 12th against
entrenched German opposition. "The attack went badly from the start."
CCB could not cross the river outside Herrlisheim while enemy artillery,
well supplied, pounded the attempts at bridging the water. The 43rd
Tank and the 66th Armored Infantry Battalions, seconding the initial
attack, were met by strong anti-tank and assault gun positions south of
town.

The 23rd Tank Battalion and the 66th Armored Infantry Battalions were thrown into the fight to try to bypass the woods where the
hostile guns were located. Late in the afternoon, the 19th's armored
infantry had managed to gain a foothold in the town, but there was no
contact established with the 43rd except for a final message around
1330 on 17 January which indicated that the battalion commander's
tank had been put out of commission. Major James W. Logan, commander of the 19th in town, reported that during the night enemy
attacks were growing stronger, with infantry, tanks, and artillery pun-
ishing his battalion. Divisional artillery tried to mitigate the desperate
situation,

> . . . but from his central command post Logan relayed that his
> units were constantly being forced to give ground. A final mes-
> sage—"I guess this is it"—told [Major General Roderick C.]
> Allen that the battalion had been overrun. Only a few of the
> surrounded infantrymen survived to escape the darkness of the
> early morning hours. But of the tank battalion there was still no
> clue.[76]

Later, an observation plane spotted a circle of Shermans in the open, some white, but others blackened from fire and then German infantry expropriating the tanks. Bob McClarren later witnessed the scene of these tanks in perfect attack formation but burned out, a distressing scene to a tank commander. The Germans also sent a message indicating the capture of more than 300 men and a lieutenant colonel. As a result of this calamity, the division had to pull back to the vicinity of the Hagenau Forest near the Moder River.

Decades later, some of the 14th veterans would suggest that units like the 42nd Infantry and the 12th Armored Divisions had not been as effective as they might have been in the fighting in Alsace. However, to be fair to both of these criticized divisions, slightly less experienced than the 14th, both had specific difficulties. The 42nd, as Richard Engler pointed out, was thrown into the fight at the Maginot Line and the two towns not only without being battle hardened but without its organic artillery, signals, and other units necessary to its success. In effect, the regiments and battalions were thrown into the battle as an agglomeration of rifle companies without sufficient support. The 14th, on the other hand, had its tanks, assault guns, tank destroyers, and both division and corps artillery reinforcing it. The 12th was simply an inexperienced unit without experienced leaders and so walked into an ambush at Herrlisheim. The failure of units of the 12th to be able to reinforce its attack group because of the impossibility of crossing drainage canals is the same as what happened at the river in Ober Otterbach in December to the 14th. Similarly the 48th Tank Battalion and the 62nd Armored Infantry was mauled in the town of Barr in November. In that case, Dr. Jeffrey Clarke and Robert Ross Smith noted the problems of inexperienced armored units advancing into built up areas.[77]

It is also important to remember the quality of the enemy. The Wehrmacht had been fighting in Europe since September 1939 and had gathered enormous savvy while fighting in many different tactical situations. German strategy has been seen primarily as blirtzkrieg: the rapid, dynamic employment of armor and mechanized infantry, along with mobile artillery and air power, woven together by radio communications into a powerful weapon of war. Scholars still discuss this offensive phenomenon, but also critical to German success when the tide turned against them were effective defensive tactics, including camouflaged armor and anti-tank guns as well as machine-gun-positions, minefields, and booby traps. Many were the casualties and equipment losses by Allied troops from the Russian Front to that of Western Europe in 1944–45 because of the infinite variety of both personnel and anti-tank mines left in place by German troops as they retreated and left a town to advancing GIs, Tommies, or Ivans. In addition, the professionalism and training of the German Army before the last desperate months of the war fostered an aggressiveness and skill symbolized by the MG-42 machine gun teams and the Mark V and Mark VI Panzers. None of this is to say that the German Army was superior to all others, but that the battle experience it had gained before, for example, the Normandy invasion, had prepared it well for the fighting that took place in Alsace in January 1945.

Withdrawal to Fight Again

To return to the 68th Armored Infantry Battalion's S-2 and S-3 Journals for 19 January, the Rear CP reported to the Forward CP that intelligence suggested two options for the Germans based on the stalemate at Hatten-Rittershoffen and the debacle at Herrlisheim-Sessenheim. The first was that "Having gained Sessenheim they may try to break thru along line Hoffen-Oberroden-Neiderbetschdorf. We are placing most emphasis on Hagenau area and withdrawing 25 Tk Bn behind 62 lnf and moving into Bischwiller area." Also put in place was the order: ". . . also moving in 36th and 103d lnf Div's to Bischwiller area, leaving us with sole defense between Voges [sic] Mts and Hagenau Forest plus 315 lnf, 222 (-25 Tk Bn)."

   The situation had become critical not only in the general area indicated above but also in Hatten. As the Journals indicate, "19AIB has been C/Atk in Hatten—hand-to-hand battles, but have beaten ey back. RR Sta in Hatten is a strong point. Any info concerning this ey position is not to be discussed over the radio or via telephone, except in case of emergency. (PW reports that all of B-315 forced to surrender completely to ey—B-315 no longer atchd to us)." Even as Command was planning on using this battalion, it no longer effectively existed as a fighting unit. The only good news for the day was that friendly tanks and infantry still controlled some pillboxes on the Maginot Line.

   The unit history of the 19th AIB presents a slightly more positive view of the problems in Hatten. After receiving about 3,000 hostile artillery rounds per hour, every building had been damaged or destroyed. Friendly artillery responded when enemy forces gathered in the woods to attack A Company, "inflicting heavy casualties." Tanks and infantry attacked B Company and forced it back, "but they managed to get out and withdraw down the street." As the unit history continues:

> Three or four houses back a line was formed by the AT Platoon, and facing the Krauts with rifles, carbines, bazookas, and hand grenades they made a heroic stand, inflicting heavy casualties, and forcing the enemy to withdraw and reorganize. The rest of the company formed another line and outposted the barns, but the enemy never got past the first line. A German, white, camouflaged tank was brought up in the field to the south of the houses, blasting into houses and barns, inflicting heavy casualties until one of our medium tanks was brought up into position, forcing it to withdraw. Pfc. Joseph Lowinger was all over Hatten that day with a bazooka, looking for any German tank. His search was rewarded when he found one. He fired a round into the turret, but didn't stay around to see the results.[78]

Unit histories are sometimes charged with doing too much cheerleading and not enough balanced reporting, but the Journal entry for the 68th confirms much of what the 19th's History reports for 18 January.

But the armored infantry battalions were taking some serious casualties. At the end of the day on the 19th, a status report for the 68th listed the following roster of effectives in its companies:

Hq Co	6 Officers	75 Enlisted Men
CoA	3	97
CoB	4	96
CoC	3	78
		Total 346[79]

A rough count would indicate that the 68th had lost approximately 30% of its effective manpower, and it should be kept in mind that shell-shock cases were not being evacuated. Captain Reed, commander of B Company, as Sgt. Jim Kneeland saw him, was weeping over the loss of his men. Reed had been known as a very tough individual, but his casualties at Rittershoffen had been calamitous.

In the last days of the combat in Hatten, the 25th TB, after providing indirect tank fire on Hatten, moved in closer to engage the enemy's tanks and infantry with the help of the men of the 62nd AIB. This task proved to be more dangerous than firing from a distance. Several tanks were damaged or destroyed, with several men, including Lt. William H. Derr (mistakenly spelled Doerr in the unit history) killed. The odds were evened by the killing of several hostile tanks and halftracks. 1st Lt. William Geneser, who was later killed in action, led the assault against enemy vehicles:

> Lt Geneser relieved Lt. Hyde and this platoon accounted for six halftracks and one tank. Many enemy personnel were killed by the accurate fire of the 76's. It was a game of "cat watching mouse." Whenever we saw enemy personnel or vehicles moving, we fired, and they retaliated. Our rcn missions were carried out daily; Lt. [John R.] Martin's AG [assault gun] platoon fired thousands of rounds, and the counter-battery fire was excessive. The doughboys of the 62nd AIB did a wonderful job outposting the tanks of both 'C' and 'A' Companies. No one can imagine the suffering that was endured those cold nights in the tanks and foxholes. 'A' Company KO'd its share of enemy tanks and halftracks. The intense cold brought on several cases of trenchfoot. . . . Jerry first showed his jet propelled plane to us during this action.[80]

The general picture for the GIs was bleak. The order to withdraw came for the 25th TB as it would for the other battalions. According to Col. Joseph Lambert, on 19 January:

> . . . the division was alerted to break contact and withdraw to previously prepared positions behind the Moder River on 48 hours' notice. At 1300 on 20 January 1945, orders were received to break contact and withdraw during the night. One Combat Command was to fight the rear-guard action and cover the withdrawing of the 14th Armored and 79th Infantry Division and attachments. Roads were to be mined and

cratered, and bridges blown during the withdrawal. Vehicles not recovered were to be destroyed. It commenced to snow at 1500.[81]

Many of the men of the 68th didn't mind withdrawing. As the unit history typifies the fight, "We were told by men who were there, that the artillery thrown into our positions was even more savage than that which they endured at Anzio. The days wore on and we fought viciously, thinking relief for us would never arrive. It didn't! Late in the evening on the 20th we received a terse operational instruction ordering us to evacuate the town." So much for a 48 hours' notice. The 68th's history takes time to congratulate the Company Headquarters' untiring efforts to insure that the battalion was well supplied and that not only the combat soldiers had artillery shells and other ammunition but also food and cigarettes "along twenty-two hundred yards of road that was continuously interdicted with artillery and small arms fire."

Then there was the same gratitude expressed to the Medical Detachment, which ran the same gauntlett as the supply personnel with the wounded. Some of these did not survive the battle. Similar thanks were also tendered to the men of the 499th, 500th, and 501st Armored Infantry Battalions, specifically: "Magnificent artillery support coupled with the saturating fire from the 4.2 chemical mortars [of the Heavy Weapons platoons] was a constant reassurance that we were not alone in the fight. Other unit histories stated the same kind of thanks for help.

The Triple A 398th (anti-aircraft) unit along with the artillery battalions had fired thousands of rounds to keep off advancing tanks, half-tracks, and especially infantry. Its quad .50 caliber machine guns inflicted terrible damage as did the German quad AAA guns turned against ground targets. Both the Assault Gun Platoon and Tank Destroyer units fired continually for nine days and often were exposed to such counter-battery fire that they had to fire quickly and then jump into their fox-holes when enemy gunners spotted them.[82]

The 14th AD's history tells the story of Lt. Robert L. Palacek, a forward observer for the 499th, who saw how "the infantrymen were being decimated by the brutal fire; he crawled all the way across that open terrain, under fire, back to the artillery, and laid down a smoke screen under which the infantrymen were able to pull back and reorganize." Unfortunately, as he was returning to the artillery position later, he ran into an enemy position and was killed.

The 14th AD's history continues to explain how, in desperation, normal radio procedures were ignored and counterattacks beaten off by heavy artillery only. For example, "Concentration 50 Nan. 62 Able. 62 Baker. Lieut. David L. Grainger of Battery B was asked for an authentication of one fire mission. [His response]: 'Authenticate, hell; shoot it!' "[83]

Since artillery depended upon telephone lines for communication between a forward observer and the gun batteries, the wire had to be repaired, as the history of the 499th AFA indicated:

> During this period, one of the greatest problems was the maintenance of wire communications. As with everything else, it was done under constant enemy artillery and mortar fire. Many heroic stories could be told of wire crews who crawled through ditches to trace breaks, while the snipers fired at them, and the artillery landing around them made new breaks when it didn't kill them. No matter what the hour or the weather, no matter what the danger involved, they toiled night and day to maintain the life-blood of artillery communications.[84]

The only reasonably safe place for an observer was inside an armored vehicle, but even that was not always secure. Lt. Phillip Wrathall, Hdqrs. Co., 500th AFA, in a tank doing observation, spotted a Mark IV, fired, and destroyed the enemy tank although several men in his tank were wounded. For fire-direction centers and the firing batteries, observers had to maintain intense vigilance, despite serious sleep deprivation, to deliver thousands of shells within even 30 seconds of an infantry call for help in stemming the tide of German infantry and armor and the thousands of rounds or mortar and artillery fired at them. On some occasions, there were as many as seven artillery battalions firing in support.

Enemy strafing, including from the new German jet aircraft, provided many anxious moments for all units involved in the fight, artillerymen included. The 398th AAA fired at incoming planes and, as indicated before, at surging enemy infantry:

The 398th AAA was doing its most savage firing of the war at the planes that came over again and again and again and turning the brutal power of the multiple .50's on ground troops; and more than once those terrible guns saved the bacon for 14th infantrymen.[85]

Liaison pilots stayed in the air in their tiny planes as much as weather allowed and directed the firing of guns of all calibers, including 240mm, to frustrate the attacks of the enemy.

Another fortunate event for the friendly side was the use of 155mm howitzers firing over sights firing with devastating results against a company of Mark VI Tiger Tanks. The more usual case, of a Tiger company of panzers fighting a company of Shermans or even the Tank Destroyers with their 90mm guns, was just the reverse. The Shermans were always outgunned until the newer versions, the "Easy Eights," with their more powerful 76mm guns were introduced in January. Even then, they were no match for the Mark V Panther or the Mark VI Tiger or the King Tiger. The armor on the Tigers was about twice that of the Shermans. There were more than a few complaints from American tankers that their rounds simply bounced off the German monsters. Their fear that they were in an impossible situation was justified. At the very end of the war, some new models had a possible chance against the Tigers. Prior to their appearance, the argument on the Allied side had been made that, "Though outgunned by German tanks and with insufficient armour to compete in the later stages of the war, the sheer numbers produced overwhelmed enemy armoured forces."[86] Considering the fact that each Sherman had a minimum of four crew members, if four Shermans were trying to defeat a Tiger at long range, the Tiger could, and did on occasion, destroy all four tanks and kill from sixteen to twenty soldiers, sometimes American and sometimes British. Belton Y. Cooper, who was a tank maintenace officer in Europe during the war, wrote a pungent book entitled *Death Traps*, the title of which represented the Sherman tanks against the German panzers. That is why American tankers would have loved to hear the story of the 155mm guns against the panzers defeating, destroying, and demoralizing the "Panzertruppen" and their machines.

But to return to the end of the battle of Hatten-Rittershoffen. It was encapsulated in the 68th AIB's history:

On the 20th of January, upon reception of the operational instruction, we gave little thought to a physical relief. Getting away from this hell was paramount in our minds. When darkness fell, platoon by platoon set out in a driving blizzard from the rear of Rittershoffen to travel the snow covered open terrain to Kuhlendorf.[87]

The men of the 68th were "proud to have fought toe to toe with some of Hitler's best, his 21st Panzer, 25 Panzergrenadier, 7th and 10th SS Paratroopers. . . ." Because the battalion was attached to the 315th Regiment of the 79th Division, its commendation for valor came from its commanding officer, Col. Andrew Schriver:

During this time, the battalion was defending it left (N) Section of RITTERSHOFFEN and the 3d Bn, 515th lnf, the right (S) section. This battalion made repeated efforts to enlarge their position in the town. Repeated enemy attacks, enemy infantry accompanied by flame throwing tanks, were repulsed both day and night in their sector, inflicting heavy casualties upon the enemy. Their aggressive attitude and high morale under such adverse conditions of continuous enemy attacks and shell fire (Arty and mortar) demonstrated a high standard of morale and efficiency. Their cooperation in every way was superior. The withdrawal from such close proximity of the enemy was brilliantly executed.[88]

The withdrawal (no source calls it a "retreat") took place in both darkness and snowfall. The winter conditions, which had tormented all the battalions in Hatten-Rittershoffen, at least helped them at this crucial time. The 68th's history quotes Gen. Jacob L. Devers, the VI Corps Commander, as saying, perhaps with some exaggeration considering the fighting at Normandy and in Russia, that this was "The greatest tank battle on the continent." Similarly, the 14th AD's History echoes some of the positive news reporting back home about the fighting in Alsace:

It was a short pull back to the Moder River, and the papers told how the Seventh Army had out-foxed Von Rundstedt, how it had fought his counter-attacks until the last second, and then pulled out and he was swinging at air and the Seventh was waiting for him again as he stumbled off balance.[89]

This is a pretty sanguine reading of what happened in the Hatten-Rittershoffen "inferno," for that is what the civilians and commentators from Alsace thought of it. Both sides in the fight had probably had enough, and the fact that the 14th Armored Division, the reserve for VI Corps, had been committed to battle and, though valorous, had been beaten up indicates that a withdrawal was a wise decision. The earlier stretching out of VI and XV Corps, from the Vosges to near the Rhine, had considerably weakened the MLR for Seventh Army. Likewise was the case for the French First Army, which with the help of the veteran 3rd Infantry Division, was holding the Colmar Pocket against the Germans. This assessment by Jeffrey L. Clarke and Robert Ross Smith of the Alsace fighting is just:

> The Seventh Army could not be strong everywhere, and the Germans probably could have penetrated Brooks' lines almost anywhere on the long VI Corps front without, however, achieving decisive results. . . . But Devers was probably accurate when he stated that "Ted Brooks [VI Corps Commander]. . . fought one of the great defensive battles of all time with very little."[90]

VI Corps had terminated the last powerful thrusts of Operation Northwind, and the analysis done by the War College in 1949 concludes that "the action was a strategic success," but it also concludes that the 14th had had insufficient time to organize. One criticism from that report argues that "CCB elected to take up what was termed an 'active defense' rather than continue the first-day's attack, a prime violation of the principle of the objective." Both sides, the report scolds, made attacks "piecemeal."[91] It is just possible that the reason for this strategy was the focus on rescuing and relieving the remnants of the 42nd and 79th Infantry Divisions holding on by their fingernails in both towns.

Col. Hans von Luck, Commander of a Kampfgruppe, who had been involved in serious fighting since Normandy, at the end of the combat, judged that "After eight days we still didn't know whether we were continuing to fight for reasons of prestige, or whether there was a tactical significance to our holding the positions." He also claimed that during the battle, "Artillery duels on a colossal scale took place every day, heavier than we had experienced in Normandy."[92] In fact, one veteran of the artillery barrages remembered that

> The artillery blasted so much that when it was over, it was hard to tell which were the streets and which were the houses. Hardly a house had a roof left and hardly a house a wall. The dead were lying on the streets, on the ground, in the cellars and in the rubbish. Kraut soldiers, American soldiers, civilians and the girl who tried to run out of her cellar and only got 15 steps.[93]

Lt. Col. James W. Lann, Commander of the 47th Tank Battalion, thought that, "for sheer bloody vicious tenseness, hour after hour and day after day, Hatten was the worst."[94]

All in all, the withdrawal was a tactical and strategic necessity. The authors of the official history of the fighting in southern France described the decision by the VI Corps Commander to get out of a bad situation:

> Brooks finally elected to withdraw. On the night of 20–21 January those units of the VI Corps north of the Hagenau forest pulled back, moving southwest toward the Moder River. The movement took the attacking Germans by surprise and prevented them from pursuing the retreating Americans, giving Brooks time to organize.[95]

Of course, withdrawals or retreats do not win battles or wars. The American soldiers fighting in Alsace were originally ordered to "establish the MLRI" something which was impossible to accomplish, given the circumstances. They were outnumbered and possibly outgunned, although American artillery did an outstanding job of supporting the infantry and fired almost countless rounds of medium artillery shells. A great number of the German losses in men and materiel were caused by swift and accurate artillery fire. The upgunned Shermans in January 1945 held their own against the hostile Mark IV's and even heavier German panzers because of the electric traverse mechanism in close-in combat. Yet the GIs stuck in the orchard and the fields and in the towns had to cope with increasing German reinforcement while the friendly reserve was more than fully committed. Further, the inexorable pressure of German grenadiers and paratroops increasingly wore down the American soldiers holding on by their fingertips. The analysis of the battle in the official history, like the Committee I report of the War College, faults VI Corps for allowing its tanks to be reduced by attrition in the confines of the towns. Clarke and Smith agree that the same thing was happening to the panzers, and conclude that General Brooks "had no choice in this matter." The dynamics of the battle determined operations and tactics, not the other way around.

With reference to the question of the effectiveness of the 14th Armored, the official history deduces that the division did much better than the 12th Armored because of its experience. It had concluded that the tragedy at Barr in November was a result of the 14th's earlier inexperience. All in all:

> Success in battle thus came down to the ability of infantry forces on both sides to attack and defend and the ability of their corps, division, regiment [and Combat Commands], and battalion commanders to position them effectively on the battlefield and make the best use of supporting manpower and machinery. In the end it was the capability of the machine to serve the foot soldier in the field, rather than the reverse, that proved decisive.[96]

That the soldiers of the 14th Armored Division, the 79th Infantry Division, and the fresh but inexperienced 42nd Infantry Division did as well as they did generates the strategic and operational question: what would have happened if in December General Eisenhower had not ordered the thinning out of both VI and XV Corps? Could VI Corps have driven the Germans back at Hatten Rittershoffen to the Rhine River with a sufficient number of divisions? An even more tempting question to raise is, what if in November Ike had allowed the fully supported Seventh Army to make a bold attack on the flanks of Patton's Third Army in the Lauterburg salient in a northeasterly direction, a possibility mentioned in the official history. General Devers, the Commander of VI Army Group, was deeply disappointed by the Supreme Commander's refusal to let him push aggressively at the end of November before the German Army had time to regroup after being chased up the Rhone Valley. It is possible that the entire campaign could have been changed on terms advantageous to the Allies.[97]

However, on the night of 20–21 January, all these speculations were moot. The withdrawing American forces had to establish a defensible bridgehead on the banks of the Moder River, a tricky maneuver in the best of times not only to withdraw safely but to dig in at a river's edge. To further complicate matters, the troops were jumbled together in two towns separated by a kilometer of open ground which had already cost lives and vehicles. Establishing and maintaining a procedure for getting out before the enemy knew of the withdrawal presented something of a challenge. Col. Joseph C. Lambert, the C-3 for the 14th, who was involved with this problem, remarks that the deep snow, the two divisions of infantry plus one of armor, including attachments, the corps engineers, the heavy artillery, the variety of vehicles, the troops walking out along with refugees while new snow fell—all these elements contributed to the difficulty of the maneuver. Lambert affirms, "It must be conceded that under the conditions the VI Corps did a magnificent job in controlling and coordinating. Owing to weather conditions and rear guard action it was two days before the enemy reacted."[98]

The perspective on the German side was sketched by Col. Hans von Luck. On the morning of the 21st, "a suspicious calm lay over and around Rittershoffen. . . . Everything was quiet; even the enemy guns were silent." At the conclusion of the battle he regretted that "There are no winners or losers here. So what was it all for? When several civilians crept out of the ruins, they had tears in their eyes. One of the officers apologized, 'We are so sorry for you and your lovely village. This damn war! For you it's now at an end'."[99]

This apology was appropriate, especially since it was German soldiers, although not necessarily under von Luck's command, who had been ordered to burn those houses which might be used for shelter by the American soldiers. The colonel said, "The Amis have gone," and the thoughtful and serious Colonel decided to visit the church and to order a lance-corporal to "tread the bellows" of the organ, which was still working. The Colonel sat down at the organ:

> . . . on the spur of the moment I began to play Bach's chorale Nun danket alle Gott [the hymn in English known as "Now thank we all our God"]. It resounded through the ruins of the

church, followed by old women and children, who knelt on the ground and quietly prayed. My men were not ashamed of tears.[100]

The old question about the German mind and culture arises: how could a nation which produced Bach and Beethoven produce a Hitler and a Himmler? Colonel von Luck's sentiments about the carnage of the battle are well taken once the fight is over, but the actions of some German soldiers were less than noble. If Captain Joseph Carter is correct about the following sequence during the struggle, it is no wonder that the attitude of some men of the American troops is tinged with bitterness:

> One German came into a house occupied by infantrymen, his hands high, and said: "Kamerad." He was told to come in; he stepped aside and a German behind him sprayed the room with burp gun fire.
> The enemy set fire to the houses with incendiary bullets. German soldiers turned the nozzle of a flame thrower into a cellar packed with Alsatian men and women and children . . . the screams could be heard above the tank fire.[101]

Carter concludes his chapter on the battle in a similarly human and humane way:

> There was relief, but not a real relief. Behind [the survivors] were their friends and their comrades, in the rubble of those towns and on those fields, and more of their friends and comrades were in the hospitals. And they were reluctant to leave. They did not want to pull out. They did not want to give up the bloody vicious towns later compared to Stalingrad. They felt a little as if they had fought and suffered and died in vain. . . . And it was a bitter grating night, that night, a night of tears in the soul, and it snowed.[102]

The orders for withdrawal given in the S-2 and S-3 Journals for 20 January are too complex and detailed to provide here, but suffice to say that the withdrawal was to be orderly. For example, "Absolutely no equipment of any kind or description to be left behind for the ey." The minefields around Rittershoffen were to be "closed," and when all was completed, the 68th AIB, which was under the command of Task Force Wahl of the 79th Infantry Division, would revert back to the control of the 14th Armored Division. The unit history of the 68th AIB summarizes casualties for the "Rittershoffen Operation":

Killed in Action	13
Died of Wounds	07
Missing in Action	18
Wounded in Action	128
Total Casualties	166[103]

Information from the Historical Division, Department of the Army, reproduced by Colonel Lambert in his article, stresses the deadliness of the fighting and compares the losses of the 14th to those in the Battle of the Ardennes suffered by a combination of the 101st Airborne Division and the 4th Armored Division in combat around the town of Bastogne. It should be remembered that the 14th's losses occurred between 11 and 20 January while the Ardennes losses happened between 10 December and 10 January, that is, about ten days compared to a full month. While the expenditure of ordnance, from 30 caliber to 81mm, indicates that the Bastogne defense expended more, the losses in killed, wounded, or missing indicates, and especially the wounded, from Lambert's perspective, that the fighting was worse in intensity around Hatten-Rittershofen than around Bastogne. Lambert pursues his parallel between the situation in the Ardennes and Alsace:

At the height of the Ardennes offensive, Allied troops were faced with superiority in numbers and fire. It was a hard, bitterly contested battle. In Alsace there was an equally aggressive and determined enemy. In addition to having superiority in numbers and fire, he had the advantage of terrain and observation, short supply lines, and a plentiful supply of ammunition. There, also, was a hard, bitterly contested battle. . . . The 14AD, undermanned and outgunned, undertook to relieve remnants of two beleaguered infantry battalions and restore a four-thousand-yard portion of the Corps MLR.

As recently as 2005, the men of the 14th Armored Division have felt that they had been slighted by historians and by those who planned and created the long delayed World War II Memorial in Washington. Representatives of the division pleaded for one of the baffle markers to reflect the baffle of Hatten-Rittershoffen, but to no avail despite the many casualties sufered by them and by both the 79th and 42nd Infantry Divisions. This feeling of neglect surfaced even before the war for the G-3 of the 14th, already quoted, knew how little attention was paid to the Alsatian campaign in the winter of '44–'45 by General Eisenhower and the staff at SHAEF. Col. Lambert's unhappiness with Ike's report to the Congress and the Houses of Parliament is reflected in his intense memories of the battle: "For the manure—, town-ridden troops disposed in the Alsatian Plains and along the rocky reaches of the Vosges, the perspective was considerably more sinister," and, he continues, the soldiers "who were occupying the ground just had an itchy uneasiness that they were being surrounded." The feeling was so strong at the beginning of OP Northwind in the mountains and remained strong as the terrible losses mounted in and around the Maginot Line.[104]

As Richard Engler, who was there, reported on the aftermath of the battle, the German engineers bulldozed the streets clear and made two mass graves, one for their dead and one for the "Amis" dead. The civilians were assigned the less than pleasant task of burying bodies. One of the townspeople, Emile Heimlich, a woodsman, volunteered along with a friend to help bury the dead. His friend asked him which of the two groups of dead he wanted to bury. "Emile replied, 'It makes no difference. There are plenty of both'." On the burial site for the GIs was the sign, "Hier ruhen 58 Amerikanische Soldaten," i.e., they were supposed to "rest in peace." Emile, a practical man, as he buried the soldiers, removed their coats, sweaters, boots, and other clothing and gave them to the freezing civilians."[105]

After the battle, the dreadful sight of what modem weapons can do to human bodies and minds impales the memory for a long time. More than half a century later, artilleryman Fred Talbot, Battery A of the 501st AFA, still sees himself riding in a halftrack "to catch up to our battery." The men in the track could see in the distance to their left a number of Sherman tanks stationary in an orchard, a scene which did not make much sense to them at the time. They dismounted the halftrack and walked over to look at the scene more closely. Talbot reframes the picture:

> I climbed up on the first one. Looking down in the open top, a sight I never want to see again, shocked me. Below me was a Commander with skin melted like wax, from top to bottom. Partially visible, at least 3 other guys were in the same condition. Unbelieving, I yelled to the other guys to check one of the other tanks. They too, had a similar sight, much to our distress.
>
> Standing on the top tank I counted, quickly, almost 75 tanks. . . .
>
> At the conservative rate of four men per tank, we were looking at 300 plus.
>
> Good God, what happened? A lot of mothers were going to get bad news.[106]

Many conclusions can be drawn about the Battle of Hatten-Rittershoffen, and several of the important ones by professional historians or by participants in the combat are recounted here. They are mostly military ones. Yet, looking at the horrors of modern industrial warfare suggests that it ought, by rational people, to be considered insane. The Homeric Age of heroism has dictated to the West its basic scale of values—with courage supreme and cowardice unthinkable. As long as men were fighting with swords, axes, and spears, there is a certain sense to Homeric values, but when men can be melted down "in the heat of battle," in this case the furnace of a burning tank, perhaps a certain degree of rethinking is necessary. This is hardly a novel or shocking sentiment, but it seems to need endless repetition.

When retired Major Bob R. McCarren, who had fought with the 25th Tank Battalion at Hatten-Rittenshoffen, returned for a visit in 2008, he was struck by the massive change. The only sign that a great battle had been fought there was the memorial in the town square.

Chapter 6

OHLUNGEN FOREST: GETTING EVEN & GETTING HURT

The Hatten-Rittershoffen struggle had forced the 14th Armored Division, along with Seventh Army, onto the defensive, with its MLR along the Moder River. The 42nd and the 79th Infantry Divisions shared with the 14th AD the responsibility of holding along this line for some time while rebuffing attacks by a determined and experienced foe through the woods and across the river and its creeks.

CCA and CCB were thus forced to be static throughout the rest of January and February in the vicinity of such towns as Wilwisheim, Saessolheim, and Furchhausen. Positions likewise in Ohlungen, Winterhouse, Batzendorf, and Pfaffenhoffen had to be maintained in this sector south of the Moder River and west of the key city of Hagenau. This town was only 24 kilometers north of the strategic city of Strasbourg, which had to be held at all costs. It was kept in Allied hands by the French First Army supported by the veteran American 3rd Infantry Division of Seventh Army.

However, much had to be done by the 14th to compensate for the losses of men, vehicles, and equipment at Hatten-Rittershoffen. Telephone lines were run and repaired, a vast number of refugees had to be processed away from contested areas, and A Company of the 84th Medical Detachment, attached to the 68th AIB, performed the critical function of receiving and medically transferring the seriously wounded to hospitals in the rear. "The Company had been receiving ever-increasing numbers of casualties from shellfire, and men suffering from trench foot, frostbite, frozen toes and fingers . . . [and] handled 367 casualties during the month of January. B Company helped out day and night for nine days."[1] And this was only for one battalion.

176

The ordnance men of various battalions and the Division Trains were also kept busy with tanks and halftracks that had been damaged, some quite seriously. Some were total losses, especially after German gunners kept firing to cause tanks to erupt in flames and thus be unserviceable. However, as many as a third of the 14th's wrecked tanks were salvaged and repaired. To increase armored efficiency in combat at this time, upgraded tank models, such as the M4 A3E8, were issued to many tank battalions in Europe. These were medium tanks but with a new, more powerful 76mm gun than the old 75mm and with a muzzle brake to protect accompanying infantry from blast. They were also fitted with wider tracks to navigate successfully on muddy ground. Happily for American tankers in the winter of 1945, the armor on these newer models on the front plate or glacis was increased to nearly three inches. By this time in the fighting ordnance was welding cradles or racks on the front and sides of tanks to carry sandbags or even concrete to fend off rounds from enemy guns and panzerfausts. Over the course of the first twenty days of January, including the Hatten-Rittershoffen destruction, ordnance for the 14th had repaired 104 tanks, 65 half-tracks, 200 wheeled vehicles, and 470 guns and instruments."[2]

The men of the 68th Armored Infantry Battalion, like their comrades in other divisions, were happy to be away from the fighting in Waldwolwisheim, but as its History remarks:

> . . . CC'B' kept us on alert and after two days ordered us to a strategic position at Batzendorf due west of Hagenau and 2,000 yards in the rear of the front line held by the infantry divisions. We were again to play the role of roving center and back up the lines in the event of a breakthrough. Corps was now holding a defensive position along the Moder River. Our attachments for this operation were 'B' Company, 25th Tank Battalion, and 1st Platoon, 'B' Company, 125th Engineers.[3]

After German troops had forced a bridgehead across the river, the battalion was committed to the fight. The attack in Ohlungen Forest designed to breach the MLR occurred either very late on 24 January or very early on 25 January, for the S-2 and S-3 Journals of the 68th report that at 0010 hours "Ey atk is under control. 79 Div has driven ey back across creek. Seems that everything will be quiet for the rest of the night." Yet a Report of Operations for the 14th AD on the 25th/26th indicates that:

> At 0140 January, the enemy was encountered in the woods north of Ohlungen, but first messages did not mention the enemy strength. An hour and a half later, Col. Lucas [Edward D. of Hdqtrs. Co.], who was maintaining liaison with the 222 Infantry, reported that the German attack was continuing. By 0415, the enemy was in the woods and the 222nd Infantry regimental reserve [42nd Inf. Div.] was being committed at the same time.[4]

Just "fifteen minutes later, the report came back that tank motors were being heard in the woods and at 0455, the 14th's CC'B' was alerted for a move at any time." Captain Joseph Carter dramatically reports that "The enemy broke through the infantry on January 25. The enemy crossed the Moder River and established a bridgehead in the Ohlungen Forest."

The S-2 and S-3 Journals of the 68th overlap their messages with the action described above. At 0345 on the 25th, CCB, in control of the 68th AIB and attachments, ordered its commander to "Send out rcn patrols by 0415 to reconnoiter routes to N. Take NW ½ km. then NE to Ohlungen . . . to first road jct S to Batzendorf. . . . Woods N of Ohlungen infested with ey." It is good to keep in mind that the woods north of the Moder River were the large Hagenau Forest while the smaller woods south of the river were Ohlungen Forest, with the MLR on the south shore of a river not difficult to cross. The 499th Armored Field Artillery had discovered that the "ey [was] feeling out entire line N of Ohlungen" and that the 25th Panzer Grenadiers were identified in this zone along with 15 tanks. The S-2 and S-3 Journals also reported that Companies E and F [the 68th] were "penetrated by ey. . . Co's B and [D] stopped at edge of woods." The 68th and its attachments were still a part of the 14th AD's CCB, which warned that "Orders may never come, but if they do, we will have to move on very short notice." To make matters worse, "Ey put bridge across creek. Unknown number of ey tks moving E to W. Reduced ey at [coded location]. Ey overran sqd just E of Neuberg," a small town on a road adjacent to the river and north-northwest of Ohlungen.

Richard Engler traced the boil-up of this threat at the edge of the river adjacent to Ohlungen Forest. The 47th Volksgrenadier Division, a regiment of the 25th Panzer Grenadier Division, troops from Parachute Infantry Regiment 20, and a battalion of Parachute Regiment 21 struck suddenly. The intent of the assault was to seize Neubourg, "push through Ohlungen Forest," take Uhwiller and doubly envelop Hagenau. In addition, the plan foresaw taking the high ground and driving into Schweighouse, also as part of the strike at Hagenau. German paratroopers aimed energetically for the firebreaks in the forest and crossings of the nearby Moder River. The men of the American 42nd Infantry Division stood in their way, without a great deal of tank or artillery support at first.

The desperate fighting began on the "freezing foggy night of January 24–25." A great number of what Engler called "little wars broke out in the contested area. . . . An armored force from the 14th Armored Division was being prepared to counter this attack." A task force composed of men from the 232nd Infantry Regiment and the 68th AIB supported by tanks was to repel the hostile advance of the grenadiers and the paratroopers. The hostile advance was conducted in a southwesterly direction, and the defenders faced it in a northeasterly direction from across the river.[5] As the 68th History continues the narrative:

> The call came on January 25th as the "Krauts" had forced bridgehead across the river and into Ohlungen Forest. Our mission was to attack and restore the main line of resistance on the Moder River.[6]

At 1230, according to the S-2 and S-3 Journals, "Troops jumped off on atk N of Ohlungen, objective to by-pass Schweighause [sic] and in a pincer movement cut ey off and prevent him from further pentrating [sic] woods along creek W and N of Schweighause, thus re-establishing the MLR." The First Platoon of D Troop of the 94 Cav Recon were "to act as a screening force on right flank for protection of 68."[7]

Richard Engler further explains the intent of the plan:

> The 68 AIB of 14th Armored Division, with supporting tanks, was to enter the woods at the southeast corner and begin, just

after noon, a push up toward the firebreak and to assist in the relief of Schweighouse—where the situation was still obscure and confused. The 232nd Infantry was also on the way to assist the infantry in securing Schweighouse.[8]

The "Report of Operations" of the 14th for the day summarized what happened in the clash: "They met little opposition at first and soon encircled the woods north of Ohlungen. First reports said some 500 enemy were in the wooded area. CC'B' was given the mission of seizing the ground west of Ohlungen and sending patrols north of the Moder at 1415. During this part of the mission, an ambulance was requested by the Fwd CP [Forward Command Post]."[9]

The S-2 and S-3 Journals also reported that tanks (the 25th Tank Battalion) were firing against enemy "burp guns in the woods," this at 1355 hours. "By 1522, the 68 AIB had moved its CP to Ohlungen [from Batzendorf], while the infantrymen and tanks continued to fight forward." The 68th began capturing prisoners, at first just a few but then many more. The enemy had been taken by surprise, and "In approximately three hours, the 68th reported that it had killed some 150 Germans and taken 50 prisoners." But the battle was not quite over yet. The Journals further record that at 1555, "Ey lnf rptd moving S along stream—unknown number." By 1600, "Troops continuing to advance to tie-in point on left."

The 68th's History records the intense motivation of the GIs:

We moved out from Bettendorf [sic] with our tank attachment looking for revenge for Rittershoffen and Ober-Otterbach. This was to be an attack in depth; 'C' Company with one platoon of tanks followed by 'B' with one platoon of tanks were to attack the woods. Headquarters Company platoons were to give supporting fire from Winterhausen [with heavy weapons] where the battalion's rear CP was set up. 499th Armored Field Artillery Battalion was in general support. The attack jumped off at approximately 1500 hours [two and one-half hours after the time in both the Journals and the Report of Operations] and the Krauts were surprised. 'C' Company had advanced to the edge of the woods and the 'Krauts' thinking they had them cut off came out of their holes; but little did they know that this was a depth attack, and they still had to face another infantry company. The tanks opened fire at point blank range and used their machine guns coupled with the deadly fire of the infantry companies. Thousands and thousands of rounds of small arms were spit out at the confused enemy, taking a severe toll by this savage attack.[10]

It is difficult to imagine how the Panzer Grenadiers could have had such faulty intelligence about the force attacking them. They knew that they faced an armored division and so should have been aware of the hostile armor. Even if they hadn't been forewarned, surely they could have heard the sound of the Sherman tanks, which were stationed not that far away from them. Whatever the reason, they were operating at a severe disadvantage.

The History of the 14th AD also provides some of the details about the initial movement of the 68th AIB:

The 68th passed through the Infantry Division troops [42nd probably] and launched its attack in depth. C Company with Lieut. [Arthur P.] Hyde's platoon of medium tanks [B Co. of the 25th TB] in the assault, B Company with Lieut. [Wilson A., B-25] Geneser's platoon following. Headquarters Company (68) and Lieut. William A. Close's platoon of B-25 were in support.

The goal of this movement was to capture Schweighouse and interdict all roads leading in and out. The Line of Departure was the axis Batzendorf Ohlungen. Fortunately, Lt. Hyde's eyesight was outstanding in that he located an enemy machine-gun position and blew it away with his 76mm gun. Often it was impossible in forests to spot concealed emplacements, as in the forests of the Vosges Mountains and, notoriously, in the Hurtgen Forest to the north. Captain Carter repeats the same episode as the authors of the 68th History in which the German infantry made their fatal mistake. "The Germans jumped from their foxholes as the first echelon passed, and were caught in a withering cross fire of tank, machine gun and infantry fire. Lieut. Close's platoon opened fire at point blank range."[11] Carter singles out Staff Sergeant Edward H. Thomas, who led his section of tanks to a clearing where he waited for the grenadiers to emerge. They did so, and his tankers round-ed up 75 of them, who were only too willing to be captured. The Journals inform us that at 1640 hours "approx 100 ey debouched from woods . . . Approx 50 ey wounded, 20 to 25 killed and balance returned into woods. Only resistance encountered was ey SAF [small arms fire] resistance."

We pick up the story again with the enthusiastic description in the 68th's *History*:

> Numerous prisoners were taken, many were killed and many more wounded. There were so many dead Germans on the field that it provided them an opportunity to employ the old Japanese trick of playing dead. Our men were nearly duped with this suicidal attempt, but in each case the deceit was detected before the malignant plot could mature.[12]

One of the toughest officers according to Bob Davies was Captain M.A. Reed, who, on this occasion, trusted no hostile troops. He stuck the muzzle of his carbine several inches deep into the stomach of a possum-playing soldier, who then jumped up "into his face."

Darkness was coming in these short winter days, and no further advance was planned, so the GIs dug in for the night. The authors of the 68th *History* commented on a change in German tactics which probably resulted from the fact that they began to realize, at least some of them, that they were losing the war. As a result, they began to observe the rules of the Geneva Convention. They permitted "us to treat the wounded unmolested."[13] It had been only recently, at the battle of Rittershoffen, that even medics were fair game for German snipers. The return to chivalry on both sides must have been appreciated by all.

As the Report of Operations for the 25th summarized the end of the day,

> At 1920, the enemy held all of Schweighausen except for two or three houses at the eastern, southern and western tips of the town. The 68th attacked north through a clearing in the woods west of the town, capturing about 40 members of the 7th Parachute Division and killing some fifty other Germans in the same vicinity.[14]

The "Report" goes on to say that a platoon of tanks from B-25 and a squad of B-68 advanced on their own to Schweighausen and made contact with the CO of the 222nd Infantry, which was situated defensively at the western edge of the town. The two "B" Companies were holding a position "1,000 meters northwest of Schweighausen." The 68th was assigned the task of deploying between the towns of Schweighausen and Neuberg and establishing a defensive position.

The plan at that stage was for Company A of the 22nd to attack in a north-westerly direction through the woods. As they fulfilled that assignment, they became "engaged in a close fire fight." The German plan was to advance over a bridge which their engineers had constructed across the Moder River north of Ohlungen, and there, as it turned out, more fighting would erupt. In opposition to that, the Third Battalion of the 314th Infantry was directed "to advance to the east and join the 68th at the midpoint of the road between Neuberg and the town of Schweighausen," for which both sides intended to fight

Because of the success of the 68th AIB in moving forward, their CP gravitated to Ohlungen, with the section of tanks from B Company of the 25th.

At the end of the day, the 68th had set up its defensive perimeter for the night and reported back to the Rear CP that the battalion "had killed approximately 150 Germans and taken about 50 prisoners."[15] The 68th's History expresses the exultation of the infantrymen in their victory over an enemy that had been difficult to defeat in all previous encounters:

> The night was cold and the snow wet as our happy warriors dug in for the night. Tomorrow we would resume the attack. Morale had been lifted; we had taken revenge for Rittershoffen and Ober-Otterbach; the boys could hardly be restrained, and they were anxious to finish the job. Nevertheless they dug their holes and loaded wounded "Krauts" on tanks for evacuation to our busy, bloody aid station where Captain Battenfeld and his angels of mercy administered to their wounds.
>
> A new trick had been acquired; one of our boys, Pfc Kenneth L. Bandy, had a very effective way of capturing Jerry prisoners. His method was to empry [sic] a clip from his Ml rifle

at a German in a foxhole, then quickly rush forward and take him prisoner before he could look out of his hole. His aim was unerring, and twelve prisoners were taken in this manner.[16]

Since a clip, when ejected from an M1 rifle, makes a distinctive "cling" sound and this would alert a German grenadier or paratrooper that the charging Gl was charging with an empty rifle, it would seem that this tactic could be quite hazardous to a soldier's health.

The Journals suggest that late the same day, at 2020 hours "Tk threat coming from NE consisting of about 10 ey tks . . . and headed SW" toward the friendly positions in the forest. The Journals then describe the Operational Instructions for 26 Jan:

> Atk at 0730. 68 takes sector and turns over to 1-314 as 1-314 turns their sector over to 2-232 in Schweighausen. We take and hold ground . . . and restoring MLR, until 1-34 relieves us. 2-232 reorganizing; 1-232 relieves us. 2-232 to cover Schweighausen. 3-232 takes 400 yd sector next to ours; keep liaision [sic] with them. LD—beginning of woods N of Ohlungen. 68 to clear woods in our sector with road as right boundary. 2-232 reorganizing; 1-232 in reserve. Our tks clear edge of woods. 79th Arty will haras our zone tonight. 3-232 will have a platoon of med tks with it. CO CCB cautions to be especially alert for atk around 2300 tonight. Coordinate our atk tomorrow with 232 on left. Clean our sector and hold along road (MLR) until relieved.

Such involved movement of so many units in such a short time in the dark must have produced many headaches for company commanders and platoon leaders, but the deployment had to be completed. A measure of how tricky all this must have been is the fact that four different original sources provide three different times for the attack. "The Report of Operations" mentions 0700 hours, the Journals 0730 hours, and both the *History* of the 14th Armored and that of the 68th cite 0800 hours for the moment to jump off. There is no indication that these discrepancies in time caused any problems for the attacking tanks and men whatever problems they might cause for historians. Thus "The Report" states, "At 0700 on the 26th, the 68th was continuing the attack and by 0930 had completed its mission by re-establishing the main line of resistance along the Moder river, while its patrols were probing the area on the enemy-held side of the stream,"[17] the last phrase suggesting the narrow width of the Moder at this location. The Journals simply track the advance methodically as it reaches, for example, "Phase Line I, all quiet," and then one hundred yards beyond that; next it is "Phase Line 2," and later "have met no opposition, so far," "meeting no opposition," and then "On objective as of 930 and organizing it." The proud writers of the 68th's *History* calmly state, "this time we pushed through what resistance they could put up with their chewed up forces, and re-established the line along the Moder River. As the afternoon wore on we were subsequently relieved by the 1st Battalion, 314th Infantry, 79th Division." Both the Fourteenth and the 79th had become familiar with each other and used to working together since the furnace at Hatten-Rittershoffen. They were both now experienced units. Happily for all the units involved in the fight in Ohlungen Forest, "Casualties for the entire mission were reported light."[18]

The 68th's *History* indicates that the unit returned to Batzendorf, "this time an elated group of fighting men. We were again to assume the role of backing up the line." In contrast to this expansive notion of the fight in Ohlungen Forest was the scheduling of a "very solemn and impressive service . . . for our fallen comrades." To further confirm the sense that fighting is killing and nothing to be happy about, "A ghastly scene was viewed when Headquarters Company's supply truck returned with its first load crammed with the torn and twisted bodies of our victims in the Ohlungen Forest."[19] Lt. Harry Kemp, in charge of the burial detail, saw a few of the victims taking gold teeth from the frozen bodies.

The pattern of fighting for the next seven or eight weeks would be active defense in that VI Corps did not have the troops to attack operationally across its front. It could not, however, sit back and absorb punishment, and so every effort was made to take the attack to the enemy. For example, C Company, the 25th Tank Battalion, attached to the 79th Infantry Division, skirmished at Kaltenhouse. As the 14th's History outlines the action:

Corp. Albert W. Miller of Lieut. William H. Kekar, Jr.'s platoon knocked out a German tank across the Moder. On the 25th [still

January], the enemy put a foot bridge across the river and penetrated the lines between Kaltenhouse and Hagenau; the 2nd
Platoon of C Company moved up, 130 Germans surrendered
and 100 casualties were inflicted; and the lines were restored.[20]

Aircraft from both sides flew when the weather was clear, with P-
47's hitting the town of Oberhoffen preparatory to a planned assault
against it, while the German jets, the Me-262's, made life dangerous for
the GIs. CCB was now attached to the 36th Infantry Division and
moved to near Oberhoffen. The intent was to employ the combined
68th AIB and the 25th TB to assist the advance of the 36th. As the
68th's History has it:

This was on February 1st and we moved up to Bischwiller
spending one night there weathering occasional artillery barrages and hearing the continuous moan of artillery directed
toward the German line. The following morning our attack
started. Our 'C' Company and 'B' of the 25th was sent out to
attack along the East of Oberhoffen. Their mission was to out
[sic] off the town from the Northeast. One platoon of 'A' of the
25th with one squad of our 'A' Company was given the mission
of attacking North parallel to Oberhoffen avoiding the town,
and then to go between the open ground and woods and to sieze
[sic] and organize the railroad in that vicinity. 'B' Company in
reserve remained in Bischwiller.[21]

Unlike the battle in the Ohlungen Forest, which is southwest of
Hagenau, this attack started from the southeast, indicating a general
movement closer to the Rhine. In January, the 12th Armored Division
had been terribly mauled at Herrlisheim, which was only a mile at most
west of the Rhine, but this time, it was hoped, the Germans could be
driven out of the vicinity of the Rhine in the Hagenau vicinity north of
the key city of Strasbourg.

Captain Joseph Carter picks up the story from the preparations
described by the authors of the 68th's unit history. The recon platoon
established an OP on the high ground over Oberhoffen while the mortar platoon went in with the 68th:

The attack jumped off; the wet ground, deceptively soft on top (the snow had begun to melt) slowed the attack; B-25 and Lieut. Walton's platoon were slowed by a series of drainage ditches. A German 88 cracked from the woods near Oberhofen, [sic] and Sgt. Thomas' tank was hit; the driver was killed and three crew members were wounded, but Thomas was unhurt. This was the third tank he had had hit.[22]

The attack was stopped simultaneously with its inception, and one of the reasons was the presence of a drainage canal, which frustrated the forward momentum of both infantry and tanks. After regrouping, the GIs returned to Bischwiller and the curious sanctuary of an insane asylum. (This is reminiscent of the account in the film *The Big Red One, The First Infantry Division,* of an infiltration into such an asylum and the elimination of an Observation Post employed by the enemy.)

The next night, after some wire laying and mine planting for defensive purposes, patrols were ordered forward "to feel out the enemy." On the morrow, A and C of the 68th, again with B-25, advanced through the town:

> Troops advanced slowly under intense enemy automatic weapon, artillery and mortar fire and systematically cleared the houses they gained. The enemy strong point [no surprise] centered around the church and street fighting ensued. Defenses were established for the night and the attack was to continue in the morning. At 0830 hours the attack was resumed and again our troops slugged it out with automatic weapons and numerous snipers to reach and conquer the church.[23]

The struggle for the town was not over by any means. After a defensive perimeter had been established, Company A received the brunt of a counterattack, which was rejected. Nevertheless the 20th's Company B was given a bad time by anti-tank guns which were concealed in the woods. For whatever reason, they did not give off a telltale flash, and these guns had caused tank and infantry losses in the Hatten-Rittershoffen fight. An Assault Gun Platoon began to fire against the gun positions in the woods, but the area was riddled with panzerfaust teams, producing double jeopardy for the tanks and the half-tracks. "Lieut. E. Q. Wood said the bazookas [the projectiles really] looked like footballs coming through the air." A seesaw struggle developed when the German foot soldiers infiltrated through the armored infantry's positions and then the GI's and the tanks had to root them out all over again. Once again, as in Rittershoffen, the Germans set houses on fire, the glare of which silhouetted the Shermans in the night. The enemy artillery began to fall on the town, and in some cases buildings collapsed on tanks. With the American infantry hugging close to the tanks and citing targets for them, they slowly ground forward with the help of P-47's that bombed the Germans. They managed to control more than seventy-five percent of the town when they were relieved by men of the 36th Division. A CCB report of the action described it in this manner:

> B-25 came under heavy fire, but in spite of losing one tank, continued on the mission. Most movements, days or night, were covered with fire by the enemy. The enemy laid down heavy artillery and mortar fire but the attack was pushed forward; patrols captured Offendorf and began clearing Herrlescheim [sic]. B-125 completed one foot bridge across the Moder southeast of Bischwiller and were working on a second.[24]

As the 68th's History characterizes this action from the night of February 2 through February 3: "Defenses were again set up for the night and 'A' Company received a counterattack which was skillfully beaten off. The following morning the attack was resumed [and] this time 'B' Company jumping through 'A' Company succeeded in taking the Northern part of the town giving us the major portion of the city. We were relieved [sic] as darkness fell by the first Battalion, 142nd Regiment, 36th Division and started our journey again to Batzendorf."[25] Total casualties for both the Ohlungen Forest and the Oberhoffen operations were thirty-one.

The next operation was directed against Pfaffenhoffen, a town at a crossroads west of Hagenau and northwest of Oberhoffen. It appeared that the 14th Armored and the 36th and 79th Infantry Divisions were working their way around Hagenau preparatory to the beginning of an offensive finally to cross the Rhine, although that would not happen until March. Concurrently with the Corps' movements, the Psychological Warfare Section, actually the S-2 Section of the 14th under Major Glynn Prine, began a campaign to weaken the enemy's will to fight and to encourage them to surrender. A part of this effort was using patrol activity to capture prisoners and gather intelligence, broadcasting appeals to enemy soldiers to give up the struggle, and firing surrender leaflets into enemy territory.[26]

At Oberhoffen, a small town about thirteen kilometers southeast of Ohlungen, the 14th was continuing to apply pressure around the Hagenau area. After crossing the Moder River on a Bailey Bridge on 1 February, the 25th Tank Battalion was fighting to take the town from the enemy. B Company had the responsibility of employing their new 76mm cannons to destroy the buildings in the town. The technique was to fire away at the opposite walls of a building until it collapsed on any German soldiers inside. Cpl. Herman Ratelle, the loader on the Sherman tank, was doing his best to make sure the rounds were hitting their mark by standing on a box of tank grenades and looking out. At one point,

> He didn't like what he saw. A German tank was coming around the building they were shelling, and it was aiming its gun right at the American tank. He recorded his reaction to the next danger:
>
> "I saw the big, red onion coming at us. It was a .88 shell, and it was red hot. There was nothing we could do."

When the .88 round hit Ratelle's tank, it exploded the grenades in the box he was standing on. He was then catapulted out of the hatch and broke both his shoulders in the process. The driver was trying to get out another hatch, but the tank was hit again, and the shell "killed him instantly."

Ratelle had more things to worry about. The shell that hit him tore off his leg. He desperately tried to stop the bleeding with a tourniquet, but he was having a difficult time. When he was assisted hopping back to the cover of another tank, the loader, Pfc. Eldon C. Drake, who would later be killed, tied off the tourniquet. Ratelle, for his part, was laughing hysterically because he thought his was "a million dollar wound." After receiving some morphine and a couple of generous glasses of Four Roses whiskey, Ratelle was placed in a body cast in Saarbourg and eventually made it home.[27]

As a part of the campaign to gather intelligence, previously mentioned, a large patrol was sent out from B Company of the 68th, and
the Battalion History explains the calamitous events that would follow:

> Our next mission was to relieve elements of the 103 Division, in
> the towns of Pfaffenhoffen, Uberach, La [Ia) Walck and
> Ringeldorf. Patrol Action and raids on the enemy's installations
> were the order of the day. On the 24th [of February] plans were
> revealed for a large patrol into the woods across the river. 'B'
> Company was assigned the job. The first and third platoons
> were to seal off the Germans in the left end of the woods, and
> the second platoon was to cover the right flank from a ditch line
> along the road that ran nearly parallel with the route of attack.
> The mission was to draw the Germans out and then take
> Prisoners needed for information on Germon [sic] troop dispo-
> sition and strength. At 2230 the patrol moved out, but had
> advanced only 300 yards beyond the foot bridge over the river
> when 'Jerries' became aware of their presence. The premature
> detection was caused by the explosion of a Schu mine, [many of
> which] were virtually scattered all over the terrain and which
> victimized three men. The patrol was then pinned down by
> heavy crossfire of machine guns. The second platoon tried to
> move forward, but the attempt was of no avail. The men lay in
> the cold mud until 0130 when the situation became worse.
> Enemy riflemen were moving in on the right flank. At 0145 the
> order to withdraw was given. The second platoon covered the
> first and third as they withdrew, then the second withdrew.[28]

The reason that this passage is quoted in such length and detail is
that it is almost identical to the story of Bob Davies' loss of his leg. The
incident above is repeated in the 14th Armored's History almost exactly, as one would expect if the Battalion History or reports on which it
was based provided the source for Captain Carter, which follows:

> On February 24 the first large patrol was ordered out;
> Company B [Bob's] was given the job. The mission was to take
> prisoners. The patrol moved out at 2230; before it had gone
> 300 yards it was discovered and pinned down by the heavy

crossfire of German machine guns. (One of the men [probably Bob Davies] had set of a Schu mine—by now the Germans had almost literally covered the area with mines, they had been there so long; you could watch across the river and see their defenses grow day by day.) The 2nd Platoon tried to move up to help the men of the 1st and 3rd but they were cut down; and enemy riflemen began to infiltrate the flank. The patrol was ordered back.[29]

Bob Davies' account of the action includes the wounding of one member of his squad, Calvin Crouch, who was struck by a bullet through one of his lungs. In the darkness Bob carried him back uphill to the crest and dropped him so that he could role down the hill to safety and medical attention. The medics managed to stabilize Crouch, but the patrol continued. Exactly when this transpired is not clear. As Bob remembered that night, his squad managed to get close to an unfriendly machine-gun position to grenade it, but in the process, he stepped on the Schu mine. The blast blew off his right leg at the ankle and left his calf shredded and bloody. He had the presence of mind to tie the wound off with a tourniquet, a step which would save his life. The same blast blinded a new replacement, Pfc. Bob Hancock. He had turned to face Bob when the mine exploded and was blinded and unable to get himself to safety after one of the German machine guns had passed them with its arc of fire.

The near tragedy of both of them being killed was averted and some wry humor kept up their spirits. On the way back, Hancock yelled, "I'm hit," and Bob asked him if he could move his legs. While suffering loss of blood himself, Sgt. Davies searched Hancock's body for a wound. Bob discovered some liquid on Hancock's back, and it happily transpired that it was from his canteen. Bob kept it as a souvenir.

But the danger was not yet over. A German patrol was out searching for whoever had set off the Schu mine. Only the most exquisite stillness in the dark saved both the private and the sergeant from discovery. Because casualties had been so frequent during this segment of the battle in and around Ohlungen Forest, there were no medics nearby. Accordingly, Bob had to crawl back about a mile and a half to an aid station at Ia Walck. He and another casualty, who was also bleeding from a serious wound, were placed on their own in the back of an ambulance. Both untended patients continued to lose blood, and by the time the two patients reached the aid station, the other man, ghostly pale from blood loss, was dead. Bob was treated by a doctor who cut off the loose tendons, ligaments, and tissue, and cauterized the wound. After all this trauma and perhaps under the influence of morphine, Bob began to shout, "I've got my ticket home. I got my ticket home." Such was the horror of combat that a man could see it as a blessing to lose one of his legs.

A replacement lieutenant soon arrived with his left leg missing, a perfect if grisly match for Bob, who had lost his right leg. When they were both stabilized and sedated, joking together, they agreed on a regular exchange of shoes when they were back in civilian life, two new shoes for the price of one.[30]

This casualty was 2nd Lt. Stanley Miller, who had been with Company B for only three days before the patrol. He was the ranking leader on the patrol, but Sgt. Davies, more infantry experienced, was the one making the decisions on this night patrol. In a letter to this author, Miller stated that he had stepped on a mine at the identical time that Bob did and suffered equally:

> I lost my left leg below the knee, had a broken right leg, [and] a piece of rock in my right eye. Eye healed in a week [so there was] no problem with it.
>
> When they got Bob and I to the aid station (Set up in a house) Bob was on a litter in a room. I was on a litter just around the door in the hail. Bob could hear them talking. Ask me, "Lt. what leg did you lose," I said my left. Bob said, "We can buy a pair of shoes. I [had] lost my right." [31]

A second letter from Stanley Miller provided more information on the deadly patrol. Miller wrote again:

"I was only with the 68th—3 days. They were in a rest area when I showed up as a replacement. Was assigned as Plt. Leader, 1st Platoon Co. B. The third night there we were sent out on patrol. The objective was to get a prisoner. If you have a 14th Armored History [cited above] the Patrol is in the Ten[th] Chapter. Starts out On Feb. 24th the first large patrol. Me and Sgt. Robert Davies, both stepped on Schu mines at the same time.

"I do have the map that I was carring [sic] that night."[32] (A copy of part of the map which Lt. Miller carried appears at the end of this chapter.)

Miller described the roundabout manner in which he joined that patrol. He had been commissioned as an officer in the Tank Destroyer battalions. His battalion became over-strength to the figure of 100% When officers were being sent to train in indirect firing, apparently in artillery, the division "broke up the TD-OCS and sent officers from the school" into various units. Seventeen Second Lieutenants transferred into the infantry. After three days of infantry tactics, Miller was sent on the ill-fated combat patrol, which would drastically change his life and that of Bob Davies.

The only ambiguity about piecing the stories together is the precise dating of the patrol on which the four men were wounded. Both the histories of the battalion and the division agree on 24 February, some time after midnight, as the date of the patrol in Pfaffenhoffen. Stanley Miller stays with the 24th in his letters but says, in a questionnaire sent to him in March 2008, that he was wounded on 23 February. The confusion is understandable after so many years and because the night patrol may have moved out before midnight but had gotten in trouble soon after midnight. It took a while for the survivors to get back to their own lines because of the severity of the German counterattack.

Phil Snoberger, a comrade of Bob's from Headquarters Company, who laid wire regularly, remained a close friend of Bob after they had roomed together in the ASTP program at the University of Cincinnati in 1943. His notion is that the wounding and the patrol occurred on Bob's birthday, 20 February. That date is incorrect. The order for the patrol, according to Phil, came from 14AD Headquarters, but the Battalion Commander, Lt. Cot. Bob Edwards, and the Company Commanders thought the patrol was a mistake. They and Phil agreed that there was sufficient information about the German positions and that the patrol was therefore unnecessary. Snoberger's words were "They knew where we were and we knew where they were." Phil Snoberger is furious about what—for him—was an unnecessary patrol which cost his buddy and lifelong friend his leg.[33]

After about a week the 68th was relieved by the 62nd and moved to Ringeldorf. The ensuing days were relatively quiet as patrolling was carried out by the Reconnaissance Platoon "alternating with patrols of the line companies." The 68th's History indicates its displeasure with what it called the "wild wire cutter of Pfaffenhoffen," who was causing no end of confusion by disrupting land line communication, but the "wild wire cutter" turned out, Snoberger discovered, to be shrapnel from friendly proximity shells. Other activities included the so-called "Hog callers," members of the psychological warfare unit who broadcast messages to the enemy suggesting that they surrender. The only result of this work was "drawing more artillery and mortar fire than prisoners."

After a week of "resting and training," the battalion moved up to the line with the rear CP in Ettendorf and the forward CP in Pfaffenhoffen. "After more patrols to capture prisoners, B Company dug in secondary positions behind the main line along the Moder." On 10 March the whole battalion was given the mission of not only holding onto its own sector but of covering that of the 62nd, which in turn had shifted to take over a sector from the 36th Infantry Division.[34]

The 62nd AIB had been busy as Captain Jack R. DeWitt commanded a raid of company size without the aid of a preliminary bombardment. The History of the 14th AD describes what happened:

> The 1st and 2nd Platoons were in the assault; the night was bright and clear, the moon almost full.
>
> The attack moved slowly, silently, the men going carefully to avoid the mines, until suddenly the 2nd Platoon was cut by the deathly flicking tongues of German machine guns, cutting across it, and the platoon was pinned to the ground; then all the German guns opened up. The 1st Platoon was pinned down by mortar and small arms fire. Corp. Gordon Johnson of the AT Platoon set up a machine gun for protection; the company was forced to pull back. Three men had been killed. . . . Lieut. Auer took out a 55 man patrol to get prisoners; they had to fire under friendly flares, and their location was disclosed. They returned without a prisoner.[35]

The frustration of the men who had to participate in these patrols must have been difficult. The Germans were just across the river and could be seen going about their business as the Americans were doing the same on their side. The patrolling had caused many casualties with little to show for it. To support friendly armor and infantry, there was a great deal of firing by the division's artillery, including the 100,000 shells fired by the division in the fighting. The First Tactical Air Force bombed Drusenheim after a particularly heavy shelling by artillery. The Germans were not idle either. There were two rail guns of 380mm which fired shells as far as thirty miles; the one called "Alsace Alice" fired rounds one night while the other, "Alsace Annie," fired on the rear area in Saverne, and one round hit C Company of the 136th Infantry in their barracks. The casualties were eleven men killed and thirteen wounded.[36]

The patrolling continued and even increased, and finally one patrol brought back some prisoners for interrogation, but there were more wounded and killed. As the history of the 68th remarked prophetically but ironically, "Our lines were now stretched very thin, and it was this fact that gave us the first inkling that a gigantic offensive would be in the offing." When the 36th Division sent "reconnaissance agents to scan our positions," it was clear to the armored infantry that something was up. The 68th's History continues providing evidence of something big:

> To materialize our suspicions the . . . on March 15 the 36th, in a coordinated attack with the 103rd Division, and accompanied by the greatest artillery preparation we had ever witnessed, jumped through our positions in an allout [sic] attack. Truck load after truck load of German PW's streamed back through our lines giving new evidence the attack was successful. When the successfulness [sic] of the attack became evident, we were ordered to assemble our forces and be prepared to jump off in an armored spearhead to exploit the break-through that the foot soldiers were sure to make.[37]

At Ringeldorf, the 14th Armored organized two task forces, one designated "Blue" and led by Major Townsend, composed of C Company of the 68th, A Company of the 25th Tank Battalion, the first platoon, C Troop, the 94th Cavalry, and the first platoon, C Company, of the 125th Engineers. The other task force, led by Lt. Colonel Bob Edwards, was designated "the 68th, which included Headquarters Company of the 68th, B Company of the 68th, B Company of the 25th, the second platoon, C Troop of the 94th Cav and Rec, and the second platoon, C Company of the 125th Armored Engineers. As the 68th's history proudly proclaimed, "We were poised and ready to strike in what we hoped to be a drive that would carry us through the Siegfried Defenses and on to the Rhine River."[38] Unbeknownst to the men, an armored patrol of the First Army had already crossed the Rhine over the Ludendorff railway bridge at Remagen and begun the buildup that would lead to the beginning of the end for the Reich. Patton's Third Army would also cross the river (ahead of Gen. Montgomery's 21st Army Group, much to the satisfaction of Patton), and with the vanguard of two armies across the Rhine in March, there was no way to stop the Allies. Yet the 14th Armored Division had been blooded at its first assault against the Westwall between 18 and 25 December. The men knew what elaborate fortifications had been erected in front of them. The task would be neither simple nor cheap to accomplish

The 68th Medical Detachment was busy but in two entirely different ways. In Batzendorf Captain Battenfeld, assisted by Staff Sergeant Schneider, Tec 5 Elliasson, Tec .3 Bopp and "sundry members of the Hq Co Assault Gun platoon," delivered a baby for a local woman. Although that event occurred in a relatively quiet context, the battle for Ohlungen Forest would provide some violent surprises to the medics:

> While at the forward aid station Tec 5 Sellen, Pfc. Boehringer and Pfc. Kerr found out what it was like to be blown out of bed by a Jerry 120mm mortar shell which blew in the side of the aid station. Fortunately the station was used more for taking care of Jerry wounded than our own. The infantry with tank support had a field day and both stations worked far into the night dressing Krauts. The ambulances and returning tanks carried load after load of enemy wounded, but very few of our own.[39]

Ken Hazleton, the medic, and the ambulance drivers were, like the 68th armored infantry, amazed that hostile fire ceased when the ambulances arrived on the scene of battle.

One of the most astounding things to happen to a medic transpired when Tec 5 Goldstein, an aid man with B Company, was caring for a wounded German soldier. As Ken Hazleton related the story:

> While he [was] bent over a wounded German taking care of him, several German medics, complete with infantry guards and

officers, approached. He slid back out of sight until they beckoned him to come forward. The Yank and the Jerries worked together for quite a while getting the man in shape. When they finished the officer ceremoniously shook hands, thanked Goldie very much, clicked his heels and then they took off dragging their wounded behind in a blanket.[40]

The war on the Eastern Front between the Germans and the Russians contained few examples of chivalry between civilized but warring nations. Russia, unlike Germany, had never signed the Geneva Convention.

Toward the end of the war on the Western Front, after the massacre at Malmedy during the Ardennes campaign in December/January of 1944/1945, prisoners on both sides, including badly wounded ones, were at hazard. At least in the case of Tec 5 Max Goldstein, a Jewish soldier, and the German medics, chivalry was still alive. Explanation of map of Pfaffenhoffen by Phil Snoberger (April 25, 2008 letter to Author):

"This is approximately the area where the 'B' C patrol crossed the river and ran into trouble.

"The woods were full of covered bunkers which protected the Krauts from tree bursts and our proximity shells.

"Incidentally it was the proximity shells that went off over the trees between Ringeldorf and Pfaffenhoffen that was the 'wild wire cutter' referred to on page 18 of the [68th] Battalion History."

The difference between tree bursts and exploding proximity shells was that the former exploded upon impact with an object, in this case, a tree branch, or because it was controlled by a time fuse. The latter were, at the time, a new development by allied engineers originally designed for the navy. The proximity shell had a built-in-radio wave which set off the explosive when the radio wave bounced off an object and returned to the transmitter. In other circumstances, the proximity fuse could be quite devastating, especially to vehicles and troops in the open.

Chapter 7

BREACHING THE SIEGFRIED LINE

The men of the 68th Armored Infantry Battalion, having been bloodied at Ober-Otterbach adjacent to the Siegfried Line, knew that another attack could be as frustrating and costly as that tactical failure. At least this time they knew what kind of obstacles they would be facing and what enormous volumes of fire could shatter them if it could not be stopped or averted. Only active and continual support from tanks and artillery, preferably with the assistance of airpower, could defeat the enemy. At the earlier battle, tank support had been limited because of a blown bridge. That mistake could not be repeated. Sometimes, and it would happen more frequently in ensuing battles, German soldiers would surrender under the impact of ferocious artillery fire if they were positioned in trenches or houses that were not especially fortified.

They were much less likely to surrender behind reinforced concrete pillboxes and bunkers. One historian, in commenting on the line near Echternach in Luxembourg, sketched them as "rat's nests, with as many as forty pillboxes per square mile, one every forty yards. . . . no fewer than a hundred other fortified positions, trenches and the ever-present mine fields."[1] This description is scary enough, but it doesn't mention the "dragon's teeth," the reinforced concrete tetrahedrons in row after row, which would stop American tanks dead if they could not be blown to allow a path for the tanks to penetrate so as to be able to fire on the German emplacements, especially the gun ports, to neutralize them.

For three tense days after the action at Pfaffenhoffen, the 68th was constantly on the alert to continue the offensive started by the 36th Infantry Division. That division was meeting with success although receiving heavy casualties from the ever-present and damnable Schu mines. Yet, it seemed that the Germans were in retreat back to the Westwall, and the armored infantrymen felt that they were ready to re-enter the battle. Suddenly the call came. The I and R Platoon was out in front of the battalion along the axis Mittersheim-Gundstadt, and it passed through the 36th ID, through Surtourg and on towards the infamous rubble-strewn battlefields of Rittershoffen and Hatten. As the 68th's History put it, on the 18th of March:

> We passed through Rittershoffen, scene of our titanic struggle [in January], now desolated and deserted, an ugly pile of stone and clay still smelling of the hectic days of the struggle. There we were told we were close behind the retreating Germans and were definitely gaining on them. They had not the motorized equipment to keep pace with us. We knew it, for we saw their dead horses laying in the streets, their wagons crumpled in heaps along the roads. The Alsatians were overjoyed. It was a real day of celebration. In the towns where we once had billeted, the people recognized us and shrieked with laughter as we passed by in our halftracks.[2]

It is truly a wonder that the Alsatian people would be overjoyed to see the GIs after their towns and livestock had been largely destroyed by American as well as German ordnance.

The 25th Tank Battalion also moved out the same day through the 36th ID, and the 25th's Recon Platoon established an OP at Schweighause "under the thunder of the Division and Corps guns that were supporting the attack with an almost endless barrage," which was being directed by that OP. The mortars of the 68th set up along the Moder River for firing.

The 25th TB's column of CCA was in the lead, proceeding resolutely through some of the same towns (like Rittershoffen) that had been passed or fought through earlier, even as far back as November, through Pfaffenhoffen and the Forest of Hagenau, Mertzwiller, Morsbronn, Surbourg and Hohwiller to Leiterswiller. A blown bridge temporarily halted the column, but the engineers replaced it and the column continued on its inexorable way. Oberroedem, Oberseebach, and Geitershof were transited. The 14th Armored Division's *History* followed the column:

The column passed through nine towns, took 18 prisoners and
met not the slightest resistance. The Germans were falling back
to the Siegfried again. The head of the column stopped at
Geitershof for the night, and Captain [Warren E. of A-68] Benoit
sent a platoon of his infantry company ahead to see if they could
reach Atenstadt. The infantrymen were later halted at a blown
overpass, pinned down by mortar and artillery fire; and pulled
back. 2nd Lieut. [Frank L.] Reissner [Hdqrs. Co., 25th Tank
Battalion] brought up his assault guns to fire on the enemy in
Wissembourg.[3]

Also on the 18th of March, the rest of the 68th linked up at
Niederrodern with the French African Division and built a bridge across
the Lauter River, diplomatically allowing the "poilus" to march across
it first. After reorganizing beyond the town, the 68th and attached units
forced a small bridgehead across the river and captured the town of
Salmbach. Completing this task, the battalion was relieved by elements
of the French Division and prepared to swing around west towards
Kapsweyer. The assault was planned, in an enveloping motion, to
breach the first belt of the Westwall.[4]

On the morning of the 19th, Company A of the 68th, still alongside
the 25th Tank Battalion, gravitated forward with its tanks and helped
spot an anti-tank gun beyond the blown overpass. The tanks fired on it
at the edge of the woods and blew it up. The column entered the town
of Altenstadt on the Lauter River on the same morning when German
artillery began to fall on them. Lt. Frank L. Reissner of Hdqrs. Co. of
the 25th TB and his driver, Pfc. Edward C. Kirstner, searched ahead for
assault-gun positions but were caught by the barrage. Kirstner was
wounded.[5]

On the afternoon of 19 March the battalion advanced via
Wissembourg to the town of Schweighofen in front of the line, where
the men billeted for the night. At the same time patrols were directed
towards Kapsweyer. In the distance to the northwest, many fires raged
through the night, especially at the always stubborn resistance at Ober-
Otterbach, where the 36th Infantry faced the same guns and fortifications that the 68th had back in December—the Westwall. The 68th
would make its assault at a different point in the Wall but could expect
the same kind of treatment.

The axis of attack for the next hazardous days was Schweighofen Kapsweyer-Steinfeld-Schaidt-Freckenfeld and through the Siegfried Line.

According to the 14th's *History*, on the morning of the twentieth, two platoons of B Company, which had been Bob Davies' Company before his wounding, went into the assault against the town of Kapsweyer, a part of the Siegfried Line fortifications. They were supported by B Company of the 25th Tank Battalion, which had been very busy in the offensive. The town was quickly taken, and the combined force advanced toward the dragon's teeth. "The infantrymen came under the same fierce artillery and mortar fire they had met on their first trip to that blood-and-concrete line, and grazing machine gun fire cut at them. They were forced back to Kapsweyer. C Company of the 68th moved into positions along the railroad south of town."[6]

A seventeen-minute artillery barrage prepared the men for the renewal of the attack. Lt. Harry T. Kemp, who would earn a Bronze Star in this action, led B Company in the attack. He saw friendly smoke rounds being fired for two minutes to protect the company. At the worst possible moment the smoke dissipated before the group could penetrate the dragon's teeth. Some of the First and Second Platoons at least reached the western edge of Steinfeld. These were eight men from Lt. James Napier's Second Platoon; he would also receive a Bronze Star. They were accompanied by fifteen men from Kemp's First Platoon, and they occupied four houses.[7] All this happened just after noon.

Captain Carter's comment on the situation was ominous: "It looked as though it was going to be a repetition of the bloody, casualty-heavy, deadly fighting the 14th had known before."[8] For the 23 men marooned in those houses, it must have seemed like a recurring nightmare. Just as before at Ober-Otterbach, the remainder of the men of the 68th were trapped in the open. They dug in while the men in the houses consolidated their position and were frozen in place by enemy fire for a day and more.

T/Sgt. Ray F. Lohof of Third Platoon of C-68, along with his comrades in B Company, was right in the middle of this attack to "test" the defenses. He characterized the event as he saw it:

> The platoon leader, Lieutenant Frank Hood [who would receive both a Bronze and a Silver Star for bravery], decided to take two

squads with a tank of the 25th Tank [Bn.] on the road leading
to Steinfeld. I, as platoon sergeant, was to take the remaining
men into the field to the right of the road toward the pillbox.
The 25th Tank proceeded up the road with the men grouped
closely behind it. I had a bad feeling about the operation and
instructed the men to wait for my signal before following me
into the field. I had selected a small hole as my first goal into an
area which otherwise afforded no protection. I had just reached
the hole when an MG-42, distinguished by its extremely high
rate of fire, opened fire from the pillbox. The fire was directed
at the men around the tank and Private First Class Bart Souther,
a BAR man, went to ground and promptly returned fire from
behind the tank. The tank went into full reverse without the
usual warning and backed over Souther and Ellenberger."[9] (Pfc.
Charles F. Ellenberger survived the war but Pfc. Earl C. Souther
did not.)

Despite this dreadful accident, Lohof, armed only with an M-1,
fired at the embrasure in the pillbox, generating a response from the
machine gunner, which sparked rounds all around his hole. Pfc. William
H. Camp took Pfc. Charles F. Ellenberger and placed him on the back
of the tank for safety although his legs were crushed.

The rest of the men from the First and Second Platoons still had to
experience the hell of finding a safe place inside of a dangerous one.

The 14th Armored *History* account reflected the sheer terror of running over the open ground under fire:

The 1st Platoon [of B-68] had 500 yards of open field to break
across and the 2nd had 700. Dug-in machine guns and the mortars and the heavy weapons in the pill boxes had the field plastered with fire and we didn't think any of us would make it.

Some of us prayed, others just stared into space. We all had
the same idea—we'll never get there.

Eighty-five men started the dash. The enemy waited until
the men were about 30 feet from the Dragon's Teeth, then
opened up with a murderous screen of machine gun fire.

Those who got that far hit the dirt among the teeth.

Bullets ricocheted with an unearthly whine on the concrete teeth and whirled crazily from one tooth to the other.[10]

Perhaps the only good thing that happened was the repair and salvaging of two Signal Corps radios back in the houses in Steinfeld. By 1230 the survivors held two houses and were able to use the radios. Water was rationed for the wounded as both American and German artillery fire landed all around them. Lt. Napier called in artillery fire against the larger pillboxes but without good effect; he then requested direct tank fire, and that eliminated fire from one pillbox. The men could not seek the shelter of the stone basements because they feared an infantry attack against them. Platoon Sergeant Dale Riggle, of B Company, after being pestered dangerously by a sniper, managed to hole the sniper's helmet. After night fell, the area was illuminated by a burning factory across the way. The men had to stay near the windows and watch for the enemy. Pfc. Manuel Lamboy, also of B Company, fired quickly at three silhouetted figures and dropped one of them. The light from the fire was saving G.I. lives.

C Company was also having its share of difficulties:

> In the meantime 'C' Company, who had to attack across open terrain, was pinned down by machine-gun and rocket fire emminating [sic] from the turreted pill-boxes on the Southwest corner of Steinfeld and from the Bien Wald forest. They could not even inch forward and held down their right flank position.[11]

The 68th's Medical Detachment was in the middle of this firestorm and did its best to treat both the wounded in the houses and those among the dragon's teeth:

> One platoon of Baker Company managed to get a toehold in Steinfeld, and Tec 5 Al Simon cared for his casualties cut off from any immediate hope of evacuation. Lt. [Glen W.] Scott organized, and led a litter party which cleared the area of the dragon's teeth of wounded and dead. Pfcs. [Phillip H.] and [Kenneth N.] Kerr with spectacular disregard of enemy fire

from the pillboxes and the forts cleared five casualties by litter in clear view of the enemy. Mortars and rockets chased the medic vehicles up and down the road. Capt. [Frank M., who would earn a Bronze Star] Lorimer's group, still attached to the blue task force pitched in and the united force found plenty to do.[12]

The fear that could be infused into a combat soldier facing the Siegfried and its murderous firepower faced other soldiers at other parts of the line at other times. Audie Murphy, as a newly minted Second Lieutenant in the 3rd Infantry Division, described his own feelings even as he was given the less dangerous assignment of Liaison Officer: "There will be small dangers, of course, and moments of minor terror. With nerves schooled to uncertainty, the hair will still rise and the flesh creep as I sense the presence of the enemy in the ruins of defeated towns. But the constant peril of the front lines is temporarily over." He stewed over the fate of the men in his former company, which was catching hell on the line. He was greeted at headquarters with the news of what happened to the captain of his company:

> At headquarters, I learn of Captain Hogan's death. He was in a captured pillbox when a mortar shell got one of his men. Badly wounded, the man tried dragging himself back to cover. The captain crawled out to give him a hand. Another shell landed, sending a piece of steel into the captain. A lieutenant went after him, the third shell landed with pin-point accuracy; and the three men died together.[13]

Murphy walked in the open toward the trench where his company was pinned down with the officers and sergeants frightened to death. He was finally able to get them out of the trench to advance closer to the enemy, where they were less likely to get hit with mortar rounds. As it turned out, there was no fire from the other pillboxes as they darted quickly ahead. The Germans had—mercifully—pulled out.

The men of the 14th Armored on the right and the 36th Infantry Division on the left on 20 March were not quite as fortunate. They were still stuck in a bad place. Although the Second Platoon's casualties of the 68th were "relatively light," the First and Third had suffered some serious casualties. One of the men was shot through the lung. T/5 Allan Simon, previously mentioned, an aid man for B Company who was with the 23 men in town, moved the casualty to a comfortable and safe place. As the 68th's *History* puts it, "By his sterling courage and medical ability he administered first aid to the wounded man and maintained a constant vigil over his comrade during the harrowing night, thereby saving the man's life.

For this action he received the bronze star award for meritorious service." Likewise, the 23 men also earned the Bronze Star for holding on in the town as long as they did.[14] The writers of these unit histories, amateur or professional in writing skills, want to ensure that bravery is recognized by those who were not there on the firing line.

But there was still work to be done, fighting in close with a determined enemy. The radio in town crackled a message to the GIs in code around 0600 on 21 March that there was to be an attack against the line after "a heavy artillery preparation, and another unidentified explosion." This latter was the exploding of a path through the dragon's teeth by the engineers. Lt. Kemp remembered it as happening at about six o'clock in the morning. The artillery fire, as the 14th's History depicted it, was "thunderous." During the night, the engineers and T/Sgt. John Sailors and Pfc. Ricardo Sanchez of A-68 had "crawled forward into no man's land to blow a path for the tanks through the Dragon's Teeth. (Sailors and Sanchez crawled over 400 yards of open terrain with fifty pounds [each] of TNT on their backs.)."[15] They would receive the Silver Star for this hazardous performance.

The History of the 47th Tank Battalion records what happened on 20 March, when two platoons of Company A of the 68th, now entering the fray, combined with C Troop of the 94th Cav Recon to "probe" the Siegfried Line. First Lt. Charles M. Bardwell with the attached 300th Engineers and nine men from his unit, the 125th Combat Engineers, managed to penetrate the Dragon's Teeth to blow out one row of them. Heavy friendly fire from 8-inch guns, 240mm howitzers, and 155mm howitzers plastered not only the line's defenses but also the towns of Steinfeld and Schaidt, which were tied in with them. One section of C-47 tanks pulled into position to the north of Kapsweyer to support the infantry, and Task Force Blue was stationed behind them. After the 36th Infantry Division seemed to be making little headway, it was the 25th Tank Battalion's turn, as its History's perspective showed:

This seemed to be the time to put in our bid, so the morning of the 22nd of March, with 'A' Company in the lead, the Battalion moved across the treadway, which had been erected over an Anti-Tank ditch, into the town of Steinfeld. Pillboxes and casements were camouflaged to look like houses and barns. Our attached TD's were blasing [sic] away with their 90mm guns and penetrating these defenses. S/Sgt [Warren F.] Roberson's tank was hit by AT fire and was knocked out. The krauts knew their ground and their artillery was accurate. A phosphorous shell hit a 'C' Company tank commanded by Cpl Hart. Sgt. [John E. Reed, 'A' Company [the 25th], while attacking an enemy pillbox and the tank spun around under the impact. Sgt. [Joseph H.] Stallings also took direct hit from artillery. Lt. [Paul M.] Kilnefelter [also of A-25] received a severe wound while making a dismounted reconnaissance of a pillbox. The infantry was having a rough time as cover was inadequate and many casualties were incurred.[16]

The fighting was ferocious, and in order to give the exposed men a chance, a smokescreen was laid down by the Mortar Platoon led by Lt. Hugh L. Ferguson of Headquarters Company of the 25th Tank Battalion. The 105mm assault guns rolled up to engage the pillboxes. Cpl. Norman N. Hall's gun was hit and "the ammo trailer started to blaze and Pfc. [Alfred D.] Crawford jumped down and released the trailer." The medics were given high praise for reaching and removing wounded under frantically dangerous conditions.

On the next morning, the 23rd, the attack resumed, with A Company, 25 TB on the right, C on the left, and B in the center, with A and the Tank Destroyers in reserve. Enemy anti-tank guns destroyed two tanks almost immediately, and a lieutenant, a sergeant, and two privates "were mortally wounded." Both A and C Companies were frustrated in their attempt to break through, but Lt. Robert R. Chrisman of C Company maneuvered his tanks to eliminate five pillboxes, which action, in turn, allowed all three tank companies to forge ahead. As they reached an anti-tank ditch outside Schaidt, smoke was laid down, and a tank dozer rumbled up to fill a ditch to allow the tanks to keep advancing. By 1100, A Company "pushed into Schaidt and on through to neutralize the pillboxes and AT guns of Jerry's last main line of defense, The Great West Wall." A reinforced recon patrol was requested to take Freckenfeld, and Lt. Chrisman's Company reduced two 88's and seized the town by 1730. The enemy was now badly disorganized.[17]

CCR moved up to support CCA, with Col. Charles H. Karlstadt in command, and Col. Daniel H. Hudelson in command of the combined 62nd AIB and A Company of the 25th along with the men of the 68th AIB. Soon the entire tank battalion was made available for the final push through the Line.

Years later there would be animated discussions about whether the 62nd or the 68th AIB "took" Steinfeld, the town which was solidly built into the German fortifications. The 14th's *History* indicates that the 62nd "passed through the 68th and took up the attack on Steinfeld." The artillery fire silenced the guns in the pillboxes, but appearances could be deceiving as the infantry surged forward:

> The men ran into the first pillbox houses—innocent-seeming farmhouses; but when artillery shells blasted against their sides, the tiles crumbled off and revealed six-foot-thick reinforced concrete walls and the windows came away and revealed tiered, recessed gun ports, nasty-snouted enemy flat trajectory guns spitting out of them. Heavy enemy counterfire rained down on the men of the 62nd in Steinfeld. The platoons attacked, not down the streets, but through backyards from window to window. The 1st Platoon and the mortar sections, the Anti-Tank Platoon, dismounted, and a section of tanks entered the town and added their weight to the fight.[18]

The fight for Steinfeld, on 21 March, continued desperately for the whole day, with weapons of all calibers and types employed to annihilate the opposition. The mortars dropped shells fifty yards in front of the infantry, and both 155mm "Long Toms" and 8-inch howitzers hammered the *Landsers*, as they were called. On the American side, the wounded were carried out of town on the backs of tanks. B Company of the 62nd reported on the fight from their immediate perspective:

> Throughout the night men fired across alleyways at fleeting targets. Two company CPs were demolished, one after the other, by artillery fire; the burning buildings fatally outlined the men

crouched near them. Every cellar was a foxhole. The machine gunners rested the barrels of their guns on window ledges, fired them without tripods, bazookas fired at pointblank ranges so you had to watch the splash; and pillboxes that had been cleared began to fire again, and had to be cleared again. Armor piercing 76mm [tank] shells ricocheted off the six-foot-thick reinforced walls, white phosphorous and fragmentation grenades were thrust by hand through the pillbox slits, lobbed into trenches.[19]

Finally, in small numbers, German soldiers with fluttering white cloths in their hands began to surrender. C Company of the 62nd arrived in town on the left, negotiating its way through a maze of half-filled anti-tank ditches, barbed wire, and the maze of pillboxes and strongpoints. "The assault squads," under veteran leadership, began to clear the houses, but in the process both Sgt. Wilbert H. Tebbe and Sgt. Elmer A. Taylor would be wounded. Tebbe would not survive but would earn a Silver Star for his gallant efforts.

Several severe counterattacks followed, and the armored infantry was hard pressed to resist the aggressive German infantry:

A night counter-attack reached the company CP itself before it was driven off. Sgt. Carl Henderson, [who would be awarded a Bronze Star] established himself on the roof with grenades and a BAR and became a one-man outpost. He lobbed his grenades while observers on the floor below gave him fire direction orders. One enemy soldier tried—unsuccessfully—to grab a machine gun by the muzzle and pull it out the window.[20]

After more surrenders to members of C Company, it was clear that Steinfeld had been taken—by both the 62nd and the 68th and supporting units. But, as Ken Hazleton insists, there was still danger for the medics:

Steinfeld was finally cleared somewhat and a forward aid station moved in. The weasel [a small tracked jeep] was the only vehicle which was able to get by the tank trap until the engineers bridged it and then the aid station personnel went riding in a half track. They held their breath all the way because of the enemy fire. The sight which met their eyes was heart rending—eleven wounded men, many seriously, had been gathered by aid man Francis, "Slim" Steinmann [who later received a Silver Star] and brought to the safety of adjoining cellars. Dressed and splintered, and with morphine and plasma, those able to walk or sit were loaded into a truck and sent back. Finally after a swift spring wreaking [sic] journey Pfc Bob Prim came in with his ambulance to pick up the seriously wounded.[21]

After heavy casualties to both A and B Companies of the 62nd AIB because of enemy artillery, the 68th's History records the satisfaction of taking Steinfeld:

We slowly realized the importance of the mission we had just completed. . . . The first phase of the battle to pierce the Siegfried Line had been won. We had suffered heavy casualties as was expected, but this time the results were quite different from those of the battle at Ober-Otterbach, where we could not even approach the first belt of the Siegfried. Reports that General Patton's Third Army had flanked the Siegfried Line and was approaching Landau, just twenty-five miles from our positions, greatly boosted the morale. These reports were substantiated by orders given to the artillery not to fire at greater than a ten-mile range because of danger of hitting Third Army men.[22]

Of course, one battle was over, but there were more to follow. The 62nd withdrew to Kapsweyer to reorganize and resupply, and the 68th then took up the baton. Early in the morning of 23 March at 0450 hours, that battalion stepped off with A and C Companies leading the attack. Headquarters Company relieved C Company of the responsibility of protecting the right flank. "After several minutes of devasting [sic] supporting artillery barrages we moved out." The soldiers had to traverse a mile of open ground to get to their objective. As the 68th's History continues:

Time seemed to stand still as we advanced across the open expanse but as dawn had not fully broken at this time, [we] were able to gain access to the fringes of town and after five hours of bitter house to house fighting the town was cleared, whereupon the tanks with Infantry mounted on them circled the town taking numerous stunned Jerries from their pillboxes and ended the operation by silencing two 88mm guns emplaced along the road leading to Freckenfeld, the next town.[23]

Although casualties were relatively light for the taking of the town, its pillboxes, and the two 88's, one armored infantryman, Sgt. Robert H. Kamm of A Company, was unlucky enough to be straddled by two rounds from an MG-42, one on each side of his torso. Fortunately, they hit no vital organs, and Kamm was safely removed from the field of battle. The 14th Armored's History described the hostile fire as "incredibly vicious: the 68th could make no headway at all, and the men were pinned down the entire day. The 25th Tank Battalion was made available to CCR; and the next morning, with the tanks, the 68th jumped off again."[24] It appears that the 68th's history version telescopes the two days into a more positive one day, and it appears that the reference to 0450 hours on 23 March should probably read "22 March."

The 14th's *History* continues the narrative. According to it, the 125th Combat Engineers built a treadway bridge for the tanks of the C-25 TB to allow them to enter the town of Steinfeld. Almost immediately, as they were exposed, three tanks were hit and knocked out and 1st Lt. Paul M. Klinefelter was wounded. The Mortar Platoon of Headquarters Company of the 68th AIB laid down smoke, and the assault guns moved up. One of the 105mm guns was hit and its ammunition trailer starting to burn. Pfc. Alfred D. Crawford jumped out of the chassis and separated the dangerously burning trailer. Medics came up and evacuated Cpl. James W. Hall, who was injured in the incident. On the morning of the 23rd, all of the 25th's tanks were brought into play. A Company of the 48th Tank Battalion was waiting in reserve. The 14th's History explained what happened next:

> In the vicious fight that followed, that started almost as soon as the tanks jumped off, B Company of the 25th lost two tanks. Lieut. Geneser, Sgt. Vincent A. Corio, Corp. Andrew Juga, Pfcs. John D. Teeters and Cleophas Swain were killed. A Company was held up in the wet marshy ground; and B Company was

stopped momentarily by the fire of the AT guns, picking off the tanks as soon as they showed themselves. Lieut. [Robert R.] Chrisman of C Company, moving on the left flank, knocked out five pillboxes and silenced the AT guns that had been holding up B. Company.[25]

It was a terrible truth of the fighting against the Siegfried that infantry on their own had almost no chance of penetrating the defenses without both the heroism and the sacrifice of the combat engineers and the tank battalions. The former had to work in the pitch black to set charges to blow the dragon's teeth, and the latter had to expose themselves to the ever quick and deadly German anti-tank guns, which took a terrible toll of the Shermans and their crews. The guns were always difficult to spot, and it was not always obvious to the naked eye that a gun had been fired.

The Wehrmacht had several different anti-tank guns of varying calibers, lengths, and velocities, and the most deadly of these was the 7.5cm Pak (Panzerabwehrkanone) 40. An enlargement of an earlier version, "It became the standard anti-tank gun remaining in service for the remainder of the war [after 1941]." Even at 1500 meters (a little less than a mile), its AP round could penetrate more than four inches in armor.[26] Neither the American nor the British Army had any vehicle that could withstand that power. General Patton's passion for a fast tank that could pierce the enemy's lines and cause havoc like old fashioned cavalry was fine in theory, but a lot of tankers lost their lives or were terribly wounded because of the vulnerability of medium tanks on the Western Front.

Another problem in the 14th and other armored divisions was the use of the American 37mm anti-tank gun against pillboxes since it lacked sufficient hitting power. It was considered "a popgun" by Cpt. Andrew Winiarczik, commander of the 25th Tank Battalion's C Company in which Sgt. Bob McClarren served. The later 57mm anti-tank gun was an improvement but still a problem.

At this point in the struggle for Steinfeld, the tanks of A-48 were sent into the bitter fight, but an anti-tank ditch stopped them. At this juncture a tank dozer was ordered up to fill in the ditch, and smoke was laid down to conceal the tanks from hostile gunfire. The 68th's History relates the story of the heroism of Lt. John P. Delmay of the 125th

Armored Engineers, for which he would receive posthumously a Silver Star:

> Preceding the attack, without regard for his own life, he took an open hatched bulldozer over virgin terrain to make a crossing over the tank barrier trap that had held up the tanks. Lt. Del May [sic] was seriously wounded in this operation and subsequently died of his wounds, he had paid the supreme sacrifice so that his comrades could achieve victory.[27]

As the contest continued, more friendly tanks were hit by various kinds of devices: one hit a mine, another was damaged by a mortar round, wounding Lt. William Kidd of the Third Platoon of A Company. The towns, Kapsweyer, Steinfeld, and Schaidt, and numbers of tanks were all blazing in what was now darkness. The engineers of the First Platoon of the 125th Combat Engineers, with the 68th, and those of the Second Platoon, with the 25th TB, and the engineers of the Third Platoon with Task Force Blue—all these moved up to drive a fatal spike into the net of the dragon's teeth with high explosives. Lt. H.B. Hewett, 125th Combat Engineers, decided, "We've got to do it tonight. . . . It's darker than all hell." The charges were prepared, and the men wore no gloves despite the cold. They proceeded at midnight toward the "teeth" with a combined load of 300 pounds of TNT, but there was still revealing light from incoming artillery rounds and burning buildings.

The party stopped at the 68th's CP and discovered how terribly difficult the day had been for both tanks and infantry. The engineers started forward at intervals of thirty yards just in case one man's explosives ignited and killed them all. If they were lucky, only one would be atomized in the blast. Their destination could barely be seen in the flickering darkness. The 14th's History paints the picture and suggests the sights and smells of the struggle:

> It was hard to see the man ahead of you in the darkness, with the flickering weird light of battle at night. The stink of burning houses was in their nostrils.
>
> It seemed they would never get there; finally, dimly, they could see the Dragon's Teeth in the light from the fires, like headstones in a graveyard.

Quickly, the first man was over the wall in front of the teeth; then the second man, and the third. Not a sound was uttered. The men tied their charges, the job was finished, finally, the men started back." [For this action Lt. Hewett would earn a Silver Star.]

Before they were [back] in town, there was a lightning flash, a terrific explosion, and 300 pounds of TNT blasted the night. The job was done.[28]

The other engineers of the 125th were called upon to perform various tasks as the fight continued. The Second Platoon of C Company built a bridge at Hunspach by exploiting an abandoned German tank, lodged in the stream, as a base. They also had to remove a ton of dynamite from a crater and filled in two others. As they advanced into the wreckage of Steinfeld, they were subjected to a heavy artillery barrage. Both Pfc. Herman A. Bounds and Lt. John C. Copes were wounded, the last by a machine gun. Copes would earn a Bronze Star for his heroism. One of his men, Sgt. Ray Hodson "suddenly charged the gun, shouting: 'Achtung, you Kraut bastards!'"

After the machine gunners surrendered, Hodson discovered that he had an empty clip in his rifle. At this point Lt. Delmay performed his heroic action with the open VTR (vehicle-tank recovery) which resulted in his death. The Third Platoon of Engineers entered Schleithal and installed 300 feet of bridging and corduroy roads so that the tanks could advance. Other engineers blew more dragon's teeth to open another path so that the division could advance. Finally, "On the 21st, the 1st Platoon was ordered to help build the bridge at Altenstadt; and on the 23rd, the company took off with CCB on that command's mad dash to the Rhine."[29]

A sure sign that the enemy was beginning to collapse was the volume of prisoners being taken, with B Company of the Engineers capturing 45 all by itself. CCB, under the command of Col. Francis J. Gillespie, "broke free at Kilgenmunster." Assault guns of the 47th TB were firing into Germany, and as the armored column wound around the wooded roads high up near the Rhine River, what in peacetime could have been a scene of gorgeous natural beauty in the spring turned into a disastrous inferno for the Germans. As Captain Joseph Carter graphically limns the dreadful picture:

It was dear and sunny—warm, actually, and a German column
had been caught on the road by aircraft, artillery, and tanks; the
unbelievable, the unending litter and wreckage lined the roads.
A German infantry column, that was horsedrawn and winding
its slow way along the dear roads of Spring before the shells
began to scream in and the men and the horses to plunge; and
as the Combat Command passed now there was the carts and
the guns tangled along the sides of the roads, and the slashed
and bloodied and bloated horses (and other horses cut loose,
munching grass in the early green Spring fields) and broken
rifles, scattered papers, field desks, sodden uniforms, all the infinite paraphernalia of an Army, and German dead and American
dead, a soldier lying by the side of the road, staring vacantly and
white-faced to the sky, the dust from the tank treads settling on
his face, his shirt torn and his chest white-bandaged where the
medics had tried to save his life; and a still form under a blanket, only muddied combat boots showing at the bottom and one
lifeless hand lying on the grass, a wedding ring glinting faintly
on the fourth finger.[30]

It would be hard to surpass the effective quality of this description
from the era of Homer to that of Remarque or Hemingway.

The action was to continue, and the 19th AIB and other units continued the fight to get to the Rhine, but it would be impossible here to
cover all of that material. This writer can only refer a reader to Carter's
History of the 14th. Lt. General Jacob L. Devers, Commander of Sixth
Army Group, commended Seventh Army, of which the 14th AD was an
integral part:

In reviewing the operations of the Seventh Army for the past 12
days, I once again wish to express to you and your gallant
troops my appreciation for the outstanding job which they have
done. As one of the tried and proven veteran Corps of our Army
you have once again demonstrated your superiority over the
enemy. You have added another victory to your already known
campaigns of Salerno, Anzio, and Southern France.[31]

The compliment was well taken by Seventh Army, but it should be noted that the 14th Armored Division started active duty after the Italian campaign in the Maritime Alps. The commendation continued by praising the "brilliant leadership" of the Army.

To get back to the 68th Armored Infantry Battalion, after its struggle at Kapsweyer, Steinfeld, and Schaidt and its casualties, its history points out that it had been prepared to assist CCB in its approach to the Rhine, particularly at Germersheim and the actual crossing of that river. Because of blown bridges, it returned to Freckenfeld and performed the dismal duty of policing the pillboxes and removing "dead Krauts." The Battalion performed maintenance and training schedules, which "kept us busy until the 30th of March." The 68th's history was pleased, of course, to record two commendations, the first dated 10 May, by Brig. General C.H. Karlstad, part of which follows:

> The actions and accomplishments of the 68th Armored Infantry Battalion during the operations of the approach to and the breaching of the Siegfried Line by Combat Command 'A' from 15 March to 24 March 1945 were most outstanding. The Battalion pursued the withdrawing enemy with a fine dash and elan from SURBOURG through NIEDERROEDERN and to the BIEN WALD forrest [sic]. . . . It then, on 20 March attacked and secured a foothold within the organized SIEGFRIED defenses at STEINFELD, GERMANY. Passing through other elements of the division, it attacked early on the morning of 23 March 1945 to capture SCHAIDT. . . . the battalion advanced over 3000 yards through an area completely covered by numerous enemy concrete bunkers . . . [and] rushed into the town and, after a period of about 5 hours, completely cleared the enemy therefrom. . . .

A special commendation was also awarded to "Officers and Men of the 68th AIB, and Co 'A', 48th TK Bn.'" from Col. D. H. Hudelson. It said in part:

> The line through which you passed was part of the greatest system of fortifications in the history of warfare. That part of the line which you overcame was one of the strongest links in this entire system. The enemy who were driven before you made a

strong and determined defense until their will to fight was broken by the force of your attack. . . .

The officers and men of the 68th AIB, 62nd AIB and Co A, 48th TK Bn, showed dogged determination and great courage in the face of intense artillery, rocket and mortar fire over a period of days; and an aggressive attitude which carried them to their successive objectives through a hail of small arms and supporting anti-tank fire. . . .[32]

There was a high price to pay for the men of the 68th in this operation:

Killed in Action	17
Died of Wounds	2
Wounded in Action	54
Injured in Action	4
TOTAL CASUALTIES	77[33]

And yet, despite the casualties, the Westwall, despite ferocious opposition, had been overcome.

Chapter 8

THE DRIVE FROM THE RHINE

After a week or more of "housekeeping" activities, the 68th AIB initiated a fighting convoy that was to motor march two hundred miles across the Rhine just north of the ancient city of Worms to Dieburg, Germany, where their fellow soldiers in the Third Army had crossed the river into Germany proper. The 14th Armored would cross on Easter Sunday, 1 April. Officially, it would not be until 23 April that the 14th Armored Division would be attached to Patton's Third Army.

The march began on the evening of 31 March, and at 0600 hours the 68th arrived in Dieburg much the worse for wear from rattling around in "deuce and a half" (2-1/2 ton) trucks and halftracks. For the remainder of that day the men had to perform more maintenance on their vehicles, guns, and other equipment. The various attachments joined to the battalion were A Company of the 48th Tank Battalion, the First Platoon of A Company of the 636th Tank Destroyer Battalion, the First Platoon of C Troop, 94th Cavalry, and the First Platoon of C Company, 125th Engineers. This varied assembly of combat soldiers and their support was placed under the control of CCA of the 14th Armored, and even Corps Artillery and Division Trains were in support. CCA had been placed under the control of XV Corps (still Seventh Army) under the 12th Army Group led by General Omar Bradley.

The 68th received the order to attack through elements of the Third Infantry Division, the much bloodied and experienced outfit which had made landings in North Africa, Italy, and in Operation Anvil on the coast of the Riviera in August. Earlier in the year it had worked with the French First Army to wrest control of the Colmar Pocket just south of where the 14th AD had been fighting since November of 1944.[1]

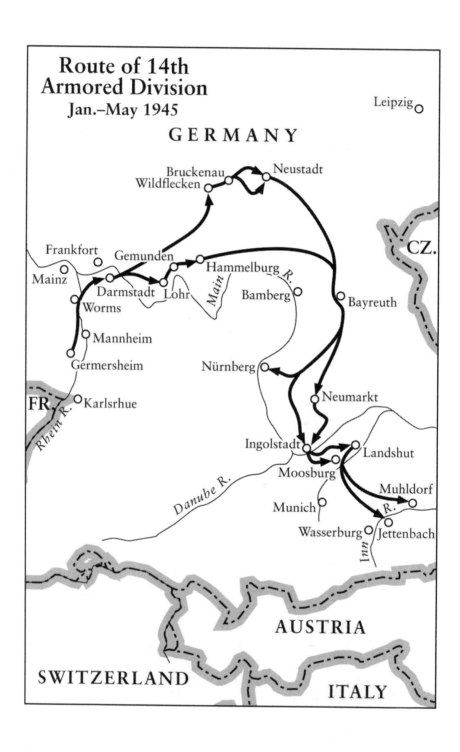

Route of 14th Armored Division Jan.–May 1945

GERMANY

Leipzig

CZ.

Bruckenau
Wildflecken
Neustadt

Frankfort
Gemunden
Mainz
Hammelburg
Main R.
Bamberg
Darmstadt
Lohr
Main
Bayreuth
Worms
Mannheim
Nürnberg
Germersheim
Neumarkt
FR.
Rhein R.
Karlsrhue
Ingolstadt
Landshut
Moosburg
Danube R.
Muhldorf
Munich
R.
Wasserburg
Jettenbach
Inn

AUSTRIA

SWITZERLAND
ITALY

The *History* of the 14th devotes a chapter to what it calls "Pursuit," by which it means the rapid advance of the division from town to town in Germany. Once the Westwall had been pierced, ideal places for the German defense were hard to come by. The Wehrmacht, always skilled in ambush and camouflage, made tactical decisions as to where to turn and face their pursuers. These would almost always be towns, and the Burgermeister and the town fathers would be placed in a difficult situation if the retreating soldiers decided to make a stand. The SS troops were often the ones to choose to make a stand, although at other times the townspeople might join them in a desperate rebuff to the strong American forces speeding to the outskirts of their town. If the town made serious resistance, it could be and often was destroyed by artillery and air bombardment. Usually there was a roadblock outside of a town trying to oppose the advancing column, and its defenders sometimes made just a show of force with small arms fire and mortars, sometimes more than that. If a white flag then appeared at the barricade, it mostly but not always meant that the town was surrendering. On some occasions this tactic was a ruse, and more than one American officer advancing to the white flag was fired upon and even killed. The result then was wholesale destruction of the town. Needless to say, the result could be a calamity for the citizens, and sometimes cooperation would appear in the most unlikely places as will be seen in examples later.

The crossing of the Rhine took place on 1 April 1945, which was then Easter Sunday, but the GIs knew it was also April Fool's Day. The eloquence of Captain Carter captures the beauty of the scene:

> For many of the men, dawn was just breaking as the long lines of vehicles turned off the good German roads near Worms, swung down the banks and onto the bridge approaches; the pink and blood red of the cold-rising Easter sun streaked the gray morning sky with strips of gentle color, and the land of Germany revealed itself, clearer and clearer, the flat slightly rolling, brown-green fertile farmland of the Rhine Valley, gray and cold that morning, the twisted gray trees marching in files over the hills.[2]

This would not be a day of glorious Resurrection but of hard marching and sudden violence. The twisted trees testified to the efficiency of the German nation, but so did its technology, manifested in the Me-262 jet fighters, which were still a problem for the advancing columns.

Fortunately for the CCA column and the men of the 68th AIB, newly attached was the 398th AAA Battalion, with its quad .50 caliber machine guns. The column was then divided, with most of the 68th allied with Company A of the 48th Tank Battalion, and A Company of the 68th with the remainder of the 48th. The Recon Platoon of the 68th along with the First Platoon of C of the 94th Cav were in the lead. As these elements passed the outposts of the 3rd Infantry Division and reached Partenstein, they were "stopped dead by sharp automatic weapons fire." B and C Companies of the 68th entered the fight and had to clear the town house by house until it was free of enemy combatants by morning.

The fighting continued without all-out resistance but with enough rifle and automatic weapons fire to slow down the column and add to the wounded and killed-in-action statistics. However, the GIs fought north until they reached Rengersbrunn. Most of these towns were set in wooded hill country above rivers, and when friendly forces won the city of Burgsinn, a town northwest of Wurzburg and southwest of Bad Kissingen, they were rewarded with the capture of the bridge across the Sinn River.[3]

The convoy crossed the river and followed a northeasterly course over mountain trails until late in the afternoon, when it encountered elements of the American 45th Infantry Division. This meeting determined that the column change course and aim in a southeasterly direction. Late that evening the task force arrived at the outskirt of Grafendorf and halted on the hillside while Lt. Graham P. Madden, who would earn both a Bronze and a Silver Star, and Lt. Robert M. Billhymer, who would earn a Silver Star, organized a patrol to ascertain whether any hostile elements occupied the town. Enemy machine gun fire from a roadblock on the edge of town forced the patrol to reverse course. In the ensuing firefight, two of 2nd Lt. Billhymer's men were killed. Permission was requested and granted to spend the remainder of the night out-posting the hillside. This was often a wise strategy, for frequently the town's defenders would decide that they had given a good account of themselves and so could then retreat to the next town. In this case, early the next morning infantry from C-68, now dismounted from the tanks, accompanied by B Company, cleared the enemy from the town.[4]

Usually such a clearance meant that there would be no more resistance in a town, but German cleverness and stubbornness determined that the men from the 68th and the 48th TB now had to fight their way out of town. Heavy fire of all kinds against the Teutonic obduracy persuaded the defenders to relinquish their hold on the town of Grafendorf. The attached 69th Field Artillery was instrumental in this effort. When the column rolled into Wartmannsroth, it received "vicious fire" from "multibarreled antiaircraft guns." It was then concluded that "discretion was the better part of valor," as an unwilling soldier in Shakespeare's Henry IV had decided. The armored convoy hastened a turn toward the town of Volkersleier. Near Waldheim, when a recon patrol was placed under heavy fire and some of the men were wounded. Sgt. Clyde R. Hazeltine and Pfc. Lloyd Montgomery of A Company of the 48th both earned Bronze Stars for leaving their tank and removing the wounded to safety. Near Polling on a tortuous road, a huge crater had been blown in the road, an obstacle which forced the infantry to advance without tank support toward the town. They were assisted by friendly artillery fire, which was especially helpful because the town was defended by SS troops. What could have been a costly engagement with multiple casualties was avoided in an extraordinary way when a tearful German boy of twelve years emerged from the woods. As the 14th's History relates the story:

> "Nichts schiessen mehr, nichts schiessen mehr" [Don't shoot. . .
> .], he wept the artillery was systematically demolishing the
> houses in town, inevitably killing civilians. (Later, many a
> German civilian, man or weeping aged woman, boy or burgermeister, was to run, stumbling, from shelled towns to the
> American guns, asking mercy.) The SS troops, the boy said,
> were forcing the fight; the townspeople wanted to surrender.
> The boy went to the forward OP, with a pair of field glasses,
> and pointed out the location of every German gun and strong
> point in the village; and the American guns blasted them out one
> by one.[5]

The fight continued through almost a dozen towns, with some fighting in vain to stop the American force and some wisely waving white flags to save themselves and their towns. When these civilians used to read about the glorious victories of the Reich in someone else's towns and cities, that was something to cheer about—but not now.

The 48th Tank Battalion, under the leadership of Major John C. Cavin, raced ahead to encounter the men of the Third Infantry Division, which evidently had little experience working with armor. Their regimental commander complained to Major Cavin, "Tanks. . . . We've had 'em before. They clog the roads, they tear up the turns, they draw fire, and they don't do a damned thing." When Cavin asked him how many tank battalions he had previously worked with, he growled, "No battalions." Then Major Cavin offered a challenge, almost a bet. He told the 3rd Infantry Officer that he would push through forty tanks in five minutes. The challenge was accepted: "Take off." When the town was cleared in five minutes and after further tactical success, the 3rd's officer then had to admit that the 48th, from where he stood, was the best armored battalion in the army.[6]

The surest sign that the German army was beginning to disintegrate was demonstrated in the town with the elegant name Aura, a town in a valley surrounded by winding roads coming down from the hills. After a certain amount of investigating which road was the best into this large town, the tanks of the 48th crested a ridge on its outskirts. They looked down on a madcap scene, with about five hundred enemy soldiers running around furiously to hitch wagons to remove artillery and frantically driving vehicles to escape. The 76mm guns of the tanks established a base of fire, and the remaining tanks rushed down the hill after the Germans. Many tried to flee, but many others surrendered under a panoply of waving white flags. The infantry of A-68 collected all the prisoners after some of the tankers chased down those fleeing into the woods. A familiar phrase in rough English was "Kamerad, Kamerad, where do I surrender?"

At Rossbach, the pleasant task of taking prisoners continued when the garrison was sitting down to a breakfast which was served by Italian prisoners. The Italians invited the Americans to enjoy the breakfast prepared for their captors. They were also eager to volunteer to fight as tankers, a request turned down, and so they picked up German rifles and joined the 68th infantry. Rupboden also fell without a struggle, but as the column moved on it was opposed by a combination of infantry, self-propelled guns, and tanks, but this resistance was eliminated with the help of artillery. A resort hospital with eighty doctors and nurses was captured without incident.

There was more serious action in Bruchenau when eighteen men were trapped in a house and subjected to heavy artillery fire, which caused several casualties. Four volunteers, Privates Bissell, Benson, Parks, killed in action, and Hoover, scouted ahead to ascertain whether there were any road obstacles and were subjected to sniper and mortar fire. They were able to reach the stranded men and then returned with information that allowed the tanks and infantry to avoid the enemy Panzerfausts which were stationed along the main road. Before they reached the next town, Romershag, two prisoners were allowed to enter the town to persuade the inhabitants to surrender. However, as happened previously, SS troops prevented that from happening. After the town was taken, the two prisoners revealed that the SS refused to allow them to offer the peace terms to the townspeople.

The hastening column, with all its parts, was primarily composed of the 48th Tank Battalion and Company A of the 68th but also included many other units mentioned before like the 94th Cav. It would be futile to try to mention all the towns passed through, and it seemed like "a rat race," with the light and medium tanks rolling at fifteen miles an hour and the halftracks of the 68th along with the armored cars of the 94th. Opposed to them in disorganized retreat, "There was the German infantry, trying to retreat, and breaking ranks and running for the woods and the tanks caught up with them; there was the artillery, German horses galloping and leaping crazily and crumpling as American mobile artillery caught them on the road."[7] Yet there could be stubborn resistance in the towns, with both soldiers and civilians firing on the speeding column.

Among the stories arising from this period was the one in which Pfc. Walter Hammonds, a driver, followed a tank into town in his quarter-ton truck. The Germans fired on the truck and wounded his passenger, but then the medics arrived. The Germans told the medics to take the passenger but not Hammonds. The medics insisted on examining Hammond's knee, claiming it needed medical assistance, which it did not. They told the Germans that the leg would have to come off, and they let both men and the medics go. One can only guess that some of the blood off the passenger must have splashed or sprayed onto Hammonds' knee.

Another episode involved a small party of men led by S/Sgt. Eilif P. Dahl, A-68, which advanced under fire to reach the home of the burgermeister of a town. Two men were wounded in the enterprise, but the burgermeister was returning with the group when he was killed. Dahl was later awarded the Bronze Star for his courage and initiative.

Still another episode about Lt. Anthony Wise, C Company of the 125th Engineers, who was instructed to examine a bridge ahead which led into Breuckenau. Nobody told him he was supposed to wait until the combat soldiers had captured the bridge. So he walked up by himself and began to examine the bridge but then found a German guard standing next to him. He took off to save his life and was lucky enough to suffer a bullet hole only in his helmet. He was awarded both the Bronze and the Silver Stars.

In another town, some Poles who had been captured and dragooned by the Germans into service joined the Italians who were already serving with A-68. The company was further enlarged by the willing Poles. T/Sgt. Charles B. Nagy, a Bronze Star recipient, whose name showed his Hungarian descent, employed his knowledge of that language to persuade 198 Hungarians to surrender.

The 94th Cav was attached to CCA and ordered to advance on roads in between the two columns, the one just described (A-68 with the 48th Tank Battalion) and the other, also part of CCA (A-48 and the remainder of the 68th). The pace was exhausting, "115 miles in three mad days, the dirt and grime and firing."

The CCA Report on the action encapsulated the advance thus:

> The 68th Infantry advanced 25 miles capturing 11 towns and seizing crossings of the Saale River at Unsleben. Some resistance was encountered in Sandberg from enemy tank fire. The 48th Tank [Battalion] advanced 14 miles capturing the towns of Unter Weissebrunn, Wegfurt, Schonau, Brendlorenzen and Neustadt. The advance progressed rapidly, destroying many enemy guns and vehicles. Intense sniper fire (soldiers and civilians) was encountered in Neustadt and the town was reported cleared at 2230 on April 7. The main Neustadt bridge was seized and held intact.
>
> The German war machine was collapsing; the German nation was being overrun.[8]

There is an amusing scene in the film Patton, when the lead tanks are sitting in a crossroad, and the tankers have trouble finding where they are on the map. Somebody finally pipes up and says, "That's because we ran off the map." But there was nothing amusing about the fighting and the wounding and the dying. The History of the 68th narrates what the battalion faced in the vicinity of Sandberg and Killanshof:

Town after town were [sic] entered and taken until we reached Sandberg. There German tank fire forced our reconnaissance elements to withdraw to Waldberg and 'B' Company attacked the town across an open valley under cover of smoke. Sandberg being now cleared, the battalion [minus Company A] set out in column once more but was soon stopped by intense machine gun and sniper fire from the woods in the vicinity of Killanshof which was subdued by TD [Tank Destroyer] and infantry attacks. Without too much interference we contacted friendly elements in Bischoffheim and were given the additional mission of seizing Unsleben and the crossings of the Streu River at Unsleben, as darkness fell.[9]

Yet worse was to come: "The honeymoon ended at Lohr" when Company A of the 68th, along with the 48th, under the Command of CCB, "encountered heavy small arms fire." As the CCB Report continued, "It was impossible to by-pass the town, and an attack was launched. Resistance was extremely stubborn." The difficulty was that Lohr is situated at the junction of the Lohr and Main Rivers, and the only way to assault it was down a valley in an exposed position. The combination of C Company of the 19th Armored Infantry Battalion and C Company of the 48th Tank Battalion led the way, with the "dogfaces" riding the tanks at 0700 hours. Lt. Felix Prieur's gunner, Cpl. William Miller, in one of the lead tanks, shot away three 75mm SP's (self-propelled guns), but in the engagement the lieutenant, who would merit a Silver Star, was killed by a sniper after his tank was hit. First Lt. Travis Cox, of B-47, took his light tank around the town and caught three horse drawn guns and put them out of action.

A brief report entitled "Hist. 14th Armored Div: June 45–Aug 15" recapitulates the difficulties which CCA was having at Lohr:

The CC [Combat Command] was having trouble all day long with the narrow mountain roads. General [A.C.] SMITH [the 14th's commander], anxious to keep pushing the attack, sent a message to Col. [Charles H.] Karlstad, now Brig. Gen., to push his attack as long as possible. CCB renewed attack on LOHR at 0615B meeting heavy SA, Arty, AT bazooka fire and blown bridges. 19th AIB and 47thTK Bn finally cleared LOHR at 1730B after meeting determined resistance. Air Forces flew several missions for CCB with excellent results. Caught an Ey column moving NE from LOHR to SACKENBACH (N3358) and STEINBACH (N340585). Ey had launched a C/Atk on LOHR at 1100B but it was beaten back with minor damage.

On 4 April, the 68th AIB moved into the attack at 0645B. The leading elements were slowed down by two undefended roadblocks but managed to pass through Fellen "after a small fire fight." At Burgsinn, "the first heavy resistance of the day" was offered by a hostile force "occupying the high ground just E of the town." The brief "Hist." of the 14th again summarizes the action:

> Lt Col Bob Edwards, CO of the 68th AIB, immediately dismounted two Armd lnf companies, B and C. The two companies attacked supported by Arty, Mortar and assault gun fire at 1245B. In 1 hour and 15 minutes the position was taken and the Bn crossed the SINN R over an intact bridge at the S end of town. At darkness the Bn occupied high ground vic (N4o576o).[10]

As Captain Carter inimitably pictured the inferno:

> The town was afire from the shelling, the flames leaping through the darkness and crackling through the madness of the firing; the smoke was in your eyes and nose, and the weird shadows of the men running, and of the tanks and of nothing at all (at night, in a burning town, in war) leapt and jumped along the walls.[11]

It was in the hills outside Lohr that two friends in Company C of the 68th experienced the terrible costs of war. Their story is quite tragic because of loss but quite memorable because of one private's telling of the story of the death of another. It is also quite typical in that such pain and suffering happened every day in the war in Europe, not to mention in the Pacific, where there were no vestiges of chivalry. In Europe, in the Middle Ages, there were serious attempts to practice a code of battle that lifted men sometimes above the level of plain barbarism. Some knights followed it, and some did not. In the ETO it was not uncommon for prisoners to be shot or for medics to be targeted by snipers. Put in simpler terms, sniping itself could be seen as a thinly disguised form of barbarism, for the combatants were not "jousting" on equal terms. One man was, from a considerable distance, executing another one who, at the moment, represented no threat to the sniper. If, on the other hand, a sniper was captured, especially after having killed a friend, he was then executed. There is little evidence that anyone complained about such a practice.

To get to the tragic story, two privates in C Company of the 68th, Richard J. Dunn and Robert D. Quinn, had gotten to know each other very well in a very short time. Quinn, a replacement in Dunn's machine gun squad, was quite green in February 1945. At first an ammunition bearer, he was elevated to assistant machine gunner after several men had been wounded or killed in the squad. (This kind of work was more than dangerous.) Dunn, a tough and cocky former resident of working-class Baltimore, to use Quinn's word, did all he could to teach Private Quinn how to be a soldier and how to stay alive in a very hazardous place. He needed to have a supply of clean socks, clean shirts, and an entrenching tool to dig foxholes quickly, an extra bandolier for his rifle, enough K rations and fresh water in his canteen, four grenades, and so on. Quinn also had to learn to distinguish "incoming" from "outgoing" artillery fire, how to time the period between the flash and the boom of the shells, how to determine when a shell is going to explode too close, how to differentiate "Kraut" machine guns from US machine guns and enemy rifle fire from friendly.

The problem for Quinn was not learning all of the above but his concern about Dunn's recklessness. He seemed not to care about exposing himself in the open. Quinn's comment was, "Dunn I think you're crazy." Dunn's response was that of a simple but fatalistic soldier. He thought that only one bullet "with my name written on it" would kill him and that it was useless to worry about all the other bullets humming through the air. Quinn reached back to a lesson in a religious class in school and complained of Dunn's fatalism that "Your death is foreordained. Fate has it written down. Until then, you are completely safe." (The Roman Emperor and General and the late Roman philosopher Boethius would have approved of the conversation.) Yet the discussion was hardly theoretical because the fatalism governed Dunn's recklessness. Dunn vulgarly called it "Yeah, fatal-shitism."

He cast a spell on Quinn, for he began to behave like Dunn, running out into the open with him to remove a wounded man from the battlefield, with Dunn the carrier and Quinn applying a tourniquet to the man's torn leg.

Later, Dunn told Quinn about his mother and how hard she worked in a laundry and how "She was always tired. Never had time to do much cooking or take care of me. I never had nothing." For Dunn, being in the Army was a step up from poverty and a life with no good end in sight. His father, who drank too much, depended on his wife for support. And so, as the saying used to go, "He found a home in the Army." He had plenty of company, for the Depression had produced millions of young men whose diet and health caused many of them not to be able to pass the Army physical, a generation of deprived kids. But they were tough.

The result was that "Everyone knew that eventually this kind of guts would get Dunn killed." The fight above Lohr for C-68 began with the lead halftrack getting hit by a panzerfaust to "turn it into a blazing funeral pyre." Small arms fire began to patter around the dismounted infantry, and a request came for volunteers to search the woods for hostile riflemen. Dunn volunteered and Quinn followed. They and the other volunteers formed a skirmish line, fixed bayonets, and "charged up the hillside into the woods." At first finding only empty foxholes, the line reformed and continued on a line parallel to the road. The two buddies alternated advancing and covering, first one then the other. They reached a field, and it was Quinn's turn to advance, which he did at a run in a tense crouch. He reached the edge of the forest, searched the dark woods for any indication of German infantry, and covered Quinn as he raced across the open field. Dunn took cover in a small depression about ten yards from where Quinn was coiled. As Dunn rose to call the other men forward, a shot exploded about twenty-five yards ahead of Quinn, and simultaneously, "Dunn lurched forward and fell." The other GIs charged forward and fired a spread of bullets from M-1's and a BAR. And then:

"A high-pitched voice cried out 'Kamerad! Kamerad! Nicht schiessen.'

"Come on zee out! Hands hoke!' I [Quinn] yelled back.

"'Nicht schiessen! Bitte! Nicht schiessen! Kamerad!'

"'Come on zee out! You killer son-of-a-bitch.'

"A rifle was lifted, just ahead of us, pointing straight up into the air. After a long pause, it was thrown out in front of the foxhole.

"A tousled boy in tattered uniform, a heavy knapsack on his back, slowly rose up, crouching, hands clasped over his head. His pack had been ripped by several of our bullets. I looked at him. He couldn't have been over 14. He hunched over, crying. He was certain I would shoot him. Fourteen! Goddam fuckin' war! Of course, I was still only 18 at the time.

"I looked at Dunn's still body. I wanted to shoot this bastard German. The combat rules are clear. A sniper doesn't shoot—kill—then surrender. No one takes snipers prisoner, especially after they have killed a buddy."[12]

Quinn was on the verge of killing him and would have done so had not Sergeant [George J.] Ringeisen, who would later be killed in action, pushed up his rifle and "cheated me out of my revenge." When Quinn was finally able to focus his attention on the badly wounded Dunn, he saw that he might be cheated again. Dunn was bleeding profusely from a wound in the throat. This was Quinn's response to the awful sight:

I looked over at Dunn, then dropped my rifle, ran over to him and lifted his head. Blood poured over both of us. The bullet had gone in where his Adam's apple should have been. It seemed to have exploded, blasted open his windpipe, ripped apart the large blood vessels in his neck. He made an effort to talk, but only red froth bubbled up. Blood poured into his open trachea. Each struggle for a breath flooded his lungs with more blood. He tried to cough, but only bright red foam sprayed over the front of his jacket and onto my lap. He looked at me and tried to raise his arm, but it was too much. He moved his mouth in an attempt to speak, but only hissing, bubbling sounds came out of his ragged windpipe.[13]

Dunn made the briefest signal with his eyes, and Quinn understood for it had been arranged between the two men that if one of them died in combat, the other would write to the mother and tell her that her son had died as a hero. Similar scenes took place on this and on other battlefields between friends, but their endless repetition could not take away the dramatic pain that would stay with the survivor for the rest of his days. Quinn would write such a letter to Dunn's mother in Baltimore.

Nevertheless, the fighting would not stop for Quinn and the men in his squad or his battalion or his division. The combat units in the vanguard had to leave messages for the support groups following: the artillery, Division Trains, and Maintenance and Supply units. Every time that the leading column made a turn in a town or near an outlying building, a machine gunner fired rounds into a wall of a building in the shape of an arrow to indicate the direction of the column. As the *History* of the 14th AD succinctly indicates, "No one got lost." At Wildflecken the advancing troops were fired upon, and soldiers of the 48th were notified that the Third Infantry Division was going to fire a TOT, a Time on Target shoot by every gun and tube into the city, with all of the shells landing at the same moment. Such a shoot would be terribly destructive to the town and also those citizens who were not offering resistance. Major Cavin, Commander of the 48th Tank Battalion, refused to allow it, and so "there were the half-tracks with the men of the 68th and the men of the 125th; armored cars of the 94th; and the whole column was smashing through a disorganized resistance."[14]

The CCB column, composed primarily of the 47th Tank Bn. and the 19th AIB, crossed the Main River at Worth on a pontoon bridge. After traversing many small towns, the column encountered lead elements of the 3rd Infantry Division. The column passed through, and in a pattern that would be repeated, it was fired on from hills that elevated from the road on either side. As the 19th's History pictured the scene:

> The column had hardly started moving when heavy sniper fire was received from the wooded hills rising on both sides of the road. Tanks, halftracks, and everyone opened up with all they had, spraying the woods; the noise through the valleys sounded like a major battle. The sniper fire continued, however, as did our own fire, but the column continued toward Lohr, where it

again ran into heavy small-arms and sniper fire at the western edge of town. The whole column along the road was an easy target for snipers in the hills; and it was unsafe to ride along the road in an unprotected vehicle. We received numerous casualties along the road, including Capt. Ernest M. Spokes of Company 'A,' who was evacuated. Lt. Francis Bingham then assumed command of the company. [Both men would receive Bronze Stars.][15]

Since snipers targeted officers above enlisted men, these casualties are not unusual, but the continuing loss of able and experienced officers, especially from the armored infantry and tank battalions, caused a serious turnover of the very men who were most effective in defeating a stubborn enemy.

Before the 19th AIB even reached Lohr, they had to face more resistance in the form of a manned roadblock. Both infantry riding tanks and those dismounting from halftracks were hit by small-arms fire. Anti-tank rounds knocked out two tanks. The crews, however, escaped and managed to join the Third Platoon of the 19th. The AT guns of the 14th AD also lost three halftracks to "bazooka fire." More casualties were incurred from small arms fire, and a tank was disabled. "T/5 A. J. Thompson voluntarily used his halftrack as an ambulance to evacuate wounded."[16]

The fight inside the city of Lohr was madness, with the combination of infantry from the 19th AIB and tankers from the 47th TB driving straight into town after a hellish artillery barrage. Again, Captain Carter's account is, as usual, vivid:

Company A-19 and the tanks met heavy and stubborn resistance, sniper and machine gun fire, and Lieut. Parko's tank, of B-47, was bazookaed [sic] and burned. Other tanks were knocked out, a driver was wounded and his tank, out of control, crashed through a stone-and-plate glass store front; tanks blocked the streets and the infantrymen fought from behind them, and smoke swirled from the burning buildings and plaster and stone poured into the streets as the buildings were blasted by the artillery and tank guns; halftracks were knocked out and German tanks were burning fiercely.[17]

Once in control of Lohr, the tanks of the 47th pushed through the streets toward the banks of the Main River with the help of the infantry of A-19. As the west bank of the river was cleared, the Germans attempted a retreat across the one remaining bridge. The main bridge had been blown, and this allowed the guns of the Americans to reduce the numbers of German infantry as they fled in haphazard fashion across the river. Air support was requested and given, and the column reached and took the small town of Sackenbach. After a reorganization of CCB, the infantry of A-19 climbed on the tanks and reached the edge of the town of Nantenbach along a road with a slope on the upper side. Hostile infantry rose from concealed trenches to attack the tanks with panzerfausts. Captain Thomas C. Beaty's tank was hit, and he was wounded. Friendly infantry "hit the ditches," and the fight turned into a melee. When the German soldiers began to roll grenades down the hill into the ranks of the GIs, causing multiple injuries, Lieut. Francis E. Marshall pushed his tank forward and began to cover the hill with heavy-gun and machine-gun fire. For his bravery, he would receive both a Bronze and a Silver Star. As Captain Joseph Carter summed up the finale:

> The Americans charged; the fiercely fighting troops closed in a deadly hand-to-hand struggle. T/Sgt Herbert J. Leese of the 1st Platoon of A-19 was found dead later, his fingers locked about the throat of a German who still had a bayonet in his right hand; Sgt. George W. Bennett and Pvt. Henry Bochner were killed going to Leese's aid. Pfc. Aubrey W. Finley [who earned a Bronze Star] was found dead in front of a German machine gun position—and in the position were four dead Germans.[18]

Although progress was being made as CCB kept advancing, further fighting, more courage, and additional wounding and dying were still a part of the equation. When the column, on 4 April, rolled out toward Langenprozelten, tanks were still being hit by anti-tank fire, and the unfortunately dangerous process of getting out of a burning tank produced more casualties. Sgt. Vergil Bardwell's tank was hit, and both he and Tec/5 Lloyd Burnett were burned as they extricated themselves. Burnett was also wounded by a sniper. (He would earn a Bronze Star.) The infantry of C-19 pushed ahead but were frustrated by sniper and machine gun fire. Fortunately, air support was available, and the combination of tank gunfire, artillery support, and bombing from the air opened things up so that the column was able to reach Gemunden. The fight at Langenprozeltin ended at 1325 hours on the fourth of April.[19]

However, instead of laurels for their efforts, the troopers faced intense opposition again. More tank officers were either killed or wounded, and there had to be a reshuffling of officers to cover all posts. A relatively new device was put into play when a rocket-firing tank, with "64 vicious projectiles," fired on the town. "Gemunden was thoroughly ablaze, afire from one end to the other; the smoke drifted up into the late afternoon sky; and still the enemy defended. Men fought house to house to inch ahead and push out the stubborn defenders. In the process, the town was destroyed. When the attackers got to the river, once again—as expected—the bridges were blown. Both the Saale and the Sinn joined north of Gemunden and expanded into the Main River, which was connected to the Rhine."[20]

Many a GI must have wondered how many towns and how many rivers did he and his comrades have to fight through and cross to persuade the German nation that it was destroying itself.

The 125th Combat Engineers were called up to put assault boats into the river to allow two platoons of armored infantry from A and C Companies of the 19th AIB to cross. Sniper fire "snapped at the streets as the men ran from house to house." More men were hit, a few captured but later freed, and the assault boats crossed the river and then a creek. Later, B Company of the 125th Engineers built a bridge "after being hindered by heavy mortar fire. . . . Bridge was ready for traffic at 2400B."[21] On the other side were enemy snipers firing from boxcars on the tracks next to the river. The tanks were called in to blast the boxcars and set them on fire. They did so. Around 1800 on 5 April the 62nd AIB was propelled into the fight, and men from the Third Infantry Division entered the town from an easterly direction. An order came through for CCB to capture and liberate a prisoner of war camp at Hammelburg, south of the town, and so "Combat Command B cut loose."[22]

Pfc. Jim Craigmile, an artilleryman with B Company of the 499th Armored Artillery Battalion, calmly assessed the scene as his company began firing:

We came along a highway that ran by a set of hills that sepa-

rated us from the community. Our M7s [self-propelled how-
itzers] were lined up along the road to fire. The target was on
an oblique. Two of us had climbed the hill and found ourselves
next to a Tank Destroyer from an attached unit. They asked us
to direct fire for them. A little out of my line, but I knew enough
to do a respectable job. They hit the target on the third round.
It was my only direct contribution to a destructive strike in the
whole tour.

I was also impressed with Lt. Criss's direction of fire on a
railroad embankment that ran along the far side of the hill that
separated the battery from the town. German soldiers were trying to move out along the far embankment. We were firing battery right. The Lieutenant laid the shells perfectly along the
area. After firing three rounds, no enemy soldiers were seen
crawling along the defilade. I talked with Criss several years ago
about that incident and congratulated his accuracy. He replied,
'It was just routine.[23]

German tanks got in the first shots at the 47th TB and crippled three
tanks. Tank Destroyers from the 636th TD Battalion came up and put
two panzers out of commission. The friendly tanks zipped ahead as
quickly as possible and reached the prison camp at 1345. The column,
led by the 19th Armored Infantry, fought its way toward the same destination. More fighting ensued as captured American Shermans fired on
the column. A combination of TD's and tanks eliminated the threat they
represented.

After bypassing some pillboxes, but firing a round through an aper-
ture just to be cautious, the column approached Hammelburg.
According to the 14th's *History*, "This is the story of the capture of
Hammelburg," from the perspective of the prisoners behind the wire:

At 0900 [on 6 April] they first heard the distant whine of a tank
engine. It sounded like an airplane. Then it stopped; and then
there was the rattle of a machine gun.

They crowded to the 10-foot wire fences and listened with
bated breath. The machine gun fire increased in intensity; then
there was the sudden sharp crack of a 76mm high velocity gun,
carrying clear on the morning air.

"They" were the men in Hammelburg; they included American lieutenant colonels down to enlisted men; Australians; British; Russians; Italians; Serbs. Over 4,000 men. A Serbian General. A Belgrade newspaper correspondent. [The History of the 14th Division points out that most American prisoners had been removed 4 days before.][24)

Some had been in German hands five years; some a few months.

They all listened to the sound of the distant firing, looked occasionally at the German guards. The guards were listening too.

Now came the sound of German artillery, the shells passing overhead; but still, in between, the tank engines whined and died away; and the firing sounded closer.[25]

The advancing American column split into two, one chasing Germans and the other crashing through fences and gates. "The prisoners roared their cheers—British, American, Russians. An American enlisted man said: "The American flag on that tank looked as good as the Statue of Liberty." A Serb prisoner obtained a 14th Armored shoulder patch and said he would frame it in his house for his children and his grandchildren. There were British prisoners in the camp from Dunkirk in 1940 and a 14th Armored lieutenant who had been captured at Lohr only days before.

But partly dampening their celebratory mood, the 14th AD liberators found an execution wall with a lead backstop to halt the bullets "stained dark red." There were also blood-stained stretchers nearby. The camp guards had been busy at their grisly work. Thirty-five of them were captured.

An article in the fall of 1988 in the 14th AD's magazine, *The Liberator*, features a letter from then General John Waters, a son-in-law of General George Patton and (on 5 April 1945) a colonel, to Staff Sergeant Joe Kapraun, who was a medic with the 47th Tank Battalion. Sgt. Kapraun was behind a tank of A Company as it broke into the camp. Staff Sergeant Tony Burclaw of A Company, helped Kapraun carry the seriously wounded Waters into an L-5 aircraft which evacuated him to a hospital in the rear of the fighting. A part of the letter by Waters follows:

How richly you deserve all that was said of you . . . on that great day. And you are still deeply grateful and always will be—as long as you live. I too feel the same way. I shall never forget my feelings when you helped me in that plane. I thank God, and you, and those who released us—a feeling one cannot put in words—but it lives within us—and always will. . . .[26]

The story behind this story concerns the famous, and to some infamous, General George S. Patton. After crossing the Rhine on 22 March, he initiated a task force, the purpose of which was to raid Oflag XIII at Hammelburg, which at the time was forty miles on the other side of the MLR. When junior officers raised questions about the raid, they were informed that Lt. Colonel John Waters was in the camp and was to be rescued along with whatever number of inmates could be taken out. A task force was formed under the command of Captain Abraham Baum composed of 16 Sherman tanks, 27 half-tracks, 3 self-propelled guns, and 300 officers and men. Setting out on the night of 26 March, they fought their way into the camp, but the German guards resisted fiercely. Casualties were inflicted on the attacking force including Colonel Waters, who was shot in the backside and the thigh. A Serbian camp doctor saved his life by an emergency operation with a kitchen knife. The camp was taken for the time being, and 5,000 prisoners, including 1,300 American army officers were freed.

The task force had room for only 250 American prisoners, and ironically, Col. Waters had to remain because of his wounds, It was just as well, for those of the task force who were not killed or mortally wounded became prisoners in the camp, about 250 more than before.[27] The story of Colonel Waters' capture began in North Africa, when Gen. Lloyd M. Fredenhall, Commander of II Corps, failed to prepare and execute a proper battle plan for the advancing panzers of General Rommel. In the debacle that later came to be known as the battle of Kasserine Pass, the American armor and infantry were routed by the more experienced 10th Panzer Division, which had better tanks and better guns. In the process, Waters, Executive Officer of the 1st Armored Division, became a casualty and a prisoner of the Germans. Eventually he wound up at Hammelburg.

The Hammelburg adventure was defended by Patton in his typically self-justifying way:

I felt very gloomy over the fact that I may have caused Waters' death, . . . but I believe that I did the right thing, and I certainly could never have lived with myself had I known that I was within 40 miles of 900 Americans [more likely 12 or 13 hundred] and not made any attempt to rescue them.[28]

Captain Baum, who was wounded in the assault, became a fellow prisoner to Waters, after his depleted force was shot up by the Germans, with an uncounted number of prisoners becoming casualties in the process. The Patton biographer Carlo D'Este described the task force as "being chopped to pieces." More important, Patton's commander, General Omar Bradley regarded the episode as "a spectacular stunt." Patton "knew damn well if he had asked me for permission I would have vetoed it . . . But I think it was doomed from the start and it was a foolhardy operation to do."[29]

However, the capture of Hammelburg prison, Oflag XIII, raised the spirits of the men of the 19th AIB and 47th TB, who had liberated the camp. Indeed, in time the shoulder patch of the 14th Armored Division would include the proud designation of "Liberators." There would be more liberations to come. But even at the time, after all the fighting, killing, wounding, and dying of the men who had reached the camp, there would be a sense of jubilation and warmth:

Next morning, after a fair night's rest, everyone took a quick look about the portion of the camp where we were billeted. It was an amazing sight to see the conglomeration of Allied P.W.'s The bulk of them seemed to be Serbians, but there were many Americans and other nationalities. It was a good feeling to see the joy and appreciation shown by all these men, who could not be grateful enough. We fed a lot of them with the food we had to spare—they were humble with their thanks. Some of them had been prisoners for as long as five years.[30]

Nevertheless, the war had to continue, and the men received orders to get organized and get back on the road to the heart of Germany. The towns the column passed included Fuchstadt, Ramsthal, Arnhausen, and Bad-Kissingen, this last town "struck into . . . on the morning of the 8th [of April]." There was fighting along the way, and at one juncture, two lieutenants drove into Munnerstadt in a jeep. They were surprised by a German officer in a Volkswagon vehicle who was driving in exactly the opposite direction towards them. He was probably doing reconnaissance as were the two lieutenants. Both drivers hit the brakes hard and reversed away. More seriously, as the column approached Wasserlossen, the enemy employed timed air bursts to catch the advancing Americans in the open. The column of the 19th AIB neared Orlenbach at dusk and saw civilians fleeing in earnest. Captain Joseph Carter wrily concluded about this scene: "That meant a fight. (If the civilians put up white flags and came out to meet you, that meant there were no German troops in town and there would be no fight; if they ran for cover it meant they were getting out of the way of the gun fire.)"[31]

The combat continued at an extreme pace, with the Germans utterly disorganized, but still the mortar and artillery rounds fell on the men of the 19th AIB as they surged ahead.

Combat Command Reserve, composed primarily of the 25th Tank Battalion and the 62nd AIB, crossed the Rhine and sped through Lohr, where the wreckage of combat remained, including the bodies of German soldiers still lying in the streets. The 62nd AIB faced the same kind of ambushes as had their comrades in the 19th. In the small village of Morleasan in the dangerous hills, Lt. Thomas R. Day led his B Company, the 62nd, along with a few tanks and recon elements into the town only to be hit by mortars and small arms fire, with one tank put out of commission. Day would earn a Bronze and a Silver Star. C-62 crossed the river in assault boats assembled by the men of the 125th Combat Engineers and assisted in the capture of Gemunden toward the end of that fight.

The engineers installed Treadway bridges, one as long as forty feet and another 35 feet, filled in ditches, cleared debris, and also suffered casualties when they had to man machine guns to stave off the enemy. Lt. Melvin O. Robinson and Pfc. George A. Bartels, his driver, were wounded when they were suddenly surrounded by German soldiers and a Mark VI tank. Before they had a chance to respond by fire, 21 Germans surrendered to them.[32] Robinson later received a Bronze Star. This sort of thing must have been unnerving: do you hold your fire in case the soldiers who just shot at you are surrendering?

The other element in the confused mix was being taken prisoner. If SS troops took an American soldier prisoner, he might not survive the hour, never mind the day. After a severe firefight, being taken prisoner was perilous for both sides. Yet as the dawn of recognition arrived for enemy troops—that the war was being lost—they might have been more inclined to keep their prisoners safe and well. They might be the ones next captured. And this scenario played out repeatedly. Two engineers were captured as they took a liberated British prisoner back for medical attention, but most prisoners were rescued later.

The unit histories of the 14th Armored Division, and especially its own detailed and expansive history, take great pains to extol the value of its artillery. In support of CCA was the 500th Armored Field Artillery (AFA), of CCB was the 499th AFA, and of CCR was the 501st. Also in support were the attached 438th and 395th Quartermaster Truck Companies (QTC), the 398th AAA Anti-Aircraft Artillery Battalion), and the 636th Tank Destroyer Battalion. Two more battalions, after Hammelburg and Gemunden, were the 69th AFA (105mm self-propelled guns (SP's) and the 975th Field Artillery Battalion, which towed 155mm howitzers. Air liaison planes were a part of these units to spot targets and adjust indirect fire. As the artillery charged ahead to keep up with the infantry and the tanks, even the artillerists were collecting prisoners. The engineers had to construct temporary airfields almost daily. When the fighting became frantic at Lohr, the 398th AAA aimed its guns at German infantry, a demoralizing development for them. "The German commander at Gemunden said one great reason for the collapse of his superior defensive position was the volume of artillery fire; it was estimated that 1,200 enemy were killed or captured at Gemunden."[33] He must have wondered as to the wisdom of the Führer's declaring war on America after it had declared war on Japan—to spring loose the enormous industrial potential of the USA to manufacture the millions of shells directed against the Wehrmacht between 1942 and 1945.

When the men of the artillery arrived at Hammelburg, American soldiers, both officers and enlisted men, walked out of the woods "and cried as the 499th received them." A story told by one of the artillerymen, George Koontz, demonstrates how, on occasion, it could be very dangerous for them at times. After he and the men of his battery had taken some prisoners who had just come driving down the road toward them, a German battery of 88's expressed its displeasure by raining down shells on the Americans. Several men were killed and more wounded. Koontz, after diving for cover, saw the need for some first aid:

Getting my aid kit, I ran up across the road to where the guns were. I took a quick look at Smitty [John D. Smith?] and knew he didn't need any help from me. More shells came and I dove under an M-7 [an SP]. I fixed up one of the men who had been hit in the leg by fragments and took him over near a wall for cover. Then I went back and got another who had been hit in the arm. Most of the vehicles had moved in [the] cover of the buildings along the street and the men were rounding up the prisoners and getting them into the cellars of the houses. One of them was a medical officer and with a little persuasion he helped fix up a few of the boys who weren't in bad shape. After making out the EMT [Emergency Medical] tags for the wounded men, I sent them out in an ambulance.[34]

As the 14th's *History* relates events, the 500th AFA had similar experiences, encountering enemy troops trying to board a train to escape the Allied juggernaut and firing on them and an anti-tank and self-propelled gun in the process. A few of the artillerymen were captured, but as in similar cases, they managed to get free. In a huge reversal of normal order, they could hear fighting behind them while friendly armor was plunging ahead of them as part of CCA. They lost Lt. Milton O. Turner in Neustadt when he opened the hatch of the armored vehicle in which he was riding and was killed by enemy tire.

The 501st, AFA, with CCR, was moving so fast that it halted at twenty-two positions on the way to set up and fire. It stopped at Neuenbach to fire in support on Gemunden. Four men in a halftrack led by Sgt. Martin B. Antaramian of Headquarters Battery entered a small village and were immediately fired upon. The GIs turned their machine guns on the stubborn enemy, who then surrendered for a total of 85 prisoners. Antaramian was given a Bronze Star.

The 14th's *History* takes pains to give credit to other support units such as maintenance companies, which were tasked to the fullest by extensive repairs to tanks, halftracks, and other vehicles. They were also involved in firefights and took captives in the process. Both the MP units and the Band members acting as MP's had their hands full directing traffic in an area of great confusion. Sending men and vehicles down the wrong road at the wrong time could get them in peril quickly. The medics of the 84th Medical Detachment took care of wounded, took care of them again when they were rewounded, and did minor repairs on their ambulance under fire all the while. The 154th Signal Company had to repair or replace at least 39 radios, haul supplies over 400 miles in a week, and string 350 miles of wire in a month. The number of messages handled was in the thousands. In addition, like all the other units, they had to handle prisoners they had captured.

Out in front as usual, the 94th Cav and Recon had its share of manic activity and danger. They, with artillery support, even took a town by themselves along with a large quota of prisoners. Between Gefall and Langenleiten, they opened fire on a column of German infantry. "The Germans were devastated."[35] But the Germans were not done; they could still inflict hurt on the advancing recon units. At Lohr, Lt. L. E. Jaeckle's armored car burst into flames after a hit by a panzerfaust, and he was captured. Worse was that Tec/5 Rex Walker was killed. Pvt. Burt H. Rolfe was killed by shrapnel while riding in his "peep." Other troopers were captured but later released by 14th Armored men.

C Troop of the 94th, with CCA, was paired with the 68th AIB and the 48th Tank Battalion, the first platoon with the former and the second with the latter. They ran into trouble almost immediately. On 7 or 8 April, tragedy hit the 3rd platoon:

> . . . the first armored car was fired on from the front by a machine gun and the commander raised himself to fire his machine gun back; then a German machine gun opened up from the rear and he was cut down. The enemy machine guns sprayed the Recon vehicles, and the peep crews were pinned down. Four men were lost in the bitter savage action. Then the tanks came up, and the enemy guns were overrun. The column moved on.[36]

It was always an extremely dangerous business to be out in front of a column in a thin-skinned vehicle like an armored car. With a determined and ingenious enemy lying in wait at his choice of place to ambush, it was amazing that more recon troopers weren't killed or wounded. The same sort of thing happened in Mitgenfeld when the enemy fired with anti-tank guns and artillery. Again an armored car and a peep were the victims, and only sustained fire from friendly artillery eliminated the hazard. In the town of Gleichamberg, the platoon encountered ferocious resistance from a combination of panzers and OCS (Officer Candidate School) students who were eager for combat. The recon troopers were even strafed from the air. And so the fighting continued against a still deadly foe. As the 14th AD's *History* concludes its chapter on this fighting in the Rhineland, it succinctly commented:

> The Squadron [the 94th] now was in possession of the river crossings of the Saale River from Bad Kissengen [sic] to Aschbach.
>
> The Division was across the Saale River, generally on a line, faced to the Southeast in the heart of Germany, and poised for the final drive. [37]

The task now for the 14th Armored and the other divisions and corps and armies of Sixth Army Group, Twelfth Army Group, and the British and Canadian Twenty-First Army Group was to plunge a dagger into the German heart and end the death and destruction of the war in western Europe.

Chapter 9

FROM COLLAPSE TO
LIBERATION

Winston Churchill, after the end of the Battle of Britain in the fall of 1940, spoke words to the Parliament of England which aptly put the situation of the British nation at that moment: "It is not the end, it is not even the beginning of the end, but it is the end of the beginning." Almost five more years would pass before England and its allies, primarily the Americans, the Canadians, the Australians, and the Russians, would be able to say that the war was over and that peace was at hand.

In some sort of inverted microcosmic parallel, the American armies in Europe, including the 14th Armored Division, were approaching the beginning of the end for the Wehrmacht in Germany from April to May, 1945. Now that the Westwall had been penetrated thoroughly and the Rhine had been crossed by a succession of American forces, it was a matter of time until the Nazi regime decided to surrender. However, that time would be determined by what overwhelming force could be applied in the speediest manner possible. The enemy could not be allowed to reorganize and reset his defenses to stop the Allied columns. However, the application of increased speed meant that advance units were going to run faster than their supporting artillery, service units, radio communications and heavy armor.

We have seen how the 14th Armored Division had run so fast and so far that it put itself in a dangerous position, It became a source of consternation to the officers that at any given moment their troops were advancing in opposite directions at the same time. It was also a matter of some concern that the Armored Field Artillery units with their various attachments or without were behind their Armored Infantry Battalions and within earshot of small arms fire to the front. At the same time Tank Battalions were behind the artillery and fighting not only to get to them but ahead of them. Artillery units were forced to fight like infantry and take responsibility for surrendering German soldiers while simultaneously performing fire missions. Medical detachments sometimes wound up in peculiar places. The result might just be a plain old mix-up, but since the tanks and infantry were frequently told to bypass points of resistance, it could be quite hazardous to face a Mark V or VI tank and infantry rolling down the road toward friendly positions. Toward the end of the war, one of the many slogans or sayings that GIs found popular was "Home Alive in '45." The hopelessness of the enemy's situation was becoming more apparent to both officers and men on both sides, and it did not seem to some soldiers that it was wise to take unnecessary chances. And so some didn't. Yet it was also obvious that being in the ETO at all was dangerous to one's health.

As Captain Joseph Carter came to the end of his *History of the Fourteenth Armored Division*, he faced the problem of trying to tell a coherent story of what was happening in April 1945:

> It is HARD ENOUGH to write the account of a battle. It is not only that there are so many stories—the story of the commander, dealing with the whole, and of his S-4, worrying about supplies, and of each of the men fighting and dying or leaving—the stories do not always agree, for each man has seen it through his own eyes; and there is so much happening at one time. . . . For there is no single specific action; there is a series of actions, some brief and some bitter, and related only in the sense that they were all in the same area and for the same end.
>
> That end was the killing of the German state.[1]

Carter records the frequently remembered question asked by the invaders of the Teutonic Fatherland, "With a country like this, what did the Germans want to start a war for?" The question became almost a lyric cry, for it was springtime:

> With nature's infinite capacity for irrelevance, the land was in the fullest flower of Spring.
>
> The milk-green streams tumbled down the hills, frothing at every turn and at every rock.

The woods on the steep hillsides, thick-grown, but without underbrush, were turning to green from the wet black of Winter. Pale grass grew in the shadows. In the gentle valleys, the fields rose softly to the far horizon, lush green of pastures or pale yellow-green of daffodils and dandelions, full fresh brown of newly turned furrows. The fields asked your eye to run a hand over them and feel them.[2]

It is almost as if this writing were produced by a poet, but these lovely pastoral passages were written by an officer who had seen some terrible combat, bodies of healthy young man exploded and scattered in sheets of blood or burned horribly in a tank. For him and others who had seen modern industrial warfare at its worst, to be able to maintain the sanity of seeing the deep value of "nature nurturing," to translate an old philosophical phrase, is just astounding, especially when the fighting was to drag on for another month. Fortunately, Hitler would take his own life and leave the decisions about the war to others in the German Army and Kriegsmarjne.

As Carter remarks, "It was a strange warfare—strange even to men who can rationalize warfare to sanity," like Frederick the Great, who decisively concluded that war should be "kurtz und leiblich"—short and lively, although the last word idiomatically means rather "intense" or "devastating." Carter, in his punctuated essay on the subject of the insanity of war in Chapter XIII, "The Battle of the Autobahn: The Death of a State, April 8–April 21, 1945," cites the example of a Wehrmacht Captain who "turned his pistol on an SS officer who had captured six Americans, shot him, then calmly turned his gun over and surrendered to the Americans. . . . Sometimes it was funny, in the bitter way that things are funny when men die for laughter."[3]

At the Division Trains Command Post, Lieut. Robert H. Thompson wondered about the utter confusion of the constantly changing situation and worried about Trains getting involved in a fight with organized opposition or even stragglers, for Division Trains, as Carter notes, was sitting on top of tons of fuel and ammunition.[4]

On about 7 April, the *68th History* writes that the battalion, accompanied by tanks, seized "crossings over the Streu River at Unsleben as darkness fell." Three of the "Streu" towns were taken by. Hdqrs. Co. Machine Gun Platoon along with the Second Platoons respectively of B and C Company, and prisoners surrendered themselves out of woods in the area. After capturing nine towns, by 11 April, the battalion "contacted friendly cavalry forces" [not specified] "on the banks of the Main River. "After fording the river, the 68th took four more towns including Dittersbrunn and Pferdsfeld.

An order came down for the battalion on 13 April to interdict the Autobahn "in the vicinity of Pegnitz." Again the 68th joined with "friendly cavalry and attacked Scheszlitz. As the 68th's *History* describes the attack, "Anti-tank and ack-ack fire caused us to dismount, and darkness had long since arrived when the town was cleared." What is characterized as a "field day" followed when a "'Kraut' convoy was caught "trying to escape." B and C Companies continued to lead the action and cleared several more towns. It was only after "heavy resistance" was overcome at Gossweinstein that the battalion took Betzenstein and paused for the night to rest and reorganize. "Stiff resistance" was met at Plech but was bypassed, and the battalion vehicles continued south on the Autobahn. At Rupprechtstegen, an entire hospital with patients and staff was captured. On 17 April the movement south continued, and after "friendly elements" joined the 68th, it aimed a course for Polling in the vicinity of Neumarkt. Travel over "muddy, treacherous mountain trails, we entered and cleared Hausheim, where we stayed for the night." On the next morning, C Company wrested the town of Berg at the same time as the rest of the battalion forged ahead toward Polling. The effort was met by "powerful SS resistance," but the armored infantrymen dismounted and overcame it. The 125th Engineers fashioned a bypass around a large crater, and the Mortar Platoon fired 81mm smoke rounds to allow the attack to succeed.[5]

The 48th Tank Battalion was paired with A-68 during the advance, and according to the 68th's *History*, the 48th "were playing a stellar role in the battalion's advance." The *History* summarizes some of its actions:

> Upon leaving Dieburg they had pushed through Gunderhausen to Ein, where two weeping prisoners told of a German Captain forcing them to kill men who refused to fight. It had become evident to them also that the Germans' defense was rapidly disintegrating. In a lightning thrust the first and second platoons with the 48th Tankers had captured Aura, but had lost valuable

time extricating their half-tracks from the muddy terrain, result-
ing from intermittent rains.[6]

The combined force of infantry and armor continued ahead and had
to fight off "stubborn resistance from enemy infantry, self-propelled
guns, and tanks." Accurate fire missions were necessary to break up this
resistance, and Lt. John Paul, commander of the Second Platoon of A-
68, who earned a Bronze Star, provided the targets. The *48th's History*
demonstrates the understanding of the men of the strategic situation:

> To us it seemed like the crossroads of the world, and Jerry, real-
> izing that we had a very strategic point and that he must have
> the main supply route in order to continue his fight for
> Nurnberg, counterattacked at numerous points. Throughout
> the night enemy movement was reported everywhere, and at the
> break of dawn the first attack was on our higher headquarters
> located in a town to our southwest. One company was sent to
> the rescue and repulsed the enemy; another came from our left
> flank and was turned back by our tanks while to our front on
> the Autobahn another was launched and repulsed but by this
> time the enemy had given it up as a lost cause.[7]

A look at the standard map depicting the routes of advance for the
14th Armored Division in some of the unit histories shows a thumb
shaped figure, starting from the landings in Marseilles at the bottom left
of the thumb and ascending into the area of Alsace north of Strasbourg
and then continuing north through the Rhineland and then dropping
south around Bruaenau and Neustadt and driving through Bayreuth,
Neumarkt and Moosburg to end in Mühldorl and Jettenbach to the east
of Munich. In the beginning, General Smith would have been amazed to
be told that this "thumb" would represent the battles his division would
fight to defeat the enemy. Not only would the division cross the Rhine
but also traverse the Danube River much to the south of where anybody
would expect them to be. The British and Canadian 21st Army Group
was entirely focused on the Ruhr and the industrial heart of Germany.
Twelfth Army Group, it appeared, was aimed, toward Berlin to excise
the heart of Nazism.

Why Patton's Third Army, now including the 14th Armored, was heading south and southwest seems strange. The apparent reason for this vector was the intelligence belief that the remainder of Hitler's forces, especially his most fanatical, were planning on retreating south into the mountains near Munich in order to construct a "National Redoubt" and maintain the war in an endless succession of guerilla actions with no victory for the Allies to savor. Patton would wind up in Czechoslovakia and stop there before bumping into the Russians, and the 14th AD and other divisions would find that the Redoubt was a chimera with no basis in fact.

Still the fighting had to continue wherever there were opposing German forces ready and able to contest the Allied advance. When the elements of the 68th coupled with elements of the 48th, battled into Bruckenau, the 68th met trouble:

> However, ill fortune accompanied the subsequent attack on Bruckenau. When after three hours of hard fighting eighteen men battled their way into the first two houses of the town, heavy bazooka firing set fire to the first house. The first platoon suffered heavy casualties from artillery, attempting to reach the besieged in the town. However, the men hung on grimly even when it became apparent that the other platoons could not reach them, and maintained their foothold until the next morning when a subsequent attack on the town was successful.[8]

A courageous patrol of four men was sent out and braved mortar and sniper fire to reach the besieged men and establish communications to relieve them later.

Other units of the 14th AD forged ahead to keep the Germans off balance and to exploit their disarray in the face of the Allied pounding. The 14th's History focuses on the 94th Cav Recon, which "played a large part in the drive south, in the shifting dissolving battle southeast through Germany." After the capture of several towns by A Troop, D Troop crossed the Saale River at Aschbach and captured two railroad trains. As far as the German supply system was concerned, the khaki foxes were in their hencoop and taking or destroying supplies that the Wehrmacht desperately needed. Even if they planned on surrendering to the Americans or British, they would clearly need food, ammunition, fuel, and other materiel if they planned on retreating in order to face the

Russians, who were rapidly approaching major German cities. The Troops of the 94th hurried in their armored cars, light tanks, and "peeps" to use the Autobahn in the Bayreuth-Nurnberg area to further drive south to end the war. At Tannfeld, D Troop had the pleasure of imprisoning 200 officer candidates at the OCS School there. The juniors had just completed a field problem and were returning to enjoy a hot meal.

When the 94th embarked again, A and D Troops were each supported by a section of Tank Destroyers to provide them with more muscle. The Squadron managed to cut off Bayreuth and Nurnberg by crossing over the Autobahn. It also encountered a column of Swiss Red Cross trucks and liberated the captured Canadian truck drivers. At the town of Pegnitz, the cavalrymen surprised and took prisoner 500 enemy soldiers. A total of 1,500 prisoners were shipped back. A factory producing aircraft, automatic weapons, and even submarines fell into the bag.[9]

At about the same time, around the 12th or 13th of April, the 68th AIB struck south and southeast around Bamberg and Bayreuth and cut the Autobahn "in the vicinity of Pegnitz" just as the 94th had done. How aware at the moment the men of the 68th were of the almost sacred, mystical character of Nurnberg to the Nazi mythmaking machine is hard to know. They did know that they wanted to excise any group attempting to flee south to set up a final fortification for the German units that still had a lot of fight in them:

> To insure security for the supply trains the Autobahn was patrolled constantly by platoon groups. Then in a fast move we flanked Nurnberg from the east and passing through Altdorf headed for Neumarkt. The purpose of our move was to cut the escape route of the Germans from Nurnberg to Hitler's National Redoubt.[10]

The 48th Tank Battalion was forcing its way from the north on Neumarkt. Its assault on the town was described in that unit's history:

> Higher headquarters considering this resistance as critical to our advances ordered a coordinated attack with an Infantry battalion in support to drive the enemy from Neumarkt. Promptly on the 19th the forces moved out with a determined effort to enter

the town. A prearranged air mission had been scheduled in the event resistance was still too strong but fortunately a few tanks and infantry were able to enter the northeast edge of town and the air support was withheld until called for. Positions were consolidated for the night awaiting the continued attack in the morning.[11]

Reconnaissance by the 68th on 19 April determined that Neumarkt was going to be defended by hostile forces. The tanks of the 48th and the armored infantry attacked and entered the town of Stanna and took heavy fire from Neumarkt. As the 14th's History characterizes the battle, "Neumarkt was one of the last German strongpoints, and it was to be a two-day nut to crack, bitter, savage fighting." Before the men in the task force ever got to Neumarkt, they had to fight through several more towns before they could try an entry into Polling. The going was tortuous and muddy, and after recon elements were frustrated in their attempt to move forward, the men of Company B, under the protection of smoke provided by the Mortar Platoon, attacked across an open field and made its way into Polling. After the engineers arranged a bypass around a crater, the vehicles were able to advance with the foot soldiers. Knowing that the city was going to fight, Company C with a tank destroyer on the right, and B Company, supported by a tank company from the 48th, advanced forward under fire toward a railroad bridge which had not been destroyed. The fighting was intense and difficult. T/Sgt. William M. Rangold of the Third Platoon of C Company led a squad to erect a makeshift bridge to get the men across the canal. S/Sgt. Richard D. Seiders, although he fell into the water, managed with Rangold's help to get to the opposite bank. From that point, Rangold led the squad several hundred yards into the town and "held off the attacks of two German tanks with bazooka fire until the remainder of the company was able to gain the protection of the town."

The First Platoon of C Company, under the leadership of T/Sgt. Walter C. Felty, led his platoon in the center, and despite being pinned down by enemy fire for some time, he directed fire and guided his men forward to the outskirts of town. "In the town," as the 68th's History continues, "Sgt. Felty exposed himself to direct the fire of a bazooka on enemy tanks. When one member of the bazooka team was wounded, he took his position of firing the bazooka at the tanks. He crippled one and

forced the others to flee." Lt. Harold Hanhard, in charge of the Third
Platoon, crossed the canal and an open field in front of his men. Their
advance was "impeded by the hail of tank and small arms fire coming
from the town." Nevertheless Lt. Hanhard forced the issue by directing
bazooka fire from an exposed position against the hostile tanks and, in
the process, killing some of them. For their extraordinary actions,
"T/Sgt. Rangold received the Silver Star Medal and Lt. Hanhardt and
T/Sgt. Felty received Bronze Stars."[12]

B-68 encountered "even more vicious fighting" as they reached the
edge of the canal and were forced under enemy fire to dig in. The CCA
Report explained what was happening:

> Advancing slowly from the west, elements of the 68th encoun-
> tered heavy small arms, automatic weapons and mortar fire
> from Neumarkt. One platoon of C Company entered the town
> at 1300 and at 1725 established contact with elements of the
> 48th Tank Battalion entering from the north. At the close of the
> day, the 68th held 10 houses. The 48th Tank attacked
> Neumarkt from the north against very heavy mortar and AT
> fire; dismounted troops of the 48th entered town at 1600
> against resistance and made contact with the 68th.[13]

During this assault on Neumarkt, B Company, the 68th, forced its
way toward the difficult canal defense and met more heavy resistance.
The men were forced to dig in for the remainder of the day. Company
A, still paired with the 48th Tank Battalion, fared better in the face of
"numerically superior troops."

The very brief "History of the 14th" attributes the difficulty of seizing Neumarkt to the stubborn and determined resistance of the 17th SS
Panzer Grenadier Division, which showered the 48th with large-caliber
antitank rounds, mortar bombs, and small arms fire delivered from the
north side of town and from high ground on the eastern side as well.
According to the "History," the 68th and the 48th met at a factory in
the northwest sector of town but were still facing "increasing heavy
resistance." After more of such resistance in Neumarkt on the next day,
a command decision was made to employ air power to subdue an unre-
lenting enemy. After the two battalions were withdrawn to a safe distance, four missions were flown.[14]

According to the 68th's History, the 65th Infantry Division was to assume the role of taking the city, and the 68th AIB withdrew to Polling on news of the planned bombing of Neumarkt. The authors of the 48th History wrote how the men in that battalion enjoyed the spectacle of the enemy being pounded by ordnance from the air:

> Seldom are troops treated to the sight of aircraft in operation against the enemy, nor are they privileged to see a bombing mission performed; higher headquarters ordered all troops to withdraw from the edge of town and the air force took over. Viewing this spectacular scene from a distance of approximately [sic] 1000 yards, although a bit dangerous, was most exciting and welcome; unfortunately for reasons unknown, we were relieved from this mission and replaced by the 65th Infantry Division. The results of the bombing were never released.[15]

CCA Headquarters, on a hill outside of Neumarkt, "watched the planes come in again and again, again and again, snarling down on the town and blasting it, and the artillery came up and began to hammer it in long volleys of explosions."[16]

The fortunes of the 68th and the 48th would continue to be intertwined. After barely a day resting and reorganizing at Polling, at 2000 hours on the next morning, all of C Company and one platoon of B-68 advanced west along the railroad track and captured Heng and Kostlbach in order "to relieve pressure on the 48th Tank Battalion, who had swung around and was now on our right flank." Two more small towns were taken, and the 68th moved to "a new assembly area." There was a fight on a hill at Dillberg, which was shared with the 48th, but neither of the two unit histories provide any details as to how the combat went. After this episode, the 68th was given the assignment of defending the rear of CCR as a mobile reserve.[17]

It was the 94th Cav Recon Squadron that continued to stick its neck out by dashing ahead into a maelstrom of confusion and danger. At Creussen, A Troop cleaned up a great deal of enemy materiel including antiaircraft weapons, ammunition, howitzers, tractors, trailers, busses, and wagons. It was time, though, for the Squadron to "tuck its tail in." Major George W. England formed the squadron defensively and requested reinforcements because information he received indicated that there was a Panzer Training School fifteen miles to the east of the 94th, which, in turn, was fifteen miles ahead of CCR. A company of armored infantry from the 62nd and a platoon of tanks from the 25th Tank Battalion were sent ahead to reinforce the cavalry. On the evening of 14 April, an enemy observation post was spotted, and at 0945 the next day two definitely unfriendly tanks appeared from the direction of Schnabelwald, and the tankers of the 25th eliminated them quickly.

The infantry and tanks were being employed as a reserve, and unidentified Tank Destroyers were responsible for the approaches to the 94th's position at Creussen. In a stroke of good luck, although the 94th was short of infantry, slave laborers, who had been making guns for the Volksturm, volunteered to fight against their former abusers. One commented about the weapons, "They aren't much good, but they're good enough to shoot Germans." Nevertheless, on the morning of the 15th, the isolated cavalry (true to American frontier tradition) was surrounded on three sides, "south, east, and north."

E Troop, in its firing position on the hills, engaged the enemy, but its assault guns were crossfired by five Panzers. Although three of them were neutralized, in the firing the Troop lost two assault guns and a half-track. E Troop then pulled back toward the town. Several officers had been captured although all but one later escaped. As the 14th's History put it,

> The Squadron situation did not look promising; a PW said that a German task force of 50 tanks and several hundred infantrymen had left the panzer training camp with the mission of recapturing Creussen and Bayreuth. By now the only route out of Creussen was to the north; A Troop, running that road, had succeeded in contacting friendly forces.
>
> The enemy attacked Creussen.[18]

Only the combined efforts of the armor, the infantry, and the recon force, along with supporting artillery and air assets, managed to hold off the enemy. Colonel Hudelson, no stranger to difficult situations since Operation Northwind, ordered in two more platoons of tanks from the 25th and two more platoons of infantry. At the town of Gottesfeld, "God's Field," the group took out five enemy tanks. The 25th's History sets the scene of the confrontation:

Two platoons from "Baker"' Company, and an Infantry platoon, were dispatched to Creussen to assist the 94th Rcn
Squadron which was being attacked. The platoons moved down
the autobahn to the town of Schwurz. Between Schwurz and
Gottsfeld [sic], they ran into direct fire from enemy tanks. Four
of our tanks were hit, two being put out of action. The infantry
then entered Gottsfeld and cleared it. By this time, the Battalion
Commander and Captain [Homer L.] Swager had made a foot
rcn to the east edge of town and noted vehicular movement in
the woods. The tanks were moved up, and suddenly three Mark
IV's rode out into the open. 'B' Company let loose, and Cpl's,
Orff and Hurl quickly accounted for two tanks, and Gunner
Stoffrigan kayoed another at a range of 3800 yards. In all, five
enemy tanks were knocked out and the pressure on Creussen
was relieved.[19] [Captain Swager would posthumously earn a
Silver Star.]

At the end of the day, the "defending forces" had struck 17 tanks
off the Panzer roster, had taken 43 prisoners, and uncounted German
dead. The four towns in the area were "levelled" and of no further use
to the enemy as assembly points. The fighting ability of the miscellaneous units thrown together had proven the ability of American forces
to adapt to circumstances and fight on equal or better terms with the
men of the Wehrmacht.

However, the fighting in the vicinity of Creussen would continue,
with enemy tanks reported in the woods nearby. There would be firefights and artillery called in to rebuff enemy activity. The 94th Cav
Recon was then switched to CCA, with the assignment of protecting its
left flank as it moved south along the Autobahn. The capture of
Wehrmacht soldiers continued, as did the liberation of slave laborers.
One of these men, after liberation from a shoe factory, walked off with
eight pairs of shoes, remarking, "I've been barefoot for four years, and
now I'm getting even with these bastards!" Hundreds of POWs were
taken, and stores of liquor and German pistols were liberated from
warehouses. As the 14th's *History* comments on the medley of men and
vehicles proceeding south,

The 3rd Platoon frequently rode the attached TDs; they had lost many of their vehicles. . . . And the 94th, by then, had picked up as many German trucks and half-tracks and trailers and sedans and Volkswagens as they had American vehicles; seeing the outfit going down the road, it would take more than a hasty glance to decide whether it was American or German.[20]

After more motoring and shifting assignments, the 94th was split, with the Second Platoon assigned to the 48th TB and the Third with the 68th Armored Infantry. As the Third Platoon led the 68th into Kirchenbirkig, it got into a scrap with retreating Germans. As they withdrew over a hill, the .50 caliber machine guns "laid in on them." The tank destroyers fired on a cluster of German barracks and set them on fire, and the only damage to the GIs was a hit on an armored car, which wounded three men and blew the commander out of the car. There is no mention of this fight in the *68th's History*. Presumably, their assistance wasn't necessary.[21]

At this stage of the fighting, it is difficult to maintain accurate chronology, for many of the unit histories including that of the Division don't always provide key dates for important actions, but a graphic image, often captured in Signal Corps film, is that of German prisoners marching down the Autobahn to POW cages:

> F Company [of the 94th] had crossed the Main [River]; the 3rd Platoon marched prisoners back along the autobahn. (To become a familiar sight, these columns of several hundred disarmed Germans, in their bedraggled field gray uniforms, led by a peep or a tank with its turret turned back, followed by a peep with a machine gun or a light tank, docilely marching to the PW cages.)[22]

A CCA Report, quoted in the Division *History*, described a generally unopposed crossing of the Main River despite the fact that all bridges had been destroyed. The dismounted infantry of the 68th forded the river near Doringstadt, with Bensfeld and the nearby hills secured. This appears to have happened on 16 April.

After this crossing, there are so many isolated but nasty fights by different units prior to reaching the Danube that it is possible here to be highly selective about which ones to explore. Concentration will be on the 68th as much as possible. After the 125th Combat Engineers of the 14th Armored Division built a bridge across the Rhine at Unnersdor, the 68th AIB and the 48th TB fought against stiff resistance at Hollfeld. Troop C of the 94th Cav, after some reconnaissance, joined with anti-tank squads of the 68th to push down further on the Autobahn. A combination of two infantry platoons of the 68th, a Tank Destroyer platoon of the 636th, and a platoon of tanks from the 48th forged ahead until it met "savage enemy resistance at a road block," the result of some anti-tank guns and riflemen.

On 16 April evidently, the 48th and 68th pushed through several towns and was again stopped at Plech, which was then bypassed. On 17 April, the CCA's command post was attacked by a strong enemy force including tanks. One of them got to within a hundred yards of the CP before it was stopped. Cooks, Company Clerks, and miscellaneous headquarters staff fought off the enemy infantry and tanks until the enemy commander thought better of his effort and pulled back.[23]

In an effort to provide credit to those units which were not always cited for performance in battle, the Division *History* cited several in the text. One of these was the 636th Tank Destroyer Battalion, which had been in action two months before the 14th AD was committed. It was attached to the division on 29 March and transported 120 miles to the Main River to fight with the 14th. The First Platoon was attached in support of the 68th, the Second in CCA Reserve, and the Third in support of the 48th Tank Battalion. Several companies had similar roles to these mentioned. B-636 took out a self-propelled gun, and Pfc. Clyde Ware spotted an enemy barge crossing the Main River and destroyed it with one round. The TD's were fortunate in having a 90mm gun but unfortunate in having very thin skin. They might be able to kill a Mark V Panther or a Mark VI Tiger if they got off the first shot, but if they were hit, it was very difficult for anyone to survive. If they got lucky, like a light tank, if an armor-piercing shell went right through the tank, they might survive, but they needed a lot of rabbit's feet for that kind of luck.

In any case, on 7 April, B Company was confronted with five American tanks captured by the Germans, "Two M-4 and three M-5 tanks were destroyed by the 90mm guns." At Mitgetfeld twelve rounds of high-explosive scared a hostile group of infantry to surrender. In the desperate fight to protect CCA Headquarters on 17 April, tank destroyers of the 636th protected a roadblock but took some casualties in the process. Around Altenhann, the Third Platoon suffered more casualties when two TD's were hit, one destroyed by bazooka and the other damaged by a grenade thrown down the hatch, which caused casualties. There were other actions not mentioned here which demonstrated both the value of the TD's and the courage of the men who were manning them.[24]

Also commended for valor and effectiveness in action, not only by the Division *History* but also by the Order of Battle of the 14th Armored, were "Organic Units" which included "CCR Rifle Company (Seventh US Army Rifle Co. No. 4, Provisional)." A note indicates that:

> CCR Rifle Company joined the Division on 27 March 1945. The all volunteer unit was African-American [sometimes referred to as "Colored" or "Negro" during the war]. Although technically not an organic unit, many of the Division's white soldiers who served in combat with the black infantrymen of CCR Rifle Company felt that they had earned the right to be considered a part of the 14th Armored Division.[25]

The Division *History* notes that this rifle company had been attached to the 19th Armored Infantry Battalion as a company of 240 enlisted men, with officers (white) from all three of the 14th's Armored Infantry Battalions. They were commanded by Capt. Derl J. Hess, a former sergeant with the 19th AIB Headquarters Company who would be honored with a Bronze Star. Since it was placed, technically, in a reserve role with CCR, it became known as the CCR Rifle Company. At the town of Frickenhausen, in its firefight in the town, the Company captured fourteen prisoners and killed two of the enemy.[26]

In its "first real engagement" at Lichtenfels, two platoons crossed the Main River and seized the town. The action, written up in the 25th Tank Battalion History, remarks on the role of the "colored doughs":

> On April 12th, we arrived near the outskirts of Lichtenfels. Here we encountered some small arms fire and bazooka fire. The bridge across the Main had been blown. Lt Col [Ernest C.] Watson, who would merit both a Bronze and a Silver Star, and Capt [Grenville T. (Jr.)] Emmet, a Bronze Star Honoree, walked

to the water's edge to look it over. Suddenly a bazooka and Machine Gun fired over their heads. Capt Emmet hit the water while the Battalion Commander lay flat on the ground. A 'C' Company tank quickly pulled up and covered them while they withdrew to safty [sic]. It was a close call. The Mortar Platoon moved into position and laid a smoke screen on the east bank of the river, while the coloured doughs of CC 'R' Rifle Company entered the town.[27]

In the combat at Creussen, a platoon traversed a wide open area 900 yards long without much cover and forced its way into the town. In addition to these other engagements, the Rifle Company, still attached to the 25th Tank Battalion, "ran into trouble." Small arms and artillery caused several casualties, including one dead. At that point, they were called on to return to Atlenfelden with a platoon of tanks, but suddenly three black platoons were called upon to join an emergency force of three platoons of infantry from A-62, eight tanks, two assault guns, and one TD. This American "Kampfgruppe" was ordered to assault the town of Allersberg to relieve pressure on other American units fighting there. They faced two Tiger tanks, armed only with bazookas, not the weapon of choice to face down a Tiger. After firing several bazooka rounds, which did nothing to the monster machines, Pvt. Percy Smith, First Platoon, fired one round which disabled the tank. He was only fifteen yards from the tank and gave his life in the exchange, and received a Bronze Star.

Not long after, orders came to rotate to Schutzendorf. Word had come down that there were SS troops about 800 yards away in a forest. All three platoons sent "strong patrols" into the woods, and within an hour, they returned with eight prisoners and reported several dead enemy left behind. "A volunteer patrol went out again to search the woods and found another group of SS troops. Four prisoners were brought back." In the attack on Landshut, under fire from across the river, the Rifle Company suffered 21 casualties although the city was taken.[28] The "coloured doughs" earned the respect of their fellow soldiers, and it is no surprise that the latter insisted that they be included in the Order of Battle of the 14th Armored Division.

When CCB got to Konigsfeld, the 19th AIB had to fight to enter that town. The 19th's *History* sketches what happened and provides a date of 14 April. Company A's tanks and men "moved to Konigsfeld, with the mission of clearing the town of any enemy troops before it could be occupied by CCB Reserve." *The History* continues the violent result:

> A combat patrol of a light tank, a half-track with one squad of infantry, and two peeps preceeded [sic] 'A'-19th to the town. As the patrol approached the town from the west, an enemy anti-tank gun fired on the leading tank at a range of 75 yards, penetrating the hull at the left front, and killing the driver instantly, and fatally wounding all the other members of the crew. With the disabled tank burning and its ammunition exploding, the rest of the patrol dismounted and moved forward on foot, while one peep went back to 'A' Company to relay the information of the anti-tank gun.[29]

Spotting anti-tank guns in the context of an embattled town was necessary before friendly armor approached within range, but it was difficult to do without infantry exposing themselves to machine gun and other kinds of fire to do it. It was the 48th Tank Battalion back in late November that had been terribly hurt because of the inability to locate anti-tank guns.

The fight continued as the peep went back and brought forward the heavy elements of A Company. After being dismounted, the medium tanks moved forward. Friendly machine gun fire was effectively directed at the site of the AT gun, and while the heads of the gunners were kept down, a tank fired one shot to dismantle the gun. It turned out that the enemy was not in a good position to oppose the force against them. On the east side of town, dug-in infantry were subjected to a combination of artillery, mortar, and tank fire, and six machine guns located on the high west side of town swept the area with fire." At this point, two infantry platoons of A-19 accompanied by a platoon of medium tanks "moved boldly" against the ridge on the east side of town. Some of the German troops surrendered—the wise thing to do—but others fatally fought back and were killed. Those making a run for it were either captured by the advancing 47th Tank Battalion coming in from the east or were cut down by machine-gun fire.[30]

On 15 April at 1700 the 19th AIB stepped off and sped through a succession of towns including Waischenfeld, Kirchahom, and finally

Weiher. The 19th was coordinated with the 47th TB, which had B-19 attached, and these units proceeded on the sixteenth to Ezelsdorf amid a dizzying number of changes of Combat Commands traveling in sometimes parallel lines but on different routes. When the 19th and the other units reached Ezelsdorf, it was joined by a section of the 94th Cav Squadron. As the friendly force surged ahead, it began receiving sniper fire and had to dig out small but hostile groups, although other enemy soldiers simply surrendered themselves as the column progressed.

An attack to clear the woods was ordered, including C Company of the 19th with attached tanks on the left and A on the right, supported in the same way. The plan was for both Companies to drive straight through the woods to a railroad track and turn towards each other to sweep up the remaining hostile forces. A Company was fortunate in that it was able to follow a road on its assignment, but C Company encountered very dense forest, which made it a dangerous patrol. Men could stumble onto machine-gun nests and be shot to pieces before knowing where they were. Nevertheless, the mission proved to be a success, with 85 prisoners and perhaps 50 killed while the 19th suffered only two casualties. Beyond that, two 76mm anti-tank guns were taken, and a plan was discovered which intended a combined tank-infantry attack against the friendly force in the vicinity of the Autobahn around the time it became dark.[31] (The Division History recorded the destruction of three AT guns in this skirmish.)

More fighting continued as the combined 19th-47th column forged ahead, but the pace of the march was picking up. Like the other "flying columns," this one was directed to make sure to interdict roads leading to Numberg:

> We found now that our immediate mission was to cut off the roads from Nurnberg to the east, denying German troops there a route of escape, for the city was being attacked and the enemy falling back. Everywhere indications that the enemy was weakening daily were growing more and more. He wanted to quit, but couldn't unless he had a good chance. Our combined penetrations had so disorganized him that he couldn't make a good defensive stand, except at strategic points, but we seemed to hit most of these. He was falling back as fast as he could, and our speed was too much for his setting up many defenses.[32]

However, when the friendly column reached the outskirts of Oberferrieden, it faced some familiar trouble. Although the men had had the satisfaction of capturing intact a passenger train all set to leave the station at Ezelsdorf, they were met by sniper fire from Oberferrieden. After dealing with that, they had to face stubborn resistance in a woods nearby and fight it off. That night, either the 16th or 17th of April, an enemy patrol surprised some engineers who were outposting a canal crossing at Dorlach. One man was killed and 19 captured, but one man escaped to report the incident. Friendly tanks then moved to the crossing, and on the next day "the C-19-A-47 team" eliminated 25 hostile troops in their foxholes.[33]

The Germans were becoming quite troublesome as they insisted on filtering back into ground already taken by friendly forces, and this was more of a problem because the area guarded by the 19th AIB and the 47th TB was quite large. There were too few friendly troops to completely cover the perimeter. It was at dawn on 20 April that the 19-47 "team," in an effort to rectify the situation and drive the enemy back on his heels, assaulted troublesome Oberferrieden. A-19, with the support of a platoon of tanks, surged ahead towards the town:

> After working up through the small town on the opposite side of the railroad tracks, from which the sniper fire was received, the company assembled for the advance across an open field into Oberferrieden. After a short artilllery and mortar barrage the company started moving into town, with the Machine-Gun Platoon supporting and following. There was scattered resistance at first and the attack progressed well until it reached the church, where a panzerfaust was fired at one of the tanks, missing it, but exploding and injuring several men. The tank backed up and fired several rounds of 76mm, while it peppered away with its machine-gun. Sniper fire became increasingly heavier from both the town and hill to the south, and, with no flank protection, casualties increased. The company was ordered to withdraw after four men had been killed and six wounded, three being from the Machine-Gun Platoon.[34]

There was frustration at seeing persistent violent resistance that would do nothing for the German Army or German nation. The

Fatherland was doomed to lose, and all the intense fighting could do was cause the certain victors more casualties. For these reasons, the American Army, toward the end of the war, adopted a policy of exchanging its steel and explosives for the flesh and blood of the enemy and the destruction of his towns. This was the inevitable corollary to senseless and bloody resistance by the Germans to the advancing foe. This is the ultimate logic of industrial warfare for a nation that seemed to have unlimited resources of ammunition and weapons, and the necessary transportation system to bring these forward to the front lines. Even the GIs could sense the tradeoff and were quite content with it. And so, after the casualties on 20 April in the town of Oberferrieden, a more devastating dynamic emerged:

> During the early morning, the town was pounded and pounded with medium and heavy artillery. The rocket tank [a new weapon] was brought up and fired into the town, as the Assault Gun Platoon poured its 105mm shells in and the Mortar Platoon cut loose with its deadly 81's. The town rocked from the shelling, and nearly every house was ablaze as the attack jumped off shortly after 0630. 'C' Company, without difficulty, moved quickly around to occupy the high ground designated, while 'A' Company moved through the town meeting very little resistance. Most of the enemy troops and civilians had vacated the town after the shelling, since it was ablaze and there was no place to stay. The town was completely cleared by 0930; we suffered only two casualties.[35]

In the copy of the 19th AIB's *History* used here, there is a-note by then Pvt. Bob Straba, who was a runner for C Company's Commander, which notes, "Kotch killed here by our own BAR." This was S/Sgt. Irving A. Koch, honored with a Bronze Star, listed as KIA in the Roster of the Division. The positive news was that there were so few casualties in the battle, but the negative was that one man lost his life to "friendly fire."

At the town of Pforring, A Company lost its commander, Capt. Richard A. Tharpe, a Bronze and Silver Star recipient, who had led the attack into town armed only with a pistol. He survived the attack and bedded down for the night in one of the houses. A round of HE hit the house and killed him, another one of the grim ironies of combat. But worse was to come when SS troops, well armed and supported, counterattacked. In the ensuing fight, two tanks and two tank destroyers were lost, "and there were many personnel casualties." This attack was rebuffed, but then the 19th was counterattacked, and that was repulsed, but the 47th was counterattacked again.[36] There seemed no end to the madness.

The death of Captain Tharpe was a sharp blow to the men of the 47th, and its History demonstrates poignantly the loss that was felt by everyone:

Able Company had in the meantime taken the small town of Pforring, here is where they had their biggest loss of the war. Capt. Richard A. Tharpe of Macon, Georgia, had taken his tanks into town that evening, walking ahead of even the infantry and armed with only a .45 cal pistol, he killed every German that stood in his path. But he wasn't killed in the attack. Not Capt. Tharpe. It was pure luck they ever got him. That night, after the town had been cleared, the enemy began to shell the town. Capt. Tharpe had gone to bed in one of the houses and an HE shell crashed through the roof killing him instantly. Gone in less time than it takes to write it was the most loved man in the company. Gone was the man who many of A Company owed their lives [to]. A man who had always taught his boys to be good soldiers, a man who never stopped working for one minute of the day for his company. There was many a man in A Company who thought he could not cry but broke down that night and wept. 1st Lt. James [R.] Deveney was sent down to take over the company, and although he had a company that had been hurt and hurt badly, he had a company who was eager to fight and wanted blood—German blood to avenge Capt. Tharpe's death."[37] Deveny would be credited with a Bronze Star.

There would only be a change of battlefield, for the 47th was switched from CCB to CCA. The attention of the Division *History* also shifted to the fortunes of the 25th Tank Battalion, which was working with the Seventh Army Rifle Platoon, the unit of black soldiers seen here before. The 25th had been ordered to proceed down the Autobahn, with C Company instructed to "join the 45th Infantry Division in a scheduled Victory Parade in the Nazi Citadel" of Nurnberg. This order turned out to be most premature, for the war was not over by any means. On the way, as the 25th History remembered, the battalion was strafed by Me-109's, clearly not a part of the Victory Parade. Plans were to be changed quickly, and the 25th motor-marched down the Autobahn towards Allersberg. Enemy artillery began firing and inflicted casualties on the men of the Rifle Platoon. As Company C's tanks approached Gogglesbruch, they fired on the church steeple just in case it was being used for observation. Even before C Company had gotten this far, enemy anti-tank guns knocked out two tanks and damaged two more.[38]

Once off the Autobahn, at 0630, three Mark V Panther tank were spotted, and the combination of TD and tank cannon fire destroyed one of them just south of Allersberg. Just outside of Gogglesbruch, a German 88 had the junction zeroed in, and Company C tanks would pay the price for being there:

> Jerry fire—88—had the spot "zeroed in," and a hit on S/Sgt. Leonard R. Shelton's tank disabled his 76mm. Close on the heels of C Company came the AG [assault gun] Platoon, Lt. [Michael] Hosak's tank escaped the enemy fire, but Tec 4 [James G.] Anderson's tank took a direct hit through the left sponson, seriously injuring Tec 4 [Edward A.] Berg and mortally wounding Pfc Gilbert [A.] Chapman. The tank went up in flames, burning Anderson, [Pfc. Raymond] Burriss and [John M.] Holt. The lead tank halted and its crewmembers jumped out to give aid to the inured members of the burning tank. Pfc. Edward C. Kistner, a Bronze Star earner, entered the burning vehicle which was still under direct fire and evacuated one of the severely burned occupants. The medics arrived quickly to take charge of the men.[39]

It is doubtful that there is any detailed record of men killed when attempting a rescue of tankers wounded in a burning or blasted tank. But it is clear that there seemed to be no reluctance on the part of comrades to make the attempt. In the case of the 25th, even when a TD advanced to "neutralize the gun position," it too was hit and "more severe casualties" were "inflicted."

Captain Homer L. Swager with his driver attempted "a personal reconnaissance," but both men were pinned down by machine-gun fire and the Captain was killed by a sniper. All in all, a very bad day.

A terrific fight was developing at Altenfelden. Lt. Col. Ernest C. Watson's tank was in position on a hill outside of Allersberg, and T/5 John Curran, a Bronze Star recipient, saw enemy infantry moving toward them. Displacing to the .50 caliber machine gun on the rear deck of the tank, he began firing on the enemy. Fortunately, the artillery observer in the Observation Post saw what was happening. He then called for a fire mission, and the Mortar Platoon laid down concentrated fire on the hostile infantry. A "hurried call" to the tanks left in Gogglesbruch brought them in a rush, daring to speed through the "88 junction" without suffering a hit. Both B Company and a platoon from C Company arrived, with the former taking a flank position, and the latter took up the same position on the ridge as the command tank. The 25th History tells us what happened next:

> One tank from 'B' Company pulled up behind the foxhole of Tec 5 [Winfield E.] Jones, Service Company [a winner of a Bronze Star]. The tank was firing over his head and the muzzle blast blew the loose dirt into the hole, while the counter fire that the tank drew was blowing the dirt from the front of his hole back in and he felt as though he was being buried alive. . . . Two direct hits on 'B' Company tanks rendered them useless. The Battle [sic] was furious and everyone that could be spared to man a gun took up positions on the eastern ridge near the mortar platoon emplacements. The fire power of the Battalion proved too great for the krauts and the attack was contained by 1500.[40]

The 14th's *History* takes space to laud the efforts of the Service Company, for many of them took their place on the ridge and fired their M4's to assist in the fiercely fought battle.

However, the danger was not over. There was a concentration of enemy troops in the area, and they had to be dealt with. The enemy was still in the woods on the left and maintained the possibility that he could cut off the Battalion's supply lines from the Autobahn. A patrol of light tanks under the command of Lt. James D. Fraser was given the assignment of patrolling the road between Altenfelden and Feuct. Two nights later, his tank was demolished by "a bazooka team," with Lt. Fraser and his gunner, Harold A. Martinez, "seriously burned." The patrol continued for the remainder of the night. In the morning, 23 April, it was discovered that the enemy had pulled out of town.

The 62nd Armored Infantry Battalion had also been busy. Driving down the road to Altenfelden, they were violently accosted by enemy fire. The tanks and halftracks, following the pattern of frontier wagons assaulted by Indians, formed a circle, and "the enemy was cut down." The First Platoon drove into Hilpolstein and while there, both a German truck driver and a motorcyclist drove up to the CP and were summarily captured.[41]

Similarly, the men of the 125th Combat Engineers were active. They repaired roads, dams, bridges, and fords, and guarded them as well when necessary. The Third Platoon of A Company employed an unusual method of repairing an old arched bridge. It blew the bridge into the creek and built a road over the ruins with a bulldozer. The Company also acted as guides, maintained bypasses, and hauled destroyed enemy vehicles off the roads. Two engineers noticed a body of troops at a distance on a hillside and assumed that they were friendly. They were not. When German artillery began to pour down, they dived for their foxholes and weapons to act as infantry. The engineers of the 125th began to fire on the hostile infantry, and the friendly position held for twelve hours until a pouring rain began to fall. When Pfc. Jack Rowe and Pfc. Daniel Guan went to get some equipment, a round narrowly missed Guan but wounded Rowe. During the late afternoon, the Company's air compressor had been hit, and it was necessary to get the "irreplaceable" equipment back to safety. When the men maneuvered back behind the apparent front line, they were fired on by a panzerfaust which missed the radio half-track, and they were also threatened by a grenade which bounced off the mess truck.

The First Platoon, at the town of Rasch, was guarding the canal passage there when more German infantry attacked. Pfc. Elmer Adamson "rallied the platoon" at the same time as Pfc. Gustav O. Laurel fired his .50 caliber to keep the enemy at bay. The vicious scrap continued:

A savage fight developed around the CP, rifles, burp guns, hand grenades and panzerfausts firing at point blank range. Tec/5 Augustus Witherite was killed; Tec/5 James J. Sullivan killed a German as he attempted to come in the door. Laurel was sent in to tell the men to surrender; but they refused and the fight continued. Artillery began to fall on the house; and it was obvious the men were heavily outnumbered. After four hours fighting, with many wounded, the platoon surrendered.[42]

Although combat engineers were trained to do engineering work, this is one of those examples when they fought valiantly as foot soldiers. The men, placed in halftracks, were driven back to the German lines with headlights on, and then they had to march 120 miles, sleep in barns, and eat potato soup without potatoes. Several of the wounded including Pfc. Gerhart A. A. Radtke (hit by a German vehicle), Gustav Laurel, and Tec/5 John Ryan, who were taken to a hospital. It would turn out to be a stroke of good luck for the rest of the engineers that they were taken to the Stalag at Moosburg. Pfc. Radtke would not survive.

The Second Platoon of the Combat Engineers' A Company also had their share of action. In another confused, swirling battle environment, this time in the vicinity of Altenhann. With the 47th TB, they sent out patrols in a woods. Forming a skirmish line with a tank as backup, they made their way toward a small village. Then chaos ensued—"a barrage of artillery and mortar fire falling among them, and machine guns and burp guns opened up from the nearest houses." As the fighting continues, it was clear that the engineers and the one tank were insufficient to stifle the enemy's aggressiveness. Four men were killed and one wounded in the withdrawal.[43]

The platoon had more work to do, this time more engineering than infantry action. After building a ford at Douzgstadt for the 47th's tanks, it removed two aerial bombs and cleared the post office of boobytraps. At Bonn, working with the 48th Tank Battalion and the 94th Cav, B Company encountered two roadblocks. Passing the first, undefended roadblock they were met with hostile fire. Lt. Clyde Humbert and Tec/4 Roy 0. Seitz extricated a wounded man, put him on the deck of a tank, sheltering his body with theirs. For this action they were recognized with the Silver Star. Near the unpleasant fight at Neumarkt, A Company had to build 400 feet of corduroy road in an area with a 15% grade and three days of mud "under intermittent fire." There were more hairy adventures for the 125th Combat Engineers, including the conduct of an exercise near Schreadorf where "a stream of enemy soldiers" emerged from the woods because they thought that the 125th was on the verge of attacking them.

Like most unit histories, whether Battalion or Division, that of the 14th Armored devoted space to those units which didn't always get enough attention. One of these was the Band, which had been converted to MP duty, especially important with the vast numbers of enemy prisoners who were coming out of the woodwork, so to speak. The first squad of Band MPs processed more than 5,000 POWs (what were then called PW's) toward the end of the war, with two of them, Tec/5 William Jenkins and Pfc. Heber Holland, captured by the enemy on April 17. The Division *History* implies, but does not say, that they both escaped from a prisoner cage in Amberg. The Second Squad was occupied guarding a hospital for convalescing German soldiers and kept moving with the flow of prisoners. At the town of Hersbruck, four freed Czechs volunteered to help them in their work. The Third Squad handled a huge number of prisoners, as many as 45,000, including five Generals and "several war criminals." The Fifth Squad did not handle prisoners but acted as "road guides."

The 84th Medical Battalion became victims of an enemy attack from the air, being "strafed and bombed" in Hersbruck. A Company of the 84th experienced some dangerous moments when Pfc. Joseph Barba and Tec/5 John R. Kearney were captured along with "a load of casualties from the 19th Infantry." The ambulance had turned in the wrong place and ran smack into some German foot soldiers. The 12th Armored Division liberated them at Schraudenbach, when that town was seized. B Company of the 84th was strafed by German planes, a sure indication in late April that the Luftwaffe was not done with the war. The Company was so close to the fighting that at Trockau casualties arrived at their facilities rather than at the Battalion Aid Station. C Company wound up stuck in the middle of fighting all around them.

With the melting snow and ice and the spring rains, transporting the wounded became extremely difficult for combat vehicles, especially halftracks and tanks, which were chewing up the roads and leaving holes at river crossings as deep as three feet. When B Company, with CCB, after getting medical vehicles out of the mud, set up their facility at Altdorf, they were exposed to both shelling and bombing. When fighting became intermittent, they simply kept moving with the Division Trains of CCB. Traveling during a blackout on the Autobahn, an ambulance smashed into an MP "peep," killing two MP's and injuring three men as well. A second ambulance, not seeing what had happened, crashed into the wreck and two more men were injured. The hazards of duty got even more dangerous for C Company, when in Betznstein not only were they strafed but enemy tanks approached as close as 50 yards. The Company was cut off for several hours.[44]

The 136th Ordnance Maintenance Battalion, on 11 April, sent A Company to support CCB and B Company to do the same for CCR, including two Quartermaster Truck Companies, an infantry company, and a tank destroyer battalion. The mechanics of the Maintenance Sections were quite amazing in improvising repairs. Pvt. Richard Frederick and Pvt. James Carson were sent off to haul in a damaged tank with their wrecker. On their way, they noticed another damaged tank "on its belly." Since they were looking for a power train and transmission, they decided to cannibalize the tank. Because the wrecker wasn't designed to lift a tank, the two mechanics somehow dug a hole under the tank, removed the bolts affixing the engine and power train, commandeered an abandoned German trailer, and drove to Hammelburg. There they installed the parts into the wrecked tank and drove it back to the shop.

The 136th, driving toward Nurnberg, "took prisoners," lost one of theirs as a prisoner, were strafed and sniped at, all the while trying to get vehicles back on the road. It was a demanding job. To illustrate the point, Lt. Belton Y. Cooper, who was in charge of a Maintenance Section with the 3rd Armored Division, described his unit's ability to get wrecked tanks back in action:

> It was my responsibility to prepare a Combat Loss Report showing all the tank and other vehicle losses during the day. I then took this report through bypassed German units, and delivered it to the Ordnance Battalion, thirty to sixty miles to the rear. The next morning I would return to the Combat Command with tanks and other replacement equipment lost

forty-eight hours prior to this date. Thus, we had new replacement vehicles within a forty-eight hour period after taking severe losses.[45]

In the armored divisions, with the number of wrecked tanks in the second half of 1944 and the first half of 1945, it was essential that as many as possible were put back in operation before the enemy could take advantage of a shortage. The Ordnance Maintenance Battalion did its work well and enabled the fast-moving columns to continue relentless pressure on the Wehrmacht and get the war over and stop the equally relentless count of casualties.

The 14th Armored Division's *History* concluded its "Pursuit" chapter by etching a drawing of the frenetic activities of the Division Artillery as it tried to keep up with the armored infantry and tank battalions. Much of the time it was out in the open, and on clear days it was subject to enemy aircraft. For example,

Divarty [Division Artillery] was strafed and bombed again and again—two artillery battalions and an airstrip out in the open may have been the target. Early in the morning of the 14th, nine Me-109s roared suddenly in over the tops of the trees; the attached 398th AAA got three and Tec/5 Paul C. Martin got another; and Divarty moved to Trockau with CCR; the 501s, the 68th and the 975th were firing into Creussen.[46]

The Division History records 17 April as "a bad day," with one threat after another. Two enemy SPs chased a colonel and a Tec/5 down a road, and a Lt. Colonel and another Tec/5 drove over a hill and blundered into a hostile tank only hundreds of yards away. Another pair composed of an officer and an enlisted man doing recon work, stumbled onto "a large group of enemy infantry." And yet, once the batteries were set up, on a bright and sunny day, the pilots in the observation planes could easily see and spot for the guns, the unfriendly tanks, horse drawn artillery, and infantry in the open. On the same day, in the afternoon, the column of guns was strafed as many as four times as vehicles became stuck in the mud.

On 19 April, Hitler's birthday, the artillery's airstrip was strafed, and the air section was prepared to burn its planes when enemy infantry infiltrated the area. The Service Battery of the 69th was ambushed at Minfeld. The Division *History* provides no details, but it does make a comment reflecting the oddness of the situation: "The fighting was so strange, so vicious and so quiet, so spotty and confused, that at one time two 105mm battalions were shooting directly at each other, 500 yards apart." The Autobahn was cut several times a day, and the 500th Armored Field Artillery nearly lost two batteries to the foe. Still, it was the air assaults that could be unnerving. As the Division forced its way deeper into Germany, there seemed to be more of them:

> . . . the men of the 500th [AFA] saw the AA guns of the 398th open up again and again, the heavy clatter of the 50s cut with the rhythmic pom-pom-pom-pom of the automatic 37. In one air attack, when the AA and the .50 caliber guns of the 500th itself had suddenly blasted loose at a plane, 74 SS troops came out of a wood, in columns of two and carrying a white flag.[47]

The thought of that combination of guns being turned on them and not the planes must have given them a serious moment of meditation about their possible bloody demise. Yet the artillery gunners must also have had second thoughts about the situation when they commenced firing, with two guns firing "on compass 4800 and three on compass 2400. Battery fired in opposite directions at the same time." This kind of craziness continued until the back of the enemy appeared to be broken: "The 14th Armored was on its way to the Danube."[48]

There was still more difficult fighting throughout April for all units, but on 28 April something positive was beginning to happen. B Company of the 68th teamed up with the 47th Tank Battalion and crushed enemy resistance at the town of Mauern. After the town was outposted, plans were completed to assault the town of Moosburg on the following morning at 0900.[49] The plan had to be more involved than usual because Moosburg contained a huge Lager or Stalag housing thousands of prisoners. However, at 0600, a novel delegation appeared at the Headquarters of Combat Command A, with Brig. Gen. C. H. Karlstadt ready to meet with it. The Division *History* enumerates the members:

> It consisted of a German Major, representing the commander of the Moosburg Allied Prisoner of War Camp, Col. Paul S. Goode

of the United States Army, and a Group Commander of the British Royal Air Force, the senior American and British Officers respectively, imprisoned in the Moosburg Camp; a Swiss Red Cross representative; and Col. Lann [the commander of the 47th TB].[50]

The party from the camp was given until 0900 to accept an offer of unconditional surrender with the stark alternative that the town would be attacked and the camp taken. Of course, there was a chance that any fighting in the vicinity of Stalag VIIA would create hazardous conditions for the prisoners, mostly men of the US Army Air Force who had been shot down over Germany, but also ground forces, including men captured in Normandy the past summer. The camp also contained men from as many as sixteen nations, 27 Red Army generals, and sons of four American generals.

One of the men in the camp, Keith Fuller, described the hair-raising experiences of the flyers who had already been through a great deal:

> Most of us were Air Corps officers shot down by flak or fighters. We had survived parachute jumps, civilian attacks, crash landings, interrogation and a blizzard march that taxed the limit of endurance.
>
> Now at the moment before freedom, it was awesomely ironic to think of being killed.[51]

The situation was also hazardous for those soldiers of the 68th AIB, specifically B Company and those of the 47th TB, C Company. The night before, they had been in a hard fight around Mauern. It was the second platoon of B-68 in the vanguard of the infantry attack:

> The second platoon led the assault, when S/Sgt. Harry Roberts' second squad and four men from Pfc. [Manuel S.] Lamboy's first squad crossed the bridge outside of town in the face of intense enemy small arms fire and with two supporting tanks [of C-47] engaged an estimated 250 of Hitler's fanatical SS troops in a terrific firefight. While the tanks kept the Germans pinned down the 15 men moved forward, and in the close-in fighting that followed they and the two accompanying tanks took a ter-

rific toll of the enemy."[52] Roberts and Lamboy would receive Bronze Star Medals.

It was obvious to everyone at the battle that the US Army was very short of foot soldiers for the task at hand. Fortunately, the SS troops were fighting only with small arms fire although they did have some panzerfausts.

As all this was transpiring, the Germans blew the bridge across the Isar, and between that explosion, the firing of the tanks' cannons, and the small arms fire, the prisoners could only squeeze themselves into whatever safe places they could find. Meanwhile, as B-68 and the C-47 tanks shot up the SS troops, 1st Lt. Joseph R. Luby of the infantry company, Pvt. John L. Hodges, of HDQRs Company, and General Karlstad, with their drivers, raced in peeps carrying .30 caliber machine guns into the camp. Although there were 240 guards in the camp, Luby manned the machine gun in his peep and shouted to the guards, "Achtung." The safe response of the guards was to surrender and allow the GIs and officers to disarm them.[53]

As the Division History grimly writes of the aftermath, "By 1030 the SS were lying dead in the fields and along the roads, grey-white faces and open mouths, twisted and staring sightlessly at the cold, blue sky above; and American medium tanks were roaring through the cobbled streets of the ancient city."[54] But what of the men in the camp—with all this violence? Keith Fuller remembers what happened only too well, the fear and the prayers. After he noticed two P-51 Mustangs diving and strafing near the "Kriegies" compound,

> Shells whined over camp from the American tanks of the Third Army aimed at Moosburg. Small arms crackled and a few of us were wounded. We dived for the barracks, in and under, ripping out flooring with super human strength.
>
> I lay beneath my bunk sweating and praying. You heard sobbing, cursing and praying in unison.
>
> The eternity it seemed may have been less than an hour. But suddenly it was quiet and voices drifted in from the compound. Gingerly we trickled outside again to see a Sherman tank lumber through the barbed wire. It was a moment of high emotion to see that barbed wire smashed down.[55]

The tremendous emotion which the men felt on the verge of liberation after such a long time was heightened by the fear and ignorance they experienced as the sounds of fighting and the flights of friendly fighter planes became all too present. For some of the British soldiers and airman, who had been held captive for several years, it was quite traumatic to be thrown again back into the world of sudden violence and arbitrary chaos. Lt. Frank Stewart of the Lothian and Borders yeomanry felt confused emotions both before and after the liberation:

> Most of us had experienced no real personal danger for upwards of five years, and what we had we'd forgotten. We had seen little of battle and fighting and it was one of our consolations for our generally uncomfortable life that for us, at least, the war had passed us by. I think it was this and the complete unexpectedness of it all that accounts for the shattering effect it has had on us. Naturally, we were all extremely frightened at the time, and it has taken time to recover. For days after, we've jumped at the slightest noise, everything has sounded like an aeroplane or a machine-gun, and everyone is restless and nervy. A typical case of shock, I suppose.[56]

The American prisoners, who had a radio to listen to Radio Luxembourg, the BBC, knew that there had been an agreement between German authorities and the Allied Powers that "Allied prisoners of war would no longer be moved if the Allied Governments would agree in turn that, when liberated, those prisoners would not be thrown back into the fighting." That agreement went into effect on 22 April, a week before the liberation of the camp. However, on the 23rd, the guards told the prisoners to line up in order to be transported. The prisoners told them about the agreement, and they in turn found that the prisoners could not be moved.[57] It was a small victory in a big war, but it made it certain that no Allied prisoners would be wounded or die as a result of the perils of marching down a road in the middle of the fighting, an event that did occur elsewhere.

It was also fortunate for all Allied prisoners of the Reich that the war had not continued much longer. A classified document revealed decades after the war by The World Jewish Congress after its discovery in the National Archives indicated that Hitler intended to execute all of them some time in May. As the document grimly said, "All Allied (prisoners of war) except those valuable to the German war economy would be exterminated." In an interview of Herman Goering in captivity after the war, he stated only that he supported the plan. Others in high positions in the Reich opposed it on the basis that "German (prisoners) in Allied hands would have to expect the same fate." Hitler's casual response to this possibility was that the German prisoners were of no use to the Reich and that the policy would discourage his soldiers from surrendering. "Goering believed that Hitler would have carried out the plan had the war in Europe lasted three more months."[58]

At Moosburg the prisoners had no idea of this possible calamity as they cautiously walked outside in time to see Sherman tanks with white stars on them approach the camp. When the prisoners realized that they were going to be freed, "It was like visiting heaven." General Patton, the Third Army commander, to whom the 14th Armored Division had only recently been attached, according to the story, ordered that the German flag be removed from the flagpole and shouted, "I want that son-of-a bitch cut down, and the man that cuts it down, I want that man to wipe his ass with it."[59]

A footnote to this story appeared in the 14th Armored's newsletter, *The Liberator*, written by Dr. Martin Allain, who described himself as a "Skinny GI." He had been the pilot of a B-26 bomber shot down over North Africa in January of 1943. He had been imprisoned in another camp, Stalag Luft lll, before his transfer to Moosburg. As the security officer for the American prisoners, he was given the responsibility of securing a large American flag smuggled into the camp. He sewed the flag between "two old German blankets and slept under it for the next year." It was planned that in case of air attack by friendly airplanes the flag would be placed on the ground to ward off harm from the air. He was one of 20,000 prisoners who had to walk in the cold and the snow to Moosburg. He concludes his story:

> When General Patton liberated us, my roommate and I went up to the German flag tower, took down their flag and replaced it with the beautiful American flag I had kept hidden for so many months.[60]

The men of the 14th AD had their own moving experiences during the liberation of the camp. One of them, John P. Meyer, was acting as a Forward Artillery Observer and motored into the camp right after the first two vehicles entered. As he characterized his feelings at that moment,

> I was standing in my vehicle and removed my helmet when I heard one of the prisoners call out, "John Meyer, you old so and so." I looked to where the call came from and there was Irvin Baer. He had been shot down over France and was imprisoned in Moosburg.[61]

Meyer had played high school football in Danville, Illinois with Baer, and the two of them had become "good friends."

One of the prisoners, Tec 4 Robert W. Kroupa, was himself from the 14th Armored, specifically from the A Company of the 125th Combat Engineers. His halftrack had been ambushed on the previous New Year's Day near Bitche during Operation Northwind. When the halftrack turned over, his wrist had been smashed, and he was taken prisoner. It was ten days later that an attempt was made at a German hospital to repair his wrist. After that he was moved to three hospitals and four prison camps, including Hammelburg, where he had almost been liberated by his comrades in his division. On 29 April, with sounds of baffle approaching and nobody guarding the gate, he "slipped out" and found a bicycle. Bicycling anxiously down the road, he felt that this could be his last chance to survive because of his general sickness and weakness:

> I didn't want to miss this chance. I ran into my own outfit in the first town I came to. They hadn't known if I was dead or alive. I wanted to go with them, but I was so sick and weak that they took me back to the prison camp.
>
> When I got back to the prison camp at Moosburg, our tanks were just going into the camp. An officer on one tank saw my 14th Armored patch on my shirt and had me jump on the tank. When we got to the camp, the prisoners started hugging and kissing me. They thought I was liberating them—but there I was, one of them.[62]

Then Major deWitt C. Armstrong, Ill tells the story of how his 94th Cav and Recon, after crossing a river near Landshut, encountered crowds of freed "Kriegies ("Kriegesgefangenen") in the town of Moosburg. Their thanks was both effusive and grateful as they climbed onto their light tanks, hugging the men, and asking for food. For Armstrong, the story got personal when it involved his captured liaison officer (not named in the letter), who had been captured only weeks before. Two days after that, the 94th overran the German headquarters where he was being interrogated. He was given a new peep and a new weapon and sent back into the hazardous business of coordinating units between forward and rearward positions. He was captured again but this time imprisoned in Moosburg; it was certainly a charm this time to be liberated by the men of his division.[63]

The 14th AD's *History* records other wonderful moments when the "Krieges" received their freedom. Tec/5 Floyd C. Mahoney of C-47 freed his own son, a lieutenant in the Army Air Corps, and an unidentified source has been quoted as saying that Mahoney Sr. "was particularly overjoyed upon finding that his son, an Army Air Force lieutenant, was a prisoner" and presumably "overjoyed" that he was alive and liberated.[64]

Another episode revolves around a 6-foot-4 Australian, imprisoned for some time, who shouted, "You damned bloody Yanks, I love you" as he "threw his arms around a peep driver." A captured American paratrooper kissed the tank commander, and "Tears streamed from his cheeks." The men of the 47th found eight of their men in the surging crowd of prisoners.[65]

All in all, although the fighting would continue for another week, the men of the 14th Armored quickly received the news of the camp's liberation, and that news engendered a powerful feeling of pride and satisfaction in doing something so overwhelmingly positive that it permeated the ranks and became, in essence, a part of the fiber of the Division. Later, they would officially be designated "The Liberators," and the word would appear on their unit coat of arms, over sixty years later still a source of immense honor. After all the wounding and the killing, the pain and the suffering, the defeat and the triumph, the filth and the obscenity, the hatred for those trying to cause their death and love for those who tried to keep them alive—the events at Hammelburg and Moosburg and the freeing of slave laborers there and elsewhere, their hysterical and near hysterical gratitude and that of the prisoners—especially their comrade Americans—softened their hearts and allowed them to think that perhaps the world could be made a better place after all.

Nevertheless, in the days, and especially the nights, when many of the freed prisoners wreaked their revenge on the guards not in custody and on some of the people in the town, the unpleasant other side of cruelty appeared. "There was rape that night and pillage, and plain and fancy robbery, and the German civilians hid indoors." Nevertheless, the war had to go on as the Division history reminds us:

Up through the mad bacchanalia, the combat troops were trying to move, tanks and endless lines of silent infantrymen from the 68th Armored Infantry Battalion, faces set and hardly seeing the weaving scenes about them, eyes straight ahead and with [the] trick men have who are going into battle of catching their lower lip and holding it caught between their teeth.[66]

Chapter 10

FROM ATLANTIC TO PACIFIC?

The images of dissolution at the end of April reminded Captain Carter of a cinematic phantasmagoria:

> The dying nation dissolved into a snarling, giggling montage of human shapes, like a color fantasy on a movie screen where the eye is not able to see nor to understand, but only to snatch at endlessly shifting swirling jumbles of shapes of the wildest human emotions, and joy is translated into a dissolving cone of orange fading quickly into red and black and green and ravage [sic].[1]

Carter's melodramatic rendering reflects the madness of events in most of Germany at the time: fighting between organized combatants on both sides, the enormous inkblots of Wehrmacht soldiers trying to surrender themselves out of their collapsing armies to get home, the jumble of prisoners, civilian and military, who found themselves unleashed from their captors and tormenters, and the residents of towns fearful of what was now going to befall them after false security. Most flew white flags, but on occasion a "hard case" would snipe at the advancing columns of armor.

As these rapidly ploughed forward, the armored columns reached the stage where they would just wave surrendering German soldiers toward the back of the advancing Americans. Towns and clusters of hostile enemy soldiers had been bypassed, but on occasion they would continue to fire at columns which had already gone by. Former prisoners of the Third Reich, civilian or military, some of whom had endured years of heartless captivity, could barely restrain themselves, sometimes from their joy, sometimes from their hatred of their captors. Many a prison guard was beaten to death in newly liberated "work" camps which the world would soon come to more realistically know as "death" camps.

The 14th Armored, regardless of all this, had to keep moving in order to terminate the regime that had engendered such a monstrosity. And so C Company of the 125th Combat Engineers and the 998th Treadway Bridge Company built a bridge across the Isar River. In its advance, C Company of the 47th Tank Battalion encountered and destroyed a horse-drawn convoy of Germans. At Ampfing the battalion discovered a camp where thousands of Jews had been cremated. When the American tanks arrived, the survivors set upon the Camp Commandant and beat him to death. When they saw the dead horses from the decimated convoy, they "tore at the flesh with their teeth and hands. They kissed the shoes of American soldiers."

Also uncovered was a huge complex served by slave laborers including a munitions plant and a Luftwaffe installation where aircraft parts were manufactured, with finished planes on two airfields. The factories were underground to a depth of seven stories, with sod twelve feet thick on top with trees growing on it. To the end, the Reich was ever industrious in its efforts to conceive and manufacture sophisticated weapons of destruction. If the war had been delayed several more months, both the Luftwaffe and the ballistic missile program might have tipped the balance in Hitler's favor. There were even efforts to build a missile with a huge warhead aimed at Manhattan Island.

And so it was critical for Allied forces to steamroll ahead as quickly as possible to demoralize the enemy and to terminate these programs. The 47th TB established another bridgehead on the Inn River. During the fighting Major Philip B. Daniels, the Combat Command B Surgeon, and Capt. Marvin E. Parsons were both wounded. Seeing their desperate need, the Chaplain, Paul Gebauer, rushed to give them first aid. Later the Chaplain would be awarded a Silver Star for his heroism. Combat Command B effected a crosssing ot the Danube River. Not to be outdone, Lt. Col. John C. Cavin, leader of the 48th, dashed ahead on the basis of information gathered from both civilians and German prisoners to take the surrender of a jet-propelled wing of the Luftwaffe including its 1,000-man contingent.

However, it wasn't all dash and surrender as the 19th Armored Infantry Battalion rode up the tail of a German column at Taufkirchen. The Germans in this column were not about to be overrun like others were. They responded with well aimed fire, and in the process shot up the recon force of the 19th at a cost of two tanks, a peep, and four men "in a short and savage fire fight."[2]

The 68th AIB was also quite busy in its advance to the Isar River, where the bridge had been blown by the retreating enemy. The Battalion history describes the assault across the remains of the bridge:

Under the leadership of Lt. [William C. Graves, who would earn a Bronze Star], the first platoon of 'B' Company, followed by the second, third, and then fourth, led the way across the blownout bridge and pushed on beyond the Isar to the town of Pattenau, meeting heavy resistance.

The resistance was overcome, and the forward thrust continued in what the Battalion history calls "a glorious drive," despite the fact that B Company, attached to a tank battalion in its attack on Muhldorf, had "the bridge across the Inn River literally blown up in their faces."

The 68th's History records the official end of the war at 0001 hours on 9 May 1945 and states that "We were happy in the realization that the small part which our battalion played had helped to achieve this victory in Europe." Officially the war ended at midnight of 7 or 8 May. Among the statistics was the list of dead, wounded, and missing in action:

Killed in Action	87
Died of Wounds	15
Wounded in Action and Hospitalized	348
Wounded in Action not Hospitalized	91
Injured in Action, Hospitalized	42
Injured in Action, not Hospitalized	11
Missing in Action	25
TOTAL CASUALTIES	619[3]

The count of those missing in action, as in other combat units, was subject to change as some men were recuperating in German hospitals or waiting for their freedom in a POW camp. Also, paperwork for some patients in army hospitals in Europe, England, and in the United States might not have been up to date. Many of the missing, if they were hit by any large caliber mortar round or artillery shell, had simply disappeared in the hungry maw of war.

A happier sequence of events happened to three survivors of the war. Lt Harry Kemp, who was being treated for a serious leg wound; Pfc. Marshall Whitesides, also of the 68th, who suffered a serious facial wound, and Joe Cotton of the 48th Tank Battalion, less seriously wounded, all found themselves on gurneys in the Army General Hospital in Dijon France after the battle of Steinfeld. After the formation of the 14th Armored Association, they renewed their acquaintance, on occasion after a few glasses of good liquor. They were still hail and positive, despite their wounds and the time it took for rehabilitation. Many other stories could be told of the combatants in the war, but some of them are no longer casting a shadow in the late sunlight of a summer's day.

But this is to get too far ahead of our story. Fighting continued for the 94th Cav and Recon, which as usual was out in front hunting for and harassing the fleeing foe. It was this unit which, on 17 April, not only took 200 prisoners but also uncovered a poison gas dump. (Fortunately, poison gas was not employed during the Second World War in Europe.) Both A and D Troop were held up by strong enemy forces with both tanks and anti-tank guns and were even strafed by hostile aircraft. As progress was renewed, displaced persons from all over Europe "with makeshift flags" and local children waved to the armored cars rushing ahead. More challenging were two self-propelled guns, a tank, a half-track, and a flak wagon, which were destroyed by D Troop. A Troop's report for 29 April laid out the progress and accomplishments of the 94th Cav and Recon:

> A Troop moved out, captured 21 towns. Fire fights at Pfeffenhauser, Oberneuhauser, Glain and Ergolding. Liberated two POW camps with 4041 Allied PWs, British, Polish, Czech, American, French, and Russian. A Troop met enemy column attempting to escape from Landshut at Glain and dispersed it by calling for tank and artillery fire. Cut enemy escape route. C Troop captured 6 towns. Encountered resistance in all towns.

Liberated 15 American officer POWs. E Troop supported squadron, fired five missions, drove off one enemy counterattack trying to flank squadron at Takaried. F Company broke up attack on squadron trains at Neuhauser. One section of F Company's M-24 tanks supported A Troop. The squadron destroyed: four enemy tanks, one armored car, one SP gun, six trucks, one sedan, one AT gun. Captured one locomotive, 16 box cars, eight passenger cars, one 150 MM gun, 600 PWs.[4]

As the 14th AD's history remarks, this is the first reference to the new M-24 light tank, with a 75mm gun. Belton Y. Cooper, the maintenance officer with the 3rd Armored Division and author of *Death Traps*, commented that the new 75mm gun still wasn't up to par. And so the new tank was assigned to scouting and reconnaissance. It was the first American tank equipped with the Christie suspension system, first invented by an American before the war.[5]

The 62nd AIB, also active until the end, was committed on 23 April to a struggle for the town of Stauf. The 47th Tank Battalion, to the right of the infantry, was being seriously hit by enemy fire. Somehow the 62nd managed to gain the element of surprise, and "the Kraut was completely routed with heavy loss of personnel" with C-62nd holding the town after two and a half hours of fighting. Like other units it was then held up by blown bridges over the Altmohl River.

The 62nd's history records that a week later the town of Ingolstadt was secured by the 86th Infantry Division, and the 62nd then crossed the Danube River and secured the city. After a certain number of changed orders, the armored infantrymen, with C Company in the vanguard, established a bridgehead across the Isar River. Keeping up the 14th AD's motto as "The Liberators," the 62nd liberated a camp at Vilsbiburg which was filled with American soldiers captured in the Ardennes battle during December and January. At Ampfing the 62nd freed a large number of Jewish civilians who were in desperate need of medical attention. The medics did what they could to save as many as possible, but nevertheless the deaths continued. It was here, in this grim place, that the war ended for the 62nd.

The writer(s) of the unit history eloquently summarized the meaning of that event for the survivors. After remembering those of their comrades who had not lived to see the end of the conflict, the authors saw the event as a series of doors through which they had passed:

> The first phases of nerve-shattering fear and heart-breaking reality were over, the end of the European war was as though a door had been opened, revealing in another chamber the same horrors that had just been vanquished with great expense in the first room. But, too, it meant half the world's fears were gone, warmly elating to the men who had helped make that dream a fact.

Also quite moving was the dedication of the history to the same men who had not made it through the carnage:

> We shall continue to fight in peace, as we did in war, to make this world a more decent place in which to live.
> To you buddies, we give this pledge. You will not return to your homes or loved ones. We shall remember you. With God's help we shall make this war the last one.[6]

The last serious fighting by the 25th Tank Battalion, some time in April, was a battle for a series of towns: Eichstadt, Rothenstein, Ingolstadt, and Hepberg. When an 88mm gun position escaped the notice of a recon patrol, it fired a round through the tank of Sgt. Stanley C. Kicinski. Miraculously there were no casualties. Lt. William H. Kekar of Headquarters Company was not as lucky as his tank was knocked out and he was wounded. B Company, operating on the left flank, destroyed an enemy tank and collected 200 POWs and killed or wounded 100 soldiers. After this action, the progress was likened by the 25th's history to "a road march," with the taking of many more prisoners. At the little town of Stephanskirchen, news came of the German surrender, but the tankers were not buying any relaxation: "We never relaxed our security."

When Prime Minister Churchill announced "V-E Day," "We took the news quietly, for each of us had foreseen Germany's defeat and its effect was anticlimactic." The final comment was that "Hitler stood for power, and the Siegfried Line was constructed as a symbol of his might. Our overcoming of this line was a major step leading to the downfall of Hitler's Empire and the complete submission of those people who believed themselves infallible." And yet the 25th remained vigilant and wary: "Two down—One to go; with the memory of fallen comrades still vivid, we rededicated ourselves to the task ahead."[7] It is quite remarkable that after all the violence, danger, and fear and hatred, the men of the 25th could still clearly see the need for them to stay ready for any combat tasks assigned to them. There was no mention of the Pacific theater and the possible invasion of Japan, but all the soldiers knew that that was a task they might be called upon to perform.

Their comrades in the 47th Tank Battalion had also seen some hard fighting in the last weeks of April after the liberation of Moosburg camp. Eight men from the battalion who had been listed as MIA after Hatten had been found safe from harm, and the battalion exulted in their safety. (They were: T/5 William Weichelt, Cpl. Eufor Cobbledick, T/5 Edward Kulawiak, Cpl. Gilbert Maines, Pfc. John Nestorek, Tec/5 John Wertz, Pfc. Verle A. Kruger, Cpl. Robert D. Hills, the son of T/5 Floyd G. Mahoney, an Air Force lieutenant.)

As one might expect, "There were plenty of drinks and spirits ran high as old friends got together again for 'old-fashioned [sic] bull sessions'."[8]

Yet the fighting was not yet over and in some ways more dangerous and haphazard because German soldiers were coming out of the woods and towns either to surrender or to fight. "Because you weren't on the point didn't mean [you] wouldn't be attacked or that you wouldn't take prisoners, because attacks were launched all up and down our column and prisoners came out of the woods and towns long after the leading tanks had passed." On May 1st serious action continued:

C Company sent a task force, under Lt. [Maynard LI Boucher [a recipient of a Bronze Star,] Muhldorf whose mission was to keep the enemy on the run and prevent them from digging in. Enroute to their objective the task force overtook a German convoy and destroyed it. Then, in a rapid move in which they captured two air fields with many planes, some of which the enemy had set on fire, a bridge across a large canal was captured, as was the city of Muhldorf.[9]

However, a happy surprise brightened up Bavaria when the men were instructed to prepare their tanks for inspection. The conclusion:

"Something must be up. Maybe something did happen. Something big did happen. On May 8, 1945 the Germans gave up their long and ill-fated struggle. V-E Day was officially announced."

The gentle reactions of the men, after all their violent experiences, reminded them of a life without war, but also without their "buddies" whom they had thought were lost. Each man "wondered about that buddy listed as MIA. Is it possible he might have climbed out of that burning shelled inferno of a tank? Could he have been taken prisoner?" They also wondered about their chances of having enough points in the Point System for discharge. "Questions—memories—and memories are too vivid. . . . In the afternoon we were paid, some months overdue. Night came—hot chow—mail call—letters to read and answer—poker—. The war in Europe was over."[10]

The history of the 48th Tank Battalion, for some reason yet unclear, ends with the battle of Rittershoffen although the combat for that unit continued, as it did for the others, until the end of the war. When the 47th Tank Battalion settled in Muhldorf, the 48th, paired with the 19th Armored Infantry Battalion under CCB, fought for three hours to force their way into the town of Manching. Afterwards the Command found a crossing across the Inn River and, as previously described, captured the airfields, aircraft, and Luftwaffe personnel.

After the seizure of Taufkirchen, the Headquarters of the 84th Medical Detachment was established. When fighting continued in Forscheim,

> Pfc. Marion Cochran, caught in enemy artillery fire, saw a soldier wounded in both legs. Crawling from under his vehicle, Cochran reached the wounded man, dragged him back, treated him and sheltered him with his own body until the shelling was over.[11]

This might seem to be a singular heroic action on the part of Pfc. Cochran, but it was very common for both medics and combat soldiers to shelter a wounded man with their own bodies. On most occasions, this action saved the life of the wounded man, but in some cases, the covering soldier was seriously wounded or killed outright by hostile fire. This was the true fulfillment of the Gospel maxim, "Greater love hath no man but that he lay down his life for another." Conditions were so bad on the roads because of the spring thaw and the pounding by the vehicles that any more intensive fighting would have endangered the wounded or injured again because it would have been impossible to get them to an aid station in time for treatment.

One of the sad ironies of the war was not just casualties caused by friendly fire, especially aircraft, but that some of the newly liberated prisoners were killed by strafing. Suffering casualties by friendly fire was simply an expected loss because of the ordinance being fired in the air or on the ground, but in this case the POW's would have possibly survived the war if they were still under guard in the stalag at Moosburg.

To handle many of the casualties, the 84th Medical Detachment set up operations at two German hospitals: one in Ampfing and one at Ecksburg. An account by B Company offered this gruesome picture at Ecksburg:

> Conditions in the hospital itself were indescribably bad. Sanitation did not exist. Medical attention was poor. There were no medical supplies and little food, and bedding and clothing were as bad as at Dachau. Patients were crowded 12 to a room, suffering dysentery, typhus and other diseases. There were lice, starvation, and unbelievable filth. A few nuns from a neighboring convent were doing what they could do to handle the situation.[12]

After their contretemps at Tautkirchen, the 19th Armored Infantry was instructed to search for an intact bridge over the Inn River, a difficult thing to find at this stage of the campaign. B Company did manage, at the town of Gar, to capture a guard company and free 250 American officers and 50 enlisted men. At that point the battalion's history expressed the sense of the combat infantrymen that the war was nearing its end:

> Thousands of German soldiers were surrendering; thousands of liberated Allied soldiers and ex-prisoners of the Germans also added to the mass of humanity that poured into our area. [It was] The end of the war and everyone sensed it. We knew it had to be very close, for there wasn't very much of Germany left to

fight over, and we, ourselves, were near the foothills of the Alps, as far south as we could go. . . . Official notice was received on the 5th of May that all hostilities on the Western Front could cease at 1200, 6 May, and that no offensives of any kind would be made. Only defensive measures would be made for security.[13]

The date of the notice, 5 May, is the earliest reference to a surrender in the various unit, division, and other histories related to the 14th Armored. Grossadmiral Karl Dönitz, who after Hitler's suicide on April 30 had been authorized to negotiate the surrender of all German forces, was attempting to stall for as much time as possible. He was trying to allow as many German soldiers and civilians to flee westward and not have to be placed under the control of the advancing Russians. His fears would prove to be well grounded. What he wanted on 6 May was to sign off on surrender terms with General Eisenhower, who represented all American, British, and French forces in western Europe, and to stall as long as possible with the Russians. On 6 May he gave written instructions to General Albert Jodi in this regard:

> If you have no more success than [Generaladmiral Hans Georg] Friedeburg had, offer a simultaneous surrender on all fronts, to be implemented in two phases. During the first phase all hostilities will have ceased, but the German troops will be allowed liberty of movement. . . . Try and make the interval before the introduction of Phase Two as long as possible, and if you can, get Eisenhower to agree that individual German soldiers will in any case be allowed to surrender to the Americans. The greater your success in these directions, the greater will be the number of German soldiers and refugees who will find salvation in the west.[14]

The circumstances surrounding the message to the 19th Armored Infantry Battalion on 5 May are not clear. They do, however, suggest an appropriate caution about not wasting lives in a continued attempt to annihilate the Wehrmacht. The 19th's history notes that on 7 May, at 1855, a letter from the Commander of the 14th Armored officially announced that at 0001, 9 May 1945 (the same date mentioned in the 68th's history) "the war in the European Theater would be officially over." The men brought out the bottles they were saving to celebrate. "The lights went on, not 'All Over the World,' but everywhere it was possible to get them in the European Theater."

However, like all soldiers, sailors, and airmen in the ETO, the troops knew that that the other war, in the Pacific, was not yet over.

Every branch and unit of the Division worked frantically to keep the fighting men going, to keep pressure on the remaining German holdouts so that they could not dig in and effectively fight back against the armored pressure. The 154th Signal Company had to string miles of its own wire and much more of German wire to keep all commands connected. The 125th Engineers worked feverishly to keep roads, bridges, and culverts open and to mark and disarm enemy minefields. After the surrender, German civilians and prisoners volunteered to assist in this last operation. The farmers were anxious to plant their crops and get back to normal life. However, at Altmuhl the enemy was having none of this and pounded a bridge site on which the engineers were working and damaged much equipment.

When examining a possible site for a pontoon bridge, several men were wounded by hostile fire, and M/Sgt. Willard F. Sherman of Headquarters Company was killed. He would be granted a Silver Star for bravery. A group of volunteers from the OP returned to the site with a .30 caliber and a .50 caliber machine gun and laid down suppressing fire. Lt. Richard W. Eddington was safely retrieved as was Lt. Martin S. Cullen, a recipient of a Bronze Star, who told the rescuers to get Eddington out first as he was the more seriously wounded.[15] Eddington earned a Bronze Star.

On 2 May, Division Artillery fired its last round after the 499th, the 500th, and the 501st AFA's accomplished their fire missions. Effectively, as the 14th AD's history put it, "The war was over." However, there was no extreme rejoicing. Too much had happened: too many friends lost both in the sense that they had lost their lives but also in the sense that they were missing. All of their comrades hoped and prayed that they would be found—alive and in one piece. In the exact words for the occasion:

The celebration at the end of the war was, generally, quiet. There were rumors, the endless rumors that had preceded it; and the 14th had still been fighting when divisions in other

Army Groups had been accepting wholesale surrenders. And there was—then—the threat of the other, still active, theatre.[16]

And yet there were monumental logistics problems all over Europe, including the area assigned to the 14th. The G-5 Section headed by Col. Grant T. Apthorp was responsible for running the Military Government of the now Occupation Forces. Displaced Persons were moving through the 14th's area of responsibillty, Prisoners of War had to be processed, and rules governing the interchange between American personnel and native Germans had to be worked out. There was a notable attempt to prevent fraternization, especially between American soldiers and German women, but the frauleins held such attractions that the policy was riddled with violations.

General Jacob L. Devers, who was not given the credit he deserved for leading Sixth Army Group and Seventh Army by General Eisenhower and the officers of SHAEF, was keenly aware of the awesome responsibilities he assumed after the surrender. He accepted the unconditional surrender of General Foertach, representing Field Marshall Albert Kesselnng and responsible for the surrender of Army Group G commanded by General Schulz. General Devers was struck by the terrible responsibility he had for the defeated country of Germany. In his *Diary*, apparently for 5 May (no hours cited in the margin), he expresses his dismay:

> I am in a let down mood because after seeing Dachau, Munich, and the hundreds of thousands of prisoners we have captured, our own Allied prisoners released, and the thousands of displaced persons in this part of Germany, I am convinced that with the destruction caused by the Air Force, Europe has been set back a hundred years. How we are going to feed these people is one of the major problems for there is not enough food in sight at this moment. In this army group I have taken definite action to get as many [German] soldiers as possible back to the farms to work the land and have strongly recommended that the miners and useful citizens get back to their occupations in order that food may be provided for this part of the world.[17]

Devers' attitude and policy led to the early order to cease offensive operations issued on the same date as this diary entry to close the book on the killing, at least in the area for which he was responsible.

Captain Archibald R. Schaffer, in charge of the occupation in the town of Mettenheim, was the subject of a chapter of a book about ancient Mettenheim, which is nearly 1300 years old. On 2 May 1945, with snow still on the ground, the inhabitants were anxious that there would be a fight for the airport, which "could mean total destruction of our home town for certain." Because there were still SS troops in the town, the people feared the worst. Fortunately they were suddenly withdrawn, and the town passed under American occupation without incident. The town's History indicates the joy of the citizens: "It was the 14th Armored Division APO 446 of the US Army which brought the end of the war for Mettenheim and freedom for prisoners and forced labor-camp workers."[18]

The History of Mettenheim goes on to express thanks to Capt. Archibald R. Schaffer, working in G-5, who saw to it that things returned to normal in the town as soon as possible. Houses were turned back to their owners by soldiers as soon as possible. Guards were established to prevent the "plundering and looting" which had plagued outlying farms. Most gratifying to this farming community was the transfer from the Luftwaffe to the farmers of the land which belonged to them. Plowing and planting began immediately. Schaffer also helped the local pastor provide services on Sunday after most of the pastor's stock of sacramental wines were stolen. The people of Mettenheim remain eternally grateful to the efforts of Capt Schaffer.[19]

At the end of the 14th Armored's history is a list of impressive statistics regarding the expenditure of ordnance and the achievements of the Division which could be expressed in numbers. Among them are a selected few:

150,000 prisoners processed . . .
Liberated 200,000 Allied prisoners . . .
Freed 250,000 displaced persons . . .
From Nice to Jettenbach, from Barr to Muhldorf, 581 14th Armored then lay buried. Hundreds were in hospitals.[20]

The prisoners of various kinds as well as the Displaced Persons, or "DP's," as they were called, would all be processed, and indeed the wounded would all be shipped eventually to the United States, some to be healed and able to leave the Army and Veteran's Hospitals, some never to make it back to the normal life they had left behind when they shipped out from New York City in October of 1944.

Sadly, those who were buried overseas either still lie there in military cemeteries or have been sent home and buried by their families. More than one of their commanders has felt the heavy responsibility of insuring that those lying in foreign soil have been paid proper respect. One of these CO's was Capt. Daniel R. Iannella, of A Company, the 62nd Armored Infantry Battalion. He worked very hard over the years to make sure that the Lorraine American Cemetery at St. Avold, France, properly maintained the graves of the 10,489 Americans interred there. His constant stream of letters both to politicians and to military leaders helped make the cemetery what it is today. As his daughter Peggy, who visited the cemetery around the turn of the century, said, "It's one of the most moving, most beautiful places I've ever seen." There is a towering memorial there 67 feet high and made of limestone, "with the Walls of the Missing extending to the north and south thereof." There is also on the wall both maps of the fighting and flags of all the units that participated in the fighting in the region. Several inscriptions stand out on different walls, but the one on the Walls of the Missing is quite simple yet touching:

HERE ARE RECORDED THE NAMES OF AMERICANS WHO GAVE THEIR LIVES IN THE SERVICE OF THEIR COUNTRY AND WHO SLEEP IN UNKNOWN GRAVES.[21]

Capt. Iannella's story deserves to be told as well. He was badly wounded at the ferocious battle of Hatten-Rittershofferi and also suffered frostbite to his hands and feet. He was captured but then escaped, only to suffer more wounds in the process. Retired as a Major in 1946, Iannella had earned a Silver Star, several Bronze Stars, four Purple Hearts, and the Combat Infantrymen's Badge, as his obituary noted. He joined the Veteran's Administration after the war and worked as a rehabilitation specialist with veterans returning from three wars. His ashes are interred in Arlington National Cemetery.[22]

At another cemetery in France, more members of the 14th AD are buried. The same white marble crosses seen at other cemeteries in

Western Europe also mark the graves of other deceased soldiers of the 14th. Buried at Epinal are eleven members of the 136th Ordinance Battalion, who were killed suddenly and violently by one shell, a 380mm round from a huge cannon, while they were billeted in a factory. Because of the long range of this kind of artillery, there was no warning—just a sudden explosion and 24 soldiers killed or wounded. Ordinance troops aren't usually seen as subject to this kind of shattering violence, but now eleven of them are buried in a cemetery which is maintained with the same care as other cemeteries for American and other soldiers killed during World War II.[23]

Readers may remember Lt. Harry Kemp, who was seriously wounded in the leg at Steinfeld and whose twin brother Larry was killed by a sniper while on a reconnaissance mission outside of the town of Rittershoffen back in January 1945. Pfc. Larry Kemp is buried in a grave at Epinal, Row 29, Grave 29. After the war, Harry stayed on in Europe working for the United States Army but was also clearly marked by the death of his twin. He needed a lot of surgery to repair two bones shattered in his leg by a single bullet and spent a great deal of time at Oliver General Hospital in Augusta, Georgia. Once he was released, like many veterans he took advantage of the GI Bill to earn a bachelors degree. He was also fortunate, again like so many of his comrades, to find a lovely woman, Mary Alice Bailey, whom he would marry while he was still on crutches and recuperating.[24]

But this narrative is tumbling over itself in the effort to trace the transformation of some of the veterans of the fighting battalions of the 14th Armored Division at the end of the war. The United States Army's personnel machinery had to grind on: distributing soldiers on the ground in the Ampfing area of Bavaria as occupation troops, determining whether men with particular skills were going to be transferred to other units to continue the fight against Japan, and calculating the number of points a soldier had toward discharge. Men were given credit for the time they spent in the European Theater of Operations, for promotions to higher ranks, whether commissioned or non commissioned, and for wounds suffered in the line of duty. Of course, those who required extensive therapy and rehabilitation were removed from these calculations.

The 14th Armored Division would be inactivated in September 1945, but in the meantime all ranks had to await the outcome of events that were out of their control, and on 3 July Col. Bob E. Edwards, the Commander of the 68th AIB, wrote a letter to his men expressing his admiration for them when the Battalion was in the process of being broken up and the men scattered to other units:

> Never was there a better time to say, "Here today and gone tomorrow." I don't know what my next job will be, or how much longer I'll be here—neither do you. (Over 500 of you are leaving today or tomorrow). But I do know that the outfit you go to will get some damned good fighting men and be proud to have you. I consider it the greatest honor of my life to have commanded this battalion for the past year and five months, and through six months of the most vicious fighting in Europe.[25]

Lt. Col. Edwards continues his testament to his comrades in combat, reminding them how well they had fought in the major battles and other actions to defeat the German Army. He expresses full confidence that if the division were ever called on to fight in the Pacific Theater, they would "finish taking care of the Japs like we did the Krauts."

Little did Lt. Col. Edwards or any other officers in the European Theater know what would have been involved if they and their men had to fight against the Japanese. After a message from the Japanese government indicating that it was prepared to discuss a surrender was received in Washington on August 10, Secretary of War Henry L. Stimson, General G. C. Marshall, the Chairman of the Joint Chiefs, and the President, Harry R. Truman, reacted with a little surprise at the speed of the Japanese response. The first concern in discussions was the fate of 168,500 Allied prisoners of war in Japanese hands, including 15,000 Americans. Truman expressed "deep concern" for these prisoners. Also discussed was the estimated number of casualties if an invasion of the home islands had been carried out. Known already were the number of casualties at Iwo Jima and Okinawa, and it was calculated that the assault against the main islands of Japan, as well as defeating Japanese armies in China and the Dutch East Indies (what is now Indonesia), would cost twenty times the cost of either of the two islands.

Especially worrisome was the Japanese employment of "Kamikaze" or suicide planes against American ships standing offshore during any one of several invasions. Thus, it was figured, "A score of Iwo Jimas translated to 634,160 casualties, including 171,720 killed or missing, while twenty Okinawas equals 982,660 casualties, including 250,400 dead or missing."[26] These figures were calculated without the knowledge of the Japanese Defense Plan called Ketsu-Go, which demanded of the Japanese people, including women and children, that they fight until the bitter end. There also was still a million-man army in China which was fully manned and equipped.

Hundreds of thousands of American soldiers, sailors, marines, and members of the Air Force would surely have died or been terribly wounded. And it is clear that, despite revisionist histories about the dropping of the atomic bombs, the Japanese Privy Council and the chiefs of the Army and the Navy were still intent on continuing the war whatever the consequences—even after Hiroshima and Nagasaki were destroyed. When the news of the Japanese surrender reached across the world on 2 September, there was a huge sigh of relief in all the military units in Europe that just perhaps they would all get home safely. For example, 2nd Lt. Robert R. McLarren of the 25th Tank Battalion was being transferred to the 20th Armored Division for the purpose of getting that division prepared to fight six thousand miles away. He wasn't the only one.

None of the American fighting men scheduled to be shipped to the Pacific Theater of Operations knew what might be in store for them. But they obeyed orders and boarded ship.

14TH ARMORED DIVISION DATA

Commanders:
Maj. Gen. Vernon E. Prichard (November 1942–July 1944)
Maj. Gen. Albert C. Smith (July 1944 to inactivation)

COMPOSITION

Headquarters Company
Combat Command A
Combat Command B
Reserve Command

25th Tank Battalion
47th Tank Battalion
48th Tank Battalion

19th Armored Infantry Battalion
62d Armored Infantry Battalion
68th Armored Infantry Battalion

94th Cavalry Reconnaissance Squadron (Mechanized)
125th Armored Engineer Battalion
154th Armored Signal Company

499th Armored Field Artillery Battalion
500th Armored Field Artillery Battalion
501st Armored Field Artillery Battalion

Divisional Trains:
136th Ordnance Maintenance Battalion
84th Armored Medical Battalion
Military Police Platoon
Band

ATTACHMENTS

Antiaircraft Artillery
398th AAA AW Bn (SP)   15 Nov 44-12 May 45
Cavalry
117th Cav Rcn Sq   2 Jan 45-10 Jan 45
Engineer
300th E ngr C Bn   28 Apr 45-2 May 45
Field Artillery
93d Armd FA Bn   3 Jan 45-9 Jan 45
69th Armd FA Bn   2 Apr 45-19 Apr 45
975th FA Bn (155mm How)   2 Apr 45-24 Apr 45
250th FA Bn (105mm How)   21 Apr 45-24 Apr 45
173d FA Gp   21 Apr 45-24 Apr 45
220th FA Gp   25 Apr 45-9 May 45
Infantry
315th Inf (- 1st Bn) (79th Div)   13 Jan 45-21 Jan 45
1st Bn, 315th Inf (79th Div)   17 Jan 45-21 Jan 45
Tank Destroyer
636th TD Bn (SP)   28 Mar 45-23 Apr 45

ASSIGNMENT AND ATTACHMENT TO HIGHER UNITS

1 November 1944:   Attached to 6th Army Group.
10 November 1944:   Seventh Army, 6th Army Group.
29 November 1944:   XV Corps.
5 December 1944:   VI Corps.
31 March 1945:   XV Corps.
23 April 1945:   III Corps, Third Army, 12th Army Group.

STATISTICS

Chronology:
Activated 15 November 1942
Arrived ETO 29 October 1944
Arrived Continent (D+75) 29 October 1944
Entered Combat:
  First Elements 14 November 1944
  Entire Division 20 November 1944
Days in Combat: 133

Battle Casualties	2,896
Non-Battle Casualties	1,400
Total Casualties	4,296
Percent of T/O Strength	.40.3

Campaigns: Rhineland, Central Europe

Individual Awards	
Distinguished Service Cross	5
Legion of Merit	5
Silver Star	167
Soldiers Medal	12
Bronze Star	2,093
Air Medal	46
Distinguished Flying Cross	1

Prisoners of War Taken	64,205

Source: US Army Center for Military History

ACKNOWLEDGMENTS AND SOURCES

This writer is in the debt of many people who encouraged me, a retired English Professor, to shake off the cobwebs of retirement and put myself in front of a word processor, a strange machine to me, for the last several years. I could not have gotten to the end of this road without their support and help. I ask the forgiveness of those who might not be mentioned below because of my absent-mindedness.

In sequence I thank Bob Davies, who piqued my curiosity about a fighting unit among fighting units, an armored infantry battalion among other armored battalions, if I may be forgiven the repetition, in an armored division in the greatest and worst war which this country and the world has ever seen.

The next person or persons in sequence were Howard and Averill Knapp. Howard's war career ended at age nineteen when, as a private in a lead tank, he was blown and burned out of a Sherman in November 1944. However, after a long and difficult recovery, Howard found and married Averill, both of whom had rewarding careers as teachers in the New York City school system. Their scholarly bent provided me not only with the names of 14th Armored veterans who could be of help to me but also with books, articles, and documents which they had collected over the years, some in English and some in French.

I will try to recognize, without omissions, all the other 14th veterans who narrated their experiences and provided me with a proper knowledge of the military conventions which were necessary to do this work. Terminology, titles, technical knowledge of weapons, tactics, and so on were passed on to me to supplement my own reading. I freely acknowledge here that I am not a professional military historian but I have done my best, and I hope that is satisfactory.

A new friend for me, Bob R. McClarren, a retired military officer with advanced degrees in both English and Library Science and who writes about the American Civil War, has been like a Vergil to me. He has led me through the labyrinth of military weapons, vehicles, unit functions, proper terminology and the like doggedly and patiently. His focus on the truth of what happened never wavers. He has read most if not all of the chapters following and has provided me with extraordinary assistance in getting things right. What is not right in what follows is my responsibility alone. His knowledge has provided the most accurate account of this odyssey of the 14th Armored Division from the USA to the European Theater of Operations. As a member of the 25th Tank Battalion, he provided me with a copy of that unit's history. He has been both critical in the best sense and supportive at the same time. One of my fears has been that the veterans would hear what I was saying or read what I was writing and categorically reject it as inaccurate and inappropriate. They haven't.

Thanks need also be proffered to the 14th Armored Division Association (website: www.14tharmoreddivision.org) for written works essential to this effort, which I read with great interest. The outstanding history of Captain Joseph Carter, Forward Echelon, Headquarters Company of the 14th is almost encyclopedic in its coverage of the division's fighting. Its roster of the members of the division, their correct names and ranks, and of the wounds and death suffered by young men in their prime as well as the medals awarded has been of incalculable value to me and to many others

The Association also deserves thanks for sponsoring the much later volume entitled *Memories of the 14th Armored Division* which provided this writer with some graphic and memorable stories. Grateful I am as well for its newsletter *The Liberator*, which is another trove of stories by and about the men of the Division. Verlyn Hofer, its editor, deserves special credit for the high quality of that publication.

Books that have been especially helpful include the highly productive Charles Whiting's *The Siegfried Line* and *The Other Battle of the Bulge*. This last volume focuses on the difficult combat in the Vosges Mountains during Operation Northwind around New Years Day, 1945. Richard Engler's impressive *The Final Crisis* provided excellent material on the fighting in Alsace during January and February, 1947. Keith E. Bonn's account of the same winter fighting, *When the Odds Were Even*, although not especially complimentary to Task Force Hudelson, offered another aspect of the war in the Vosges. The Official History of the campaign, *Riviera to the Rhine*, was invaluable in providing evidence from German archives released decades after the war. Col. Hans Von Luck's *Panzer Commander* also vividly presented the German soldier's view of the war against what they called the "Amis."

Other books and articles, including Kenneth Hazleton's account of the fighting from a medic's point of view, assembled or written by combat veterans of the fighting, helped this writer as well. Even as late as 2008, Vernon H. Brown's *Mount Up! We're Moving Out,* was vital to understanding the hazardous life of a trooper in the 94th Cav Recon (Mech'zd) in late 1944 and early 1945.

Two relatively recent books which happily bring attention to the fighting in southern France after Anvil/Dragoon and in the Vosges Mountains and Alsace are *First to the Rhine: The 6th Army Group in World War II* by Harry Yeide and Mark Stout, and *Decision at Strasbourg: Ike's Strategic Mistake to Halt the Sixth Army Group at the Rhine in 1944* by David P Colley. Both of these works, the former quite thorough and the latter quite controversial, focus the kind of attention appropriate to the contribution made by American (and French) combat forces between August 1944 and the end of the war in May 1945.

On a highly specific matter pertaining to the 68th Armored Infantry Battalion, in my effort to sort out the details of the tragic patrol in February 19, 1945 which seriously wounded not only Bob Davies but others as well (in Chapter Seven), I am indebted especially to former Lieutenant Stanley Miller, who officially led it. He also stepped on a Schu mine almost at the same time as did Bob Davies. He has written me several letters about his experience and sent me the very map he took with him on the patrol. Philip H. Snoberger, a close friend of Bob Davies, who was a member of the 68th AIB's Headquarters Detachment, was especially critical on the details of the deadly patrol.

Other 14th Armored veterans who have been particularly helpful include the late T/Sgt. Dudley R. Partrick, formerly with the 500th Armored Artillery Battalion. He has been an informative conversationalist and sent me his copy of a book describing the weaknesses of the M-4 Sherman tank. Former Lt. Harry Kemp, of the 68th, offered insights into the action at Kapsweyer and Steinfeld and the breaking of the Siegfried Line in which he participated. He also allowed me to read his brief work on that subject and read and checked my chapter on it for accuracy. Like Mr. Partrick and Mr. Kemp (really Dudley and Harry), Bob Straba, veteran of the 19th AIB, provided me with a copy of his unit history and enlightened and entertained me with anecdotes of battle. His penetrating and challenging view of all things military was both useful and amusing. I believe it was Roy Roberts who made available the history of the 47th TB. Let me also not forget Fred Harshberger, a Sergeant in the 62nd AIB, a crewmember of an assault gun who supplied me with a copy of his unit history. So, too with Fred Shattuck, of the 500th Armored Field Artillery Battalion, who loaned me several books which were quite informative. I would also like to thank Joe (Raymond D.) and Mary Ann Cotten for their unwavering and cheerful support for my efforts over the last several years as well as Morris Berman. I am sure I am omitting a few veterans who also contributed to my efforts here, and I beg their indulgence for any lapses on my part.

My friend Glibert Gagne's essential translation of documents in French was a sine qua non for the tragedy in Barr in November 1944. Two absolute treasure troves of military history were National Archives II in College Park, MD and The Center For Military History in Carlisle, PA (website: www.history.army.mil). Their staffs were more than helpful to an amateur like myself. The original historically important documents they found for me proved invaluable.

I wish to also thank the folks at Casemate Publishing for their conscientious and professional assistance in the production of this book. I am thinking especially of Steven Smith, who steered me through some unexpected difficulties, Tara Lichterman, who assisted in solving practical problemsn, and Libby Braden, who "made" the book for me.

Finally I must thank my wife Marilyn, who carefully proofread my text and wisely suggested corrections. The book could also never have been written without the support and approval of her sister Jo (Olive) Davies. Her special knowledge of her husband's life after the war created a perspective for me that was of great help in understanding the sacrifices that families made both during and after the war.

Once again, I have to take responsibility for any errors or misunderstandings in the text. Writing about combat is writing about subjective chaos. Each soldier sees what he saw or thought he saw a little differently than someone else a foxhole away. No civilian can ever see things from that unique perspective.

NOTES

Chapter One: First Days of Battle in the Maritime Alps

[1] Lt. Graham E. Madden and Pvt. Ralph Kovanda, *Unit History: 68th Armored Infantry Battalion: From Embarkation to V-E Day* (Altolling: Gebr. Geiselberger, n. d.), p. 31.

[2] "Baker 499th from Marseille to Erding: The View of an Artillery Man," *The Liberator* 39.3 (Spring 2005), 15.

[3] *68 History*, p. 4.

[4] *68 History*, p. 4.

[5] *68 History*, p. 5.

[6] Lt. Walter R. Dickson and Sgt. James W. Hanifin, *Combat History of 19th Armored Infantry Battalion, October 12, 1944 To May 9th, 1945* (Munich: J. G. Weiss, 1945), p. 5.

[7] *68 History*, p. 5.

[8] Telephone call from Russ Taylor, April 10, 2004.

[9] Captain Joseph Carter, *The History of the 14th Armored Division* (n. p. Whipporwill Publication, n. d., 1946?), n. p.

[10] *68 History*, p. 5.

[11] Conversation with Bob Davies, sometime in May 2005. See Robert Asahina's book, *Just Americans: How Japanese Americans Won a War at Home and Abroad* (New York: Gotham Books, 2006). The two wars of the title were the combat in Europe, especially in Italy, and the war at home in order for the Nisei (Japanese-Americans) to be accepted as loyal citizens (hence the title).

[12] *68 History*, p. 5. See also Samuel Eliot Morison's discussion of the First Airborne Force in volume two of his standard-setting work, *History of Naval Operations in World War II* (Edison, N.J.: Castle Books, 2001) in fifteen volumes: *The Invasion of France and Germany, 1944–1945*, for the airborne component of the Anvil/Dragoon operation.

[13] Carter, n. p. See also 19th *History*, p. 5.

[14] *19th AIB History*, p. 5.

[15] *68 History*, p. 6, and conversation with Bob Davies, August 20, 2005.

303

16 "68th A.I.B. Medical Detachment HISTORY, From 12 October 1944 Embarkation To 8 May 1945 V-E Day," unpublished typescript, n. d., p. 2. The other designation for this unit is the 84th Medical Battalion. I am indebted to Ken Hazleton for sending me this pamphlet.

17 Carter. n. p.; *68 History*, pp. 6–7. The embarrassing episode for Capt. Reed was revealed by the ever mischievous Bob Davies in a conversation on December 11, 2005.

18 Carter, n. p.

19 Carter, n. p.

20 *68 History*, p. 7. "Alsatian" presumably refers to that dialect of German, but that is assuming that GIs would recognize French. The Reich had outlawed the speaking of French after taking over Alsace in 1940.

Chapter Two: The Tragedy at Barr

1 Keith E. Bonn, Commentary in Georg Grossjohann, *Five Years, Four Fronts: A German Officer's World War II Combat Memoirs*, trans. Ulbrecke Aberle (New York: Ballantine Books, 2005), p. 179.

2 Jeffrey J. Clarke and Robert Ross Smith, *Riviera to the Rhine: The European Theater of Operations, United States Army in World War II* (Washington, D.C.: Center of Military History, 1994), p. 368.

3 *Riviera*, pp. 454-455.

4 T/Sgt. Dean B. Robinson and T/Sgt. Vernon G. Brown, "We Came to Fight," (Munich: Oldenbourg, 1945), n.p.; Captain Joseph Carter, *The History of the Fourteenth Armored Division* (n.p. Whipporwill Publications, 1946?), n.p. It is a pity that many of these unit histories have no pagination.

5 Carter, n.p.

6 Christine Huffschmidt, *La Liberation de Barr lors de Ia IIe Guerre Mondiale*, (n.p.: n.p., 1988/89.), pp. 9–10 of translation by Gilbert Gagne (2006). The original is a pamphlet published by the author. Several citizens of Barr were interviewed, and unattributed copies of maps of the town and battle are included in the loose leafed pamphlet. No indication is given of where it was published. It depends heavily on Dr. Marcel Krieg's account and on Captain Carter's history. I am indebted to my friend, Gilbert Gagne, for the translation.

7 La Liberation de Barr, p. 12.

8 "We Came to Fight," n.p.

9 Carter, n.p.

10 "14th Armored Division Monthly Report," NARA II 16349, 614-TK (48)oz.

11 "Recollections of WW II," *The Liberator* 37.3 (Spring 2003), 14.

12 Carter, n.p.

13 "A Memorial Day Tribute to My Father-in-Law," *The Liberator* 34.1 (Summer 1999), 9. Originally an article in the *Lake George (NY) Mirror* (May 29, 1998).

14 Carter, n.p.

15 *Chariots of Iron: 50 Years of American Armor* (Louisville: Harmony House, n.d), p. 32. Philip Trewhitt, *Armored Fighting Vehicles* (London: Friedman

Fairfax, 1999), p. 31.

[16] Carter, n.p.

[17] Carter, n.p.

[18] *La Liberation*, pp. 9–10.

[19] *La Liberation*, p. 12.

[20] "We Came to Fight," np.

[21] Interview with Howard Knapp on 20 January, 2005, at the Jacksonville Beach Southeast Reunion of the 14th Armored Division. I owe a great debt of gratitude to Howard and his wife Averil for generously loaning me many books and other materials essential to the writing of this chapter.

[22] "A Lifelong Friendship," *Memories of the 14th Armored Division* (Paducah, Ky. Turner Publishing Co., 1999), p. 39.

[23] *Memories*, p. 47.

[24] "The Hospital of Barr at the Center of Combat . . ." trans. Gilbert Gagne, 2006, originally in French in *Societe D' Histoire et D'Archaelogie: De Dambach—La-Ville. Barr. Obernai* (n.d. n.p) n.p. Dr Krieg published his account a few years after the war, and Mr. Gagne recently translated it for me.

[25] Krieg, p. 6 (of translation as are later notes).

[26] Krieg, p. 7.

[27] Krieg, p. 8.

[28] Krieg, p. 11.

[29] Krieg, p. 12.

[30] Krieg, p. 13.

[31] Quoted in Huffschmidt, p. 27.

[32] Krieg, another edition of "The Hospital . . ." paying homage to Dr. Krieg in *Annuaire de la Societe D'Histoire . . .* 36 (2002), 164.

[33] Quoted in Huffschmidt, p. 20.

[34] Krieg, p. 17.

[35] Krieg, p. 18.

[36] Quoted in Huffschmidt, p. 20.

[37] "Monthly Report," n.p., NARA II. 614-TK (48)-0.2. Box 16349

[38] *Riviera*, p. 456.

[39] "Recollections," p. 14; "The End of the War," *Memories*, p. 47.

Chapter Three: Offen-Ottenbach: The Onslaught

[1] The spelling of the town's name with the hyphen is taken from military sources contemporary with the end of the war. The spelling in a modem atlas is "Oberotterbach," one word. The name means "upper otter [the animal] brook."

[2] Captain Joseph Carter, *The History of the 14th Armored Division* (n. p.: Whipporwill Publication, n. d. 1946?), n. p.

[3] Jeffrey J. Clarke and Robert Ross Smith, *Riviera to the Rhine: The European Theater of Operations in United States Army in World War ll* (Washington, D.C.: Center of Military History, 1995), p. 481.

[4] "14th Armored Division Diary," (2 Oct. 42–31 Jan 45), NARA II. 614-0.30.

There is no indication of the provenance of this document, but the typing is exactly the same as other documents in the files. It is a pity that this "Diary" wasn't maintained throughout the Division's deployment in Europe.

[5] *14th History*, n. p.

[6] *14th History*, n. p.

[7] "Diary," (December 15), n. p.

[8] *Unit History: 68th Armored Infantry Battalion: From Port of Embarkation To D-Day* (Altolling: Gebr. Geiselberger, 1945?), p. 7.

[9] *14th Armored History*, n. p. The term "Greater Germany" includes those areas annexed by force by Nazi Germany including the Rhineland, before the war began in France in May 1940.

[10] "Diary," (December 15), n. p.

[11] *14th History*, n. p.

[12] Charles Whiting, *The Siegfried Line* (Washington, D.C.: Office of the Chief of Military History, 1963), p. xix.

[13] *Company Commander* (Short Hills, N.J.: Burford Books, 1947), p. 10.

[14] Quoted in Whiting, p. 42.

[15] *14th History*, n. p.

[16] *14th History*, n. p.

[17] *14th History*, n. p.

[18] *14th History*, n. p.

[19] "Diary," (December 16), n. p.

[20] *68th History*, p. 8. See also *14th History*, n. p.

[21] *14th History*, n. p.

[22] Carlyle P. Brown, "My Memories of WW II," *Memories of the 14th Armored Division* (Paducah, Ky.: Turner Publishing Co. 1999), p. 24.

[23] "Medical Detachment [of the 68th AIB] History: From leaving States to VE Day," Unpublished report, p. 2. Hazleton gives credit to many other medics and ambulance drivers, too numerous to mention in this text.

[24] *14th History*, n. p.

[25] *68th History*, p. 8; Ken Hazleton, p. 4.

[26] *Siegfried Line*, p. 229.

[27] *68th History*, p. 9.

[28] *68th History*, p. 9.

[29] Clifford Hansford, "Chaplain's Comments," *The Liberator* 31.1 (Summer 1996), 4.

[30] Hansford, p. 4.

[31] *68th History*, p. 10.

[32] "Medical Detachment," p. 4.

[33] *14th History*, n. p.

[34] *68th History*, p. 10.

Chapter Four: Task Force Hudelson and Operation Northwind

[1] *D Day to VE Day, 1944–45: General Eisenhower's Report on the Invasion of*

Europe (London: The Stationer's Office, 2000), pp. 248, 252, 260 ff. As with any correspondence, personal reports, or diaries by generals after a war, a reader has to be aware of the human tendency toward self-justification.

[2] Wolf T. Zoepf, *Seven Days in January: With the SS-Mountain Division in Operation NORWIND,* Forward by Gen. Theodore C. Mataxis US Army (Retired) (Bedford, Pa.: The Aberjona Press, 2001), p. 69.

[3] Roger Cirillo, "Ardennes-Alsace: The U.S. Army Campaigns of World War II." http: //www. history.army. mil/brochures/Ardennes/aral.htm. pp. 23–24.

[4] *Diaries* in US Army Collection, Carlisle, Pa. Archives Collection 01 Restricted Circulation, Box One, OCLC 47184665. The comment in note one applies here as well.

[5] John Nelson Ricard, *Patton at Bay: the Lorraine Campaign, 1944* (Washington, D.C. Brassey's Inc., 2004), pp. 213-214.

[6] Douglas Porch, *The Path to Victory: The Mediterranean Theater in World War II* (New York: Farrar, Straus and Giroux, 2004), 609–610. See also Charles Whiting, *The Other Battle of the Bulge: Operation Northwind* (Havertown, Pa.: Casemate Press, 2002), pp. 16–17, and John D. Eisenhower's *The Bitter Woods* (New York: Ace Publishing Co., 1969), p. 493. Rick Atkinson's recent book *The Day of Battle* notes DeGaulle's comment that French troops would go no farther in the war in Italy than Genoa. Thus they were available for Anvil/Dragoon.

[7] Eisenhower, pp. 251–252.

[8] Devers' *Diary,* 19 December 1944.

[9] Gen. Eisenhower, pp. 250–251, and John Tolland, Battle: *The Story of the Bulge* (New York: Random House, 1959), p. 31. See also Cirillo, pp. 37–38.

[10] Porch, p. 608. For example, see *Bitter Woods,* Danny S. Parker's *Battle of the Bulge: Hitler's Ardennes Offensive, 1944–1945* (New York: De Capo Press, 1991), and Charles MacDonald, *A Time for Trumpets: The Untold Story of the Battle of the Bulge* (New York: William Morrow & Co., 1985). However, more recent work supports Porch: David P. Colley's *Decision at Strasbourg: Ike's Strategic Mistake to Halt the Sixth Army Group at the Rhine in 1944* (Annapolis, Md.: Naval Institute Press, 2008) and Harry Yeide and Mark Stout's *First to the Rhine: The 6th Army Group in World War II* (St. Paul, Mn.: Zenith Press, 2007).

[11] *The Bitter Woods,* p. 493.

[12] Qtd. In *The Other Battle of the Bulge,* p. 11.

[13] *Bitter Woods,* pp. 494–495.

[14] Zoepf, p. 62.

[15] Zoepf, p. 65.

[16] *Bitter Woods,* pp. 495–496.

[17] Devers, *Diaries,* 19, 20, 21 December 1944.

[18] Devers, *Diaries,* 25 December 1944.

[19] Seventh Army Intelligence Report, Reproduced by Hq 14 AD G-3m I and E, later published as "Now It Can Be Told!" and "prepared at /Seventh Army head-quarters at the request of the "ARMY AND NAVY JOURNAL," p. 1. Much of the following account of Task Force Hudelson and other components of the 14th

AD and VI Corps is based on this report and another Seventh Army Report cited in the next note. I am indebted to Staff Sgt. Donald L. Haynie, Company A, the 68th AIB, for my copy of this valuable document. Thanks must also be rendered for an originally printed copy of this report from Pfc. Frederic A. Shattuck, 500th Armored Artillery Headquarters Battery, received later.

[20] "Now. . . ," p. 6; and Lt. Col. William B. Goddard, 7th Army Historian, "Hudelson Task Force, 21 December–2 January," Headquarters Seventh Army Historical Section (4 June 1945), p. 2, hereafter cited as Goddard.

[21] "Now," p. 8.

[22] *Diaries*, 27 December 1944.

[23] Goddard, p. 2.

[24] *Diaries*, 28 December 1944.

[25] *Other Battle*, p. 19.

[26] Hitler speech, quoted in Col. Joe E. Lambert, "Armored Rescue," *Armored Infantry Journal* (Jan./Feb., 1949), 37–38. Colonel Lambert was G-3 for the Fourteenth, and he was concerned that General Eisenhower's comments on the war in Europe gave little or no credit to the men of his division and of Seventh Army. His article, based on considerable primary materials, was an attempt to redress that grievance.

[27] Jeffrey J. Clarke and Robert Ross Smith, *Riviera to the Rhine. US Army in World War II* (Washington, D.C.: Government Printing Office, 1993), pp. 502–504. Charles Whiting argues that another aim of Operation Northwind was to emasculate and neutralize the DeGaulle Free French Government-in-exile (p. 120). Apropos of Lambert's concern with the neglect of the 14th AD and Seventh Army, the official history cited above was published a half century after the war in Europe and decades after all the others.

[28] "Now. . . ," p. 4.

[29] Devers' *Diary*, 30 December 1944.

[30] "Diary—Armd Div," (28 December, 1945), NARA II, Box 614-0.30.

[31] "Now. . . ," p. 4.

[32] Goddard, p. 2. Keith E. Bonn, *When the Odds Were Even: The Vosges Mountain Campaign, October 1944–January 1945* (New York: Ballantine Books, 2006), p. 191, argues that the Task Force was "Arrayed more as a screening force than as one for defense" and that its organization was a departure "from the American practice of habitual relationships between maneuver and supporting unit." It is true that the 117th Cav Recon Battalion was attached to the 14th hastily and that it was not the usual task of this and the 94th Cav Recon Battalion of the 14th to stand its ground against overwhelming odds.

[33] Vernon H. Brown, Jr., *Mount Up! We're Moving Out! The World War II Memoirs of an Armored Car Gunner of D Troop, 94th Cavalry Reconnaissance Squadron . . .* (Bennington, Vt.: Merriam Press, 2008), p. 57.

[34] Richard Engler, *The Final Crisis: Combat in Northern Alsace 1945* (Hampton, Va.: Aegis Consulting Group, 1999), pp. 96–98. Written by a combat veteran of the fighting in Alsace, this is an incisive and penetrating study.

[35] *Riviera,* p. 505.

[36] Engler, pp. 97–98.

[37] "Burp Guns at Midnight," *Memories of the 14th Armored Division* (Paducah, Ky: Turner Publishing Co., 1999), p. 46.

[38] Goddard, p. 3.

[39] Captain Joseph Carter, *The History of the 14th Armored Division* (n.p.: A Whipporwill Publication, n.d.), n.p. There are several editions—really issues—of this same text published after the war by a variety of publishers, and so publishing information is less than clear. When the attached 117th Cav Recon battalion broke, it left exposed the right flank of the 399th Infantry, as Keith Bonn points out (*Odds,* p. 219).

[40] Goddard, pp. 3–4.

[41] Engler, p. 97.

[42] Goddard, p. 4.

[43] Carter, n.p.

[44] Carter, n.p. and Goddard, p. 5. The information on this episode was gleaned by Goddard through his interview with 62 AIB staff officers soon after the battle.

[45] Carter, n.p.

[46] Carter, n.p.

[47] Goddard, p. 5.

[48] Goddard, pp. 5–6.

[49] Howard A. Trammel, Lt. Col. US Army (Ret.), "The Battle of Bannstein," *The Liberator* 39.1 (Summer 2004), 6. This is the second and last installment of his article, but, inexplicably, I have not been able to find the first.

[50] Trammel, p. 16.

[51] Trammel, p. 17.

[52] Trammel, p. 18.

[53] Goddard, pp. 6–7.

[54] *Other Battle,* p. 27.

[55] Goddard, pp. 9–10.

[56] Goddard, p. 10.

[57] Goddard, p. 11.

[58] "Diary—14th Armd." 2 January 1945, n.p.

[59] Goddard, pp. 11–12.

[60] Goddard, p. 12.

[61] Goddard, p. 13.

[62] "Jim Minn Honored on Veterans' Day by University Associates," *The Liberator* 37.3 (Spring 2003), 7–8. This article is based on Minn's diary kept during the war, and the article was assembled by his university associates at the University of Mississippi. Jim retired as a chemist from Hercules, Inc. in 1991 and then worked as a research chemist at the university.

[63] Goddard, pp. 14–15. Goddard quotes the CCR Report of the 14th Armored written about this battle.

[64] Goddard, pp. 16–17.

[65] Goddard, p. 17.

[66] Goddard, p. 17.

[67] Trammel, Part Two, 18–19 versus *Riviera,* pp. 529–530.

[68] *Diaries,* 20 December 1944.

[69] *Riviera,* pp. 529–530.

[70] *Diaries,* 20 December 1944.

[71] S-2 and S-3 Journals, 68th AIB, 1 January, NARA 614-lNF. These Journals, a record of daily communications between the 68th Battalion CP, OP, artillery units, CCR, 14th AD Hdqrs., etc., document the actions of the Battalion. In the following pages of the text of this chapter and the next, dates are simply given in the text for reference. Hours of the day are cited as in the original.

[72] The reader is encouraged to read Wolf T. Zoepf's *Seven Days in January*: With the 6th *SS-Mountain Division in Operation Nordwind* for an excellent detailed account of the fight for Reipertswiller. Zoepf points out a puzzling fact about Hudelson and the intelligence situation (argued above): that Hudelson failed to mention to staff at the 275th's headquarters that an attack was imminent even though the date of the visit was on or about 30 December, p. 81.

[73] *Riviera,* p. 505.

[74] Goddard, p. 17; and Trammel, Part Two, p. 18.

[75] Lt. Walter R. Dickson and Sgt. James W. Hanifin, *Combat History of 19th Armored Infantry Battalion, October 12, 1944 To May 9th, 1945* (Munich: J. G. Weiss, 1945), p. 16.

[76] Dickson, p. 17.

[77] Dickson, p. 18.

[78] Dickson, p. 19.

[79] Dickson, p. 20–21.

[80] Odds, pp. 232–233.

[81] Wolf T. Zoepf, *Seven Days in January: With the 6th SS-Mountain Division in Operation Nordwind,* p. 257. This impressive book, by a former Battalion Adjutant of the 3rd Battalion of the 6th SS-Mountain Division, already cited, provides a well researched and meticulous account of the battle for Reipertswiller in the first week of January 1945 by someone intimately involved in the fighting. It is just to say that this SS battalion behaved in a most civilized manner toward several hundred American prisoners including wounded during that week. Needless to say, not all SS units at that time could be so credited.

Chapter Five: The Hatten-Rittershoffen Inferno

[1] Roger Cirillo, "Ardennes-Alsace," US Army Center of Military History. *http://www.army.mil/brochures/ardennes/aral. htm* (12/19/2008), p. 18.

[2] *Diaries* in US Army Heritage Collection, Carlisle, Pa. Archives Collection 01 Restricted Circulation Box One, OCLC 47184665.

[3] Richard Engler, Jr. *The Final Crisis: Combat in Northern Alsace, January 1945* (Hampton, Va: Aegis Consulting Group, 1990), pp. 143, 144, 145.

[4] Engler, pp. 149–150.

[5] Committee I, Armored Officers Advanced Course, The Armored School 1949–1950, "The Battle of Hatten Rittershoffen: 14th Armored Division, 12–20 January 1945" (Fort Knox, Ky.: US Army, 1950), pp. 5–6.

[6] T/Sgt. Dean B. Robinson and T/Sgt. Vernon G. Brown, "We Came to Fight," (Munich: Oldenbourg, 1945), n. p.

[7] Vernon H. Brown, Jr., *Mount Up! We're Moving Out!* (Bennington, Vt.: Merriam Press, 2008), p. 57.

[8] *The Final Crisis,* especially Chapters Ten and Eleven, "Village Aflame in the Maginot Line," pp. 141–167, and "The Flames Come to Rittershoffen, pp. 168–191.

[9] Robinson and Brown, n. p.

[10] Robinson, n. p.

[11] Robinson, n. p.

[12] Quoted in Robinson, n. p.

[13] Engler, pp. 172–173.

[14] Colonel Hans von Luck, *Panzer Commander: The Memoirs of Hans von Luck* (New York: Random House, 1989), 229–230 (No translator).

[15] Robinson, n. p.

[16] Von Luck, p. 231.

[17] Von Luck, p. 232.

[18] Qtd. in Engler, p. 173.

[19] "Presidential Unit Citation," *The Liberator* 28.3 (Spring 1994), 6.

[20] McGrane, qtd. In Robinson, n. p.

[21] Robinson, n. p.

[22] Von Luck, p. 232–233

[23] Darrell E. Todd, "From Air Corps to Tanker in Record Time," *The Liberator* 39.1 (Summer 2004), 12–13.

[24] Todd, p. 13.

[25] *The History of the 14th Armored Division* (n. p.: A Whipporwill Publication, n. d.), n. p. There are multiple issues of this book by different publishers, but none of them have page numbers.

[26] Lt. Graham P. Madden and Pfc. Ralph D. Kovanda. *Unit History: 68th Armored Infantry Battalion* (Altolling: Gebr Geiseberger, n. d.), p. 11.

[27] Madden and Kovanda, p. 11.

[28] Madden and Kovanda, p. 11.

[29] S/Sgt. William D. Rutz, "Three Sergeants and Now One," *Memories the 14th Armored Division* (Paducah, Ky.: Turner Publishing Co., 1999), pp. 41–42.

[30] Quoted in S/Sgt. Donald L. Haynie, "The 14th Armored Division and the Battle of Rittershofen/Hatten . . ." (Arvacia, Co, Co.: dlhaynie@JUNO.com), p. 57.

[31] Qtd. in Haynie, pp. 16, 17.

[32] Robert H. Kamm, Conversation with author on September 22, 2006 at 14th Reunion.

[33] Haynie, p. 37.

[34] Joseph Carter, n. p.

[35] Col. Joseph C. Lambert, "Armored Rescue," *Armored Cavalry Journal* (Jan/Feb 1949), 42.

[36] *The Final Crisis*, p. 176.

[37] "The 'Battle of Hatten'. . .," *The Liberator* 32.1 (Summer 1997), 12.

[38] *The Siegfried Line*, a self-published book, n. d.

[39] Many conversations with Sgt. Bob Davies at various times in 2005 and 2006. Bob kept coming back, like many comrades, to what happened to them during this battle. He also pointed out that the Ober-Otterbach shelling for four to five days turned his hair white. It later grew back normally.

[40] Carter, n. p.

[41] "We Came to Fight," n. p.

[42] William Z. Breer, "A War Experience," *Memories,* p. 37.

[43] Madden and Kovanda, p. 12.

[44] Madden and Kovanda, p. 12.

[45] Committee 1 Report, p. 33.

[46] Lambert, p. 43.

[47] Carter, n. p.

[48] Qtd. In Committee I Report, p. 33.

[49] Carter, n. p.

[50] Lt. Walter R. Dickson and Sgt. James W. Hanifin, *Combat History of 19th Armored Infantry Battalion, October 12th to May 9th 1945* (Munich: J. G. Weiss, 1945), p. 34.

[51] Authors Unknown, *47th Tank Battalion History: From New York/o/Hudson to Muhldorf o/Inn* (Muhldorf: Druck von D, Geiger, n. d. [1945?]), p. 23.

[52] "The Battle of Hatten," *The Liberator* 38.3 (Spring 2004), 8.

[53] Dickson and Hanifin, pp. 34–36.

[54] Committee I Report, pp. 43, 44.

[55] "Armored Rescue," p. 43.

[56] Madden and Kovanda, p. 13.

[57] Qtd. in *Riviera*, p. 520

[58] Committee I Report, p. 33.

[59] Conversation with Sgt. Robert Kamm, September 22, 2006.

[60] "The Battle of Hatten," *The Liberator* 38.3 (Spring 2004), 8.

[61] "The Battle of Hatten," Copyright 1992, a small pamphlet, p. 2.

[62] Carter, n. p.

[63] Dickson and Hanifin, pp. 37–38.

[64] Carter, n. p. and Committee I Report, p. 33.

[65] "The Battle of Hatten," *Liberator,* p. 9.

[66] Dickson and Hanifin, p. 39.

[67] *47th Tank Battalion History,* p. 27.

[68] "Armored Rescue," p. 43.

[69] Carter, n. p.

[70] Carter, n. p.

[71] Madden and Kovanda, p. 12.

[72] Carter, n. p.

[73] 47th Tank Battalion History, p. 27.

[74] Carter, n. p.

[75] *Crisis*, pp. 203–204.

[76] *Riviera*, pp. 524–527.

[77] *Riviera*, p. 531.

[78] Dickson and Hanifin, pp. 43–44.

[79] Madden and Kovanda, p. 12.

[80] *History of the 25th Tank Battalion*, p. 11.

[81] "Armored Rescue," p. 44.

[82] Madden and Kovanda, pp. 13–14.

[83] Carter, n. p.

[84] Qtd. in 68th AIB History, pp. 13–14.

[85] Carter, n. p.

[86] Philip Trewhitt, *Armored Fighting Vehicles* (London: Friedman Fairfax, 1999), p. 34.

[87] Madden and Kovanda, p. 13.

[88] Qtd. in *68 AIB History*, pp. 13–14.

[89] Carter, n. p.

[90] *Riviera*, p. 528.

[91] Committee I Report, pp. 62–64.

[92] *Panzer Commander*, p. 185.

[93] No author, no title but account organized by Lt. Col. James W. Lann for *Memories* (p. 15) from the 47th Tank Battalion's History. Lann was the commander of that unit.

[94] Lann, p. 15.

[95] *Riviera*, p. 526.

[96] *Riviera*, p. 532.

[97] For a vigorous argument that General Eisenhower made a mistake in not allowing Sixth Army Group to cross the Rhine and go on the offensive in November 1945, see David P. Colley's *Decision at Strasbourg: Ike's Strategic Mistake to Halt the Sixth Army Group at the Rhine in 1944* (Annapolis, Md.: Naval Institute Press, 2008).

[98] "Armored Rescue," p. 44.

[99] *Panzer Commander*, p. 235.

[100] *Panzer Commander*, p. 236.

[101] Carter, n. p.

[102] Madden and Kovanda, p. 15.

[103] "Armored Rescue," p. 44.

[104] Lambert, p. 45.

[105] Lambert, p. 45.

[106] "Bad Day at Black Rock," *The Liberator* 38.1 (Summer 2003), 15.

Chapter Six: Ohlungen Forest: Getting Hurt and Getting Even

[1] Ken Hazleton, 68th A.I.B Medical Detachment HISTORY: From 13 October 1944 Embarkation To 8 May 1945 V.E. Day, unpublished pamphlet, p. 7.

[2] Captain Joseph Carter, "Defense: January 21–March 15, 1945," The *History of the 14th Armored Division*, n. p.

[3] Madden and Kovanda, *Unit History: 68th Armored Infantry Battalion*, p. 14.

[4] "Report of Operations 14th D, 25–26 Jan 45 Ohlungen Forest," NARA II. 614–0.3.0.

[5] Richard Engler, *The Final Crisis: Combat in Northern Alsace, January 1945* (Hampton, Va.: Aegis Consulting Group, 1999), pp. 294–295.

[6] *68th AIB History*, pp. 14–15.

[7] "Report. . . ," p. 2.

[8] Engler, p. 301.

[9] "Report," p. 2.

[10] *68th History*, p. 43.

[11] *14th AD History*, n. p.

[12] *68th History*, p. 15.

[13] *68th History*, p. 15.

[14] "Report," p. 3.

[15] "Report," p. 4.

[16] *68th History*, p. 16.

[17] "Report," p. 3.

[18] *68th History*, p. 16.

[19] *68th History*, p. 16.

[20] *14th AD History*, n. p.

[21] *68th History*, p. 16.

[22] Carter, n. p.

[23] Carter, n. p.

[24] CCB Report, quoted in Carter, n. p.

[25] *68th History*, p. 16.

[26] *68th History*, pp. 17–18.

[27] Al Zdon, "He Saw It Coming," *The Liberator* 42.2 (Winter 2008), 11–13, 16–17.

[28] *68th History*, pp. 17–18.

[29] Carter, n. p.

[30] Several interviews with Bob Davies over many months on and off in 2004 and 2005. Each interview would either confirm previous details or else provide other details not previously presented.

[31] Letter from Stanley Miller to author dated April 4, 2005, p. 1.

[32] The same, dated March 13, 2007, pp. 1–2.

[33] Interview with Philip Snoberger (formerly Hdqrs. Co., 68th AIB), November 4, 2006. He was frequently at the side of Lt. Col. Bob E. Edwards, the Commander of the Battalion.

[34] *68th History*, p. 18.

[35] Carter, n. p.
[36] Carter, n. p.
[37] *68th History*, p. 18.
[38] *68th History*, pp. 18–19.
[39] Hazleton, p. 6.
[40] Hazleton, p. 7.

Chapter Seven: Breaching the Siegfried Line
[1] Charles Whiting, Siegfried: *The Nazi's Last Stand* (London: Pan Books, 2003), p. 186.
[2] *68th History*, p. 19.
[3] Captain Joseph Carter, Chapter XI, "Breakthrough," in *14th History*, n. p.
[4] Carter, n. p.
[5] *68th History*, p. 19.
[6] Carter, n. p.
[7] Conversation with Lt. Harry Kemp, 20 January, 2005.
[8] Carter, n. p.
[9] S/Sgt. Ray F. Lohof, "A Siegfried Pillbox," *Memories of the 14th Armored Division* (Paducah, Ky.: Turner Publishing Co, 1999), pp. 46–47.
[10] Carter, n. p.
[11] *68th History*, p. 20.
[12] Ken Hazleton, "68th AIB Medical Detachment History: From 13 October 1944 Embarkation To 8 May 1945 V-E Day," unpublished report, p. 8.
[13] *To Hell and Back* (New York: Henry Holt and Co., 2002), 263–264.
[14] *68th History*, pp. 20–21.
[15] Carter, n. p.; Conversation with Lt. Harry T. Kemp (above).
[16] Ralph Cardinal, *History of 25th Tank Bn.* (no publishing information), p. 15.
[17] Cardinal, p. 25.
[18] Carter, n. p.
[19] Qtd. in Carter, n. p.
[20] Carter, n. p.
[21] "Medical Detachment," p. 8.
[22] *68th History*, p. 22.
[23] *68th History*, p. 22.
[24] Carter, n. p.
[25] Carter, n. p.
[26] Ian V. Hogg, *German Artillery of World War Two* (London: Greenhill Books, 2002, p. 197. The one exception to this armored vulnerability for the Americans was the introduction of the M26 Pershing almost at the end of the war. "The M26 was the closest thing we had to the German Panther. It had four inches of cast steel armor on the glacis plate at forty-five degrees, whereas the Panther had three and a half inches of plate armor at somewhat less than thirty-eight degrees, the nominal angle below which armor-piercing shot would ricochet." Belton Y. Cooper, *Death Traps: The Survival of an American Armored Division in World*

War II [Novato, Ca.: Presidio Press, Inc. 2001], p. 212.) I am indebted to the late Dudley Partrick, a veteran of the 14th, for his kindness in forwarding this informative book to me. It should also be mentioned that the British Army developed a Sherman tank called the "Firefly," equipped with a 76.2 mm. gun with a long barrel which was competitive with some German armor.

[27] *68th History*, p. 22.
[28] Carter, n. p.
[29] Carter, n. p.
[30] Carter, n. p.
[31] Carter, n. p.
[32] *68th History*, pp. 23–24.
[33] *68th History*, p. 24.

Chapter Eight: The Drive From the Rhine

[1] *68th History*, pp. 24–25.
[2] *14th History*, Chapter XX, "Pursuit: Lohr, Gemunden, Neustadt, Hammelburg," n. p.
[3] *14th History*, n. p.
[4] *14th History*, n. p.; *68th History*, p. 25.
[5] *14th History*, n. p.
[6] *14th History*, n. p.
[7] *14th History*, n. p.
[8] Quoted in *14th History*, n. p.
[9] *68th History*, p. 26.
[10] "Hist. 14th Armored Dlv: June 45–Aug 15 (1 Apr–9 May)," NARA II 6140.2, pp. 3–4.
[11] *14th History*, n. p.
[12] Dr. Robert Quinn, *My Best Trip* (Victoria, C.: Trafford Publishing, 2003), pp. 5–11.
[13] Quinn, p. 11.
[14] *14th History*, n. p.
[15] Lt. Walter R. Dickson and Sgt. James W. Hanifin, *Combat History of 19th Armored Infantry Battalion: October 12th to May 9th, 1945* (Munich: J. G. Weiss, 1945), p. 67.
[16] *19th Combat History*, p. 68.
[17] *14th History*, n. p.
[18] *14th History*, n. p.
[19] *14th History*, n. p.
[20] *14th History*, n. p.
[21] "Hist.—14th," p 5.
[22] *14th History*, n. p.
[23] Jim Craigmile, Pfc., "Baker 499th From Marseille to Erding: The View of an Artillery Man," *The Liberator* 40.3 (Spring 2006), 7.
[24] "Hist. . . .," p. 6.

[25] John Nichol and Tony Rennell, *The Last Escape: The Untold Story of Allied Prisoners of War in Europe 1944–1945* (New York: Viking Press, 2000), pp. 201–202.

[26] "Heroism by 14th A. D. Member Remembered," *Liberator* 23.2 (Fall 1988), 1.

[27] Stanley P. Hirshson, *General Patton: A Soldier's Life* (New York: Harper Collins, 2002), pp. 307–308.

[28] Qtd. In Hirshson, pp. 621–623.

[29] Qtd. In Hirshson, p. 623.

[30] *19th AIB History*, p. 74.

[31] *14th History*, n. p.

[32] *14th History*, n. p.

[33] *14th History*, n. p.

[34] *14th History*, n. p.

[35] *14th History*, n. p.

[36] *14th History*, n. p.

[37] *14th History*, n. p.

Chapter Nine: From Collapse to Liberation

[1] *14 A.D. History*, n. p.

[2] *14 A.D. History*, n. p.

[3] *14 A.D. History*, n. p.

[4] *14 A.D. History*, n. p.

[5] *68th History*, pp. 26-27.

[6] *68th History*, p. 27.

[7] *68th History*, p. 27; "We Came To Fight," *Unit History of the 48th TB* by T/Sgt. Dean B. Robinson and T/Sgt. Vernon G. Brown (Munich: R. Oldenbourg, 1945), n. p.

[8] *68th History*, pp. 27-28.

[9] *14 A.D. History*, n. p.

[10] *68th History*, pp. 28-29.

[11] *48th TB History*, n. p.

[12] *68th History*, pp. 29-30.

[13] Qtd. In *14th History*, n. p.

[14] "History: 14th Armored Division: June 1945–Aug. 1945," NARA 11, 614. 02, pp. 13–14.

[15] *48th TB History*, n. p.

[16] *14 A.D. History*, n. p.

[17] *14 A.D. History*, n. p.

[18] *14 A.D. History*, n. p.

[19] Ralph Cardinal, Lt. 25th Tank Bn, "History of 25th Tank Bn." (no publishing information, probably published in 1945 in Germany), p. 16.

[20] *14 A.D. History*, n. p.

[21] *14 A.D. History*, n. p.

[22] *14 A.D. History*, n. p.

[23] *14 A.D. History*, n. p.

[24] *14 A.D. History*, n. p.

[25] "Order of Battle: Fourteenth Armored Division, In The European Theater of Operations," 14th armored division. Org/ob 14 adeto. Htm. (3/2/2005), p. 1.

[26] *14 A.D. History*, n. p.

[27] *25th TB History*, p. 16.

[28] *14 A.D. History*, n. p.

[29] *Combat History of 19th Armored Infantry Battalion: October 12th, 1944 To May 9, 1945* (Munich: J. G. Weiss, 1945), p. 79.

[30] *19th History*, p. 79.

[31] *19th History*, p. 79.

[32] *19th History*, p. 80.

[33] *47th Tank Battalion History: From New York o/Hudson to Muhldorf o/ Inn,* (no publishing information), p. 36.

[34] *19th History*, p. 81.

[35] *19th History*, pp. 82–83; *14 A. D. History*, n. p.

[36] *19 AIB History*, p. 82.

[37] *47th TB History*, p. 36.

[38] *25th History*, p. 17; *14 A. D. History*, n. p.

[39] *25th History*, p. 17.

[40] *25th History*, p. 17.

[41] *25th History*, p. 18; *14 A. D. History*, n. p.

[42] *14 A.D. History*, n. p.

[43] *14 A.D. History*, n. p.

[44] *14 A.D. History*, n. p.

[45] *Death Traps: The Survival of an American Armored Division in World War II* (Novato, Ca.: Presidio Press, 2001), pp. vii–viii.

[46] *14 A.D. History*, n. p.

[47] *14 A.D. History*, n. p.

[48] *14 A.D. History*, n. p.

[49] *68th History*, pp. 31-32.

[50] *14 A.D. History*, n. p.

[51] "Condensed Milk Toast Reminds Former POW's of Captivity," *Waterbury Republican* (missing publishing information).

[52] *68th History*, p. 32.

[53] Lankford, p. 12.

[54] *14 A. D. History*, n. p.

[55] Keith Fuller, n. p.

[56] Qtd. In John Nichol and Tony Rennel, *The Last Escape: The Untold Story of Allied Prisoners of War in Europe 1944–45* (New York: Viking Press, 2003), p. 280.

[57] *Last Escape*, p. 284.

[58] Andy Soltis, "Hitler Plotted Final Bloodbath," *The Liberator* 32.3 (Spring

1998), 12.
[59] *Last Escape,* p. 284.
[60] Dr. Martin Allain, " 'Skinny GI' speaks Up: Ex POW tells about hoisting American flag," *The Liberator* 28.1 (Summer 1993), 8.
[61] John P. Meyer, "Lots of Memories," *Memories of the 14th Armored Division* (Paducah, Ky.: Turner Publishing Co., 1999), p. 45.
[62] Robert Kroupa, "A Captive in Moosburg," *Memories,* p. 50.
[63] DeWitt C, Armstrong, Ill, "Helped feed liberated POWs at Moosburg," *The Liberator* 33.1 (Summer 1998), 15.
[64] *14 A. D. History,* n. p.; *Liberator* 33.1, 13.
[65] *14 A.D. History,* n. p.
[66] *14 A.D. History,* n. p.

Chapter Ten: "From Atlantic to Pacific?"

[1] "Chapter XNI: The Battle of the Autobahn, The Death of a State, April April 9–21, 1945," *The History of the 14th Armored Division* (n. p.: A Whipporwill Publication, n. d.), n. p.
[2] Carter, n. p.
[3] Lt. Graham P. Madden and Pfc. Ralph D. Kovanda, *Unit History: 68th Armored Infantry Battalion: From Port of Embarkation To V-E Day* (Altolling: Gebr. Geiselberger, n. d.), p. 32.
[4] Quoted in Carter, n. p.
[5] *Death Traps: The Survival of an American Armored Division in World War II* (Novato, Ca.: Presidio Press, Inc., 2001), p. 24.
[6] Unsigned, *62 Armored Infantry Battalion History* (no publishing info.), pp. 107, 3.
[7] Lt. Ralph Cardinal, *History of the 25th Tank Bn.* (no publishing info.), pp. 17, 18.
[8] "Editors," *47th Tank Battalion History: From New York ol Hudson to Muhldorf o/Inn* (Muhldorf: Druck von D. Geiger, n. d.), p. 37.
[9] *47th TB History,* p. 37.
[10] *47th TB History,* p. 10.
[11] *14th AD History,* n. p.
[12] *14th AD History,* p. 10.
[13] Unsigned, *Combat History of 19th Armored Infantry Battalion: October 12th, To May 9th, 1945* (Munich: Printer: J. G. Weiss, 1945), pp. 90–91.
[14] John Toland, *The Last 100 Days: The Tumultuous and Controversial Story of the Final Days of World War II in Europe* (New York: Modern Library, 2003), p. 570.
[15] *19th History,* p. 91.
[16] *14th AD History,* n.p.
[17] "Diaries" of the 14th AD, May 5, 1945, NARA II 614–0.3.0.
[18] Qtd. in "Schaffer Featured in German History Book," *The Liberator* 28.1 (Summer 1993), 16–17.

[19] "Schaffer," p. 17.

[20] *14th History*, n. p.

[21] Editor, "Lorraine American Cemetery," *The Liberator* 34.2 (Winter, 1999), 15.

[22] "Daniel R. Iannella, Commander of A Company, 62nd AIB, Dies in Saarbrucken, Germany at 86," *The Liberator* 35.3 (Spring, 2001), 8.

[23] Editor, "Locates, Visits Grave of Cousin in Epinal Cemetery," *The Liberator* 35.2 (Winter, 2000), 7.

[24] (Lt.) Harry Kemp has described his life in this context in several places: his small unpublished book, *The Siegfried Line,* (n.d.) an e-mail from "Harry Kemp," <htk 207@Webtv.com>, and also in several articles in *The Liberator*.

[25] "From Your 68th BN. CO. AIB., Ampfling, Germany 3 July 1948," made available by Ken Hazleton, Medical Detachment, 68th AIB.

[26] Richard B. Frank, *Downfall: The End of the Japanese Empire* (New York: Random House, 1999), 257.